Daylight Performance of Buildings

Edited by Marc Fontoynont
Ecole Nationale des Travaux Publics de l'Etat, Lyons, France

European Commission Directorate General XII for Science, Research & Development

Daylight performance of buildings

Copyright	©1999 European Commission
Edited by	M. Fontoynont, ENTPE, Lyon, France
Published by	James & James (Science Publishers) for the European Commission Directorate General XII for Science, Research and Development
Printed by	Magnum International Printing Co. Ltd., Hong Kong
ISBN	1-873936-87-7
EUR no.	18895

Daylight Performance of Buildings documents a major outcome of a comprehensive European research program, Daylight Europe JOU2-CT94-0282, 1994-97, a project of the European JOULE III Research Program. The project was funded by the European Commission DG XII for Science, Research and Development, Rue de la Loi 200, B-1049 Brussels, Belgium, and individual member states participating in the project.

Preface

For more than two decades the European Commission has strongly supported a wide range of Research and Development and dissemination activities to improve the energy efficiency and environmental performance of our buildings, which account for almost half of Europe's total energy use and consequent impact.

Daylighting has become a major topic in energy conscious design. By optimizing the potential of daylight the energy for lighting our buildings can be drastically reduced, especially in buildings used mainly during the day, and the use of air conditioning can be reduced or eliminated.

In 'Daylight Performance of Buildings' the daylighting behaviour of sixty buildings throughout Europe, new and old, large and small, with a wide variety of functions has been monitored and objectively assessed. The resulting case studies provide a valuable resource for building designers and incorporate quantitative and qualitative assessment of a range of daylighting solutions.

This collection of case studies of buildings with notable daylighting features illustrates the complexity and range of issues which need to be taken into account in good daylighting design. In addition to its potential for significant savings in energy use and consequent environmental impact, good daylighting design can dramatic-ally improve our living and working conditions.

Dr Georges Deschamps
European Commission,
Directorate General XII
for Science, Research and Development

Until the beginning of this century, daylight was the most important light source for daytime use for factories, offices, domestic and public buildings. The availability of affordable artificial lighting led to a building designs primarily dependent on electric lighting in deep-plan buildings with smaller windows.

Daylight is now reassuming its importance and desirability in design criteria for buildings used mainly during the day. People prefer daylight, and daylight use can offset the need for artificial lighting, saving running costs and reducing the environmental impact of energy use in buildings. Daylight design of buildings is becoming an integral part of the concept of sustainable buildings, along with improved indoor comfort and working conditions.

Daylight use in buildings requires daylight admission and distribution in the building to be considered. Shallow buildings are preferable, window design and size are important and solar control and shading systems are essential. An integrated design approach has to be adopted.

Throughout the predominance of artificial lighting, the daylight design tradition among architects and engineers was lost. The EU Daylight Europe project was begun to disseminate techniques of good daylight design to architects and engineers. Good examples of daylit buildings need to be documented, as do appropriate designs. The two main deliverables of the Daylight Europe project: Daylight Design of Buildings, and the present book, seeks to fulfill this need.

Much can be learned by studying older examples of buildings that were built with daylight as their primary light source. This book of case studies contains several historic examples of buildings, such as the two thousand years old Pantheon in Rome, and the beautiful seventeenth-century Trinity College library in Cambridge, United Kingdom. Most examples are from this century, and many newly completed buildings are included, such as the United Kingdom's Stansted Airport, and Alex Tombazis' office in Athens, Greece.

The 60 buildings documented in this book represent a unique source of information, since this is the first time that so many daylit buildings have been monitored and documented. We hope that the book will find use as a source of inspiration in architects' offices, and thereby contribute to the design of buildings that are more comfortable and inspiring to be in, and have a smaller environmental impact.

Poul E Kristensen
Daylight Europe scientific coordinator
Energy Center Denmark
Danish Technological Institute

Contents

Acknowledgements

This book was published within the JOULE programme, called the 'Daylight Europe' Project of the European Commission Directorate General XII for Science, Research and Development. The project was supervized by Dr Georges Deschamps.

General coordination by:
Poul Kristensen
Edited by:
Marc Fontoynont, ENTPE, Lyons, France.
Coordination of the case study subprogramme:
Marc Fontoynont and Vincent Berrutto.

Participating teams:

Building Research Establishment,
Watford, UK

Conphoebus,
Catania, Italy

Faculty of Architecture,
Cambridge, UK

The Martin Centre,
Cambridge, UK

Danish Building Research Institute,
Copenhagen, Denmark

Fraunhofer Institut für Bauphysik,
Stuttgart, Germany

BBRI,
Brussels, Belgium

EDAS, Dept of Architecture,
Glasgow, UK

University College Dublin,
Dublin, Ireland

Royal Institute of Technology,
Gävle, Sweden

Danish Technological Institute,
Copenhagen, Denmark

ESBENSEN Consulting Engineers,
Copenhagen, Denmark

Chalmers University,
Building Services Engineering,
Gothenburg, Sweden

LNEC,
Lisbon, Portugal

Simos Lighting Consultants,
Carouge, Switzerland

A.N. Tombazis & Ass. Arch.,
Polydroso, Athens, Greece

National Observatory of Athens,
Athens, Greece

ESRU, University of Strathclyde,
Glasgow, UK

Faculty of Architecture,
Trøndheim, Norway

Norwegian Electrical Power Research Institute,
Trøndheim, Norway

LESO - PB, EPFL,
Lausanne, Switzerland

UPC - Architecture,
Barcelona, Spain

Ecole Nationale des Travaux Publics de l'Etat,
Lyons, France

Those involved in the preparation of this book include:

Editing
Marc Fontoynont (ENTPE) with John Goulding (ERG)

Design
Energy Research Group / ENTPE

Coordination of case study material
Pascale Avouac Bastie (ENTPE)

Typesetting / desktop publishing
Sinéad McKeon (ERG),
Pascale Avouac Bastie (ENTPE) and Cécile Demé (ENTPE)

Secretarial Assistance
Cécile Demé (ENTPE)

Additionnal contributions
Vivienne Brophy (ERG),
Pierre Jolivet (ERG),
Liz Fleming (ERG),
Prof. Joe Clark (ESRU),
Staffan Hygge (KTH).

Introduction

by Marc Fontoynont

This book attempts to provide an original view of the built environment, whether it concerns modern architectural landmarks or architecture representative of the end of the 20th century. The objective is to offer some understanding of the way daylight penetrates and propagates in a building, and to determine the causes of the effects which can be observed: the reasons for bright spaces, shadows, contrast, glare, and, more generally, the way occupants, lighting requirements are fullfilled by daylight.

In this respect, the built environment around us can be considered as a large laboratory in which lighting phenomena can be observed and understood.

The 60 case studies which are presented have been proposed by participants of the "Daylight Europe" programme, which has been supported by the European Commission, DG XII for Science Research and Development, consists of within the JOULE Programme. The range of buildings selected for study comprises those which were accessible to the participants and is thus more supply-led than demand-led. The sample is therefore rather heterogeneous - but such is reality! We have presented them according to themes to allow more interesting, topic-related, discussions.

The spirit of our work has been to offer as objective as possible an analysis of the daylighting qualities of the buildings studied. The measuring campaign which has been undertaken will provide valuable data in the future for building designers and daylighting scientists.

The measuring campaign required the development of a precise procedure which is described in this document. The level of experience in undertaking lighting measurements was rather heterogeneous among members, and various difficulties may have lead to some errors in the measurements, although, in most cases, inconsistent results have been re-evaluated. The major potential source of error has been in the simultaneous measurement of indoor and oudoor illuminance under very precise overcast sky conditions. This task becomes difficult if the studied building is far from the location of the monitoring team, or if access to the building was limited. Sometimes sky conditions, which were required to be continuously overcast, were unsuitable for measurements.

As coordinator, I tried my best to collect the most useful data concerning the monitored building. Sometimes this led to difficulties since the measuring teams had to visit the building again and perform measurements in locations difficult to access.

The work which is presented here is the result of a three-year long international task, with all the difficulties that entails in the management of the measuring campaign and collection of the data.

A significant level of expertise has developed among the participants, with improved confidence in their measuring capabilities and processing of the data. It is anticipated that this work will be continued in the future by participants or by other teams, once the book is published.

We hope that our document will find a place on your bookshelves and that you will use it regularly, and that it will inform and encourage you in future daylight design and monitoring activities.

I woud like to thank the participants of the Daylight Europe Programme for all their efforts to produce information of high quality in sometimes difficult circumstances. I would like to thank John Goulding from University College Dublin for his advice and his assistance in the detailed reviewing of the text before publishing; Vincent Berrutto from ENTPE, France, for his coordination of the monitoring campaign and his involvement in the definition of measuring procedures; Pascale Avouac-Bastie, from ENTPE, for collecting the data from all participants, adapting them to our requirements and producing the DTP version of the results.

▽ Marc Fontoynont, editor and coordinator of the monitoring subtask of 'Daylight Europe'.

Daylight performance of buildings: 60 European case studies

The results of a three-year monitoring campaign of buildings throughout Europe are presented in this book. We present here a summary of them, obtained through the observation of the daylighting behaviour of 60 buildings. Various types of buildings were involved, from offices to museums, libraries to churches and more specific buildings such as airports or factories. Classical buildings (such as the Pantheon in Rome built in 128 AD) are included, some of which are historical landmarks (such as Ronchamp church by Le Corbusier), others are more recent (such as the Stansted Air Terminal by Foster & Associates). The sizes range from one single room of 11 metres (Anatomical Theatre, Gothenburg, Sweden) to a large-scale office building (100,000m² floor area of the Tractebel building, Brussels). The study shows the extraordinary potential of daylighting techniques, to improve amenity and energy performances for the benefit of building occupants and managers. However, opportunities are often missed, with performance of daylighting solutions sometimes overestimated by designers, or with significant problems of overheating and insufficient attenuation of glare. Above all, this monitoring campaign shows the broad scope of daylighting design, and the importance of careful assessment of side effects which need to be analysed with the benefit of experience and knowledge of the physical principles; and appropriately managed.

A three-year monitoring programme throughout Europe

For a period of three years between September 1994 and August 1997, a large scale monitoring programme was conducted at European level, dealing with the daylighting performance of 60 buildings throughout Europe. More than 10 organizations were involved in the task which required about 30 people to carry out measurements, process the data and supply the results to the coordinator. The task included observations, indoor luminous measurements for specific climatic conditions and calculation of performance indicies. For some buildings, a specific Post Occupancy Evaluation study (POE)

The understanding of the behaviour of a ▷ building with respect to daylight requires the measurement of specific parameters sometimes in locations with difficult access.

to assess the effects of daylighting strategies on the occupants. In parallel, a simulation group conducted detailed energy calculations for six monitored buildings aimed at comparing the energy saving potential of the proposed daylighting techniques with a reference case or other options.

Using reality as a source of information

In recent years, there has been a growing concern about the development of tools to provide assistance in daylighting design. The oldest and most used tool is still the scale model (light propagation follows the same rules in a scale model and in full scale reality). Now, various computer programs have been proposed either to simulate the daylighting behaviour of a building with well characterized daylighting sources, or to assist designers in their strategic decisions. For any tool used, there is always some doubt about its validity, and concern about its limited field of investigation.

It is clear that the performance of daylighting systems can be judged objectively and subjectively, and that energy aspects are partly visible and partly invisible. However, only on-site observations and measurements can detect some aspects of daylighting which are difficult to predict with tools: exact final optical performance of systems, rendering of the indoor space, quality of views, dynamics of daylight, and above all, the global impression given to the visitor as well as the occupants. Finally, it has been found that a database of buildings, some of them well known and most of them accessible to the public, would be of great interest to building designers.

Selection of 60 buildings

The 60 buildings were selected for their interesting daylighting features, either generally or at least regarding a specific feature. Ease of access also played a part in their selection. All participants made proposals regarding the buildings they intended to monitor and it was decided that 60 buildings appeared to be the maximum achievable number with respect to the allocated budget. A decision was made to include standard building configurations and not to focus only on cases where the solution was elaborate or unusual. It was decided to offer a large range of buildings and applications, with solutions offering a large variety of ways to bring daylight into building interiors.

A standard procedure for collecting information

In order to extract useful information from the 60 buildings, a monitoring procedure was established. It dealt with a series of measurements and observations, and with their analysis. The following is a summary of the tasks conducted:

Tasks

1 Geometric assessment (glazing area/ dimensions)

2 Daylight factor assessment, through the simultaneous measurement of indoor and outdoor illumination under overcast sky conditions.

3 Material characterization: measurement of reflections and transmissions of opaque surfaces, glazing materials and awnings.

4 Visual comfort assessment, through the determination of luminances in the field of view of the occupants.

5 Homogeneity of daylight penetration, through the comparison of vertical illuminance measured in the centres of rooms.

6 Assessment of luminous flux penetration through various apertures, under standard overcast conditions (external horizontal illuminance equal to 10,000 lux)

7 Photography, with wide angle lenses and fish-eye lenses to display the patterns of daylight penetration in the space, for diffuse light and sunlight.

8 Recording of occupants' comments

9 Energy calculations for various daylighting options

The procedure developed for this task required some training seminars to help teams master the various aspects of daylighting measurement. The sensors used by the teams were calibrated together. However, errors can still occur, particularly if measurements are taken in non-standard climatic conditions. The recording of material properties on site also required some specific conditions of incident light on the surfaces. It is clear that some errors may have still occurred in the monitoring campaign, although a great effort was made to minimize these.

The importance of objective assessment

Any example of architecture can be considered as an optical element allowing some daylight to penetrate it and then reflected it by the indoor surfaces. In order to compare two buildings, a reference light source needs to be defined, regardless of its significance with regard to the local climate. The best reference sky condition is a totally overcast sky, the luminance of which is larger near the zenith than near the horizon (typically two to three times). Since we are mainly interested in relative values, such as ratios of indoor to outdoor values (daylight factors), or ratios of indoor to indoor values (luminance contrasts, homogeneity, etc.), the global brightness of such skies has no importance, and measurements can be conducted any time during the year: a sky twice as bright as the reference one leads to indoor spaces two times brighter. This also means that measurements under overcast sky conditions apply for Mediterranean buildings, even if such skies are rare in these climates.

Objective assessment helps us to discover the difference between the perceived brightness of a space and the exact amount of daylight used to light it. This started useful discussions about the comparison of the performance of daylighting systems and about the role played by material finishes.

Finally, it was decided that objective assessment was probably the best method for a large-scale monitoring programme, to reduce the differences in assessment between participants, and to provide useful data to the largest possible audience.

A typical exercise which was conducted for many case studies was the assessment of the luminous flux provided by daylighting systems under standard overcast conditions (representing an outdoor horizontal illuminance of 10,000 lux). This allowed a quick comparison of the amount of light admitted by facade windows and secondary lighting windows. The value could also be compared with the amount of light provided by luminaires to give an idea of the potential of daylighting to replace artificial lighting.

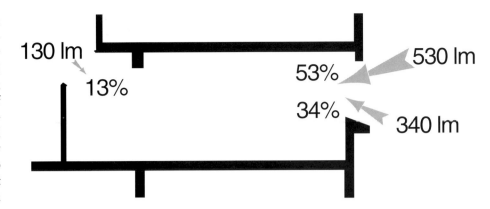

△ Example of assessment of the origins of natural light fluxes entering a room per 1,000 lux of total incoming light flux. This technique clearly displays the amount of light provided by the secondary daylighting window by comparison with the facade window.

Simple systems often perform better.

The amount of natural light entering a building is related to three major factors:

1) the luminance of the section of the sky as seen from behind the window,

2) the associated solid angle of this section,

3) the capacity of the window to bring daylight inside (area and transparency).

The final amount of light available inside is related to the area of the absorbing surfaces (by comparison with the window area) as well as their reflectances, and particularly those of the surfaces directly hit by the incident daylight.

For this reason, most systems with additional surfaces, even if reflective, tend to globally decrease daylight penetration through the reduction of the solid angle of light collection (2), and adding additional light absorptions in process (3). This means that greater control of daylight often leads to a reduced overall luminous performance. In this way, the best performance remains that of the horizontal roof aperture collecting daylight from a large section of the sky with very little obstruction. But we all know that protection against sunlight and the provision of a view to the external environment are needed in most buildings.

For this reason, it was found that a combination of simple systems (roof and facade apertures for instance) performed better than advanced facade systems attempting to deviate diffuse daylight deep into the building

▷ A combination of simple systems and bright indoor finishes was found to perform rather well.

▷ Corridors of the Reiterstrasse Office building in Bern are lit with natural light, partly hidden from the field of vision, filtering between obstructions, leading to a low luminance level, glare-free, but pleasant space.

△ In the bright Baroque church of the Neresheim Monastery, daylight factors range between 1 to 1.5%, values higher than usually found in cathedrals where values around 0.5% or below are common.

△ The Architects Office in Athens is a good example of a building where facade window area has been reduced to a minimum size because of the climate, still achieving a bright work space near each window. The rest of the room benefits from ambient light admitted by a central roof monitor equipped with shading devices.

through the addition of reflective surfaces.

Furthermore, complex systems involving highly reflective surfaces have performances which are very dependent on maintenance and durability of the components. Dust, condensation or surface deterioration quickly reduce optical efficiency, sometimes by more than 50%.

Some spaces perform well with rather low levels of light

If we take away the cases for which high illuminances are required (such as about 500 lux on the work plane for instance, or more for some factory work), many spaces can appear bright

at modest levels of illuminances. The reason can be that the general brightness of the space is higher than that expected due to its function. This is the case in the church of the Neresheim Monastery, where indoor finishes are particularly bright, and stained glass has been replaced with clear windows.

Circulation spaces frequently do not need a high level of illuminance. Values of 10 to 50 lux may be acceptable as long as the eye of the occupant is adapted to the luminance of the indoor surfaces, and not to the outdoor luminance, which is usually much higher. This suggests that apertures should be partly hidden from the field of vision, with

natural light pouring in behind architectural elements.

Adding small apertures gives better performance than increasing window sizes

Increasing window sizes leads to more daylight being admitted, but can also cause more glare and more constraints regarding the shading systems. Beyond a certain level of daylight penetration, increasing window area may in fact generate far more problems than the benefits of letting some additional natural light in.

For instance, increasing daylight factors from 3 to 4% (through an increase in window area of 33%) will only lead to

△ These secondary daylighting windows are clearly undersized with regard to their potential to add extra daylight to the corridors from the daylit offices.

△ In Collège La Vanoise, Modane, France, the most attractive daylighting feature is the tilted secondary lighting system allowing daylight to penetrate from the atrium roof to the interior. The tilt angle of the windows leads to a transmitted light equal to 3 times that transmitted by vertical windows. Daylight distribution in classrooms becomes balanced and the general impression is of a very bright space.

▷ The translucent floors and ceilings of the Waucquez Department Store in Brussels allow daylight to penetrate deep into the building, because their area (comparable to the area of the glazed roof) compensates for the optical losses associated with the triple absorption of light coming from the outside. At ground level, daylight factors reach values above 1%.

an increase of the daylighting period during the year of less than 5%. The challenge therefore is in bringing more daylight into areas where daylight factors are low, and lighting requirements high. Examples can be found among the case studies, where roof apertures, secondary daylighting windows or double side lighting solutions are used instead of single side facade solutions.

◁ In Stansted Air Terminal, the rooflight elements associated with the supporting columns are the major aesthetic feature of the large square hall (120m x 120m).

▽ In the Trapholt Art Museum, Denmark, daylight is brought from the ceiling through hanging canvas 3D forms, a unique and remarkable design.

Translucent floors

Secondary daylighting is of great interest, as an accepted way to bring daylight deep into a building. Internal walls or ceilings can be transparent or translucent. However, the light falling on these surfaces can be 10 to 100 times lower than the illuminance on a vertical window on the facade. This suggests that secondary daylighting can be applied only if the daylight factor on the surface concerned is sufficient (typically more than 1%) and the glazing area should be as large or larger than the original window area on the roof or the facade. Ideally, a secondary lighting window should occupy the entire surface of the indoor wall or partition.

Daylight, a large contributor to the amenity of the space

The daylighting system can also be considered as a piece of sculpture, in the same way as a chandelier behaves with artificial lighting. It becomes an aesthetic object on its own. However, it needs to be assessed in terms of its ability to fulfill visual criteria such as glare control (moderate luminances) and

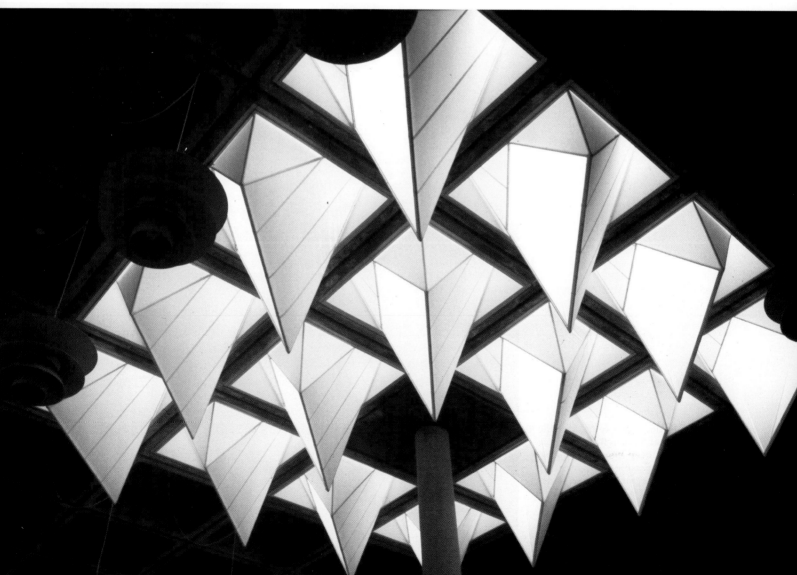

overall performance (production of a luminous flux and distribution in the space). Among the 60 buildings which have been studied, some of them have integrated aesthetic elements, such as the rooflights of Stansted Air Terminal, UK, the hanging pyramids of Trapholt Museum, Denmark, the occuli of Bibliothèque Nationale in Paris, etc. Sometimes they integrate artificial lighting so that artificial and natural lighting are associated in the final rendering.

Sizing of daylighting systems needs to be based on visual specifications for the users

The larger the window area in the facade, the higher the risk that occupants will be exposed to glare and overheating in summer. Hence, shading devices, which must operate in glare situations and provide the desired attenuation, have a crucial role. If their luminous transmittance is too high (above 10% in general), the risk of glare is significant, with luminance reaching more than 1,000 cd/m² for an illuminance on the awning of 40,000 lux.

Increasing use of computer screens make luminance control more critical

Vision on computer screens with typical maximum luminance values in the range of 80 to 120 cd/m² is sensitive to veiling reflections due to luminous elements around them

A daylight source generates high luminance. First, through direct vision of the sky (2,000 to 10,000 cd/m²) or the outdoor environment (similar values if lit by sunlight). Second, because it causes high levels of illuminance on surfaces near the aperture (1,000 to 5,000 lux typically, and more if there is a sun patch). If the receiving surface is bright (reflectance above 60%), its corresponding luminance can reach values in the range of 200 to 1,000 cd/m². Even if the typical reflectance of a computer screen is low (less than 5% usually), the luminance of the reflection on the screen may be 50 cd/m² for a 1,000 cd/m² light source, and 100 cd/m² for a 2,000 cd/m² light source. This is significant by comparison with the maximum brightness (about 100 cd/m²)

of the screen. The resulting situation is a veiling luminance or reflection which makes reading the screen difficult.

Atria: buffer spaces which may also work as light boxes

Various monitored buildings included atria, designed mainly for thermal reasons, acting as buffer spaces with temperatures warmer than outdoor temperatures in winter. While heat losses can be reduced, overheating needs to be avoided through high ventilation rates and proper shading.

▽ Overglazed facades and poor shading may lead to indoor spaces with extreme glare or overheating. Occupants may have no other option but to install their own protective measures.

◁ Multiple apertures tend to be preferable to create bright interiors. However, this may lead to more veiling reflections on computer screens if the apertures are not hidden or if the surfaces receiving most of the light are too bright.

The addition of an atrium as a refurbishment of a courtyard may lead to a reduction of daylight to the adjacent windows by more than 50%.

The main difficulty is that illuminance levels on atria walls are much lower than on external facades (often a third to a fifth). Daylight falls on the windows surrounding the atria at a high incident angle, leading to poor penetration in the interior (daylight penetrates two metres typically). Also, shading on the atrium roof will affect the amount of light available. Secondary daylighting windows facing into the atrium need to be large, at least 50% of the wall surface, to offer any significant contribution of daylight to lighting needs.

The role of surface finishes was assessed. It was found that the reflectance of the floor of the atrium was a significant factor in the daylighting of the two lower floors surrounding the atrium.

Specific problems at high latitudes

At high latitudes, the sun's trajectory is closer to the horizon. If one wants to collect sunlight during the heating season, which is predominant across the year, south-facing clerestories are more appropriate than horizontal roof glazings.

On the contrary, sunlight is a serious source of glare, and fixed overhangs on south facades would need to be large and would reduce significantly the penetration of diffuse light from the sky.

However, the fact that the sun is closer to the horizon leads to shading from obstructions, which can be significant throughout the year.

Thermal trade-off often affects perception of global performance by occupants

Although no specific monitoring was performed regarding the energy performance of the 60 buildings, the thermal trade-offs have been part of our concern: when it was possible, occupants and users were interviewed, and for six selected buildings detailed thermal analyses were performed to assess the energy impacts of the daylighting features.

The energy performance of the buildings as they are today was computed using the energy simulation programme ESP-r (ESRU, 1997) and comparisons were made for configurations without the daylighting features. The RADIANCE programme (Ward, 1993) was used both for the generation of optical parameters for ESP-r and for specific assessment of glare issues.

△ In the atrium of the Beresford Court office building, daylight reflections on the bright floor contribute substantially of the light penetrating the lower floor.

▽ In Göteborg, Sweden, the south-facing clerestory above the atrium of a law court building collects low-level sunlight and reflects it downward.

For most cases, it was found that the savings in annual lighting consumption tended to be large, but that the thermal impact is slightly positive in the case of atria, but negative with light redirecting facade systems. When an increase in thermal loads was reported, they tended to be smaller than the benefits of savings in lighting electricity. However, glare and reduction of diffuse light penetration was found to be critical. For instance, glare was found to be significant when atrium walls would receive direct sunlight.

Conclusion

Working together within a group of about 30 people for three years has led to the establishment of a common know-how in daylighting monitoring which will benefit all participants, their colleagues and institutes, while a significant and valuable resource has been created for building designers and daylighting specialists. No doubt these references will also facilitate the advancement of knowledge when experts and teachers will refer to them when explaining daylighting principles. It is expected that other daylighting monitoring campaigns will be launched in the future, and be more ambitious in terms of their assessment of performance.

Acknowledgements

Thanks are due to: Vincent Berrutto from the National Engineering School of State Public Works (ENTPE, France) for his contribution in the selection of the case studies, and the coordination of the monitoring procedure; Pascale Avouac-Bastie (ENTPE, France) who had the tedious task of collecting the data provided by all participants, checking the quality, and modifying the graphs when necessary; and John Goulding (UCD, Dublin) who provided assistance in editing and reviewing text. The task was conducted with the financial contribution of the European Commission, Directorate General XII for Science, Research and Development.

△ In Trondheim, Norway, the sun's elevation above the horizon is low. This leads to frequent shadowing effects by neighbouring buildings, and severe risks of glare when the sun is visible.

References

ESRU, Energy Simulations Research Unit 'ESP-r, A building and plant energy simulation environment, user guide version 9 series', ESRU publication, University of Strathclyde, Glasgow, 1997.

Ward G., The Radiance 2.3. Synthetic Imaging System, Lawrence Berkeley Laboratory, 1993.

List of participants
Building Research Establishment, Watford
United Kingdom
Conphoebus, Catania
Italy
Faculty of Architecture, Cambridge
United Kingdom
The Martin Centre, Cambridge
United Kingdom
Danish Building Research Institute, Copenhagen
Denmark
Fraunhofer Institut für Bauphysik, Stuttgart
Germany
BBRI, Brussels
Belgium
EDAS, Dept of Architecture, Glasgow
United Kingdom
Energy Research Group, University College Dublin, Dublin
Ireland
Royal Institute of Technology, Gävle
Sweden
Building Services Engineering, Chalmers
Sweden
Danish Technological Institute, Copenhagen
Denmark
ESBENSEN Consulting Engineers, Copenhagen
Denmark
Chalmers University of Technology, Gothenburg
Sweden
LNEC, Lisboa
Portugal
Simos Lighting Consultants, Carouge
Switzerland
A.N. Tombazis & Assoc. Arch., Polydroso, Athens
Greece
National Observatory of Athens, Athens
Greece
ESRU, University of Strathclyde, Glasgow
United Kingdom
Faculty of Architecture, Trondheim
Norway
Norwegian Electrical Power Research Institute, Trondheim
Norway
LESO -PB, EPFL, Lausanne
Switzerland
UPC - Architecture, Barcelona
Spain
Ecole Nationale des Travaux Publics de l'Etat, Lyons
France

Daylight performance of buildings: monitoring procedure

This section presents a procedure which was developed to allow the assessment of the behaviour of buildings and building components with respect to daylight. The goal was the characterization of windows as 'daylighting luminaires', in relation to the space lit and the materials used. Reasons for the success or failure of daylighting options can be deduced from site measurements. An objective analysis of the resulting visual environments is proposed, a means of investigating how they are adapted to the visual needs of occupants. This information should be seen as complementary to subjective assessment, where aesthetics and amenity are of concern. The proposed procedure has been developed within a European monitoring campaign which studied 60 European buildings, and ran from 1996 to 1997 [1].

It focuses on various buildings, old and new, including offices, museums, schools, houses, glazed streets, churches, factories, etc.

Introduction

There is a gap between the large amount of discussion associated with daylight in architectural magazines and the often small amount of useful, scientific information which can be gleaned by readers from these articles. Photographs can give an instant impression of the quality of daylight in a space, but the image depends so much on the skill of the photographer and the selected climatic conditions at the time that it is sometimes difficult for the reader to really understand the dynamics of daylight: is the building bright or dark? In the building are the levels of illuminance well adapted to the activities of the occupants? Are shading devices efficient? This introduces the concept of the 'performance' of a building, or a component with respect to daylighting. This suggests that there is a way to go beyond the image to report the quality of lighting.

On the other hand, light propagation is a well-known phenomenon today, and there are measurement tools to characterize it. A building can be seen as an optical system in which light propagates. Window sizes, surface shapes and finishes affect this propagation, and it should be possible to identify, on site, the exact role of each element in the

▽ The aim of the monitoring procedure has been to understand the optical phenomena involved and how they have created the luminous environment we see in the building.

process. By determining the influence of each element in the final success or failure of architectural options, we can provide useful information to the design community.

Geometric description

The first consideration in daylighting is the dimension of the window with respect to the space to be lit. But the most useful parameter is the exact glazing area, which needs to be adjusted by the transmittance of the glazing. When performing on-site monitoring, it is useful to have access to architectural drawings when they are available. Measurements can then be easily written onto the drawings.

Of great interest is the ratio of the glazed area to the floor area; this is called the 'glazing ratio'. Typically in the range from 5% to 30%, this ratio gives a rapid idea of the general brightness of the space over the year, and also the sensitivity of the space to outdoor climatic conditions.

However, some tinted or diffusing glazing used today may have a transmittance of less than 50%. This means than the glazing ratio needs to be corrected to take account of the transmittance of the glazing. On the other hand, brightness of finishes may multiply amount of light in areas of rooms situated away from apertures by two or three times.

Characterization of opaque and translucent materials

The most important aspect of the optical properties of materials is the difference in behaviour with a point light source (such as the sun for instance) and a diffuse light source (such as an overcast sky or, in general, the luminous conditions inside a building). During a monitoring campaign, it is easy to determine the transmittance of non diffusing glazing perpendicularly to the glazing plane (normal-normal transmittance). It is also useful to assess the transmittance of any glazing (clear, tinted or diffusing) for a diffuse light source such as an overcast sky: this is the hemispherical-hemispherical transmittance. Indoor finishes can be characterized by their reflectance under diffuse light, such as the indoor lighting when the sources of light are not in one direction (for instance when point-light sources such as lamps are well dis-

▽ Windows are the sources of daylight. Their size needs to be compared with the floor area of the zone they illuminate. The ratio of the glazed area to the floor area is the aperture ratio.

tributed over the space, or when daylight comes from two opposite directions). When mirrors are used, it is possible to measure their specular reflectance for given angles.

Measurements require luxmeters, measuring illuminance (lux) incident on the sensor, and luminance meters, measuring the luminance (cd/m^2) of surfaces as they appear from specific points of observation.

Overcast sky as a reference light source to characterize architecture

Although often more appealing, the indoor luminance environment under sunny conditions cannot be easily recorded. Overcast sky conditions are the most standardized conditions in which to perform monitoring. This is

the only way to draw comparisons between different daylighting features installed under different climates. Such skies are typically brighter near the zenith than near the horizon. For this reason, a luminance range check should be performed prior to the measurements. This means ensuring that the average horizon luminance is no more than half the zenith luminance.

Daylight factors for assessment of daylight penetration

Indoor light distribution can be characterized through the measurement of illuminance on all useful surfaces: workplane, walls, paintings, copy-machines, computer screens, etc. However, since the intensity of natural light varies, it is necessary to consider the ratio of the local illuminance to the

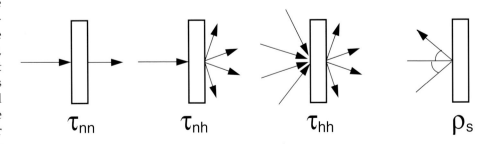

△ Various definitions of transmittance of glazing: normal-normal transmittance, normal-hemispherical transmittance (for diffusing glazing only); hemispherical-hemispherical transmittance; and reflectance.

△ On-site determination of normal-normal transmittance (τ_{nn}) of clear glazing, which the ratio of the luminance of an object seen behind the glazing (L_{in}), in a direction perpendicular to the glazing plane, to the luminance of the same object, in the same direction, without the glazing (L_{out}). $\tau_{nn} = L_{in}/L_{out}$. Practically, the measurements are taken once with the window closed, and once with the window open.

△ On-site determination of the hemispherical-hemispherical transmittance (τ_{hh}) of clear or translucent glazing, which the ratio of illuminance behind the glazing (I_{in}) and in front of the glazing (I_{out}), with the luxmeter being located outside. $\tau_{hh} = I_{in}/I_{out}$. This measurement needs to be performed under overcast sky conditions.

△ On-site determination of the hemispherical-hemispherical reflectance (ρ_{hh}) of materials: the luminance of a given wall surface (L_{wall}) is compared with the luminance of reference samples (one white- L_{white}, one grey L_{grey}). The luminous conditions should be as diffuse as possible: no artificial lighting, no daylight at low/high incidence, etc.

$$\rho_1 = \rho_{white} \cdot \frac{L_{surface}}{L_{white}} \qquad \rho_2 = \rho_{grey} \cdot \frac{L_{surface}}{L_{grey}} \qquad \boxed{\rho_{hh} = \frac{\rho_1 + \rho_2}{2}}$$

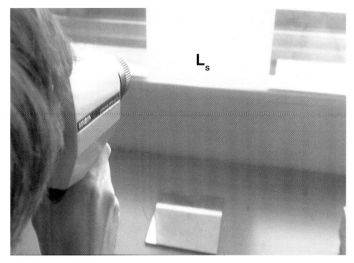

△ On site determination of the specular reflectance (ρ_s) at a given angle: the luminance of the reflection (L_r) is compared to the luminance of the source of light (L_s) , seen from the sample. $\rho_s = L_r / L_s$

simultaneous outdoor horizontal illuminance due to an unobstructed sky, and this ratio is called the 'daylight factor DF(%) [2]'. For this reason, two luxmeters are needed, as well as a way to guarantee that the two readings are performed simultaneously. Typically two people are needed, one inside , one outside. They can communicate by radio or the person outside can record the illuminances at regular steps, every 15 or 30 seconds for instance. Such a measurement procedure was proposed by the Building Research Establishment [3]. During illuminance measurements, sky conditions are continuously checked to make sure that the sky is close to a CIE standard overcast sky, so that measurements are reproducible.

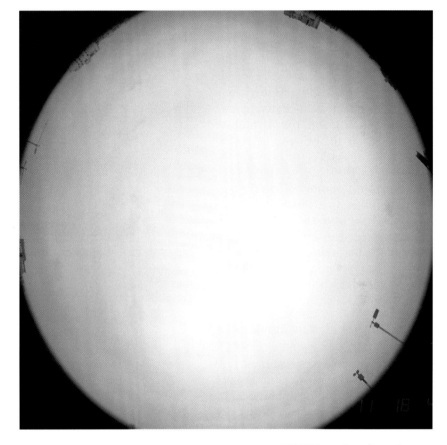

▷ Picture taken with a fish-eye lens. An overcast sky is a practical reference light source allowing comparison of performance between various daylighting systems.

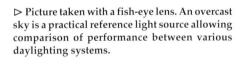

◁ In order to be considered as suitable for monitoring, an overcast sky should have a luminance near the horizon not exceeding half that of the zenith luminance.

△ Daylight factors are obtained by performing indoor illuminance measurements and simultaneous outdoor measurements and expressing the result as a ratio. The outdoor sensor is positioned horizontally, in an unobstructed location, such as the roof of the building for instance. Indoor illuminance (I_{in}) measurements are performed at all locations where they can be compared with specifications of lighting requirements: work places, paintings, computer screens, floors, etc. Simultaneously, the outdoor horizontal illuminance (I_{out}) is recorded, to eliminate errors due to fluctuations of daylight.

On the reference plane, the grid of measurement points needs to be equally spaced in both directions across the room. Across the width of the room, a bigger spacing is reasonable, compared to the spacing in the direction perpendicular to the windows. The distance between points must be adapted to the size of the space, however a minimum of 15 points is recommended to draw contours of equal daylight factor to produce a plot of the distribution of daylight throughout the room. Daylight factor contours are plotted using logarithmic interpolation between points as well as a logarithmic scale.

Light flux provided by daylighting systems

The comparison of the light fluxe (lm) provided by various apertures is of great interest. Incoming light flux is the product of the average illuminance behind a glazing facing outside (I_{in}) and the area of this glazing ($A_{glazing}$). With this technique, it is possible, for instance, to assess the benefits of secondary daylighting windows by comparison with facade windows. For simplicity, the reference climatic conditions used for this assessment are those of an overcast sky providing an outdoor horizontal illuminance of 10,000 lx.

Characterization of the luminous environment

One further stage in the assessment of daylighting performances deals with the attempt to characterize the indoor luminous environment as the occupants

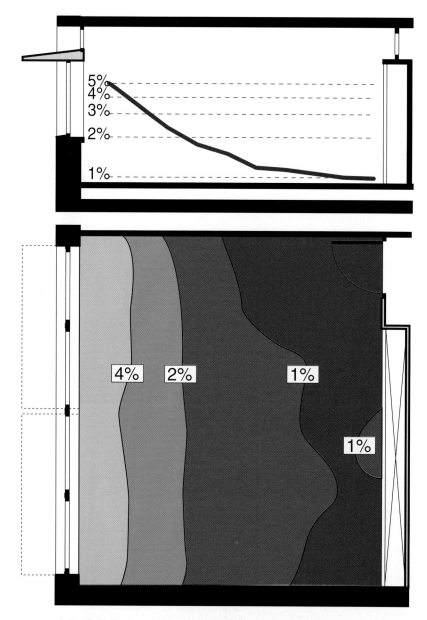

△ Daylight factors are then plotted along a cross-section or with isolux contours on a plane (such as the typical workplane height of 0.8 metres above floor level) to describe daylight penetration. The display of daylight factor (DF) contours provides a clear interpretation of daylight penetration in the monitored room. DF (%) = I_{in} x 100/ I_{out}

△ Determination of the contribution of light reflections on the external ground. The luxmeter is oriented upward and downward to compare light coming from the upper and lower hemispheres.

see it. The measurements are vertical illuminance, and luminance in specific directions.

As far as visual performance is concerned, luminance distribution can cause disability glare and transient adaptation problems [4]. Formulae are proposed in the literature to quantify these two physiological phenomena [4] [5]. However, they require knowledge of some characteristics of the glare source which cannot be easily measured with our spot luminance meters.

As far as visual comfort is concerned, poor luminance distribution can cause discomfort glare which is a different physiological phenomenon than disability glare. However, no index has actually been recommended for assessing discomfort glare due to windows. The Daylight Glare Index (DGI) was proposed for evaluating the discomfort glare produced by the direct view of an unobstructed sky (but not by sunlight) [6]. However, there are four elements which suggest avoiding using this index:

1) it is based on very few experimental data

2) some studies carried out in realistic situations failed to replicate the results which had led to the definition of DGI [7]

3) DGI formula cannot integrate the unmeasurable psychological influence of the prospect viewed through the window;

4) it is not feasible to measure, with standard spot luminancemeters, the parameters required for the

△ Under standard sky conditions adjusted for a horizontal external illuminance of 10,000 lux, the luminous fluxe entering the space can be computed by multiplying the illuminance behind the windows by the area of the glazing. This leads to comparison of the performance of various daylighting systems in terms of lumens brought to the space.

calculation of DGI. Several other glare evaluation systems have been used worldwide [8]. However all of them, even the most such as the Unified Glare Rating, are designed for artificial lighting and are not recommended for use with daylighting.

For our procedure, it was decided to conduct a few luminance measurements in relevant directions, particularly in buildings with work places. At chosen reference locations, luminance was measured in 5-6 typical sight directions simultaneously with the horizontal illuminance outside, as for daylight factor measurements. Then the luminance would be readjusted for a reference overcast sky providing 10,000 lux on the horizontal plane outdoor. The measurement points should be located on the visual task, the surrounding area of the field of view and the remote surfaces. Luminance values are divided by external illuminance values, where upon they are multiplied by 10 klx and reported in wide-angle pictures taken at the chosen reference locations. While this procedure allows us draw general comparisons between different day-lighting design systems, it also enables an assessment of whether the ratio of the task background luminance to the adjacent surrounding luminance lies between 0.3 and 3, and whether the ratio of the task background luminance to the remote surface luminance lies between 0.1 and 10, as is often recommended to prevent disability glare and transient adaptation problems especially at work stations [5]. There are, however, three major drawbacks to this procedure:

1) it may be difficult to locate the surfaces which have the highest (or lowest) luminance in the field of view

2) assuming that these surfaces have been located, it may be impossible to correctly measure them with the luminance metre

3) it may also be difficult, especially for remote surfaces, to determine exactly whether the selected surface causes problems or whether it is necessary for visual interest and distant eye focus. It is indeed recommended to provide in a luminous environment small visual areas which exceed the luminance-ratio recommendations [5].

Vertical illuminance measurements are performed to assess the homogeneity or non-homogeneity of the luminances distribution in the field of view of an observer. They lead to the rating of the ability of a daylighting system to attenuate glare. The measurements are conducted under standard overcast conditions, and adjusted for a reference outdoor illuminance of 10,000 lux.

Veiling reflections are disturbing light reflections on a screen, a table, a painting due to the specular nature of its surface. The origin of the veiling reflection is identified in installing a mirror on the medium displaying the light source.

Sunlight penetration

There are some measurements or visual assessments which can be performed objectively under sunny conditions.

Pictures and measurements conducted under sunny conditions with and without shading show the attenuation of light due to the sunshading system: sun patches may still exist even if attenuated, or awnings may become a

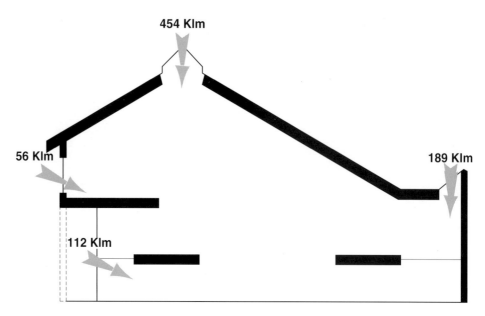

△ Values of fluxe in lumens allow a quick comparison with the theoretical number of lamps or luminaires providing an equivalent light flux. The typical performance index used for this comparison is 60lm/W corresponding to modern fluorescent or metal halide sources in efficient luminaires (values shown for an overcast sky leading to a horizontal illuminance of 10,000 lux).

▷ Luminance measurement from an observer's point of view allows the determination of excessive contrasts. For instance, luminance values larger than 10 times the luminance of the task will appear as sources of disability glare and would lead to transient adaptation problems. If the luminance surrounding the task is below 10% of the task luminance, eye strain may also be caused, since the task itself will become a source of glare.

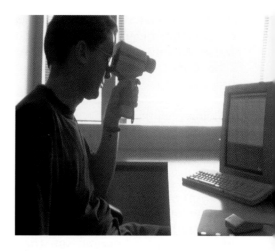

▷ A fish-eye lens is best suited to display all elements in the field of vision.

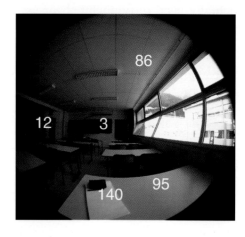

△ Assessment of hemispherical - hemispherical transmittance of diffusing awnings. No direct sun beams should hit the window pane - overcast sky conditions prefered.

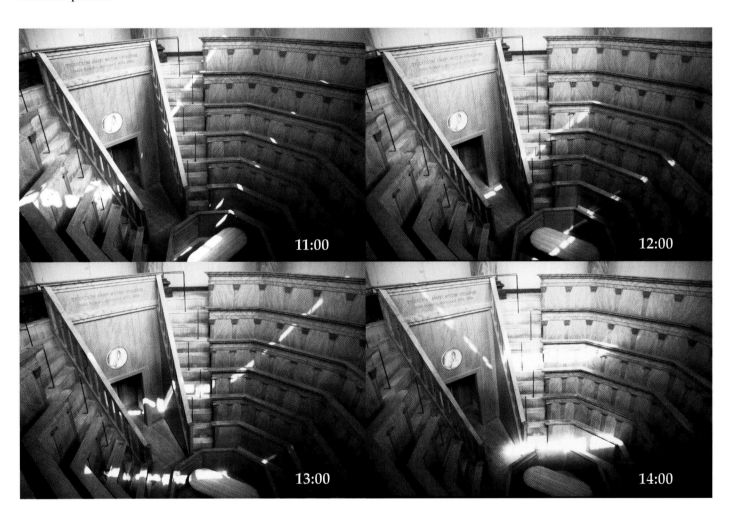

glare source if they are both brightly coloured and diffusing. It is suggest that recording and observation should be done for equinoxes and solstices.

Sequences of pictures may show the varying patterns associated with the movement of sun patches in the interior.

△ Sequences of pictures of sunlight penetration at referenced dates such as solstices and equinoxes showing the response of the architecture or the daylighting system to incoming sunlight.

▷ Veiling reflections on glossy surfaces are identified using a mirror surface. It shows the image of the disturbing light source. If no light source is visible in the mirror, it shows that it is located in such a position that no veiling reflections are generated.

Conclusion

This procedure has been tested and used for 60 buildings throughout Europe. It has required cross-checking of the calibration of the instruments, and training sessions. Regular discussions at meetings between participants occured during the three years of the programme. Further details regarding the procedure, the results, and the equipment will be found in [9].

Using simple measuring equipment was a real challenge undertaken by the participants of 'Daylight Europe'. The procedure described in this section was successfully tested in a pilot study and is currently being applied all over Europe. A companion volume to this book dealing with daylighting design guidelines has also been prepared within the Daylight Europe project [10].

Acknowledgements

The work described in this book forms part of the Daylight Europe Project, funded by the European Commission, DGXII for Science, Research and Development, and coordinated by Esbensen Consulting Engineers (DK). The participating teams are:
Esbensen(DK), The Martin Centre (UK), ENTPE (F), UPC (E), SINTEF (N), LNEC (P), CTH (S), Univ. of Athens (Gr), SBI (DK), IBP (D), LESO (CH), BRE (UK), BBRI (B), Conphoebus (I), ESRU (UK), KTH (S), UCD (IRL), A.N. Tombazis & ass. Architects (GR).

References

[1] P. E. Kristensen, "Daylight Europe", Proc. 4th E. C. SolarEnergy in Architecture and UrbanPlanning, Berlin, 1996.

[2] R. G. Hopkinson, P. Petherbridge, J. Longmore, "Daylighting", Heinemann, London, 1966.

[3] P. J. Littlefair, M. E. Aizlewood, "Measuring daylight in real buildings", to be published in Proc. CIBSE National Conf., Bath, 1996.

[4] Commission Internationale de l'Eclairage, "An analytic model for describing the influence of lighting parameters upon visual performance", CIE 19/2.1 & 19/2.2, 1981.

[5] Illuminating Engineering Society of North America, "Lighting Handbook", ed.: M. Rea, IESNA, 1993.

[6] P. Chauvel, J. B. Collins, R. Dogniaux, J. Longmore, "Glare from windows - current views of the problem", Lighting Res. Technol. 14 (1), pp. 31-46, 1982.

[7] T. Iwata et al., "Subjective response on discomfort glare caused by windows", Proc. of the CIE 22nd Session (Melbourne), pp. 108-109, 1991.

[8] Commission Internationale de l'Eclairage, "Discomfort glare in interior lighting", CIE 117, 1995.

[9] Marc Fontoynont Editor, Daylight Performance of Buildings, James and James Science Publishers Ltd, London, 1998.

[10] Nick Baker, Editor Daylighting Design Guidelines, James and James Science Publishers Ltd, London, 1999.

Daylighting systems used

Category	Building	Country	Page	Glazed roof	Roof monitors	Translucent ceiling / floor	Atrium / courtyard	Glazed street	Glazed wall facade	Windows	Clerestories	Light-shelves	Prismatic devices / optical	Secondary daylighting	Passive sunlight control	Active sunlight control	View versus glare	Video Display Units (VDU's)	Bright indoor finishes	Colouring effects
Glazed Streets	SAS Headquarters	SWE	29	●				●	●					●					●	
	St Hubert Galleries	BEL	33	●				●						●						
	Galleria V. Emmanuele II	ITA	37	●				●						●						
Transportation buildings	Stansted Airport	GBR	41		●			●							●				●	
	Waterloo International Terminal	GBR	45	●				●	●									●		
Churches	Saint Jean Cathedral	FRA	51							●	●									●
	Chapel Notre Dame du Haut	FRA	55							●	●				●				●	●
	Baroque Church	DEU	59							●	●								●	
	Sainte-Marie de la Tourette Convent	FRA	63		●							●			●					●
	Pantheon Dome	ITA	67		●										●					
Museums	Neue Staatsgalerie	DEU	73	●		●									●		●		●	
	Wallraf-Richartz-Museum	DEU	77		●										●		●		●	
	Byzantine Museum	GRC	81		●						●				●				●	
	Musée de Grenoble	FRA	85		●										●				●	
	Trapholt Art Museum	DNK	89		●								●		●				●	
	Waucquez Department Store	BEL	93	●		●	●							●	●				●	
	Modern Art Centre	PRT	99						●		●				●		●		●	
	Sir John Soane's Museum	GBR	103		●						●				●				●	
	Louvre Museum	FRA	107		●										●				●	
Offices	Tractebel Building	BEL	113						●							●	●	●		
	Sukkertoppen	DNK	117	●			●		●						●		●			
	Trundholm Town Hall	DNK	121				●		●						●		●			
	Domino Haus	DEU	125	●			●		●						●		●			
	Architects Office	GRC	129							●	●				●		●			
	Beresford Court	IRL	133	●			●		●						●					●
	EOS Building	CHE	137								●	●			●	●	●			
	Reiterstrasse Building	CHE	141		●		●			●					●		●			
	UAP Insurance Building	CHE	145							●					●	●	●			
	Victoria Quay	GBR	147				●			●					●	●	●	●		
	National Observatory of Athens	GRC	151							●							●	●		
	Statoil Research Centre	NOR	153							●					●		●			
	Kristallen office building	SWE	157	●			●			●				●			●		●	
	CNA-SUVA Building	CHE	161							●			●	●	●					
	Gothenburg Law Courts Annex	SWE	165		●					●				●	●					
	LNEC Main Building	PRT	169							●	●			●	●	●	●			
	Irish Energy Centre	IRL	173				●			●					●	●	●			
Educational buildings	Dragvoll University Centre	NOR	179	●			●			●					●	●				
	Pharmacy Faculty	PRT	183		●		●			●					●	●				
	Queen's Building	GBR	191								●	●			●		●	●		
	Anatomy Lecture Theatre	SWE	197								●									
	Collège de la Terre Sainte	CHE	201		●		●								●	●				
	Collège La Vanoise	FRA	205		●		●					●			●	●			●	●
	Berthold Brecht School	DEU	211		●		●								●				●	
	Training Centre-Agricultural Bank	GRC	215		●						●	●			●				●	
	Teachers Training College	PRT	219		●										●	●			●	
Libraries	Stockholm Public Library	SWE	225								●				●					
	Darwin College Library	GBR	229							●	●						●	●		
	Bibliothèque Nationale de France	FRA	233		●					●					●					
	Trinity College Library	GBR	237							●							●			
	APU Learning Resource Centre	GBR	241	●			●				●	●			●					
Houses	La Roche House	FRA	247							●	●								●	
	Architect's House	GRC	251		●					●	●			●						●
	Casa Serra	ESP	255		●					●	●			●						
	Hawkes' House	GBR	259							●	●			●						
Demonstration projects	German Pavilion	ESP	265						●						●				●	
	Conphoebus Office Building	ITA	269								●	●			●	●				
	Brundtland Centre	DNK	275		●						●			●						
Others	The Palm House	GBR	281	●			●		●											
	Fagus-Werk	DEU	285		●	●			●							●				
	Paustian House	DNK	289		●		●			●	●								●	

21

What will you get in this book ?

Daylight factor variations.

Expressed in % of the outdoor horizontal illuminance simultaneously measured for an unobstructed sky. They have been measured for specific overcast conditions (see section on the monitoring procedure for more details). Under overcast conditions the indoor illuminances are proportional to the out-door horizontal illuminance: when the outdoor illuminance is doubled, all indoor illuminances are also doubled. The daylight factor is a quantity which describes best the ability of a building to let natural light in. It can be used to assess the fraction of the operating time during which given illuminance thresholds are exceeded.

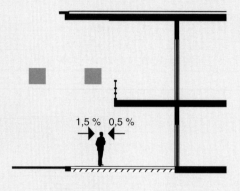

◁ Vertical daylight factors are measured either to assess the corresponding average luminance in the field of view (L = E/p), or to assess the amount of light penetrating vertical windows.

▽ Daylight factors variations displayed in plan, using iso-DF lines. This presentation gives an indication of the areas concerned by daylight penetration, or its absence.

▽ Daylight factors variations displayed along a cross-section. Note that the vertical scale is logarithmic, since such is the perception by the human eye.

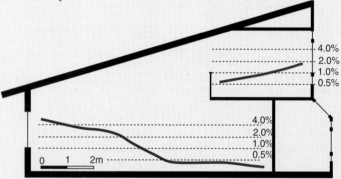

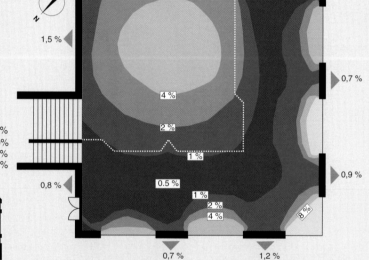

Assessment of luminous fluxes

A luminous flux is expressed in lumen (lm). For instance, a 60 W incandescent light bulb produces around 900 lm, a 36 W T8 fluorescent tube around 3,000 lm. We present sometimes the luminous fluxes penetrating windows for one standard overcast sky condition, the one which would lead to an outdoor horizontal illuminance in the absence of obstructions of 10,000 lux. The value of the luminous flux (lm) crossing a surface S is the product of the value of its area (m²) by the illuminance (lux) measured in its plan.

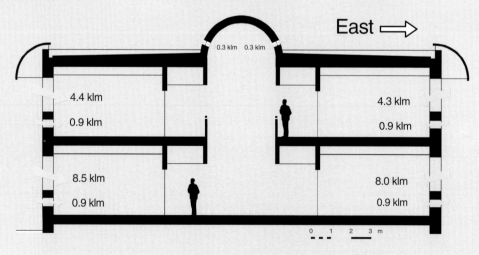

△ Comparison of luminous fluxes penetrating a room through various openings under a standard overcast sky condition providing an outdoor illuminance of 10,000 lux. It could be compared with fluxes supplied by luminaires equipped with fluorescent tubes. A luminaire equipped with a 36W T8 tube produces around 1.5 Klm.

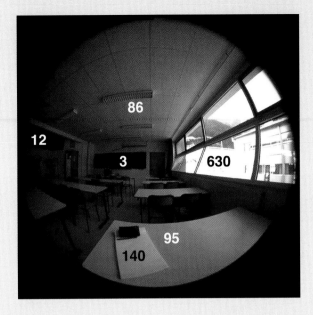

△ Comparison of luminances of windows and indoor surfaces for assessment of glare. Left: with fish-eye lens, right with 20mm lens.

Luminance distribution (cd/m²)

The luminance is a quantity which can be measured (with a luminance meter) to describe the 'brightness' of a surface, such as a wall, a desk surface or a transluscent window. It is sometimes useful to measure the luminances of surfaces in various directions in the field of view of an observer, to characterize the homogeneity or non-homogeneity of the luminances. It should be remembered that the sensitivity of the eye to light is logarithmic. Typical luminances of surfaces in a building are in the range of 1 to 100 cd/m², 100 to 1,000 cd/m² for surfaces of bright appearances: clear walls under daylight, lampshades when lamps are turned on or dark skies seen from the interior of a building. In the range of 1,000 to 10,000 cd/m² are most light sources (sky, reflections of sunbeams on construction elements or clear indoor finishes and luminaires (unless 'low luminance luminaires'). In this range of luminances, the sources are often glary if they are in the field of vision. The filament of an incandescent light bulb, or the sun, reach much higher luminances, above 100,000 cd/m².

Materials properties assessed on site

	Colour	Hemispherical-hemispherical reflectance
Floor	light grey/white	51%
Ceiling (concrete)	dark grey	19%
Wall	white	84%

	Normal-normal transmittance	Hemispherical-hemispherical transmittance
Double glazing	71%	78%

▷ Bright finishes lead to substantial increase of illuminances particularly in areas far away from apertures.

▽ Bookshelves and walls made of wood absorb daylight penetration.

Material properties

Indoor finishes and glazing materials contribute to final illuminance levels in a building. In areas far away from the apertures, indoor finishes may be the major contributors to the amount of light available. The transmittance of glazing or shading has a direct effect on the amount of light penetrating a building. On-site characterization of material's optical properties has been conducted for each case study. The detail of the procedure is described in the section 'Monitoring procedure'.

Map of Europe

●147 *Number indicates page of case study*

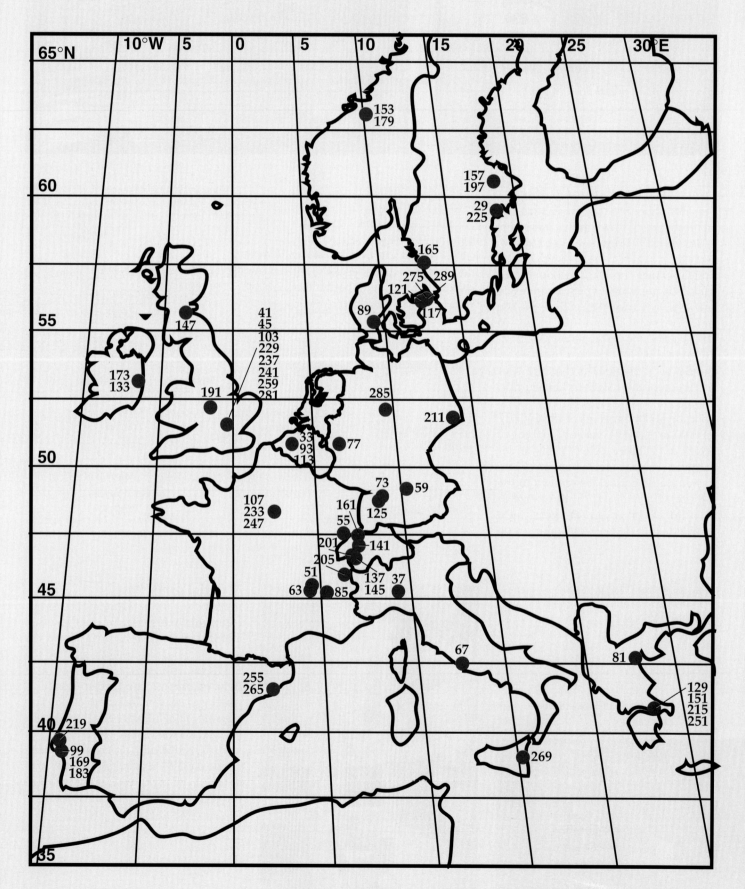

Buildings monitored by each organization

Team	Case study building	Team	Case study building
BBRI	Tractebel Building, Brussels Waucquez Department Store, Brussels St Hubert Galleries, Brussels	FIB	Fagus-Werk, Alfeld an der Leine Neue Staatsgalerie, Stuttgart Wallraf-Richartz Museum, Cologne Domino Haus, Reutlinger Baroque Church, Neresheim Monastery Berthold Brecht School, Dresden
BRE	Queen's Building, De Montfort Univ., Leicester Waterloo International Terminal, London		
Camb	Stansted Airport, Stansted, Essex The Palm House, Royal Botanic Gardens, Kew Darwin College Library, Cambridge Trinity College Library, Cambridge APU Learning Resource Centre, Chelmsford Hawkes' House, Cambridge Sir John Soane's Museum, London	LNEC	Pharmacy Faculty, Lisbon Modern Art Centre, Lisbon Teacher's Training College, Setbal LNEC Main Building, Lisbon
		SBI	Trapholt Art Museum, Kolding Sukkertoppen, Valby Trundholm Town Hall, Trundholm Paustian House, Copenhagen
CONPH	Conphoebus Office Building, Catania Pantheon Dome, Rome Galleria V. Emanuele II, Milan	U. of Athens	Byzantine Museum,Thessaloniki Architects Office, Polydroso, Athens National Observatory of Athens, Athens Architect's House, Kifissia, Athens Agricultural Bank of Greece, Athens
CUT	Anatomy Lecture Theatre, Uppsala Stockholm Public Library, Stockholm SAS Head Quarters, Stockholm Kristallen office building, Uppsala Göteborg Law Courts Annex, Göteborg		
EFI	Dragvoll University Centre, Trondheim Statoil Research Centre, Trondheim	UCD	Beresford Court, Dublin Irish Energy Centre, Dublin
		UPC	Casa Serra, Barcelona
ENTPE	Bibliothèque Nationale de France, Paris Musèe of Grenoble, Grenoble German Pavilion, Barcelona Saint-Jean Cathedral, Lyons Chapel Notre Dame du Haut, Ronchamp Sainte Marie de la Tourette Convent, Eveux La Roche House, Paris Collège La Vanoise, Modane Louvre Museum, Paris		
EPFL/LESO	EOS Building, Lausanne Reiterstrasse Building, Berne UAP Insurance Building, Lausanne CNA - SUVA Building, Basle Collège de la Terre Sainte, Coppet		
ESB/SBI	Brundtland Centre, Toftlund, Denmark		
ESRU/EDAS	Victoria Quay, The Scottish Office, Edinburgh		

BBRI	= Belgian Building Research Institute	**ENTPE**	= Ecole Nationale des Travaux Publics de l'Etat	**EDAS**	= Energy Design Advisory Service
BRE	= Building Research Establishment	**EPFL**	= Ecole Polytechnique Fédérale de Lausanne	**SBI**	= Danish Building Research Institute
Camb	= University of Cambridge	**LESO**	= Laboratoire d'Energie Solaire et de physique	**FIB**	= Fraunhofer-Institute für Bauphysik
CONPH	= Conphoebus		du bâtiment	**LNEC**	= Laboratório Nacional de Engenharia Civil
CUT	= Chalmers University of Technology	**ESB**	= Esbensen, Consulting Engineers	**UCD**	= University College Dublin
EFI	= Norwegian Electrical Institute	**ESRU**	= Energy Systems Research Unit	**UPC**	= Universitat Politècnica de Catalunya

Glazed streets

Developed in the 19th century because of the emergence of steel construction and glazing technologies, glazed streets allow us to enjoy shopping in European city centres sheltered from rain and bad weather. They reduce daylight penetration compared to open streets by at least 50% due to obstruction by steel beams and glazing bars, reduced transmittance of glazing and dirt deposits. The importance of bright facades and floor finishes is significant, and daylight distribution in neighbouring buildings requires larger glazed areas than in open streets.

A central atrium becomes a 170m long planted street

SAS Headquarters, Stockholm, SWEDEN

Eight building aisles join together along a central street, leading to a micro-urban environment.

Innovative management of office spaces

The SAS Headquarters is one of the first examples of the new Scandinavian floor plan type called *combi-office*. In the SAS case, each employee has his own private zone, and accesses a semi-private zone which is designed to encourage contacts within groups. The central street is designed to create the feeling of urban environment within the building. It houses various stores: bank, grocery, bakery, restaurants, etc as well as services, not to mention a sports hall and a swimming pool.

▽ The central glazed atrium can be seen as a resurrection of the 20th century covered street in Europe.

A glazed street, where white wall finishes contribute significantly to daylight penetration

Daylight penetrates mainly from the sloped triple glazed roof and partly, but to a much lower extent, from openings on the higher floors between each of the individual buildings. In the main part of the street the daylight factor is constant with levels around 16%. In three areas of the glazed street sidelighting has a major impact on the daylight factor on floor level, with values reaching 25% locally. The north-western end seems to get additional daylight because of reflections from the small lake outside. Local obstructions such as trees or gangways reduce daylight factors value to about 4%.

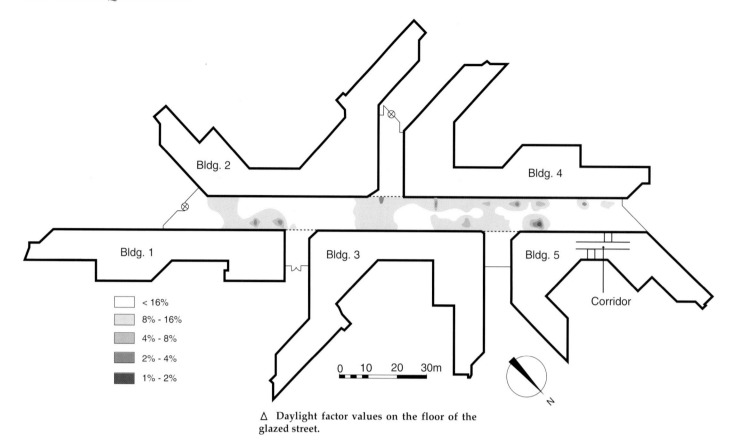

< 16%
8% - 16%
4% - 8%
2% - 4%
1% - 2%

0 10 20 30m

N

△ Daylight factor values on the floor of the glazed street.

◁ The central street distributes light to six floors.

△ Aerial view.

It should be noted that wall finishes are extremely bright (reflectance 0.75) allowing atrium windows to benefit from reflections on atrium walls, particularly for lower floors. Vertical daylight factors in the middle of the street are around 10%.

Cross-section of buildings of 12 metres for office spaces

The individual offices are about 4m deep, with a central corridor 3m large. Partitions between corridors and offices are fully glazed, allowing daylight to penetrate in the corridor. There, the resulting daylight factors are low (about 0.5%) but sufficient for circulation. On the fifth floor, the amount of daylight

△ Fifth floor office near the atrium showing award-winning luminaire.

Fifth floor office near the facade, △ showing glazed partition towards central corridor.

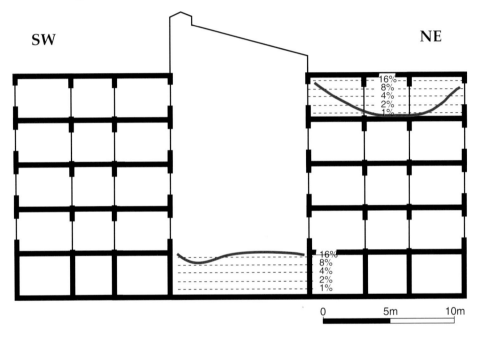

SW

NE

16%
8%
4%
2%
1%

16%
8%
4%
2%
1%

◁ south-west/north-east section of the SAS Headquarters buildings 4 and 5.

0   5m   10m

coming from the atrium appears a little bit higher than the one coming from the facade, due to larger glazed area and better transmittance. It should be noted that all windows facing the atrium are equipped with external moveable awnings for solar protection and privacy.

Heating, ventilation and air-conditioning systems

The building complex has a water/air air-conditioning system with individual cooling through cooled free-convection beams in each office room. Through these cooling beams cooled water is constantly circulated. The heating in the office rooms is mainly supplied by direct electric resistance radiators under the windows. The heating and cooling supply of the building complex uses the aquifer that the building is located on. In summertime the aquifer is used for cooling the water supplied to cooling beams and air cooling coils. In winter, the aquifer water is used as a heat source for heat pumps that supply air coils, the hydronic radiator system and service hot water. The heating and cooling supply systems have been extensively monitored and evaluated. The result is that it works well and delivers cooling at a low cost.

Award-winning indirect luminaires

The building complex has a standard lighting system with no daylighting controls, although there is manual lighting control in each office room. To avoid reflections on computer monitors nearly all office rooms have floor-mounted up-lights, with a small amount of directed down-light. These fixtures, specially designed for SAS HQ, received prizes for good lighting design and became popular in Sweden after the SAS HQ was finished. Here are two useful references:

- Jansson, Ingemar 1988 "SAS Frösundavik - A Creation in Glass and Light with 15 Light Sources per Employee". *Ljuskultur, No 3-1988, pp 4-9.* Ljuskultur, Stockholm, Sweden (in Swedish).
- Anonymous 1988 "Light of the Year 1987. First Prize - Office Rooms at SAS Frösundavik". *Ljuskultur, No 6-1988, pp 5-7.* Ljuskultur, Stockholm, Sweden (in Swedish).

They include three 38W compact fluorescent lamps aimed at the ceiling and one 38W lamp aimed downward, toward the round section of the working table.

SAS HEADQUARTERS

△ The entrance at the south-eastern end, showing painted aluminium trellises for solar protection.

▷ The restaurant at the north western end.

Daylighting monitoring

The daylight measurements were carried out 25 to 26 May 1995 and concentrated mainly to the glazed street and two office rooms on the 5th floor in the northernmost building, Building 5. Daylight factors were measured at a height of 0.8m above the floor of the glazed street in grids of 2m by 2m. Measurements were taken at almost 600 points. In the office rooms daylight factors were also measured 0.8m above the floor, with a grid of 0.5 x 1.0m.

Material properties assessed on site

	Hemispherical-hemispherical reflectances
Atrium walls	75%
Atrium floor	35%
Office walls	76%

	Hemispherical-hemispherical transmittance
External facade glazing (triple glazing)	65%
Atrium facade glazing	73%
Atrium roof glazing	81%

CREDITS

Building description
The building is located in Frösundavik in Solna, a suburb of Stockholm
Gross floor area: 63,500m²
Net floor area: 40,000m² with the possibility to add a similar area on the grounds
Office space: 1,450 rooms each 12m²
Construction period: Nov 1985 - Dec 1987
Windows: triple glass with a slight green colour.

External solar shading: light, painted aluminium trellises, inclined 45°, so arranged that they cast characteristic horizontal light strips on the walls.

Climate
Stockholm (Latitude: 59°21'N, Longitude: 18°04'E) is located on the Swedish Baltic coast, which means that the climate is somewhat more continental than the temperate north European coastal type. The monthly average temperature is around -3°C in winter and around 17°C in summer. During October to February there are on average 15 to 20 totally cloudy days per month whereas during the rest of the year there are on average 8 to 12 totally cloudy days per month. The clear days are maximum during March to August with an average of 5 to 7 clear days per month. During November and December there are only about 2 clear days per month.

Acknowledgements
National funding for the monitoring from the Department of Energy Efficiency (DOEE) at the Swedish National Administration of Technical and Industrial Development (NUTEK) and from the Swedish Council for Building Research (BFR) is gratefully acknowledged.

Client
SAS - Scandinavian Airlines Systems
S-185 95 SOLNA

Architect
Niels Torp A/S Arkitekter MNAL, Olso, Norway
Artificial lighting design: Lighting Design Partnership/Niels Torp A/S
Furnishing on office floors: PLAN 5 Arkitekter AB/Ahlström & Kock

Monitoring organisation
Chalmers University of Technology, Department of Building Services Engineering and The Monitoring Centre for Energy Research - S-412 96 GÖTEBORG, SWEDEN

References
Hultin, Olof. 1985 "The Competition about SAS Headquarters". *Arkitektur* No. 3-1985, pp 16-24. Arkitekturförlag, Stockholm, Sweden. (in Swedish)

Brady, Michael. 1987 "Niels Torp - Norway's Master Builder". *SCANORAMA* July/August 1987, pp 78-84. SAS, Copenhagen, Denmark.

Torp, Niels. 1988 "SAS Headquarters, Frösundavik". *Arkitektur* No. 5-1988, pp 6-16. Arkitekturförlag, Stockholm, Sweden. (in Swedish)

Edblom, Mats. 1988 "Norwegian Mirror". *Arkitektur* No. 5-1988, p 17. Arkitekturförlag, Stockholm, Sweden. (in Swedish)

A 19th century glazed street with unobtrusive but efficient natural ventilation

St Hubert Galleries, Brussels, BELGIUM

The high transmittance of the cylindrical glazed roof of the St Hubert Galleries admits a large amount of daylight to the ground level. Bright facade finishes help to increase daylight penetration in adjacent spaces.

Bright and elegant shopping streets protected from the outside climate

The St Hubert galleries are a set of three covered streets built in 1847 in Brussels. The building of the galleries was one of the most successful embellishments of the centre of Brussels. Their simple, elegant and rational architecture in an Italian neo-Renaissance style attracted the public and with its set of fine stores it became a fashionable meeting place from the beginning. Completed in 1847, the gallery was the biggest in Europe. The gallery is composed of shops on the ground floor, offices and apartments below the glazed roof, and mansard rooms above the glazed roof. The glazed roof is made of 450 semi-circular self-supporting cast-iron arches which create very little obstruction to the incoming daylight. The floor is dark, but the walls are bright. The general feeling is that the level of brightness is very similar to that of an uncovered street. The daylight factor in the centre of the gallery is about 17%. Though daylight factors are high in the gallery, they decrease rapidly to below 1% behind the shop windows. This causes the shop windows to appear underlit and consequently they require electric lighting all year round to enhance the display of their products.

Hot air is naturally extracted through spaces between panes in the glazed roof

The glass roof was designed in order to allow sufficient natural ventilation of the galleries and to prevent dripping condensation and dirt from the roof. The system consists of overlapping panes combining ventilation and the automatic drainage of condensation and rain water to the outside. To obtain a good natural ventilation, the roof was additionally split up into two parts with a bigger gap between them (see cross-section).

◁ A neo-Renaissance shopping center of the 19th century, roofed over by a semi-cylindrical self-supporting roof structure.

ST HUBERT GALLERIES

▷ The cylindrical roof above the street is made of overlapping glass panes with waterproof gaps allowing easy exhaust of hot air. Condensation is drained to the outside automatically.

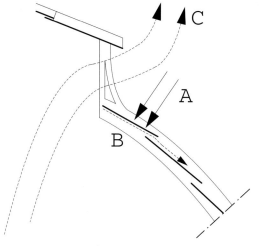

△ Sectional view of the glazed roof explaining its three functions (A: protection against precipitation; B: condensation drainage; C: natural ventilation).

▷ Daylight factor distribution in the gallery and the neighbouring spaces.

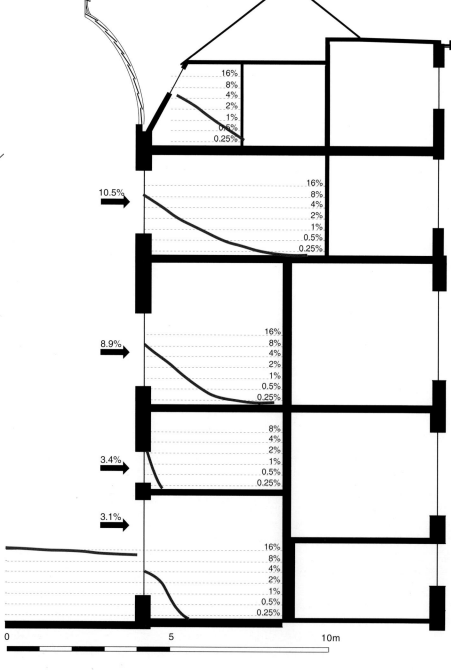

▷ Indoor view of office space lit by the gallery.

▷ Powerful artificial lighting and different colours of light are needed in shop windows to eliminate veiling reflections.

Sharp decrease of illuminances on facades due to the narrowness of the gallery

Illuminance values on facades rapidly decrease from top to bottom of the facades due to the increasing obstruction of the opposite building. Vertical daylight factors decrease from a value of 10.5% at the upper window level to 3.1% at 1.5 metres above the gallery floor. If this is compared with the horizontal daylight factor of more than 12% on the floor, it leads to the conclusion that no useful light is being reflected from the floor to the facades.

The high obstructions facing the windows cause shallow penetration of daylight at each floor. The brightness of the facade finish is not sufficient to compensate for this phenomenon.

For instance, a daylight factor of 2% is barely reached at about one metre from the windows on most floors. This suggests that window sizes need to be enlarged in the case of such a double attenuation of daylight from the glazed roof which reduces the incoming light by about 30%, and the obstructions which may reduce this amount to a ratio as low as 1/10. Single glazing is used throughout the gallery.

◁ Bright facade finish and high windows lead to an increase of daylight penetration into interiors.

Daylight monitoring

Daylighting monitoring was conducted during two overcast days: 11 April 1996 (approx 10 Klux) and 2 May 1996 (approx 20 Klux).

Material properties assessed on site

	Colour	Hemispherical-hemispherical reflectances
Facade	white and light grey	65%
Floor	black	16%

		Normal-normal transmittance
Roof glass		90%
Interior glazing		90%
Shop vitrines		90%

CREDITS

Building description
The St Hubert Galleries are composed of three galleries: the King's Gallery and the Queen's Gallery are in line with each other and the later Prince's Gallery is perpendicular to the two others and differs from them by its smaller size and the simpler double-pitched roof.

King's and Queen's Gallery:
Construction: 1846 to 1847
Total length 213m, width 8m, height 18m.

Prince's Gallery:
Construction: 1860
total length 54m, width 4.5m.

Climate
Minimal monthly temperature: 2.4°C (January)
Maximal monthly temperature: 17.1°C (July)
Annual sunshine duration: 1600 hours
Latitude: 50°N, Longitude: 4°E
Altitude: 100m

Client
Galeries Royales Saint-Hubert sca
Galerie du Roi 5
1000 Bruxelles
Tel: ++32.2-512 2061
Fax: ++32.2-514 5355

Architect
Jean-Pierre Cluysenaar (1811-1880)

Monitoring organisation
BBRI (WTCB-CSTC)
Violetstraat 21-23
1000 Brussels
Tel: ++32.2-502 6690
Fax: ++32.2-502 8180

A daylit gallery which fosters urban life in downtown Milan

Galleria Vittorio Emanuele II, Milan, ITALY

This gallery is more animated (although darker) than neighbouring streets of similar dimensions, its attraction being largely related to its glazed roof, and the decorated floor.

250 metres of covered streets, with facades which are brighter near the ground

The gallery Vittorio Emanuele II was designed by the architect Giuseppe Mengoni and it was built from 1865 to 1878 by the Milan Municipality. It connects Piazza del Duomo with Via Manzoni where the Teatro alla Scala is located.

The gallery is the traditional centre of the Milanese social life and it houses elegant cafés, boutiques and book-shops. Mengoni designed the Gallery in the form of a Latin cross crowned at a height of 47 metres with a glass cupola having a diameter of 37.8 metres. The plan of the imposing work is characterized by a central octagonal square with two traverse wings both 13.6 metres wide and 32 metres high and respectively 166 and 100 metres long. The longer wing is north-south oriented and it ends on the south side. The structure of the work is completely made of iron with wired glass 6mm thick.

The floor of the gallery is decorated with ceramics in various patterns with average reflectances of 20%. The finish of the upper part of the facades is light brown with a reflectance of 30%. The lower part of the facades is brighter, with a reflectance of 40%.

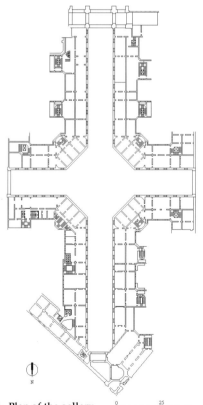

△ Plan of the gallery.

◁ The gallery and the uncoverd street on the same axis (with DF values of 15% on the floor of the former, and around 35% for the latter.

37

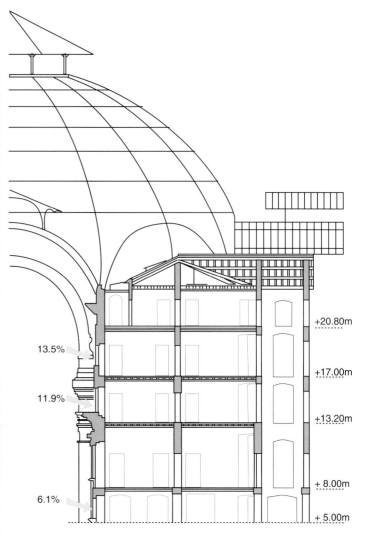

◁ Tiled patterns on the floor below the rotunda.

△ Daylight factors along the facades of the glazed street.

Daylight factors from 10% in the gallery to 20% under the cupola

The horizontal daylight factor was measured at 1.7 metres above the floor. In the central octagonal square, under the glazed cupola, the horizontal daylight factor is 20% at the centre and 15% on the border line of the square. In the wings, the average value is of the order of 15%. Such values are similar to those found in the halls of railway stations built at the same period. By comparing values with the similar ones in uncovered streets, it suggests that the overall transmittance of the cover is about 40%. (In fact, a value of 45% was obtained with laboratory measurements).

Daylighting monitoring

Daylighting monitoring was performed on 7 May 1997 from 15:00 to 15:30 solar time, and on 8 May 1997 from 9:00 to 10:00 solar time. The sky was overcast and the average horizontal external illuminance was 17,000 lux. The reference exterior point was placed on the roof of a building located in the south wing of the gallery.

Material properties assessed on site

	Hemispherical-hemispherical reflectances
Upper facade finish	30%
Lower facade finish	40%
Floor tiles	20%
	Hemispherical hemispherical transmittances
Roof cover (with wired glass - 6mm)	45%

CREDITS

Building
Two glazed streets 166 metres and 100 metres long, 13.6 metres wide and 32 metres high. The rotunda, has a diameter of 37.8m and a is located at a height of 47m. The gallery was built from 1865 and 1878. It belongs to the Municipality of Milan.

Climate
The location is Milan: Latitude: 45°45′N, Longitude: 9°18′E, Altitude: 122m.
Minimum monthly average temperature: 1.7°C (January).
Maximum monthly average temperature: 25.1°C (July). Annual sunshine duration: 1869 hours/years.

Architect
Giuseppe Mengoni

Monitoring organisation
Conphoebus, Energy in building Department Zona Industriale, Passo Martino 95030 Piano d'Arci, Catania, Italy
Tel. +39.95-291407
Fax: +39.95-291246

Transportation buildings

Airports and railway terminals tend to be large halls housing a wide range of activities. For most travellers, their concerns are to find the right information on notice boards or displays, proceed to the gates or platforms, and occupy the waiting time. It is a time of mixed activities, sometimes under high stress (looking for the information, getting the tickets or boarding passes, proceeding to the embarkation areas) and other more relaxed activites such as shopping or simply waiting.

Good lighting design responds to these needs by seeking to provide the best quality of lighting for the presentation of information, directions, etc. together with pleasant, interesting environments for the waiting spaces and service areas.

Of particular interest for daylighting designers is the pleasantness of the space in general, the quality of the lighting environment and appropriateness of the lighting at information displays or signage. Unwanted reflections, sunlight penetration or back-light may become highly disturbing. But the general quality of daylight can help reduce the stress levels experienced by the travellers, and provide a pleasant moment in a journey.

Light surface finishes compensate for moderate size of roof apertures

Stansted Airport, Stansted, Essex, UNITED KINGDOM

The Stansted Air Terminal is like a gigantic light box, with daylight and artificial light integrated around tree-like columns.

▽ Stansted terminal, with its spectacular ceiling 12 metres above the floor.

Space frame roof 'floats' on top of four glazed walls

From a distance, the terminal seems like a line drawn above the flat countryside. The low height and the high percentage of glazing on all sides invites the visitor to enter the bright interior space. As one approaches the large square terminal, the vast roof unfolds and seems to float above the ground with very little support from tree-like steel columns in groups of four containing the service pods on a 36m² grid. Light fills the interior, which if not for the security panels dividing the check-in area from the duty free area, would be one large room. The high roof (12m), the clear glazing and the structural system create

a forest canopy, making an exciting space.

121 square roof apertures equipped with light filtering panels

Looking up, the 36m² grid is divided into four squares of 18m² and each of these is a shallow dome which has four triangular roof lights. These rooflights have an area of 11m² or 3.5% of the total roof area. Light comes through these to be diffused and deflected by perforated triangular planes which hang below and look like hovering kites, as Brawne suggests in the RIBA Journal (1991). Although only 8.5% of the roof is glazed, the entire space is filled with daylight, producing a feeling of

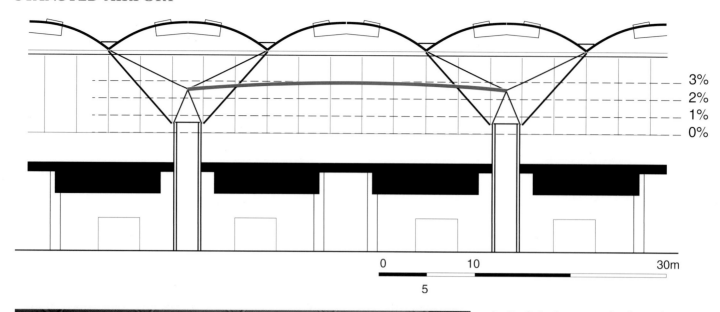

3% — 2% — 1% — 0% —

0   10   30m

5

△ Daylight factor on the floor of Stansted hall.

◁ One of the 121 square roof modules, located at the top of a 18m x 18m square dome.

calmness and airiness. 'The most powerful thread running through our buildings', says Fosters' director Spencer de Grey 'is the use of natural light. Even on a dull day like today, the difference it makes is astonishing. It's much better for the staff too. They can feel the changes of the day'.

Large glazed facades with insulating glass

The authorities claim that Stansted is 22% more energy efficient than any other UK airport terminal. This is due mostly to the daylight design of the terminal. The sides of the 'box' are double glazed with toughened glass. The latter has a low emissivity coating and an inert gas filling. This provides a curtain wall with a U value of 1.6.

A bright space lit with small roof apertures

The rooflights have clear transparent glazing. In order to overcome glare, it was necessary to reduce contrast between the bright sky and the darker ceiling. The solution is simple and elegant. Triangular metal panels, suspended on cables beneath the rooflights, bounce the daylight back to the adjacent ceiling. This suspended perforated metal shade has a light transmittance of 50%. As a whole, the calculated daylight factor for the combined rooflights and shade is 3%. As the roof aperture is only 3.5% of the floor area, this suggests that the bright

floor and ceiling finishes compensate for the low daylight penetration (with standard floor and wall finishes, the daylight factor would be about 1 to 2%).

The good penetration of light is supported by the specular floor (38% reflectance) and the high reflectance finishes of the roof panels and the steel columns (35%, 51% reflectance respectively) which bounce the incoming light to all directions.

The very satisfactory light levels give the building operator the opportunity to use minimal or no artificial light in the terminal even on overcast days, with obvious energy savings.

Information displays affected by daylight penetrations

Daylight entering the space from the roof openings is a source of veiling reflections on the screens of the video display terminals. Discomfort glare situations are also found when observers face the display panels with the glazed curtain walls behind. In this situation, there is a large difference in luminance between the display (around 100 to 120 cd/m^2) and the windows, which can reach luminances of 1,000 to 5,000 cd/m^2 even under overcast

Entrance to Stansted terminal (south, south-east). △   △ Internal view of entrance area.

High contast between clock face and glazed wall behind. ▽   ▽ VDU screen integrated in service pod.

conditions. For the facade equipped with translucent glass, this luminance is divided by two on overcast days.

Daylighting monitoring

The performance was assessed in one of the central bays, along the check-in desks. The grid was extended only on half of the bay area due to the symmetry of the space. Finally the grid was defined by the floor tiles, and the measurements were taken on the 23 April 1996, at 0.75m height from the floor. Reflectance measurements and transmittance measurements were taken on the same day.

View of Stansted terminal from south, south-east. ▽

△ Luminance values (Cd/m²) under standard overcast conditions.

Material properties assessed on site

	Colour	Hemispherical-hemispherical reflectances
Check-in desk	dark grey	6%
Floor	light grey	38%
Desk behind check in	grey	26%
Columns	light grey	51%
Panel opposite check in	white	87%
Roof	grey	35%
Perforated panel	white	50%
		Hemispherical-hemispherical transmittance
Green glass		55%
Clear glazing		88%

CREDITS

Building description
Stansted Air Terminal was constructed in 1991. It is a large square building (196 x 162 metres), with an indoor ceiling height of 12 metres.

Climate
Stansted Airport is situated in Stansted, Essex (Latitude: 51°7'N, Longitude: 01°00'E). The site is flat as is most of the Essex countryside. The climate can be described by the Cambridge one due to their proximity. Thus, the monthly average outdoor temperature is close to 5.43°C in winter and 14.9°C during summer. The average daily sunshine duration is 4.18 hours.

Acknowledgements
We would like to thank Ms J King of the Public Affairs Department, Stansted Airport Limited, and Mr P Buckle for approving the monitoring of the airport. Furthermore we are grateful to Mr A Searles, Engineering Support Officer, Department of Engineering, Stansted Airport Limited, for supplying us with the drawings of the building. Finally we would like to thank Foster and Partners for allowing us to reproduce their drawings.

Architect
Foster Associates, Riverside Three, 22 Riverside Three, London SW11 4AN, UK

Client
Stansted Airport, Essex CM24 12W, UK

Monitoring organisation
The Martin Centre for Architectural and Urban Studies, Department of Architecture, University of Cambridge, 6 Chaucer Road Cambridge CB2 2EB, U.K.

References
Best, A., "Taking flight", The Architectural Review, Vol. CLXXXIX, No. 1131, May 1991, pp. 58-61.
Brawne, M., Frontis, R.I.B.A. Journal, May 1991, pp. 4-12.
Davey, P., "Airports come of age", The Architectural Review, Vol. CLXXXIX, No. 1131, May 1991, pp. 35-57.
Davies, C., "How it was built", The Architectural Review, Vol. CLXXXIX, No. 1131, May 1991, pp. 62-73.
Design, "Back to basics: the Stansted story", Design, March 1991, pp. 34-40.
Fisher, T., "Against entropy", Progressive Architecture, January 1991, pp. 54-63.
Fordham, M., "Servicing the spaces", The Architectural Review, Vol. CLXXXIX, No. 1131, May 1991, pp. 77-82.
Manser, J., "National awards: Stansted airport terminal", R.I.B.A. Journal, 6 January 1993, pp. 17-19.
Owens, R., "Fit for take-off", The Architects' Journal, Vol. 193, No. 13, 27 March 1991, pp. 24-27.
Whitby, M., "Stansted: keeping it up", The Architectural Review, Vol. CLXXXIX, No. 1131, May 1991, pp. 74-76.
Williams, A. & Partners, "Stansted airport", Building, Issue 19, 10 May 1991, pp. 49-60.

Daylight streams into International Railway Terminal

Waterloo International Terminal, London, UNITED KINGDOM

A modern railway station in the tradition of the daylit stations of the 19th century.

▷ External view of the glazed west facade of the new Waterloo terminal.

▽ View looking south down the length of the curved platform.

A 300m long daylit hall

Waterloo station has been remodelled to handle international rail passengers using the Channel Tunnel. The platforms of the new Waterloo International Terminal are housed in a boomerang shaped enclosure, 300 meters in length and 50 meters in width.

In a cross-section perpendicular to the tracks, the western third of the roof contains almost uninterrupted glazing while the remaining two thirds contains narrow linear bands of roof lights. Underneath the platform area are the non-daylit arrivals concourse and departure lounges. These are linked to the platforms by moving travelators.

The sleek Eurostar trains, the graceful arch of the roof and the high quality surface finishes make this an exciting space to pass through. The effect is enhanced by very strong daylighting. Daylight factors everywhere are high and the asymmetric glazing distri-

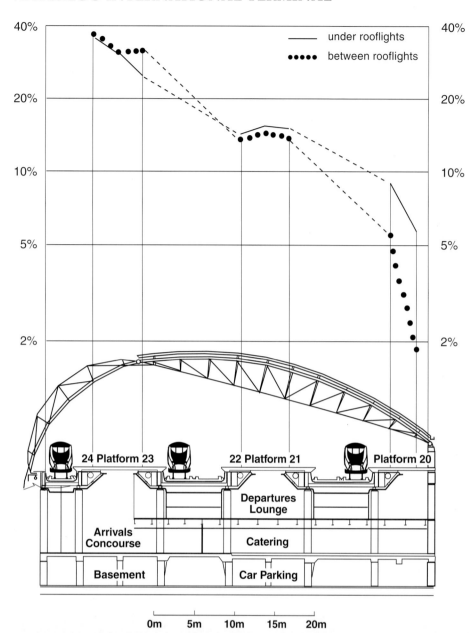

bution produces a dynamic flow of light across the space.

The ratio of daylight factors on the platforms ranges from 1 to 6

Daylight factors are high everywhere throughout the platform areas. The continuous roof glazing to the western side gives very high daylight factors (over 25 to 30%) on platforms 23 and 24. The narrower bands of roof lights on the eastern side admit less light but daylight factors are still high: around 15% on platforms 22, and 21 and 2 to 10% on platform 20.

The asymmetric arrangement of the roof lights gives a vibrant but not overpowering flow of light across the space. For example, on platforms 21/22 the vertical daylight factor facing east was 8%; facing west towards the continuous glazing it was 10%.

◁   Cross section of platforms showing measured daylight factors.

▽ View looking down platform 21.

Looking down the travelator to the arrivals concourse. ▷

Looking up the travelator towards the platforms from the concourse. ▷

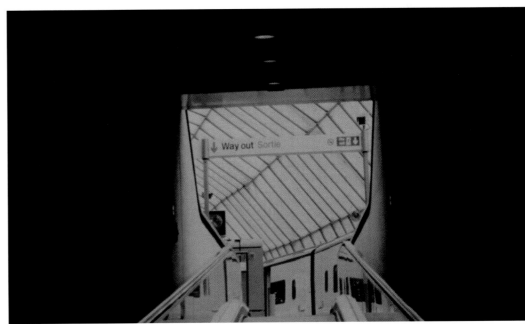

A sharp luminous frontier between the station hall and the underground concourse

There is a big contrast between the brightly daylit platforms and the dark tunnels leading to and from the arrivals concourse and departure lounges.

Passengers leaving the UK go into a non-daylit departure lounge where they wait until their train is ready for boarding. They then travel via travelators or escalators up to the daylit platform areas. Arriving passengers go down the escalators and travelators through a control area on the departures level then further down to the non-daylit arrivals concourse. Passen-

ger circulation is similar to that in an international airport.

The travelator ramp to the platform areas passes through a sloping tunnel. There are large contrasts between the low light levels inside the tunnel and the brightly daylit platform areas. For example, vertical illuminances at eye level facing up the ramp varied from 250 lux in the depth of the tunnel to 2,850 lux when emerging onto platform 24. The corresponding horizontal illuminances ranged from only 54 lux inside the tunnel to 7,300 lux on the platform. These measurements were taken on a bright overcast day with an outdoor horizontal illumin-

ance value of nearly 20,000 lux. This sudden transition enhances the impact of the daylit space, and heightens the excitement of departure, but it could cause momentary glare or adaptation problems on bright days. Conversely, arriving passengers experience a feeling of moving from a semi-outdoor enclosure to a much darker subterranean space.

Glazed roof causes unwelcome reflections on VDU screens

Some of the information screens on the platforms were difficult to read because of veiling reflections from the roof lights.

Departure information is displayed on illuminated VDU screens mounted above standing eye height. Because of the high levels of daylight and reflections from bright roof lights, these screens were often difficult to read. The luminance of the screens (lower than 100 cd/m²) must compete with reflections generated by the roof glazing, with luminances typically of the order of few thousands of cd/m².

Daylight factors in the vertical plane of the screen ranged from 2% on platform 20, through 8% on platform 22, to a very high 15% on platform 24. Large black hoods over the screens would improve their readability considerably.

Field measurements

Because of the use of the building, and the fact that the platform areas are not normally accessible to non-passengers as they are beyond customs and passport controls, field measurements were limited to one hour. They were carried out in March 1996.

△ Reflection patterns on video screens make information difficult to read.

▽ Display of direction in dark letters on bright background.

Material properties assessed on site

	Hemispherical-hemispherical Reflectances
Platform	22%
Silvery grey roof elements	19%
	Normal-normal Transmittance
Glazing linear bands	92%
Western glazing	86% to 90%

CREDITS

Building
Waterloo International is a rail terminal designed by Nicholas Grimshaw and Partners, Architects and completed in 1993. The 59,000m² station is designed to handle 15 million passengers per year and up to 3,000 at any one time.

Climate
Waterloo International Terminal is in the centre of London. Its climate is best represented by the Kew Test Reference Year. The monthly average outdoor temperatures are around 5°C in winter and 16°C in summer. The average daily sunshine duration is 4.2 hours over the year and 1.4 hours in December.

Client
European Passenger Services Limited
Waterloo Station
London SE1 8SE

Architects
Nicholas Grimshaw and Partners
1 Conway Street
London W1

Monitoring organisation
Building Research Establishment
Garston, Watford, UK.

References
M Field "International station for fast track travellers" Architect's Journal 18 August 1993, pp 15-17.

In churches, daylight can play a large symbolic role. Daylight factors tend to be low (0.5 to 2%) to encourage meditation, but also to enhance lighting effects, such as the presence of stained glass windows and the emphasis of light on the altar or in neighbouring chapels. Light-coloured indoor finishes may profoundly change the general atmosphere, making it brighter and more uniform. Coloured glass and stained glass using saturated colours can give the space unique qualities, different from other spaces. Glazed areas are often rather moderate, typically in the range of 5 to 10% of the floor area.

Daylight-related adjustments during the two-century construction of a medieval cathedral

Saint-Jean Cathedral, Lyons, FRANCE

Design adjustments performed during the construction suggest that builders learned ways to increase daylight admission.

Like all Christian houses of worship, this cathedral built between the end of the 12th and the beginning of the 15th centuries was designed with the idea that daylight, (symbol of transcendance), is radiated by God ('God is light', John 1.1). As typical in medieval religious architecture, large stained art glass windows, strongly contrasting with adjacent stone walls, admit and colour the light and convey to worshippers the Message of God through translucent illustrations and inscriptions. However, what is particularly interesting in Saint-Jean Cathedral is the evolution of daylight treatment during the long period of construction. The apse was built in the Roman style with massive walls and focused daylighting, whereupon the nave was built in the Gothic style with a tendency to pierce walls as much as possible. Some details illustrate this evolution and make art historians believe that builders strove to increase daylight penetration through the ages.

△ Stained glass windows illustrate the Message of God.

◁ Highly contrasted nave.

△ Narrower mullions and tracery in a more recent window.

◁ Massive mullions and tracery in a former window.

More reflective stones in the apse embrasures

The apse embrasures were built with a stone called 'choin'. This stone is more reflective than the one called 'stone from Lucenay' which was used above the embrasures. Although the surface of the 'choin' is now irregular, it used to be polished and was, consequently, even more reflective.

Narrowed mullions

The mullions and traceries separating and supporting the former windows were hewn directly from the facade stone walls. Their section is therefore thick. In the nave part of the building, mullions and traceries have no supporting function. They were built as slender elements, after which windows were opened. As a consequence, their section was reduced and less daylight was occluded.

Enlarged rose window

Careful observation of the internal envelope of the cathedral reveals that the radius of one arch of the transept southern aisle was increased during the construction phase, after that the arch was raised slightly above impost level. According to historians, this decision was probably taken to enlarge the transversal rose window located in the same aisle.

◁ Increased arch radius in the transept southern aisle.

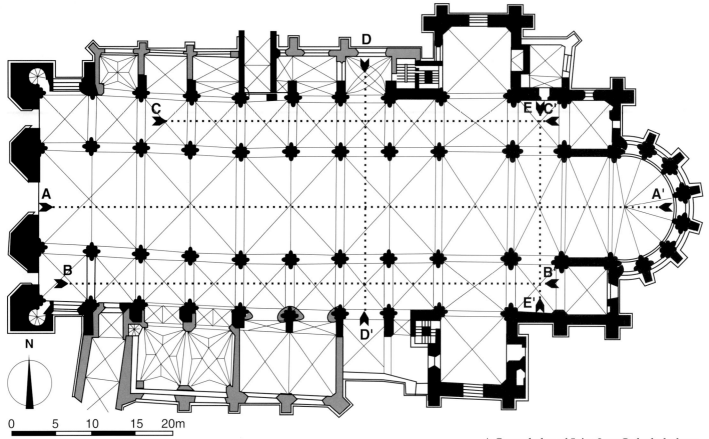

△ General plan of Saint-Jean Cathedral, showing the five sections used to display daylight factors.

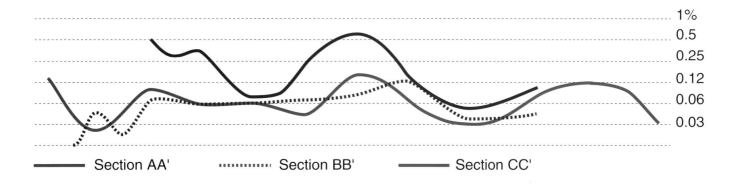

——— Section AA'   ·········· Section BB'   ——— Section CC'

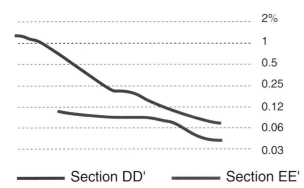

——— Section DD'   ——— Section EE'

◁ △ Daylight factor variations across the cathedral showing the imbalance caused by the new colourless translucent glazing in D for example.

Time-altered light distribution

When looking at light distribution within the cathedral, one notices that gothic nave clerestories create a relatively bright zone in the upper part of a visitor's field of view. This is emphasised by the fact that clerestories are less obstructed than lower windows by external obstructions. However, the horizontal daylight factor distribution is somewhat unexpected because of the intervention that occurred after the 18th century. One notices that the brightest zone is located in the north aisle, and that light distribution is unbalanced between the south and north aisles. This odd distribution is due to the fact that south-facing adjoining chapels are deeper than north-facing ones, but it is due also to modern interventions, i.e. the new colourless translucent glazing installed in some chapels adjacent to the north aisle and the fact that obstructions are lower on the north side than on the south side.

Daylighting monitoring

The monitoring was conducted on 6 October 1997.

▷ Eastern view of Saint-Jean Cathedral on the banks of the river Saone. On the hill, in the background, is Fourviere Church.

△ White translucent glazing in D.

◁ Example of stained glass window.

CREDITS

Building description
The cathedral without its chapels has an overall floor area of about 1,900m². The maximum indoor height is 32m and the overall length is 80m.

Climate
Saint-Jean Cathedral is located in downtown Lyons (Latitude: 45°45'N, Longitude: 4°51'E, Altitude: 170m). The monthly average outdoor temperature ranges from about 2°C in January to 21°C in July.

Monitoring organisation
ENTPE/DGCB
Rue Maurice Audin
69518 Vaulx-en-Velin- France

Acknowledgements
Prof. N. Reveyron

References
N. Reveyron "La Cathédrale de Lyon et sa place dans l'histoire de l'art (1170 to 1245)" PhD dissertation under the supervision of Mrs Anne Prache, Univ. Paris IV Sorbonne, France 1992.

Material properties assessed on site

	Hemispherical-hemispherical reflectance
Lucenay stone	40%

Mastery of daylight in an emblem of modern architecture

Chapel Notre Dame du Haut, Ronchamp, FRANCE

A sculptural architecture designed by Le Corbusier, playing with wall thickness, daylight and colours.

Le Corbusier became attracted by the site and the programme of this building. On top of the Ronchamp sacred hill, there was a need for a church for a congregation of 200; three small chapels, and one outdoor altar for thousands of pilgrims. Realised in 1954, Notre Dame du Haut which has been said to be non-symbolic but expressive, has quickly become an emblematic building of 20th century religious architecture which is characterized by an absence of strict rules and typology, and by a plurality of styles and light treatments. It has also become one of the most famous illustrations of the modern mastery of daylight by an architect who claimed that 'architecture is the clever and magnifi-

cent assembly of volumes under light'.

A symphony of lights

The monumental south wall which, together with the massive roof and the stone pavement gives the visitor the impression of entering a cave, is pierced with 27 splayed rectangular window bays each with a relatively small glazed area whose design recalls Indian and North African vernacular architecture. These windows, which have different sizes and internal or external embrasures, are emphasized by their almost random spare distribution in this relatively dark space. Their internal embrasures create intermediate zones of luminance which attenuate the contrasts

▽ Twenty-seven windows animate the impressive south wall, photographed during clear sky conditions.

◁▷ During at least half of the year, deep window embrasures prevent direct solar penetrations through the south wall (external and internal embrasures photographed on 24 March).

between the glass and adjoining wall surfaces. They also prevent, during at least half a year, the penetration of direct sunbeams through the south wall: observations carried out around the spring equinox show that sunlight is either projected onto the surface of the embrasures or on the roof overhang.

Le Corbusier painted some windows with metal oxides and left the others colourless. He used the same colours as those of the door (i.e. cobalt blue, vivid yellow and red, emerald green, deep violet and grey) and he completed this coloured composition with patterns and praises to Mary: moon with human face, birds, butterflies, flowers, leaves, sun, stars, clouds. However, Le Corbusier reserved the term 'stained art glass windows' for ancient architecture and preferred to speak about 'coloured glazing'.

A wall of stars

The east wall opens outside to the 'external nave'. The morning light goes through it and illuminates a multi-coloured 17th century statue of the Virgin Mary that worshippers have called 'The Morning Star'. This statue is placed into the east wall in a window whose embrasure is painted green, yellow, and red. It is surrounded by dazzling, star-like light spots created by small openings which were left by the construction scaffold beams.

A light slit emphasizes the sail-like roof appearance

A narrow continuous opened slit, inspired by the Saint-Sophia Basilica in Constantinople, separates the east and south walls from the roof. It is only perceptible from inside and it gives some lightness to the large curved concrete roof, making it appear like a sail, and reinforcing the whole dynamic of the interior space.

'A well-adjusted polychromy'

Le Corbusier mostly used either unfinished concrete (dark grey) or whitewashed concrete, but he also added colours, considering that 'a well-adjusted polychromy is necessary to make the white appreciable', claiming also that 'polychromy is as strong a medium

◁ In the morning, the statue of the Virgin Mary is highlighted.

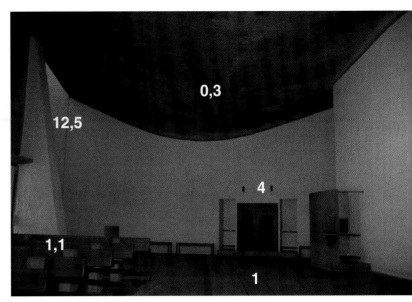

The east wall is animated by a high range of luminances. The statue of △ the Virgin Mary is surrounded by bright 'stars', which are small holes in the facade.

△ On the other hand, the luminance distribution toward the west wall is much smoother.

Details of a light periscope located above ▷ one secondary chapel.

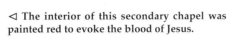

◁ The interior of this secondary chapel was painted red to evoke the blood of Jesus.

of architecture as the plan and section'. These colours can cover relatively large areas (e.g. the violet wall adjacent to the sacristy, the carmine red secondary chapel) or be applied sparingly (e.g. stained glass windows, main door).

Light periscopes
Each of the three secondary chapels is lit by a 'periscope' which has also a ventilation function and which recalls light

and ventilation towers present over peasant houses on Ischia (near Naples). These periscopes admit daylight through one long vertical slit and the 'brise-lumière'. Light is then projected down to chapel altars.

Contrasted chapels
The nave is characterized by low daylight factors (around 1%) with most daylight close to south wall windows.

The three secondary chapels are treated very differently. The one located in the south-western corner, and illuminated by the north-facing periscope (the biggest one), receives significantly more light than the others (maximum 10%). It is the brightest part of the chapel. The east-oriented secondary chapel, painted red, is the darkest zone of the building (daylight factors around 0.1%) which tends to emphasized candle light. As for the west-oriented chapel, which is similar to the east-oriented one but with white surfaces, it has an intermediate average daylight factor of 2% (which is closer to light levels measured in the nave). This clearly emphasizes the important effect of internal reflectance on light penetration, especially with this kind of daylighting feature.

Daylight monitoring
Monitoring was performed on 2 May 1996.

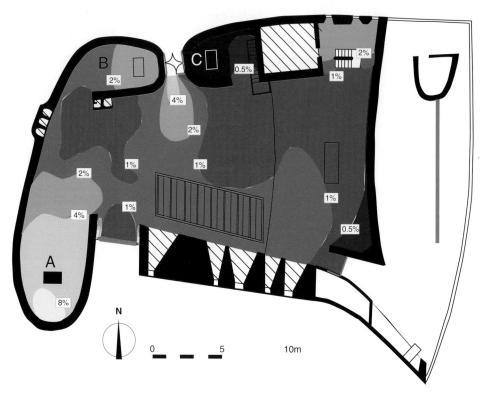

▽ Light periscopes over the three secondary chapels.

△ Contrasted horizontal daylight factors in the three chapels A, B and C.

Material properties assessed on site

	Colour	Hemispherical-hemispherical reflectances
Wall	white	88%
Floor (nave)		22%
Floor (chapel)		37%
Wall	red	24%

CREDITS

Building description
Built in 1954.
The envelope is made of a concrete shell, made with a 'mortar gun' whitened with lime. The major chapel can house 200 people. On the sides, there are three little chapels, and one exterior altar against the east wall allow the gathering of large crowds of pilgrims.

Climate
The village of Ronchamp is located 25 km west of Belfort in the north-eastern part of France (Latitude: 47°42'N, Longitude: 6°39'E, Altitude: 497m).

The monthly average outdoor temperature ranges from about 1°C in January to 19°C in July.

Client
Le Corbusier was commissioned by Fathers Couturier and Régamey.

Architect
Le Corbusier

Monitoring organisation
ENTPE/DGCB
Rue Maurice Audin
69518 Vaulx-en-Velin-France

References
Pauly D. "Ronchamp lecture d'une architecture", Paris: Ophrys, 1980.
Le Corbusier Oeuvres Complètes 1910-1929.
Baker G. "La Corbusier, An analysis of form", Van Nostrand Reinhold (UK) Co. Ltd., 1985.

Copyright FLC - Adagp, Paris 1998.

Sunlight and daylight play on baroque interior features

Baroque Church, Neresheim Monastery, GERMANY

The principal objective in this church has been to use daylight to focus attention on the splendour of its Baroque interior.

Baroque architecture with large windows and bright internal finishes

'Benedictus montes amabat': Benedictine monks loved to build their castle-like abbeys on high points in the landscape. Hence the location of this abbey on a hill above the town of Neresheim in the eastern Swabian Alps, in southern Germany.

The church is part of a monastery which dates back to the early 12th century. From 1750 to 1792, in the course of the renovation of the monastery, the church was constructed in the Baroque style by the renowned architect Balthasar Neumann at the height of his career. He died however before the church was completed and not all his ideas were put to work, due to savings needs and the change of styles from Baroque to Classicism. The interior design is therefore not totally comparable with the much more glossy design of churches in the decades before the construction of this church was finished. Nevertheless, the bright interior appearance was not diminished by this, since the walls are painted in a very bright white (monitored reflection of 81%). It's just a little less gold that was used.

The floor plan of the church takes the form of a Latin cross, with an overall length of 83m. The aisle divides the nave into three parts, with the eastern part accomodating the choir and altar,

▽ General view down the nave, towards the main altar in the east.

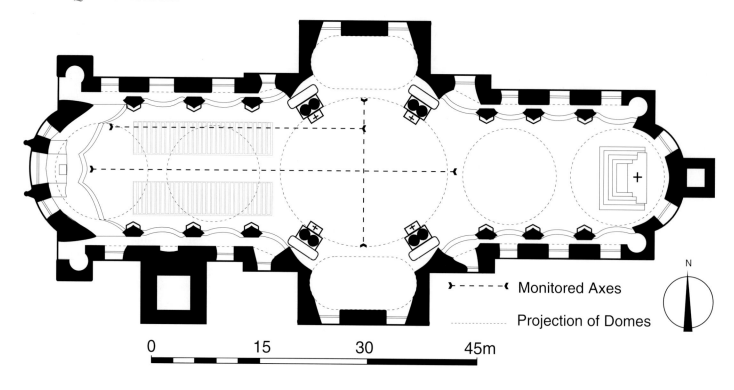

0   15   30   45m

△ Plan of the church.

Monitored Axes

Projection of Domes

N

▽ Daylight factor distribution in the church showing high uniformity.

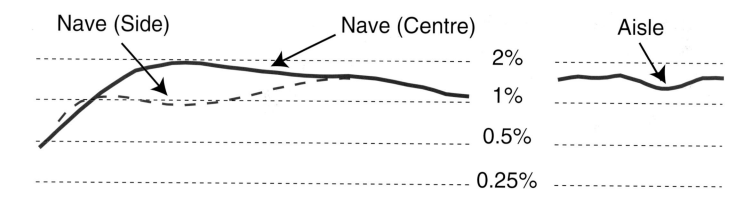

Nave (Side)   Nave (Centre)   Aisle

2%

1%

0.5%

0.25%

the western part the seating and an open floor area at the crossing of the nave and aisle.

Indoor finishes maximize light reflections

By contrast with medieval churches, those of the Baroque period often have ornate, impressively daylit interiors, thus serving the desire of the Catholic Church to show its magnificence in a reaction to the criticism by Luther. Window areas are designed to be larger than previously, indoor materials are bright with white walls, golden statues and marble. Hidden surfaces are often glossy in order to increase the effects of

light reflections in the space. The resulting luminous environment is the opposite of softness. Typical luminance distributions have been measured in this survey. For overcast sky conditions, typical indoor surfaces have rather high luminance levels of 15 to 40 cd/m^2, when luminances levels of the reflections can reach few hundred cd/m^2 and luminance of windows are around 300 to 1,000 cd/m^2. By comparison, a Gothic church would have luminance values in the range of 2 to 5 cd/m^2 in many areas for the same daylight conditions.

Ceiling paintings simulate infinite height

Large frescoes in the seven roof domes seem to open the church to infinity. The paintings with religious motifs either extend the space with perspective drawings of continuing columns and domes or show scenes of heaven. These elaborate frescoes are especially emphasized during winter when snow covering the ground reflects light into the domes. In general, the bright-ness of the church allows these frescoes to be visible at all times. Daylight factors are generally around 1% to 1.5%, which is higher than in the churches designed before the Baroque period.

△ Luminance measurements (altar region in the eastern part of the nave) seen under standard overcast sky conditions.

Sun patch moving on the choir organ ▷ near the north facade, in March.

An indoor space which is animated by the variations in daylight

It is necessary to spend some time to fully observe the various indoor light patterns associated with the changes in daylight outside. With its many sculptures, cornices and glossy surfaces, the space is very sensitive to the directionality of the incoming daylight, and especially to sunlight.

For instance, western light during the late afternoons of summer accentuates the different architectural details, especially at the two altars on the eastern side. Sun patches move across the choir organ at the facade during the mornings in spring.

Daylighting monitoring

Monitoring of the Neresheim abbey church focused on one part of the nave and the aisle. Due to the religious and monastic life in the abbey the altar and choir area could not be accessed. Monitoring was performed on two days in May 1996.

△ Ceiling fresco in the east dome, above main altar.

▽ View of the abbey of Neresheim from the east side.

CREDITS

Building description
The church is part of the monastery, which origins date back to the early 12th century. From 1750 to 1792, in the coarse of the retrofitting of the monastery, the church was planned in the Baroque style by the renowned Baroque architect Balthasar Neumann at the height of his carreer. Unfortunately, only three years after the construction began, he died, and not all his plans and ideas were realized. The floor plan of the church corresponds to a Latin cross, with an overall length of 83m.

Climate
The abbey in the eastern Swabian Alps, Latitude: 48°8'N, Longitude: 10°3'E, Altitude: 530m.

The climate of Neresheim is best represented by the Würzburg Test Reference Year. The monthly average outdoor temperatures are coldest month: January with a mean of -1.3°C, warmest month: August with a mean of 18.3°C

Monitoring organisation
Fraunhofer Institute for Building Physics, Nobelstraße 12, 70569 Stuttgart, Germany

References
900 Jahre Abtei Neresheim 1095 -1995, Text: Norbert Lieb, Verlag Schnell & Steiner, Regensburg, 3. Edition 1995

Balthasar Neumann, Abteikirche Neresheim, Text: Christian Norberg-Schulz, Photos Peter Walser, Ernst Wasmuth Verlag, Tübingen / Berlin, 1993

Material properties assessed on site

		Hemispherical-hemispherical reflectance
Floor	marble	24%
Benches	dark wood	9%
Walls	white	81%
	Normal-normal transmittance	Hemispherical-hemispherical transmittance
Glazing (single blown panes)	93%	79%

Vivid colours under focused and sparse daylight

Sainte-Marie de La Tourette Convent, Eveux, FRANCE

In the church of the convent, the dramatic focusing of daylight is reinforced by colourful surfaces.

Vivid colours counter-balance bare concrete austerity

Designed in 1960 by Le Corbusier to house members of the Dominican Order, this convent includes around its central cloister a hundred cells, common rooms and one church. The church is a massive box-like austere volume where the omnipresent grey concrete is brightened by touches of vivid colours. These colours, close to where daylight enters, constitute the only ornament in the church. According to Le Corbusier, they 'possess the walls and qualify them with the power of blood, or the freshness of the prairies, or the shining sun, or the depth of the sky and the sea'.

Original light-focusing features

The penetration of light in the church is concentrated through different types of daylighting systems characteristic of Le Corbusier's architecture. Three conical lightwells - so-called 'canons de lumière' (lightguns) by the architect - are angled in different directions and focus the light into the crypt and the church north aisle. Seven trapezoidal light ducts - so-called 'mitraillettes' (submachine-gun) - are slanted toward the south and redirect the light vertically the light above the sacristy. As for the horizontal slits lined up in the western part of the church, they direct daylight toward the monks' reading places.

▽ Vivid colours in the north aisle of the church. The internal surfaces of the lightwells are painted white, red or black.

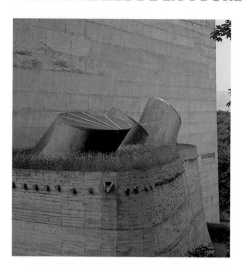

◁ Conical 'lightguns' seen from outside.

'Lightguns' seen from inside the crypt. ▷

Trapezoidal lightwells seen from outside. △   △ Lightwells above the sacristy.

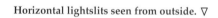

Horizontal lightslits seen from outside. ▽   ▽ Lightslits seen from inside (back of the church).

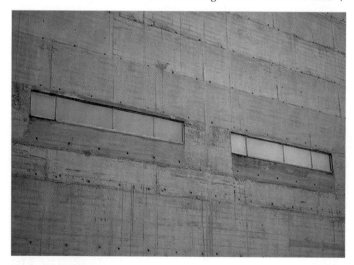

Dramatic light variations

Daylight focusing features generate an uneven horizontal distribution of light. Overall daylight factors are very low in the nave (0.2% on average) with a little more light very close to the eastern full-height vertical slit as well as below the horizontal slits (where daylight factors are around 0.5%). However, the north aisle and the adjacent crypt benefit from the significantly higher contribution of the 'canons de lumière' which cause daylight factors to exceed 2% in some places. There, measurements suggest that the white lightwell focuses daylight onto the north aisle altar, even if the peak illuminance is slightly off the altar centre. As a consequence, this altar gets much more emphasis than the one located in the middle of the nave, in an area where daylight factors are below 0.1%. The attractiveness of the north aisle is also evident when looking at the vertical daylight factor distribution and the highly contrasted luminance distribution measured from the western part of the church. This distribution shows that, although the eye adaptation luminance is equally low in the western part of the nave whatever the orientation,

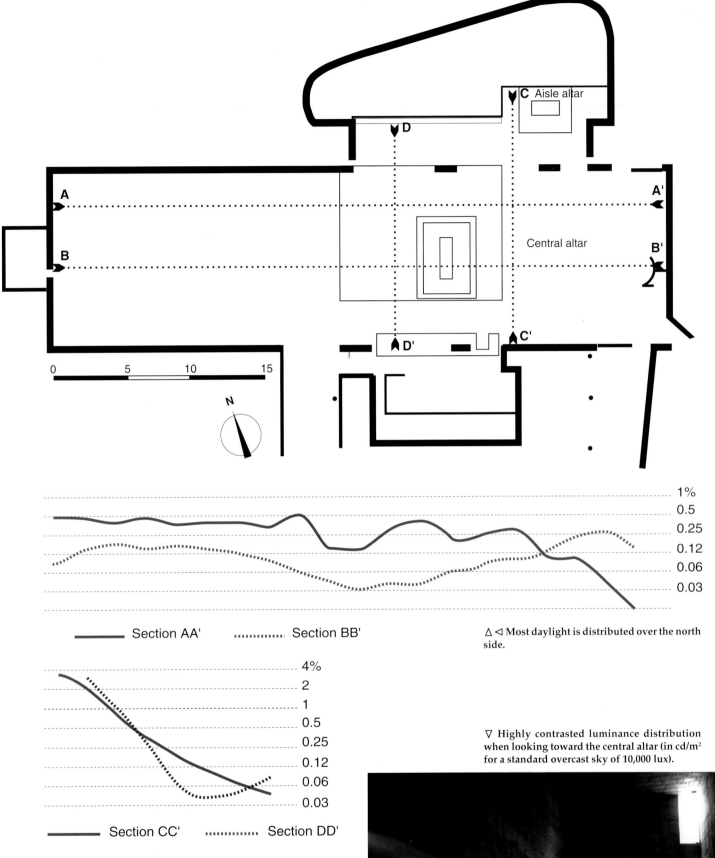

Central altar

C Aisle altar

——— Section AA'   ·········· Section BB'

1%
0.5
0.25
0.12
0.06
0.03

△ ◁ Most daylight is distributed over the north side.

——— Section CC'   ·········· Section DD'

4%
2
1
0.5
0.25
0.12
0.06
0.03

▽ Highly contrasted luminance distribution when looking toward the central altar (in cd/m² for a standard overcast sky of 10,000 lux).

◁ Contrasting red, white, yellow or green horizontal lights at the back of the chapel.

▷ Interior view of one cell.

◁ South facing monks' cells on the first and second floor.

◁ Horizontal daylight factors distribution in one monk cell.

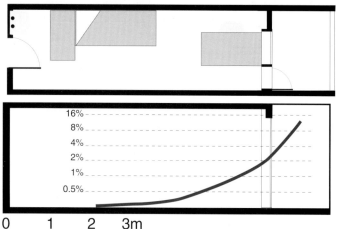

it becomes significantly higher toward the north aisle when standing close to the central altar. As for the luminance distribution, it clearly reveals the high contrasts between the openings and the north aisle surfaces on one hand and the predominant rough concrete on the other hand.

In monks' cells, furniture is arranged in response to low daylight levels

The height, length and width of the monk cells were chosen by Le Corbusier in accordance with his 'Modulor' measuring system based on mathematics and human proportions. The attenuation of the daylight by the loggia explains the fact that the daylight factor is relatively low (only 1%) near the window. Together with the large depth to width ratio and the roughly plastered walls and ceiling, this provides very little natural lighting in the back of the cell. Nevertheless, furniture is judiciously arranged with respect to light distribution: the brightest zone is reserved for the work plane whereas the bed and the closet are placed deeper into the room. As for the desk, it is set perpendicular to the window, minimizing the negative effect of reflections.

CREDITS

Building description
The building has an overall floor area of 5,000m². It is placed in the midst of nature, in a small vale that opens out onto the forest.

Climate
La Tourette convent is located in Eveux, 26 km west of Lyon (Latitude: 45°50'N, Longitude: 4°37'E). The monthly average outdoor temperature ranges from about 2°C in January to 21°C in July.

Acknowledgements
The Dominican Community and the Fondation Le Corbusier for authorizing measurements in the Convent.

Client
Communauté Dominicaine
Couvent Sainte-Marie de la Tourette
Eveux BP 105
F-69210 L'Arbresle

Architect
Le Corbusier

Monitoring organisation
ENTPE/DGCB
Rue Maurice Audin
69518 Vaulx-en-Velin- France

Material properties assessed on site

	Colour	Hemispherical-hemispherical reflectances
Floor	concrete grey	38%
Walls	concrete grey	35%

A two thousand year old example of daylighting with the 1% daylight factor standard

Panthcon Dome, Rome, ITALY

This well known construction offers a unique daylighting effect, and a way to illustrate solar geometry.

▽ **The Pantheon dome with its 8.8 metre occulus.**

An imposing dome, with a height equal to its diameter

The Pantheon, a magnificent Roman temple dedicated to all the gods, was built from 118 to 128 AD by Emperor Hadrian. In the middle ages the monument was converted into a Christian church and at present it contains the tomb of Raffaello and those of some Italian kings. The building is an architectural unit consisting of a rectangular colonnade tympanum pronaos attached to the large circular hall with the big hemispherical dome. The internal part of the dome is subdivided into 28 lacunars arranged in five layers above which is located a circular zenithal opening.

At ground level, the circumference of the walls gives access to seven niches and eight aedicule. The height and the diameter of the hall are both equal to 43.2 metres. The diameter of the circular opening is 8.8 metres. It is the only daylighting feature of the entire space. The entrance to the monument faces north, and the aisle connecting the entrance with the altar lies on a north-south axis.

A uniformly lit floor with a daylight factor of 1%

Daylight factors were measured on the floor for overcast conditions. Daylight factors are almost constant (1%) across the section of the dome, due to the

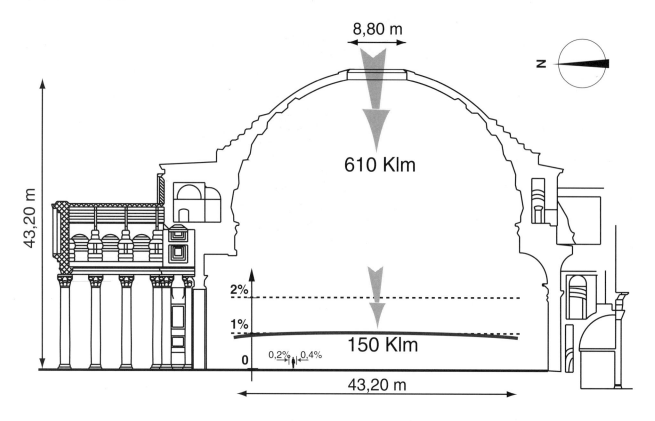

8,80 m

610 Klm

2%

1%

150 Klm

0

0,2% 0,4%

43,20 m

43,20 m

△ The floor of the Pantheon dome is uniformly lit, with a daylight factor around 1%, vertical daylight factors are around 0.2% and 0.4%.Under overcast sky conditions, with an outdoor illuminance of 10,000 lux, the occulus brings in a luminous flux equivalent to the one produced by 10 KW of metal halide projectors. The luminous flux incident on the floor is about one fourth of this amount.

◁ The floor level is free of obstruction and accessible to the public.

height of the building: the angle of incidence of light from the occulus on the floor varies from 0° to only 27° at the edges. Taking into account additional light reflections from the side walls, this explains the extreme homogeneity of the daylight distribution in the space. The 1% value should be compared with the aperture ratio, equal to 4% (the ratio of the area of the occulus to the area of the floor).

The flux balance was assessed from these values for standard overcast conditions (representing an horizontal outdoor illuminance of 10,000 lux). The luminous flux incident on the floor is equal to about one fourth of the flux incident on the top of the occulus. To give an idea of the magnitude of the flux on the oculus, it is roughly equivalent to that produced by projectors equipped with metal halide lamps with a total power of 10 KW. At solar noon in summer, and under sunny conditions, the incoming flux can reach values six to ten times higher.

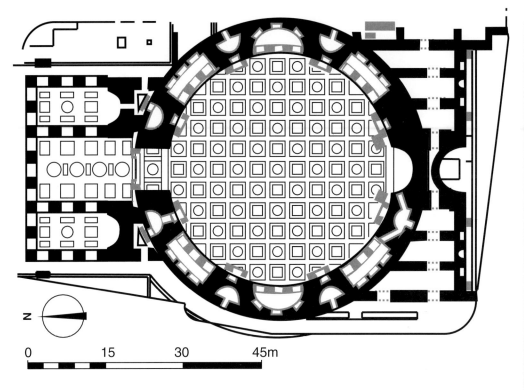

△ Plan of the Pantheon.

▽ Sunlight penetration at solar noon for the winter and summer solstices and the equinoxes.

▷ Sunlight penetrations during the summer solstice at 12:00, 14:00, 16:00, 18:00 solar time.

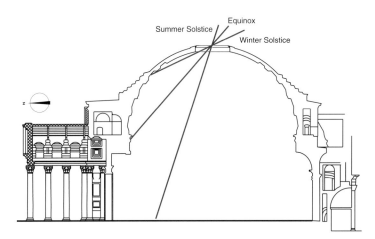

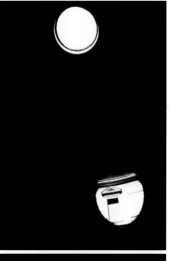

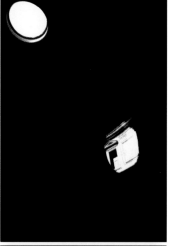

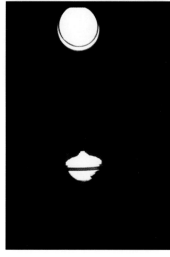

A cascade of daylight

Vertical daylight factors were also measured, at a height of 1.70 metres above floor level. They are much smaller than horizontal ones, between 0.2 and 0.4%, versus 1% horizontally. This demonstrates that most of the incident light on vertical surfaces (such as visitors; faces for instance) comes from the zenith.

The Pantheon: a solar clock and calendar

In the Pantheon the solar light indicates exactly the date of the equinoxes and solstices, showing likewise the hours of the day. The solar beams reach the lower zone located below the attic at the summer solstice, the upper zone of the dome at the winter solstice and the intermediate zone between the attic and the first order of lacunars during the equinoxes.

Material reflectance moderate contrasts

Daylight coming from the zenithal opening is also diffused by the internal surfaces of the monument, with a reflectance of about 30%. The consequence is a rather uniform distribution of luminances. Under standard overcast conditions (horizontal outdoor illuminances equal to 10,000 lux), the typical indoor luminance ranges typically between 5 and 15 cd/m², leading to the feeling of a very moderate luminous environment, in comparison with the luminance of the occulus, around 3,000 cd/m².

Daylighting monitoring

Daylighting monitoring was performed in April 1996, under a dark overcast sky (approx 5,000 lux). Indoor horizontal illuminance was measured along two axes: north-east/south-west and north-west/south-east.

△ View of the occulus from the centre of the floor.

▽ North facade of the Pantheon, with the tympanum.

Material properties assessed on site

	Colour	Hemispherical-hemispherical reflectances
Floor marble (as a chessboard)	grey, brown & light brown	30%

CREDITS

Building description
Built at the beginning of the second century AD, the Pantheon dome is 43.2m in diameter and 43.5m in height. It is located at Piazza della Rotonda in Rome.

Climate
Rome is a city with a latitude of 41°88'N and a longitude 12°47'E. The altitude of the site of the Pantheon is 20m above sea level. The climate is Mediterranean, with a minimum monthly average temperature of 7.6°C in January and a maximum monthly average temperature of 25.7° in July. Annual sunshine duration is 2480 hours/year.

Client
The Pantheon is a public monument belonging to the Italian State.

Architect
Emperor Hadrian and his architects

Monitoring organisation
Francesco Aleo
Conphoebus, Energy in building Department
Zona Industriale, Passo Martino 95030 Piano d'Arci, Catania, Italy
Tel: +39.95-291407
Fax: +39.95-291246

Museums represent one of the most difficult building types to light with daylight due to the difficult compromises to be found between the expectations of visitors for whom high illuminance levels are preferable to perceive the details of the works of art, and the preservation of the light-sensitive artworks requiring the least possible exposure to light (or as few lux.hours per year). Although daylight should be avoided for the presentation of highly light-sensitive materials such as drawings, collages, pastels or watercolours, it can often be acceptable for oil paintings, especially if they are protected with varnish. In these circumstances, daylight factor values on works of art in the range of 0.5 to 2% appear acceptable in most European countries, with best results when at least some seasonal, daily or even hourly attenuation can be provided such as 1.5% in winter and 0.6% in summer. Sunlight should be avoided in all circumstances on light-sensitive artwork due to the high illuminance levels which can be reached (over 30,000 lux) and resultant heating of the painting's surface which may lead to deterioration.

Daylight penetration attenuated by a sophisticated daylight control system

Neue Staatsgalerie, Stuttgart, GERMANY

A combination of highly glazed roof and controls ensures that conservation criteria are met for all climatic conditions.

2,200m² of art galleries daylit from translucent ceilings

Located in the center of Stuttgart this gallery for modern art has been integrated in an historic district with other museums, a school of music, theatre and a palace housing the state government of Baden Würtemberg. The Neue Staatsgalerie was built in 1984 by British architect James Stirling. It offers 3,000m² floor area of exhibition rooms and houses modern paintings and sculptures. It is an extension of the Old Staatsgalerie built in 1843.

A glazed attic with control of daylight and sunlight penetration

15 rooms are daylit from the ceiling. Typical room dimensions are 10.6m x

14.6m and the ceiling height varies from 4 to 6m. From the interior, the appearance of the ceiling is a large rectangle of semi-transparent glass. Visitors can guess the various elements of the attic: the upper roof glazing, the arrays of slats, the luminaires.

The inner layer is made of semi-translucent triple glazing: 4mm float glazing, 4mm special glazing (without green additives), and a 9mm security compound glazing. This glazing offers thermal insulation to the space which is heated and ventilated but not cooled. It also contains a UV absorbing film.

Above are luminaires, using fluorescentlamps (colour temperature: daylight white, and colour rendering

▽ View of the ceiling construction, with half-opened shading slats, luminaires, and the diffusing glass used for the ceilings of the gallery rooms.

◁ View of a typical gallery room daylit by the semi-translucent ceiling.

▽ Four typical positions of the blinds for control of daylight penetrations.

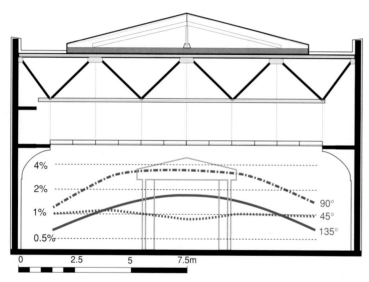

Horizontal daylight factors on an axis normal △ to the slats in the middle of the room for different slat tilt angle.

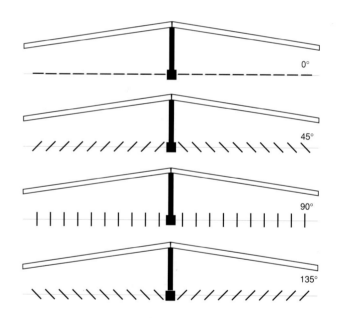

indices: 80<Ra<90). These lamps are located in the path of the incoming daylight to offer similar lighting pattern as daylight. The artificial lighting can also behave as a 'daylight booster', when daylight is insufficient.

Above the luminaire is a sophisticated system aimed at controlling daylight penetration and preventing direct sunlight penetration: it consists of horizontal aluminium blinds, mounted on horizontal bearing rods which can be tilted in an angular range from 0° to 135° to the horizontal plane. Attached rubber seals enable almost total blocking of daylight. The blinds are controlled by electric motors. Finally, the outer weather protection layer consists of single pane diffusing therm-olux glazing.

Daylight factor values are sensitive to the position of the blinds

Daylight factor distribution on the horizontal plane peaks in the centre of the rooms and decreases toward the walls. With blinds in the vertical position (90°) the daylight factor on the horizontal plane (0.8m obove the floor) peaks at 3.5%. For 135° the value is lower, 1.7%, and even lower for an angle of 45°.

Near the walls, daylight is more stable, with horizontal daylight factors ranging from 0.7% to 1.2% as a function of the position of the blinds. This is more or less proportional to the global amount of daylight penetrating the room, and rather insensitive to the direction of daylight passing through the blinds.

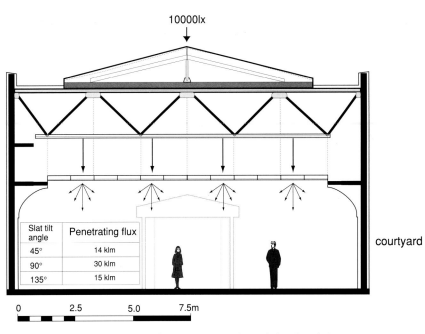

Slat tilt angle	Penetrating flux
45°	14 klm
90°	30 klm
135°	15 klm

Luminous flux penetration through the glazed △ attic (klm), as a function of the slat tilt angle. Sky conditions: overcast sky providing 10,000 lux on an horizontal plane outside.

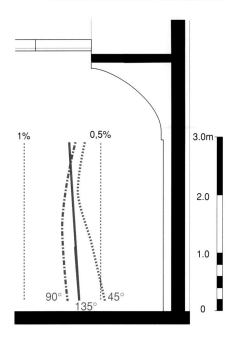

◁ Vertical daylight factor distribution along an axis in the middle of an exhibition wall for different slat tilt angles.

Daylight factors on exhibition wall with slats at 45° and 90°. ▽

Horizontal daylight factors in gallery room, 0.8m ▽ above floor, for blind tilt angle of 90°.

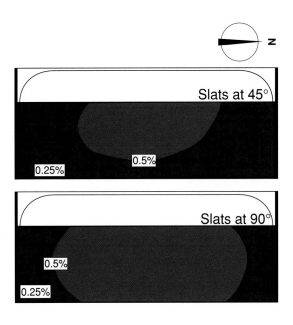

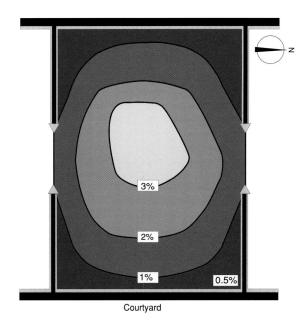

Due to the low reflectance of the floor (grey carpet, reflectance 20%), little light is scattered from the floor area onto the walls. The resulting daylight factors on walls do not vary much as a function of the blind position, between 0.5% and 0.7%. They are rather low for the presentation of oil paintings for the climate of Stuttgart, giving priority to conservation. It shows also that the blind systems does not provide a possibility for high attenuation levels, which would be required to adapt to skies of different luminances (overcast skies with luminances of 2,000 to 10,000 cd/m^2 for instance). Daylight factor distribution on the walls is however rather uniform, with a decrease toward the corners no less than 0.25%.

Blind position controlled with daylight sensor

A roof-mounted sensor system reads horizontal illuminance due to the sky brightness. The position of the blind is then regulated as a function of the sensor reading and position of the sun.

Although indoor illuminance sensors are installed, these are not linked to the control system. Neither is the artificial lighting system connected to the control unit. Thus no closed-loop daylight-dependent artificial lighting control is installed. Two artificial lighting levels can be switched manually (two luminaire groups in each room).

The lighting power density in the gallery rooms is about 18.7 W/m^2, with an annual consumption of lighting electricity estimated at 39 KWh/m^2.

◁ Luminances in an exhibition room with the slats half open (45°) for a 10 klux external illuminance.

Daylighting monitoring

Monitoring concentrated on the behaviour of the translucent ceiling construction. Thus a gallery room on the second floor without side openings towards the courtyard was selected. Measurements were performed in January 1996.

▽ Facade view of the Neue Staatsgalerie.

Material properties assessed on site

	Colour	Hemispherical-hemispherical reflectances
Walls	white	66%
Carpet floor	grey	20%
		Hemispherical-hemispherical transmittances
Outer layer (Thermolux)		33%

CREDITS

Building description
The building was constructed as a museum for modern painting and sculptures by the British architect James Stirling. It was opened for the public in 1984.
Usable area: 6,800m²

Climate
Stuttgart, the capital of the Bundesland Baden Württemberg, is located in the valley and on the hills around the river Neckar in the south-western part of Germany at elevations between 200 and 400 metres. Its climatic conditions are best described by the Würzburg Test Reference Year. The monthly average temperatures is -1.3°C in January, and 18.3°C in August. In spring and autumn the centre of the town, located in the Neckar valley, is often covered by fog, whereas smog is often predominent in summer.

Client
State of Baden Württemberg
Staatliches Hochbauamt 1
D-70182 Stuttgart

Architect
James Stirling - Michael Wilford and Associates,
Stuttgart

Daylight consultant
Institut für Tageslichttechnik, Dr.-Ing. Hanns Freymuth,
Stuttgart

Monitoring organisation
Fraunhofer Institute for Building Physics, Nobelstraße 12, 70569 Stuttgart, Germany.

References
Neue Staatsgalerie und Kammertheater Stuttgart, Publisher: Finanzministerum Baden-Württemberg, Neues Schloß, Stuttgart, 1984.

James Stirling - Die neue Staatsgalerie Stuttgart, Verlag Gerd Hatje, Stuttgart, 1984.

Architektur und Licht für moderne Kunst, Die Beleuchtung der neuen Staatsgalerie Stuttgart; W. Prahl, G. Roessler, Licht 3/1988.

More than one kilometre of north-facing rooflights filter and control daylight penetration in a museum

Wallraf-Richartz-Museum, Museum Ludwig, Philharmonie, Cologne, GERMANY

The rooflights designed for the Wallraf-Richartz Museum filter daylight through a triple-layer security glazing. External blinds block sun penetration, internal blinds adjust to the variation of daylight.

▽ **View of one of the gallery rooms daylit by the north facing sheds.**

The museum has emerged as a main feature of the reconstruction of the urban environment around the Gothic cathedral of Cologne. The museum complex was designed to replace the old Wallraf-Richartz Museum, destroyed in the Second World War, and to house modern art provided by several collectors, and the AGFA historama, a renowned collection on the history of photography. This allows for a broad presentation of art, from the fourteenth century up to modern times, in one building. In addition to the art galleries, the Köln Philharmonie has been accommodated in the building complex.

Triple-layer glazing with motorized roller blinds provides good control of daylight penetration

Fifty-three roof monitors, oriented to the north, with a total length of 1,100m filter light to the upper-floor galleries. The glazed portion is inclined at 53° to the horizontal plane. To shield rooms from direct sunlight which might penetrate the rooms at low sun angles, fixed, external sheet metal blinds have been mounted vertically on the glazing frames of the roof monitors. Illuminance levels on the exhibition walls can be reduced by internal textile blinds. For protection of exhibits, a UV-absorbing foil is

△ Bright wall finishes contribute to the high homogeneity of daylight distribution, here in a small gallery.

▽ Horizontal daylight factors distribution across the gallery.

▷ Shadows on walls due to spaces between sheds are attenuated by curvature of ceiling.

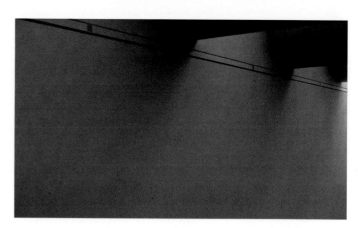

▷ Daylight factor distribution on the north and south facing walls, with and without blinds.

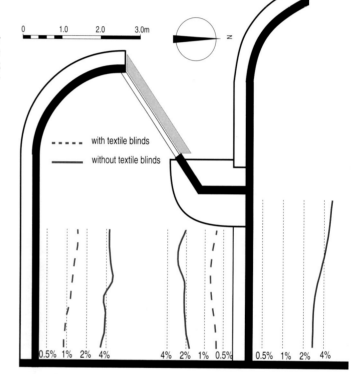

with textile blinds

without textile blinds

0   1.0   2.0   3.0m   N

0.5% 1% 2% 4%   4% 2% 1% 0.5%   0.5% 1% 2% 4%

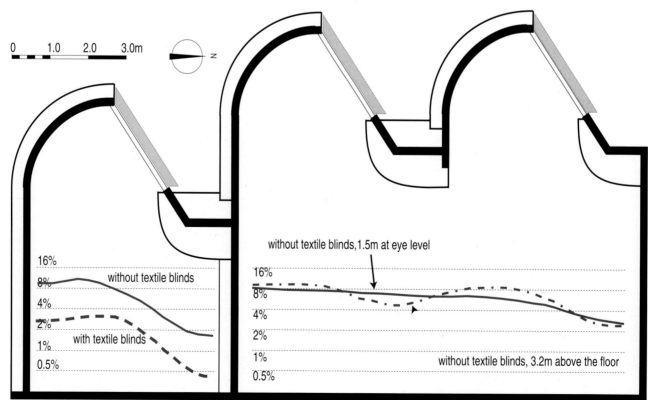

0   1.0   2.0   3.0m   N

16%
8%   without textile blinds
4%
2%
1%   with textile blinds
0.5%

without textile blinds, 1.5m at eye level

16%
8%
4%
2%
1%   without textile blinds, 3.2m above the floor
0.5%

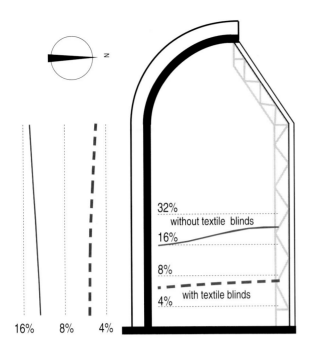

△ Vertical and horizontal daylight factors in a room with a north facing glazed facade.

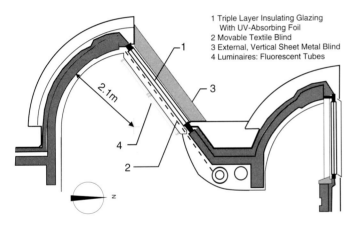

1 Triple Layer Insulating Glazing With UV-Absorbing Foil
2 Movable Textile Blind
3 External, Vertical Sheet Metal Blind
4 Luminaires: Fluorescent Tubes

△ Detail drawing of rooflight construction.

△ Room with north-oriented glazed facade. Due to high daylight penetration it cannot be used for standard exhibitions.

embedded in the triple-layer security glazing. The overall luminous transmittance of the glazing is 58%. The textile blind has a transmittance of 35% allowing attenuation by a factor of 3 when fully lowered.

Fully integrated artificial lighting extends the perception of natural light over time

Fluorescent tubes are located below the inclined frame elements of the glazed shed areas. They are almost invisible and distribute light in approximately the same way as daylight comes through the roof monitors. As a result, their curved shapes present similar luminous conditions during the day and night. Of significant inter-est also is the capability of the artific-ial lighting to 'boost' daylighting when it is insufficient during dark overcast days, or at the beginning and end of the day.

Curved rooflights redirect and scatter the penetrating daylight

The curved shape of the roof monitors is a major aesthetic feature of the museum. The indoor concave surface has a radius of 2.10 meters, and is painted white (reflectance: 77%). It allows a smooth var-iation of luminance on the top part of the exhibition walls. It also redirects light toward the north side of the museum to compensate for the fact that daylight comes mainly from the north side. As a consequence, daylight factors on south-facing walls, although they obtain no direct light, are 45% lower than they are on north-facing exhibition walls.

Daylight factors offer good compromise between protection of exhibits and pleasure of the visitors

When roller blinds are up, daylight factor values on the southern walls, receiving direct daylight from the rooflights, are about 3.2% 1.5m above ground. These values increase with height to reach about 4.4% at 3 metres (5.3% at 4m) above the floor. By comparison, the values on the floor are about 3%. Knowing that the specified illuminance for oil painting is 150 lux (ICOM), this means that the museum can be satisfactorily daylit with outdoor illuminances of about 4,300 lux. Since higher illuminance values are common, roller blinds are needed to allow some adjustment. It is interesting to note that excess daylight will penetrate when outdoor diffuse illuminance exceeds 9,000 lux, a situation which occurs for at least 1,500 hours per year.

Good savings in lighting electricity can be achieved through extensive use of daylighting

In theory, the museum offers significant opportunities for energy saving, but this requires careful control of the blinds to protect against excess daylight and over-heating. However, due to poor management of the blind controls, the blinds tend to be closed most of the time which requires the artificial lighting to be in use for longer than is necessary.

Some galleries are also sidelit, which leads to daylight factors in excess of 10% on some walls. The result is that these exhibition areas tend not to be used or the glazed areas are obstructed by portable exhibition panels.

△ Location of the museum, near Cologne Cathedral.

Daylighting monitoring

Monitoring concentrated on the behaviour of the roof lighting concept. Two representative gallery rooms, daylit only by rooflights, were selected on the second floor. In addition one room being roof lit as well as sidelit on the north facade was monitored. Measurements were performed in late September 1996.

CREDITS

Building description
The building complex is located in the centre of Cologne, situated 40 metres away from the banks of the river Rhine and directly adjacent to the Cologne Cathedral. The museum and the included underground Köln Philharmonie offer alltogether 25,000m² of space. The building was opened for the public in 1986.

Climate
Latitude: 51°N, Longitude: 7°E, Altitude: 50m. It's climatic conditions are best described by the Essen Test Reference Year, coldest month: Febuary with a mean of 1.8°C, warmest month: August with a mean 17.7°C.

Client
Stadt Köln, der Oberstadtdirektor, Cologne

Architect
Peter Busmann and Godfrid Haberer, Cologne

Daylighting Consultants
Institut für Tageslichttechnik, Dr.-Ing. Hanns Freymuth, Stuttgart

Artificial Lighting Design
Lichtdesign, Hans Theo von Malotki, Cologne

Monitoring organisation
Fraunhofer Institute for Building Physics, Nobelstraße 12, 70569 Stuttgart, Germany

References
Zwischen Dom und Strom, Neubau Wallraf-Richartz-Museum, Museum Ludwig und Kölner Philharmonie, Publisher: Der Oberstadtdirektor, Hochbaudezernat, Stadt Cologne

Wallraf-Richartz-Museum und Museum Ludwig mit Philharmonie Köln, Glasforum 4 - 87.

Lichtblick zwischen Dom und Rhein, Wallraf-Richartz-Museum / Museum Ludwig in Köln, Wolfgang Prahl, Georg Roessler, Licht 8/1987

Oberlichtsäle im Wallraf-Richartz-Museum / Museum Ludwig in Cologne, Hanns Freymuth, Licht 3 / 1988

△ North facade of the Museum.

Material properties assessed on site

	Colour	Hemispherical-hemispherical reflectances
Walls	white	77%
Floor	wood	19%

	Normal-normal transmittance	Hemispherical-hemispherical transmittance
Glazing	65%	58%
Textile blinds		35%

A variety of roof daylighting solutions for a museum in a Mediterranean climate

Byzantine Museum, Thessaloniki, GREECE

The daylighting solutions incorporated have created a variety of different luminous environments.

▽ Gallery with clerestories and facade windows (Picture taken at the end of the construction).

Daylight features designed for the display of artwork

The building was completed in 1993 and houses art objects of the Byzantine period including sculptures, paintings and fabrics, the latter being most sensitive to light. This led to the unfortunate obstruction of most windows a few years after opening of the museum. The majority of the windows have been blocked up while the walls have been painted brown, so that the interior has been significantly modified in comparison with newly constructed building presented below.

The original general daylighting strategy focused on the design of two families of apertures: clerestories and facade windows looking towards internal courtyards. The latter are small in size and are mainly used as circulation spaces.

Bright-coloured surface finishes compensate for the contrast with the outdoor luminous environment

Floors are finished in pale grey marble, while walls and ceilings in the galleries are painted white (in the early version of the building). In the

BYZANTINE MUSEUM

▷ Daylight factor distribution across central gallery (B). Roof monitors are shaded with vertical concrete fins.

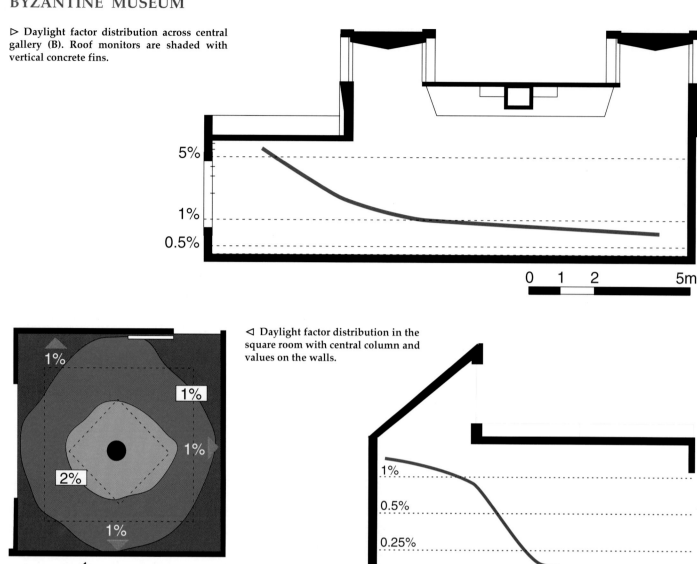

5%

1%

0.5%

0   1   2   5m

◁ Daylight factor distribution in the square room with central column and values on the walls.

1%

1%

1%

2%

1%

0   0.5   1.0   1.5m

▷ Daylight factor distribution in single clerestory room (A).

1%

0.5%

0.25%

▽ View of square room (C) with central column.

concrete frame and red-brick infill panels are exposed. Visible external surfaces are painted a deep terracotta colour, reducing glare from light reflections in courtyards.

Clerestories facing in two opposite directions balance the directionality of daylight

The central gallery is one of the largest in the museum. Located on the first floor, it is 25m long and is lit by two arrays of clerestories screened by fixed exterior vertical fins to reduce excessive solar gain. Furthermore, glazing is translucent to prevent the risk of sunlight penetration. The horizontal daylight factors were measured at a height of 0.8m. and vertical values on walls at 1.65m from floor. Daylight factors ranged from 0.8% to 1.8% on walls. These values may appear low, but they are common in

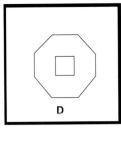

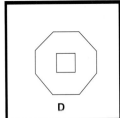

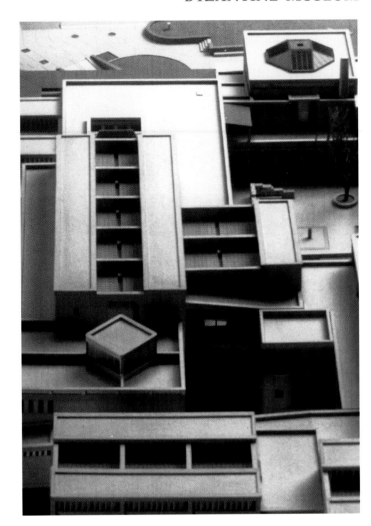

◁ Location of monitored rooms
  A: Single clerestory room.
  B: Central gallery.
  C: Square room with central column.
  D: Room with octogonal roof system.

△ Aerial view of scale model showing in the foreground the roof windows of room C, and in the background the hidden clerestory of room A. One room with an octagonal roof can be seen on the right.

▽ View of room with octagonal clerestories and hanging screen (D).

lighting and are rather high for the Greek climate. Facade windows significantly increase local illuminances on the plane 0.8m above the floor, with values exceeding 5%. At the north-west end of the central gallery is an exterior daylit with a south-east facing clerestory, equipped with diffusing glass. Horizontal daylight factors range from 0.6% to 1.2%. Such a design is only suitable for works of art with very low sensitivity to light exposure.

Vertical column catches daylight from center roof aperture

In the square room (C), the roof aperture is located just above the column, resulting in a play of light between beams and the column. Horizontal daylight factors vary from 0.6 to 3.2%. Here walls are painted grey (reflectance 0.5). Vertical daylight factors on walls are around 1%.

Horizontal sliding screen attenuates daylight penetration

Two square galleries are roofed by octagonal pitched structures with translucent glazing. Below is a horizontal sliding screen which attenuates incoming daylight (transmittance: 36%).

Daylight availability in Greece significantly reduces requirements for artificial lighting

In Greece, daylight is not only more intense than in the rest of Europe (due to the high angles of the sun in the sky), but it is also more intense and available for longer periods during from September until March. It is, therefore, easy to reach high fraction of daylight use between 9hr and 17hr. For this building, the fraction reaches approximately 84%.

Daylight monitoring

Daylight measurements were performed only in the upper floor of the museum, in rooms shown on the plan as room A, room B, room C and room D. The measurements took place on 25 January 1996 under overcast conditions.

◁ External view of the museum with the city of Thessaloniki in the background.

◁ Luminance distribution (cd/m²) in the main gallery (B) adjusted for a standard overcast sky, leading to an exterior horizontal illuminance of 10,000 lux, showing the rather high uniformity of the luminous space.

Material properties assessed on site

	Hemispherical-hemispherical reflectance
Wall	86%
Ceiling	86%
Floor	60%
Interior structural elements	54%

	Hemispherical-hemispherical transmittance	Direct-direct transmittance
Translucent glazing	36%	48%
Clear glass	72%	83%

CREDITS

Building description
The building is located on an urban site in Thessaloniki (Latitude: 40°33′N, Longitude: 23°00′E) on the Aegean coast of northern Greece at sea level. The site is open on all sides so that there are no significant external obstructions to sunlight or daylight. The building was completed in 1993 and houses art objects of the Byzantine period throughout its area of 12,000m².

Climate
The climate is Mediterranean with mean annual temperature 15.7°C. Annual maximum monthly average temperature is 20.6°C while the minimum one is 9.4°C. Heating degree days (base: 18°C) are 1,800 per year.

The maximum value of sunshine duration is in July with 11.4 hours/day. The least sunny days occur in December with 3.3 hours/day. Mean daily global radiation is 4649 Wh/m² and mean daily sunshine duration is 6.7 hours.

Client
Greek Ministry of Culture

Architect
Kyriakos Krokos, 1993.
Filopappou 27
Athens
Tel: 0030.1-9215195
Fax: 0030.1-9242398

Monitoring organisation
Aris Tsangrassoulis
National Observatory, Athens
N. Tsakiris
Aristotle University of Thessaloniki

Awnings controlled by 27 light sensors, oriented according to the operation of each daylighting system

Musée de Grenoble, Grenoble, FRANCE

This museum features various roof aperture solutions blocking sun penetration passively, and actively allowing adjustment for daylight penetration as a function of climatic changes.

The largest national museum outside Paris

With a total net area of 10,600m², the Musée de Grenoble was, in 1994, the largest national museum to be built outside Paris. Located at the edge of the old city of Grenoble on the banks of the river Isère, it houses a large permanent collection of classical and modern paintings, as well as Egyptian art. It is structured around a central street, separating classical art galleries and temporary exhibitions, and leading to 20th century art rooms located along the circular wall facing the river Isère.

Passive protection against sunlight, and dispersion of diffuse light

Except for sculptures which are lit from facade windows, and highly sensitive materials which are displayed in windowless galleries, all exhibition galleries are daylit via roof apertures. Classical art galleries are daylit from combinations of linear roof monitors, facing south and north. No sun can penetrate the rooms due to obstructions created by cylindrical lamellae hanging from the ceiling. Above the 20th century art galleries, daylight comes through north-facing roof monitors. This design, in association with the high obstructions due to the surrounding mountains prevents sunbeams from penetrating the exhibition areas.

Construction elements below the apertures have been designed to distribute diffuse light to the interior and make daylight factors on walls more uniform.

Active control of daylight penetration

Sunlight is prevented from penetrating through fixed elements, and diffuse light is controlled by movable shades made of diffusing white awnings. Four positions can be selected: open, 30% closed, 60% closed and fully closed. These positions are automatically selected on the basis of readings of illuminances provided by external sensors. External sensors were preferred to indoor sensors because they provide information on daylight penetration independently from artificial lighting and awning position. Readings are taken continuously, but

◁ View of the north wall, lit by a continuous clerestory. Sunlight is blocked by beams and movable shades.

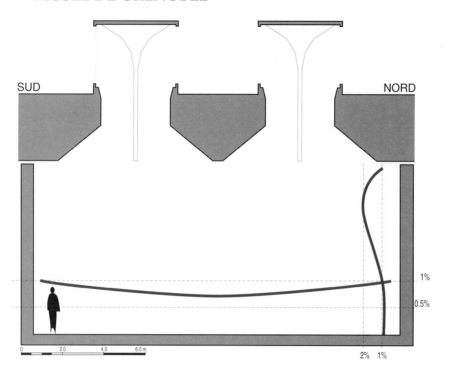

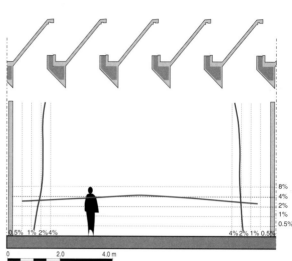

△ Daylight factors along a cross section of one of the 18th century rooms dealing with French & Italian paintings.

△ Daylight factors below the north facing roof monitors of room 38, 20th century painting area.

▷ Daylight factor distribution on surfaces of one of the 18th century rooms.

deployment of the awnings can be modified to reduce the disruptive effects of shading movements for visitors. Typical intervals are of 30 minutes. The deployment of awnings compensates for diurnal and seasonal variations in diffuse light, typically in a ratio of 1 to 4 at noon for overcast sky conditions between January and June.

Direction and orientation of sensors have been adapted to each daylighting system

One major difficulty in the control of shading with external sensors, is that the control strategy depends on each daylighting system. In order to achieve as linear as possible a relationship between the reading of the sensor and the illuminance on the painting, the outdoor sensor needs to face the area of the sky which supplies the light energy - the photons - which will ultimately reach the paintings. For this reason, each one of the nine families of daylighting systems is controlled by its own individual sensor system. Three sensors have been used for each of the nine systems. This is to ensure the quality of the external illuminance reading: a faculty sensor would therefore be easy to detect.

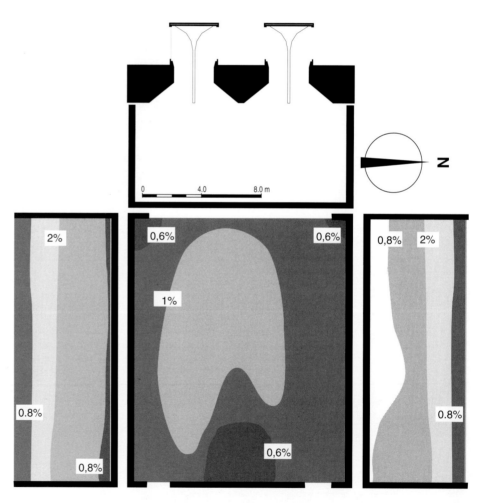

▷ View of one of the 'classical paintings' rooms, with south- and north-facing roof monitors. French and Italian painting, 18th century.

▷ West end of the 'classical paintings' aisle, for display of sculpture with side lighting.

▷ View of the north-facing roof monitors above room 38 of the '20th century painting' section.

△ For each of the nine major daylighting systems, three light sensors are used to control the movement of awnings. They face the section of the sky providing most of the light in accordance with the design of the daylighting system.

△ Difference of colour temperature between north and south sections of sky leads to a change of tint on the east-west lamellae of the roof monitors above the 'classical painting' rooms.

Daylighting monitoring

Measurements were conducted in spring 1996 with additional optical measurements in September 1997.

▽ South and west facade of the museum, 'classical painting' aisle.

Material properties assessed on site

	Colour	Hemispherical-hemispherical reflectances
Wall (20th century room)	yellow	50%
Wall (18th century room)	white	80%
Floor	wood	30%

	Normal-normal transmittance	Hemispherical-hemispherical transmittance
Double glazing	75%	—

CREDITS

Building description
Building area: 10,600m²
6,500m² for exhibition only
Open January 1994

Climate
Latitude: 45°11'N, Longitude: 5°43'E, Altitude: 240m. The maximum average temperature is 20°C in July and the minimum average temperature is 1°C in January. The sunshine duration is 2200h/year.

Architects
Olivier Félix Faure (Groupe 6 Architects), with Antoine Félix Faure, Macary. Assistance of Lorenzo Piqueras, delegated architect by the Direction des Musées de France.

Client
Musée de Grenoble
City of Grenoble
Place Lavalette
38000 Grenoble

Daylighting consultants
Marc Fontoynont, Bernard Paule, Richard Mitanchey
ENTPE-DGCB
Rue M. Audin - F 69120 Vaulx en Velin

Daylighting Controls Systems
SOMFY
8 avenue de Margencel - 74300 Cluses

References
Marc Fontoynont, Bernard Paule, Richard Mitanchey, Integration of daylighting and artificial lighting in Musée d'Intérêt National de Grenoble, ASES Conference proceedings, Washington, 1993.

Acknowledgments
We would like to thank Serge Lemoine, Director of the Museum and Mr Foglieti for their cooperation for helping the monitoring activities.

Special prism-shaped roof lights mix sunlight and skylight

Trapholt Art Museum, Kolding, DENMARK

The coolness of light from the northern part of the sky is mixed with the warmth of reflected sunlight to enrich the luminous environment.

Roof systems with hanging prism of canvas animate the space of room 8. ▽

A 'Running Fence' on the northern slopes of Kolding Fiord

The architect's main theme is a moving wall, a Running Fence, which wanders across the site, on the northern slopes of Kolding Fiord. The 'museum path' lead the public through the museum from the main entrance. The floor of this path follows the slope of the terrain, while the vaulted ceiling runs horizontally above, giving an increasing ceiling height as one moves through the building.

A large variety of daylighting solutions, from roof to facade

The lighting design and sizing of every window and skylight opening has been determined according to the actual size of the items exhibited. Minor individual works, applied art, furniture, etc. are given limited space with limited and adjustable light openings, while major works and paintings, where context and breadth of view are crucial, are given larger rooms and bigger lighting openings. However, in larger rooms, the light is configured so that it also retains the painting and sculpture's properties, depicting the details of form and texture.

In Trapholt's exhibition spaces, the lighting architect arranged the exploitation of daylight to be manifold and to give rhythm and renewed interest to the works of art displayed.

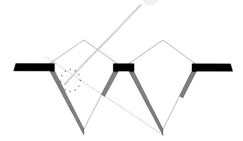

△ Principle of the shaft element in room 7.

▽ Principle of the shaft element in room 8.

△ Skylights above room 8.

Daylight factor distribution on the floor and ▷ on the exhibition wall, in room 8.

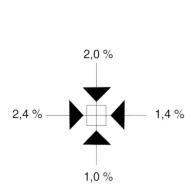

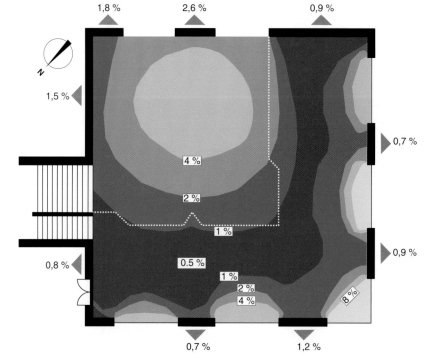

△ Vertical daylight factor in the center of the room, 1.50m above floor.

Various principles of daylight illumination have been used, ranging from rooms with ordinary sidelight windows to rooms with specially designed skylights taking the form of glazed opaque prisms which project above and below the roof plane. The sidelighting windows are of different sizes, placed both high and low in the facade, and their orientations are adapted according to the room's use and the varied nature of the works of art on display.

All windows have white interior louvre systems which direct and adjust the light, to make parts of the exterior walls semi-transparent, when necessary, or completely opaque. All daylight measurements were conducted with the louvre system (large venetian blinds) in their normal open position (sidelit windows only).

Roof elements mix reflected sunlight and diffuse light from the northern

Approximately 45% of the exhibition area is equipped with these specially formed prism-shaped elements, so that direct sunlight does not reach down to the exhibition halls, but stops at the inner surface of the shaft walls. The same applies to the reflected sunlight from the exterior sidewalls of the surrounding prisms. These special formed skylights filter the relatively cool light from the northerly quadrant of the sky with warm light reflected from their light-coloured internal surfaces and the white exterior sidewalls of the neighbouring skylight element. This gives, depending on the variation of light intensity from the sky, a varied supplement of reflected sunlight to the interior. The colour of the skylight element by the combination of incoming warm reflected

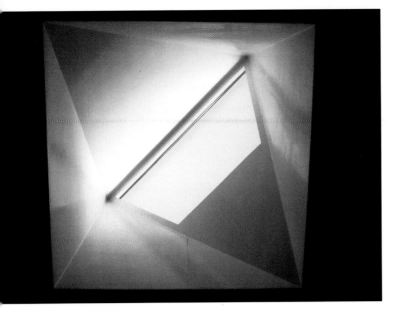

Skylights of room 7 seen from below. △   △ Roof systems seen from the roof (room 7).

Daylight factor distribution on the floor and on the exhibition wall of room 7. ▽

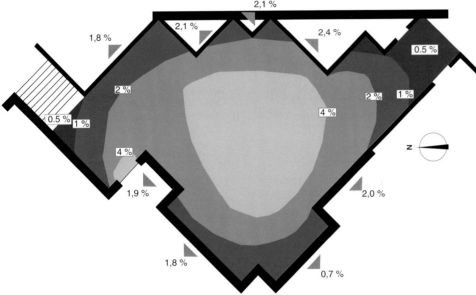

▽ Room 7.

sunlight and cool skylight, can resemble the colour of mother-of-pearl. On clear days, the sunlight and the bluish light from the sky give the exhibition walls a moderately additive colour mixture which accentuates the paintings displayed.

Louvre on sidelights attenuates daylight penetration for preservation of art (room 5)

The windows of the sidelit room's are of full room height and oriented both to the south-west and to the north-west. During measurements, the white louvres were fully closed in the lowest 2m section of the window while adjusted to a horizontal slat angle position for the remaining top part of the window. Horizontal daylight factor measurements showed a uniform light distribution throughout the room varying from 2% in the majority of the room area to 1% near the sidewalls and at the back of the room. Measurements showed that daylight factors along the sidewalls varied from 1.6% to 3.9%, being highest close to the large windows. Such values are typical in museums for the exhibition of oil paintings in northern Europe. However, areas with daylight factors values above 2.5% would require shading in summertime.

Skylights concentrate daylight on the floor rather that the exhibition walls (room 7)

The specially formed skylight elements provide the interior with light of little variation and uniform luminance distribution on the floor and sidewalls. The horizontal daylight factor distribution showed a daylight factor varying from 1 to 4%, being highest in the centre of the room below the skylights. Assessment of the vertical luminance distribution on the sidewalls was conducted by taking measurements in 3 positions (1.5m, 2.5m and 3.5m above floor) at every main surface where the paintings were displayed.

Measurements showed a uniform luminance distribution and small daylight factor variation from the highest to the lowest measurement position (0.5 to 1%).

Daylight in the central hall with balcony, skylights and sidelighting

The central hall is separated by a balcony at the exterior wall whereas the middle of the room towards the 'museum path' has a two-storey high ceiling. The middle of the room receives daylight mainly from the skylights (the hemi-hemi global transmittance=17%), while windows in the exterior wall admit daylight to both the balcony and the area below it. The skylights have integrated hanging prisms of white canvas to filter incoming light. Measurements in the middle of the room at full height showed a uniform horizontal light distribution with daylight factors varying from 2.5 to 5%.

Daylighting monitoring

The monitoring of the indoor illuminances was conducted in December 1996, under overcast conditions. Typical outdoor illuminance levels were around 5,000 lux. Pictures were taken March 1997.

CREDITS

Building description
Built in 1988
Gross floor area: 3,085m²
Exhibition area:1,790m²

The Trapholt Art Museum's new buildings near Kolding in Jutland, Denmark, were inaugurated in 1988 as a result of a national architectural competition in 1982. In the period 1995-96 a comprehensive extension including an underground furniture museum and a hall for special exhibitions was added.

Climate
Minimum monthly average temperature: -0.6°C
Maximum monthly average temperature: 16.7°C
The average daily sunshine duration is 0.9 hours in winter, 8.1 hours in summer and 4.9 hours averaged over the year.

Client
Kolding Art Society
Lesbygade 56
6000 Kolding

The Trapholt Foundation
Aeblehaven 23
6000 Kolding

Kolding City Council
Akseltorv
6000 Kolding

Architect
Boje Lundgaard and Bente Aude
Pilestraede 10
1112 Copenhagen K

Lighting architect
Sophus Frandsen
The Royal Danish Academy of Fine Art
Institute of Building Science
Philips de Langes Allé 10
1435 Copenhagen K

Landscaping consultants
Svend Kirkegaard
Nyhavn 31 D
1051 Copenhagen K

Monitoring organisation
Danish Building Research Institute
Energy and Indoor Climate Division, Project Group: Daylight in Buildings
P.O. Box 119 2970 Horsholm, Denmark

References
A brochure of the museum in Danish with English and German summaries
is available at The Trapholt Museum of Modern Art, Aeblehaven 23,
6000 Kolding, Denmark.

Kunstmuseet Trapholt, Kolding, 1986-88, (in Danish with English and
German summary), Arkitektur DK, 4/89

△ Axonometric view of the Trapholt Art Museum. Daylight measurements were conducted in rooms 5, 7 and 8.

◁ Outdoor view of the Trapholt Art Museum.

Materials properties assessed on site

	Colour	Hemispherical-hemispherical reflectance
Floor	light grey/white	51%
Ceiling (concrete)	dark grey	19%
Wall	white	84%

	Normal-normal transmitance	Hemispherical-hemispherical transmittance
Double glazing	71%	78%

Two-stage daylight transmission admits light to deep core areas of building

Waucquez Department Store, Brussels, BELGIUM

This art nouveau textiles depart-ment store in Brussels was con-verted into a comic strip museum in 1989. It features decorated light-wells below glazed domes which provide a major architect-ural attraction.

Extraordinary daylight penetrat-ion lights two floors

As daylight is the only light that allows the colour of textiles to be properly appreciated and as its psychological effect was well known, architect Victor Horta favoured its penetration deep into the store. Moreover, artificial lighting was expensive in the early 1900s, so the store was originally completely lit by daylight. Most daylight enters via two large glazed vaults. These vaults are protected by two glasshouses on the roof, whose glass was replaced by armoured glass (transmittance: 76%) during the renovation in 1989.

The glass of the vault was replaced by diffusing polycarbonate panels (trans-mittance: 52%) fitted to the original steel frames. The space between the glass-house and the vault serves as a buffer space reducing heat losses in winter. In summer, it is ventilated by automatic windows at the top of the glasshouses. The horizontal daylight factors above the vault reach values from 45 to 50% in both glasshouses. Thus the effect of the glasshouses is to halve the amount of light reaching the domes.

Both vaults then distribute daylight into the exhibition halls on the first floor. The brightness is extraordinary, and this phenomenon is enhanced by reflection from the light-coloured walls which are painted broken white (reflectance: 57%) and from the white ceiling (reflectance: 84%). The floor reflectance varies bet-ween 20% for the parquet floor and 40% for the marble mosaics.

The daylighting effect of the vaults is remarkable. The daylight factors achie-ved are extremely high and the result is impressive. As was suitably express-ed by a staff member, sometimes the museum looks brighter than the outside street. Under the larger vault, daylight factor values vary from 6% to 18.5%. This light illuminates the big central hall at the first floor and is partly trans-mitted toward the ground floor. Under the smaller dome, daylight factor values are found to be only slightly lower: they vary from 4% to 15%.

◁ Daylight directs the visitor towards the central reception hall.

◁ Protective glasshouses on the roof.

◁ Although the diffusing vaults are un-avoidably covered with dust, they still have a transmittance of 52%.

◁ View on the translucent floor under the larger vault, made of diffusing white glass tiles.

View of the lattice windows under the translucent floor made of diffusing white glass tiles. ▷

Translucent floors extend daylight penetration into the core areas of the building

The next stage in light distribution occurs through the light-well illuminating the central reception hall, and the additional luminous transmittance through the surrounding translucent floor (transmittance: 18%). The light-well is situated slightly off-axis from the middle of the largest vault towards the back of the building. Though the main contribution to the illumination of the hall comes from the light-well, the translucent floor has an important function, extending the floor surface lit by the light-well without reducing floor surface at first floor level. By this process, light now comes through an area which is four times larger. The translucent floor also softens the transition in illumination levels from the spaces directly under the floor aperture to the nearby fully-covered spaces. Moreover this is a very beautiful example of a translucent floor, decorated on the ceiling side with curved lattice glazing.

A similar strategy is adopted for the light coming from the second, smaller vault, part of the light being used for the illumination of the back of the first

floor and the other part illuminating one of the most monumental stairs Horta ever designed.

Two dramatic luminous effects are achieved on the ground floor below these light wells: the luminaire in the centre of the entrance hall is emphasized by the daylight, as is the monumental staircase under the second vault. The daylight factors on the ground floor reach values up to 8%.

High illuminance levels achieved with no energy use

With these high daylight factors on the ground floor and the first floor, it is common to observe illuminance levels in the range of 2,000 to 4,000 lux in these areas without any artificial lighting. The thermal effect of these glasshouses is also very important, reducing approximately by half the winter heating consumption. A major disadvantage is the hot temperatures reached in summer. The automatic windows for natural ventilation of the glasshouses on the roof can not prevent the high light performance from leading to summer overheating. Mainly on the first floor and the mezzanine overheating temperatures were recorded during the whole

summer period, with peaks over 35°C, very hot for the Belgian climate.

High contrast makes neighbouring areas look darker

On all floors, the areas away from the vaults and from the light well are much darker and daylight factors are decreasing rapidly to values below 0.5%. The fast decrease of daylight levels leads to a strong contrast with the very well-lit central spaces and gives the neighbouring areas a darker aspect than the daylight factor values may suggest.

The open architecture with very few partitions between the lighter and darker spaces attenuates this phenomenon, but can not completely set off the problem. For the actual use of the building these darker areas are most useful. Most of the permanent exhibition walls and display cases are placed in zones with low daylight factors to prevent the comic strip originals from degradation due to excessive exposure to daylight. The result is that nearly all showcases are artificially lit, strongly contrasting with the very nicely daylit central parts of the building, where no artificial light is needed at all.

◁ The smaller diffusing vault seen from inside the protecting glasshouse.

◁ The smaller diffusing vault seen from below.

◁ In the latter added mezzanine, thick cast glass tiles were used as translucent floor.

▷ Daylight factor distribution along a transverse cross-section through the centre of the first floor aperture.

A: Protecting glasshouse.
B: Diffusing vault.
C: Translucent floor 1, white diffusive glass tiles, decorated with lattice windows.
D: Glazed partition.
E: Translucent floor 2, semidiffusive cast glass tiles.
F: Facade windows.

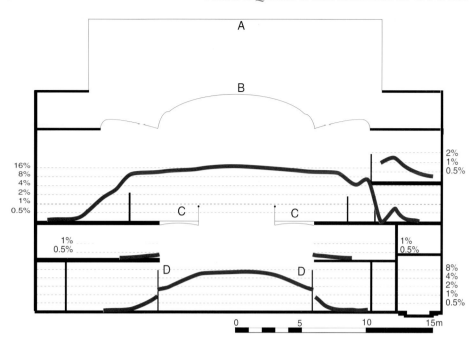

▽ Daylight factor distribution along a longitudinal cross-section through the centre of the first floor aperture.

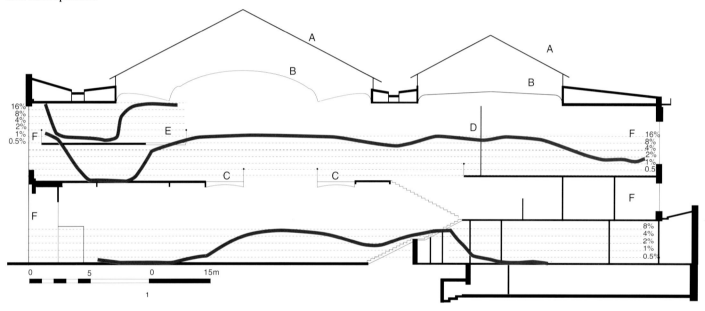

Exhibition walls adjacent to light wells do not require specific additional lighting

In the central parts of the building the exhibition walls are not provided with artificial lighting because of the excellent daylight conditions there. The vertical daylight factors measured in the middle of the exposed images, are in general satisfactory for a good view of the exposed material, varying between 2 and 6%. Visitors, however, notice their own reflections in the show cases, but this phenomenon is limited. More bothersome are the direct reflections of the light vaults on the tilted or horizontal show cases, sometimes obstructing any view of the comic strips on display.

Refurbishment reduces daylight from facade windows

In the original concept, the light coming from the vaults was supplemented by the light from large facade windows in the front and rear facades. The light coming from these sources could easily penetrate into the building because of the open architecture, using columns instead of bearing walls and glass for the limited number of indoor partitions.

In the current state, however, very low daylight factors (<0.5%) were measured in any area away from the vaults. This is mainly due to the earliest renovation of the store (1913), when a mezzanine and in-between floor were needed to expand the floor surface of the commer-

cially successful store. Although the architect paid attention to the integration of these additions in the whole, the original daylight concept was lost. Both additional floors cut the front facade windows in two, reducing the daylight penetration on the first floor and the ground floor to 2% at less than 3m from the windows. On the intermediate floor and the mezzanine the situation is even worse, because the windows were not designed for these floors. The light enters at floor height and does not penetrate further than one metre. It should be noted that electric lighting was first introduced during this initial renovation. In the actual situation, the little daylight left is blocked by the exposition walls that are mainly

◁ Horta's design included every detail of the building such as stairs, balustrades, lattice windows, floor mosaics, furniture and even lamp posts.

installed in these darker parts of the building.

At the rear facade, the high windows were not blocked by addition of the in-between floors, thus showing how good the original concept was. Unfortunately, the rear facade windows are now continuously covered with white curtains with a measured transmittance of 27%.

Even with this obstruction the daylight factors in the room don't fall below 2%. This means that before the extra floors were added the building must have offered a very bright and balanced luminous environment.

Daylight monitoring

The building was monitored 13 May 1996, under overcast conditions. The external horizontal illuminance was between 10 and 40 Klux.

CREDITS

Building description
Art nouveau department store, originally designed for a textile vendor. Departs from the state-of-the-art in large department stores design and the extensive use of daylight at the time.

Climate
Minimal monthly temperature: 2.4°C (January). Maximal monthly temperature: 17.1°C (July). Annual sunshine duration: 1600 hours. Latitude: 50°N, Longitude: 4°E, Altitude: 100m.

Client
Original building: Magasins Waucquez
Restoration: Belgian Ministry of Public Works, Buildings Direction-Residence Palace
Wetstraat 155 - 1040 Brussel
Current use: Belgian Centre for Comic Strip Art, museum, exhibition space, Zandstraat 20 - 1000 Brussels

Architect
Original building: Victor Horta, 1906
Intermediate floor and mezzanine:
Charles Veraart in 1912/13.
Restoration 1988-89:
Cooparch, J.DeSalle
426, Chaussée de Waterloo, 1050 Brussels
P. Van Assche
13, Rue du Président, 1050 Brussels
J.Y. Frateur
46, Rue de l'étoile, 5032 Bossière

Monitoring organisation
BBRI (WTCB-CSTC)
Violetstraat 21-23 - 1000 Brussels
Tel: ++32.2-502 6690
Fax: ++32.2-502 8180

References
Van Assche, P., Lelubre, C., et al., Restauratie van de Magazijnen Waucquez, 1989, Regie der Gebouwen
Auquier, J., 1990, Belgian Center of Comic Strip Art, information folder

Material properties assessed on site

	Colour	Hemispherical/hemispherical reflectance
Ceiling	white	84%
Walls	broken white	57%
Floor	parquet, mosaics	20-40%

	Material	Hemispherical/hemispherical transmittance
Glasshouses	armoured glass	76%
Vaults	diffusive polycarbonate	52%
Translucent floor 1	white diffusive glass tiles	18%
Translucent floor 2	semidiffusive cast glass tiles	59%
Facade windows	double glass	66%
Glass indoor partitions	single glass	85%

Four arrays of north-facing clerestories designed to bring daylight without sunlight to a museum

Modern Art Centre, Lisbon, PORTUGAL

Permanent diffusing blinds are required continuously to attenuate daylight penetration and protect works of art.

▽ Indoor view of the main gallery of the Modern Art Centre, with the north-facing clerestories.

A gallery totally daylit from the north-facing windows, 80% of them being clerestories

The Modern Art Centre is located in the Calouste Gulbekian Foundation Campus in the centre of the city of Lisbon.

The main complex of the centre occupies an area of approximately 6,200m², distributed in two principal areas - the Galleries of the Museum and the Centre for Documentation and Artistic Creation. The entrance area is connected to a restaurant overlooking a park and opening onto an external terrace with water features.

The main exhibition hall is 7m in length and 23m in width at ground level (total area: 1590m²). The hall extends towards the south facade through another level (length: 70m, width: 11m, area: 751m²). The entire hall is daylit both from north-facing clerestories (glazed area: 350m²) and north-facing windows (glazed area: 70m²) The glazing ratio relevant to the north-facing clerestories is therefore 15%.

Clerestories obstructed with interior diffusing curtains

Although facing north, the clerestories tend to be oversized for daylighting

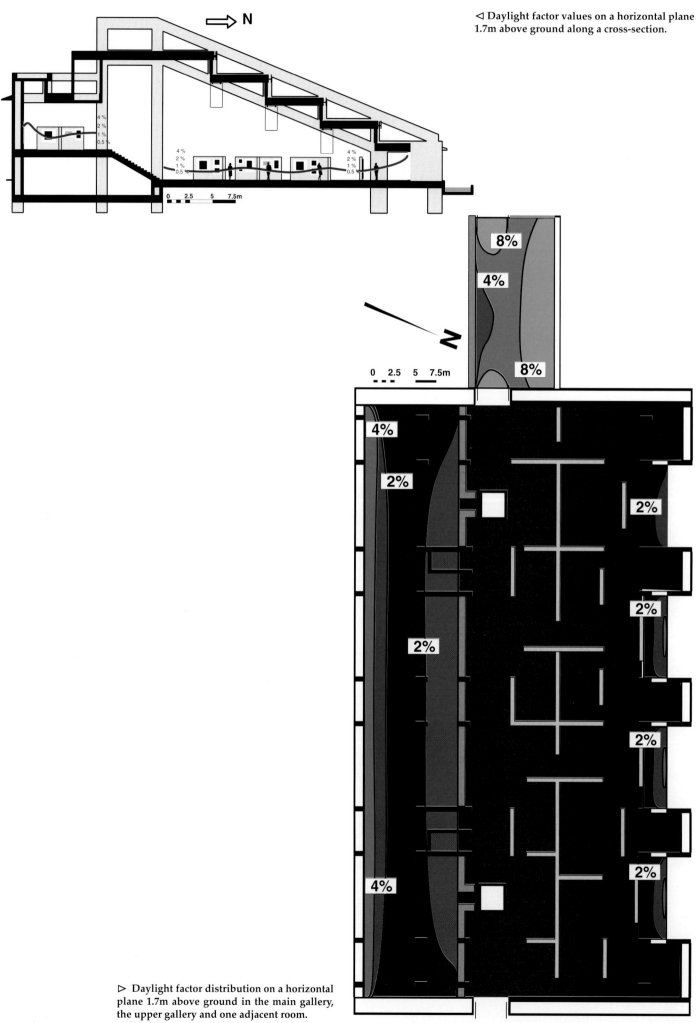

◁ Daylight factor values on a horizontal plane 1.7m above ground along a cross-section.

▷ Daylight factor distribution on a horizontal plane 1.7m above ground in the main gallery, the upper gallery and one adjacent room.

▷ South wall, daylit from north-facing clerestories.

▷ North-facing window in the main gallery, at ground floor level.

works of art, particularly drawings and photographs. For this reason, all clerestories are permanently shaded with interior translucent vertical blinds. Their luminous transmission appears low (less than 20%).

The resulting daylight factors at floor level are consequently low: around 0.5% in the centre of the room. The unshaded clerestory above the upper gallery on the south side leads, however, to daylight factor values of 1 to 2% on a horizontal plane, and 2 to 4% on the wall.

Daylighting monitoring

Monitoring was performed in February and May 1997 for overcast conditions (5Klux to 30Klux), and in August 1997 for clear sky conditions.

The outdoor illuminance sensor was located on the roof of the building, with no obstructions.

MODERN ART CENTRE

▷ External view of the north facade of the Modern Art Centre, surrounded by vegetation.

◁ Location of the Modern Art Centre.

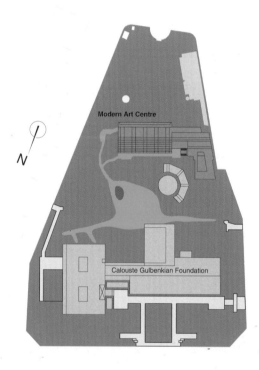

CREDITS

Building
Total area: 13,800m². Main gallery: 1,590m².
Upper gallery: 751m².
Built in 1983.

Climate
Latitude: 38°46'N, Longitude: 9°08'W, Altitude: 100m. Minimum monthly average temperature 12.2°C (January) and maximum monthly average temperature 20°C (July). The average sunshine duration is 143.1 hours in January (48%) and 321.3 hours in July (72%).

Architect
Sir Leslie Martin

Building owner
Fundaçion Calouste Gulbekian - Centro des Arte Moderna
Faculdade de Farmácia da Universidade Técnica de Lisboa
Av. das Forças Armadas
1600 Lisboa - Portugal
Tel : + 351.1-848 2131
Fax : + 351.1-840 1581

Monitoring organisation
LNEC - Laboratorio Nacional de Engenharia Civil
Av. Brasil, 101
1799 Lisboa Codex, Portugal
Tel: +351.1-848 2131
Fax: +351.1-840 1581

References
'Daylight Monitoring of the Modern Art Centre', Lisbon, LNEC Report 1997

Acknowledgements
We would like to thank the director of the Modern Art Centre, Dr Jorge Molder, for allowing the monitoring of the building and Architect Cristina Sena da Fonseca for her help and collaboration.

Material properties assessed on site

	Colour	Hemispherical-hemispherical reflectance
Exhibition walls	white	93%
Concrete pillars	medium grey	36%
Wall and ceilings	white	87%
Marble-tile floors	medium grey	31%

	Normal-normal transmittance	Hemispherical-hemispherical transmittance
Single glazing	79%	73%
Double tinted glazing	38%	36%
Shading device (blinds)	-	32%
Shading device (courtins)	-	35%

A study of daylighting devices at the beginning of the 19th century

Sir John Soane's Museum, London, UNITED KINGDOM

This museum features an amazing combination of daylighting devices and materials with specific optical properties. It shows that its designer, Sir John Soane, had a good understanding of the way to play with concealed daylighting sources.

The combination of a private house and a museum

The Sir John Soane's museum is an exquisite and eccentric collection of spaces, lighting devices and objects, which the architect, Sir John Soane (1753 to 1837) designed and lived amongst. His wish was to use his house as a museum and he designed it specifically to display the antiquities and works of art he had collected. It consists of a house at the front of the site, on three floors, and a single-storey 'museum' across the rear of the site. On his death in 1837 it became a public museum and since then it has been preserved by a Board of Trustees.

Lately it underwent a five year refurbishment programme (1990 to 1995), during which much of the coloured glazing, lost in the years since Soane's death, was reinstated and the octagonal lantern-light in the Breakfast Room repaired. The north and south Breakfast Room skylights (inadequate softwood skylights installed after damage in the Second World War) were replaced. The Picture Room lantern lights and central skylight were repaired as part of this restoration programme. Due to the extent of the museum, it was decided that the study would be concentrated on two main rooms of the house situated on the entrance level: the Breakfast and Picture Rooms.

Windows for view, roof lights and mirrors to control daylighting of works of art

The house is designed to be predominately side-lit in order to provide visual contact with the external environment, and the museum is essentially top-lit to maximize wall space for the display of Soane's collection. This is obvious in the two spaces chosen to be monitored: the Breakfast Room and the Picture Room. Furthermore in the case of the first, Soane followed Vitruvian principles on the orientation of habitable rooms: the room which is used mostly in the morning has large openings towards the east.

◁ View towards the north side of the Breakfast Room. Light comes in from the window on the right (not in view), from the octangular lantern and from the north skylight. Slide courtesy of the Trustees of the Sir John Soane's Museum.

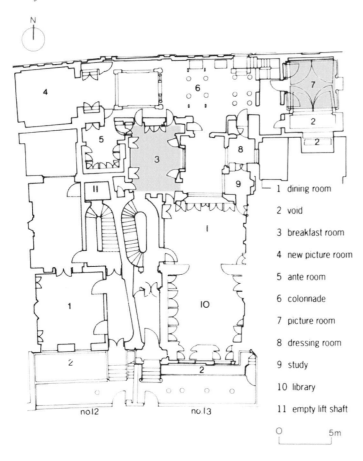

Ground floor of the Sir John Soane's Museum, and in grey, the two △ monitored rooms. Drawing courtesy of the Architects' Journal and the Trustees of the Sir John Soane's Museum.

1 dining room

2 void

3 breakfast room

4 new picture room

5 ante room

6 colonnade

7 picture room

8 dressing room

9 study

10 library

11 empty lift shaft

△ Drawing of the east and south side of the Picture Room (1823). Notice the arched canopies of the ceiling and the hinged panels of the south wall which open to display further paintings. Drawing courtesy of the Trustees of the Sir John Soane's Museum.

Soane's use of skylights throughout the house (see first floor plan) seems like a study of daylight penetration. Rooflights of different shapes and sizes, clerestory lights, concealed light, coloured and mirrored glass are the techniques that he employed to 'compose his poetry'.

Clear, diffusing and coloured glass manipulate daylight

Sir John Soane used a wide variety of glass types to manipulate the transmission of light into the house and the museum. These were either clear, translucent, coloured or etched. In the servants' quarters crown glass was considered adequate, while in the principal rooms he used large panes of expensive plate glass. The replacement of such diverse types of glass raised problems during the restoration planned by the architect Julian Harrap. In the case of the yellow glass used in many of the skylights above the museum and in those in the Breakfast Room, Harrap decided to replace it with a glass constructed by the flash method, which produced a shade of yellow called 'primrose'. With this method, one side of the plain glass sheet is coated

with a chemical which, when heated in the kiln, turns yellow. In the rooflight of the Picture Room, we find both translucent and plain glass. The original translucent glass (destroyed) was either acid-etched or blasted and cut with a foliage pattern. This type of glass was easily replicated during the restoration.

The Breakfast Room: luminous contrast and colouring of daylight

The Breakfast Room was built in 1812 and is a highly characteristic example of Soane's personal style. Its general dimensions are 3.80 x 5.50m and its height is 3.30m. In the centre of the room there is a domed ceiling. The ceiling is supported by four segmental arches on four pilasters. Within each spandrel of the dome is a large convex mirror and the soffits of the arches are decorated with small convex mirrors. In the dome there is an octangular lantern-light with painted glass. At the north and south ends of the room there are skylights with yellow glass. Finally there are two windows - the larger one set within a canted recess, which overlook a small courtyard, named the Monument Court. As Soane himself describes it: 'The view from this room into the

Monument Court and into the Museum, the mirrors in the ceiling, and the looking-glass, combined with the variety of outline and general arrangement in the design and decoration of this limited space, present a succession of those fanciful effects which constitute the poetry of Architecture'.

The Breakfast Room receives the largest part of its illumination from the east facing window overlooking the Monument Court. We can observe from the daylight factor contours on the plan that daylight drops from 4% to 1% from the opening to the centre of the room (see drawing of daylight factor contours on plan and section of the room). The linear rooflights illuminate both paintings from Soane's collection and articulate the composition of the ceiling planes. By raising the lanterns above the line of the main ceiling, the architect creates a concealed lighting effect that extends the boundaries of the room and evokes an impression of the scalloped ceiling hovering over the main space. Furthermore the skylight on the north side of the room has a larger glazing area causing the higher daylight factor on that side of the room (2% as opposed to

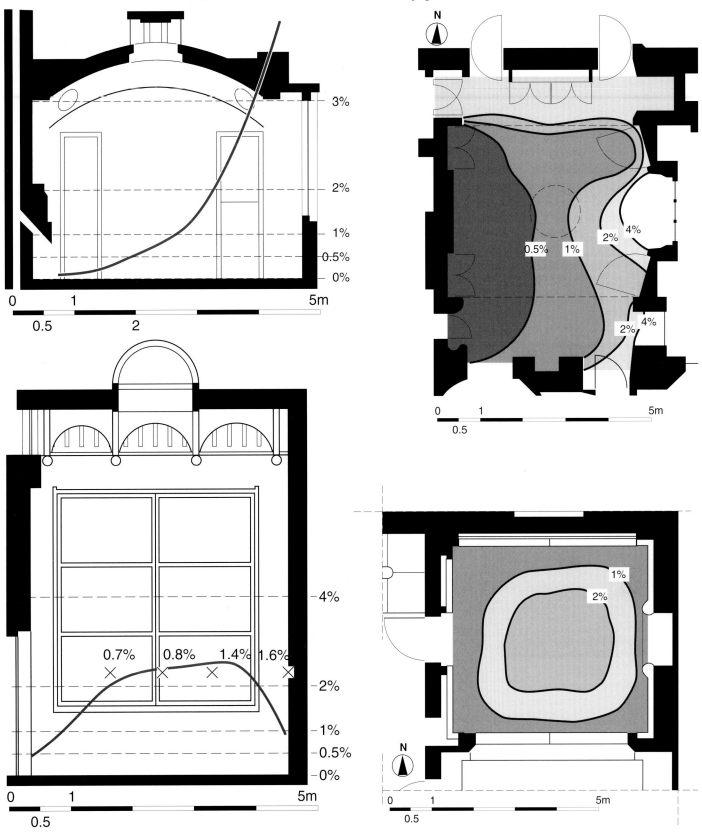

Section of the Breakfast Room. ▽

▽ Daylight factor distribution in the Breakfast Room.

Section of the Picture Room. △

△ Daylight factor distribution in the Picture Room.

0.5% on the other side). Finally the yellow colour of the glazing gives a warm effect in the room.

The Picture Room: homogeneity of light obtained from clerestories of various orientations

The Picture Room was built in 1824 and illustrates Soane's last style phase. Its general dimensions are 4.60 x 4.80m and its height is 5.85m. The ceiling with its arched canopies and the fireplace with its 'Early English' foliage, are examples of his endeavour to merge Classical and Gothic themes. It has clerestories as a continuation of the walls on the west, south and north sides and a central half-round rooflight. The great peculiarity of the room is that three of the walls (N, S and W) contain hinged panels which open to display further pictures. When the south wall opens, all its 'layers' overlook a lightshaft leading to the Monk's Cell in the basement.

The Picture Room was designed in order to provide the appropriate luminous setting for Soane's artworks. He constructed high level clerestory lights to the north, south and west walls to illuminate the adjacent wall surfaces. As we notice from the vertical daylight factor measurements, there is a drop of vertical daylight factors on the west wall due to the fact that there are no clerestories on the east wall (0.7 to 0.8% at eye level as opposed to 1 to 1.6% on the remaining three walls of the room). Furthermore, in order to restore a more uniform distribution of illuminance Soane introduced a central linear rooflight (0.9 x 2.4m) with semi-circular glazing, to provide an increased daylight factor (2%) on the ground level.

Finally he introduced clear and translucent glazing of high (48%) and low (19%) transmittance, so that the light is diffused before reaching the artworks' planes.

Furthermore, even though the room has a height of almost 6m, when the visitor tries to view the paintings positioned higher up, he experiences problems of veiling reflections from the daylight coming through the clerestories and bouncing on their protective glass.

Daylighting monitoring

The performance was assessed in the Breakfast Room and the Picture Room. Daylight factors were measured 0.85m from the floor on 31 January 1997.

◁ Detail of the Breakfast Room south skylight and arched ceiling. Notice the coloured light effect due to the yellow glass of the skylight. (Slide courtesy of the Trustees of the Sir John Soane's Museum).

CREDITS

Site and climate
The Sir John Soane's Museum is located at 13 Lincoln's Inn Fields, London (Latitude: 51°28'N, Longitude: 00°19'W). It actually extends behind Nos. 12 (built in 1792) and 14 (built in 1824) which were also designed by the architect. The climate in London has a monthly average outdoor temperature close to 5°C in winter and near 15°C during summer. The average daily sunshine duration is 4.18 hours.

Building
The Sir John Soane's Museum, occupying a site of 1,880m², was the residence of the architect, Sir John Soane, and was completed in 1812. It was his home for 25 years after which he left it in trust as part of his endowment. It has four stories and a basement (except for No. 13 which has no fourth floor). The areas open to the public are on the basement and the two floors above. The second floor of No. 13 is used by the curatorial staff of the museum while the third floor forms a flat for the Resident Warden. These rooms were originally bedrooms.

Client
Sir John Soane

Architect
Sir John Soane

Monitoring organisation
The Martin Centre, 6, Chaucer Road, Cambridge CB2 2EB, United Kingdom.

Bibliography
J. Summerson, *A New Description of Sir John Soane's Museum*, 9th Revised Edition, Board of Trustees of Sir John Soane's Museum, London, 1991.

J. Harrap, 'Using technology to save Soane', *The Architects' Journal*, Vol. 197, No. 9, 1993, pp. 36-44.

N. J. Craddock, *Sir John Soane and the Luminous Environment*, Dissertation for the M.Phil. in Environmental Design in Architecture, Department of Architecture, University of Cambridge, 1995.

Acknowledgements
We would like to thank Ms Margaret Richardson (Curator), Ms Helen Dorey (Deputy Curator) and the staff of the museum for their permission and help while we performed the monitoring. Furthermore we would like to thank the Trustees of the Sir John Soane's Museum for giving us copyright permission for the use of slides in this publication. Finally we would like to thank the Architects' Journal for providing us with the drawings of the museum and the Trustees of the Sir John Soane's Museum for allowing their reproduction.

Materials properties assessed on site

	Colour	Hemispherical-hemispherical reflectance
Breakfast Room		
Floor (carpet)		14%
Furniture	dark wood	8%
Wall /Ceiling	light wood	29%
Picture Room		
Wall panel	dark wood	5%
Floor	wood	22%
Wood and walls	grey	10%
		Normal-normal transmittance
Yellow rooflight		57%
Translucent clerestory		19% to 48%

Three successive translucent layers adjust daylight penetration for display of paintings

The 'Sept Mètres' Room, Louvre Museum, Paris, FRANCE

The lighting solution keeps the principle of translucent ceilings of the 19th century, but improves its visual aspect and performance, for daylighting throughout the year.

The 'Sept Mètres' room has been through continuous changes since its first construction in 1863 to 1864. It can be visited prior to the access of the 'Grande Gallerie', coming from the staircase with the statue of the 'Victory of Samothrace' or as a specific loop. Two cavities created by U-shaped partitions are equipped with showcases with anti- reflection glass. These allow observers to avoid visitor traffic. It allows the simultaneous display of large-scale paintings (on walls) and small-scale ones in the showcases. The partitions perpendicular to the axis of the room bring a museographical transversality, and a hierachy to the spaces.

A former system was a source of disturbing visual effects

The former system can be seen as a typical design of the 19th century. Most art galleries of this period were daylit with transluscent horizontal glazing below a glazed attic. The major problem with such a design is related to the aging of the glazed ceiling, and the fact that dirt and objects on the glazing surface can be seen from below. This results in disturbing shadows. Another problem associated with the aesthetics of the glazing cover is that sun patches can be seen on the glazing, and that the daylight distribution tends to be largely asymetrical under sunny conditions. Finally, the artificial lighting which was

▽ View of the 'Sept Mètres' room, with the translucent ceiling and the newly built transverse partitions.

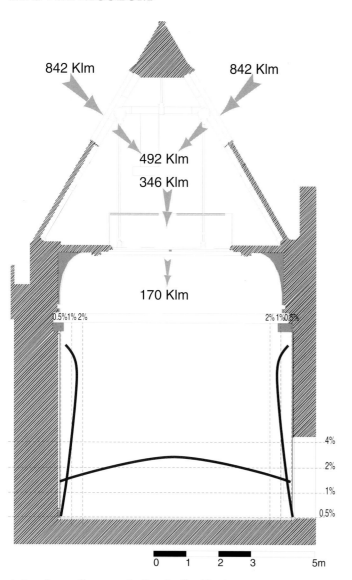

842 Klm   842 Klm

492 Klm

346 Klm

170 Klm

0.5% 1% 2%   2% 1% 0.5%

4%
2%
1%
0.5%

0   1   2   3   5m

△ Luminous flux penetration in the 'Sept Mètres' room before renovation. The sky is overcast, and values are adjusted for a standard outdoor horizontal illuminance of 10,000 lx.

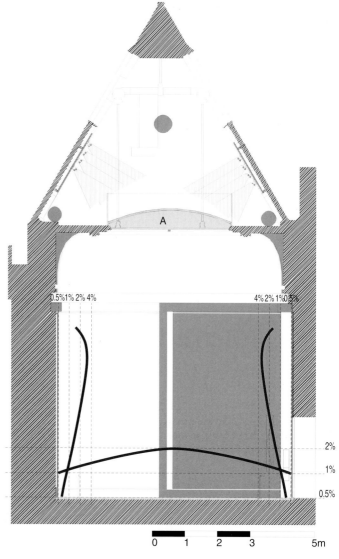

0.5% 1% 2% 4%   4% 2% 1% 0.5%

A

2%
1%
0.5%

0   1   2   3   5m

△ Cross-section of the 'Sept Mètres' room after renovation, with daylight factor distribution. It shows the principle of artificial lighting and the light diffusing box.

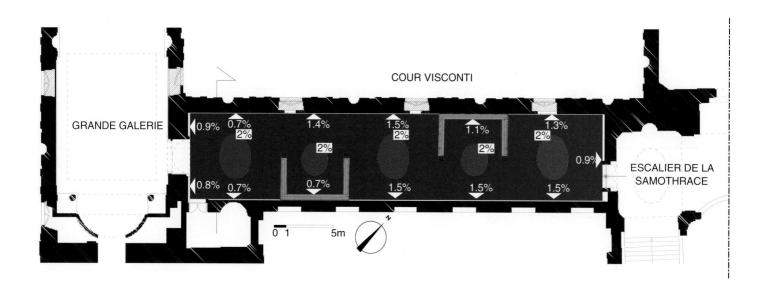

COUR VISCONTI

GRANDE GALERIE

0.9% 0.7%   1.4%   1.5%   1.1%   1.3%
      2%   2%   2%
        2%   2%
0.8% 0.7%   0.7%   1.5%   1.5%   1.5%
                                          0.9%

ESCALIER DE LA SAMOTHRACE

0 1   5m

△ Plan of 'Sept Mètres' room with daylight factor contours.

▷ Show cases are equipped with anti-reflection coatings, and their background is slightly darker than the walls.

▷ View of the roof lantern, after renovation, showing the additional transluscent cover and the luminaires moved under the roof.

added later often consisted of suspended luminaires. Under sunny conditions, shadows of these structures can be seen from below. Furthermore, it was found that illuminance on paintings was only a fifth of that on the floor.

A new design aimed at increasing visual quality

In order to obtain the most uniform luminance distribution across the transluscent ceiling, the principle of a double translucent layer was selected: a shadow or a sun patch on the first layer would not be seen by an observer situated in the room below. The difficulty is the limitation of the transmittance of diffusing glass: high dispersion of light through a glass panel usually leads to poor transmittance. For this reason, a compromise was sought. Each of the two layers of the diffuser (the first diffuser above, and the laminated glass below) was specified with moderate dispersion of light so that the combination of the two reaches the required dispersion. The solution includes a first layer made of double layer polycarbonate panels, 6mm thick, sand-blasted on the surface underneath, for optimal dispersion of light. The second layer consists of a laminated glass, made of two glass panes 3mm thick, with a light dispersing film.

The global efficiency of the former solution was estimated at 35%: 35% of the luminous flux entering the glazed attic actually penetrates the museum space under overcast conditions, leading to daylight factor values of less than 1% on the walls. One goal of the new design was that the addition of a new layer of diffuser should slightly increase the amount of diffuse light reaching the paintings. For this reason, it was decided to use a new laminated glass slightly less diffusing than the earlier material; to use a polycarbonate panel of high transmittance; to remove the luminaires above the diffuser; and to paint the attic walls in white. The results show that the daylight factors were changed in the process in the as predicted.

Although shading elements were desired by the design team to moderate daylight penetrations in summer, it was decided not to use any movable elements, to avoid problems of maintenance. For this reason, the daylight levels on walls often exceed recommended values during summer (the months with the largest number of visitors).

Daylighting boosted by artificial lighting

In locating luminaires on the sides of the attic, the diffuser was given a better access to daylight. In moving lamps at a higher distance from the diffuser, another advantage was that the fluorescent tubes become invisible from below. The location of the luminaires on the sides also gave the possibility to aim the luminaires toward the paintings instead of the floor of the museum, as was the case before. Artificial lighting consists of two groups of 90 luminaires, each equipped with two 58W T8 fluorescent tubes, with a colour temperature of 4,000K. Globally, the association of polycarbonate and laminated glass tend to reduce the colour temperature of the incoming light. More precisely, under a standard light source equivalent to daylight at 6,500K, the colour temperature of transmitted daylight is lower by 370K.

Daylighting monitoring

The monitoring prior to the restoration of the 'Sept Mètres' Room was conducted in May 1994. The next monitoring activities concerning the finished construction were conducted in December 1997 and January 1998.

CREDITS

Building
The 'Sept Mètres' room is perpendicular to the 'Grande Gallerie', in the Denon Aisle of Louvre. Its floor area is 270m². It was first built in 1864. The last modifications were conducted in 1997.

Climate
(Latitude: 48°52'N, Longitude: 2°20'E, Altitude: 25m). The monthly average outdoor temperature ranges from about 3°C in January to 19°C in July.

Client
Louvre Museum
1 Place du Carrousel
75001 Paris
Tel: +33.1-40 20 97 55

Architect
Lorenzo Piqueras
54, rue de Montreuil
75011 Paris
Tel/Fax: +33.1-43 67 26 11

Lighting Consultant
Dr Marc Fontoynont
ENTPE DGCB
Rue Maurice Audin
F 69518 Vaulx-en-Velin, Lyon, Cedex

Engineers
OTH Bâtiments, Alain Collet

Daylighting organisation
ENTPE DGCB
Rue Maurice Audin
F 69518 Vaulx-en-Velin, Lyon, Cedex

Material properties assessed on site

	Colour	Hemispherical/hemispherical reflectance
Walls	light yellow	62%
Wall edges	grey	41%
Walls in showcases	beige/yellow	55%
Wooden floor		24%
Ceiling	natural plaster	60%

		Hemispherical/hemipherical transmittance
Roof glazing		65%
Polycarbonated panel		68%
Laminated glass		64%

Daylight quality can be judged by its ability to satisfy the requirements of occupants at their work space; in terms of:

- *a view toward the outside,*

- *the supply of sufficient light on the work plane: (200 to 600 lux as often as possible) requiring daylight factors in the range of 2 to 4% if possible for most European locations.*

- *Glare control using adaptable shading devices, with typical transmittances of awnings below 20%, to provide enough attenuation of sunlight for instance*

- *reduction of disturbing reflections ('veiling reflections') on computer screens, avoiding daylight coming from behind the terminal user.*

- *Balanced luminances in the field of view near the workplane, with surounding luminances not exceeding 10 times the one of the task luminance. The energy-saving potential can be achieved with automatic controls of lighting in response to daylight or occupation. High energy savings can be achieved if lighting is separated into ambient lighting (easily controlled in response to daylight) and task lighting.*

Circulation zones can easily be daylit using secondary daylighting windows since they may be considered as well-lit even with daylight factors as low as 0.5 or 0.25%.

Glazing adapted to each facade orientation provides different levels of daylight attenuation

Tractebel building, Brussels, BELGIUM

Glazing types and blinds largely modify the daylight distribution in rooms as well as visual comfort conditions.

◁ Aerial view of the Tractebel building.

62,000m² of office floor for 2,600 people

The Tractebel building is a contemporary office building built in 1990 and designed by M. Jaspers & Partners. The building, of 62,000m² floor area, is occupied by 2,600 people mainly employed by Tractebel, a large Belgian engineering company. Functionality and flexibility were principal issues in the design. The internal layout consists of fixed and moveable offices, modular furniture, modular moveable walls, ceilings and lighting. The general shape of the building is a double cross with facades facing NW, NE, SW and SE. The junction of the two crosses forms a courtyard. Facades have large glazed areas: window area is equal to 44% of the facade area. Glazing types differ according to the orientation of the facade. SE and SW facades use double glazing with selective heat-reflecting glass on the exterior pane. NE and NW facades use double clear glass.

In addition, the acoustic properties of the glazing are adjusted depending on the adjacent noise conditions. Acoustic insulation is greatest on facades facing the local highway.

The effect of the difference in glazing properties was monitored on the 1st and the 3rd floor of wing E of the building, which has NW and SE facades.

▽ A typical standard office for two persons in the Tractebel building.

Daylighting from facades with heat reflective glass

The three windows of the monitored office are 1.60m high and 2.60m in width. The typical glazing ratio of office space is rather high at 21% (ratio of glazing area to floor area). Although the luminous transmittance of the glazing is only 43% (compared to 76% for the double clear glazing with a low-E coating), daylight penetration is rather good. The selective properties of the glass make the radiative transmittance significantly lower at 23%, which is close to the theoretical minimum value by comparison with the luminous transmittance. The rather high illuminance values which are reached are due to bright wall finishes (wall reflectances vary from 60 to 90%).

Viewed from the outside, the heat-reflecting glazing gives a slight silvery reflection. However colour rendering toward the inside is very good (CRI=96)

and the glass appears to be clear to occupants sitting in their office. For occupants in the middle of wing E and seeing NW and SE facades simult-aneously, the tint of the heat reflective glass is hardly noticeable; one notices only the difference in transmittance.

Daylighting from facades with clear glass

Clear glass was used to the NE and NW facades.

In wing E, the north-west facade faces a courtyard. From the first floor, the obstruction is significant: 38 degrees above the horizon at the level of the work plane.

In room 4, the measurements demonstrate that the good luminous transmittance of the clear glass roughly compensates for the reduction of daylight due to the building wing across the courtyard.

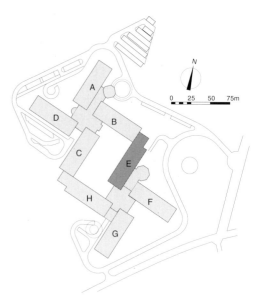

△ Site plan, showing location of wing E where measurements were taken.

▽ Daylight factor distribution on the work plane in rooms 1, 2 (Third floor) 3 and 4 (First floor). NW facade is equipped with clear glass, SE with heat-reflecting glazing.

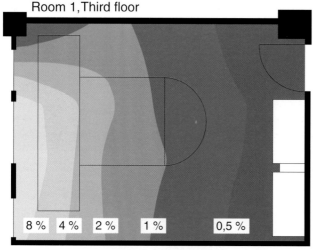

Room 1, Third floor

8 % 4 % 2 % 1 % 0,5 %

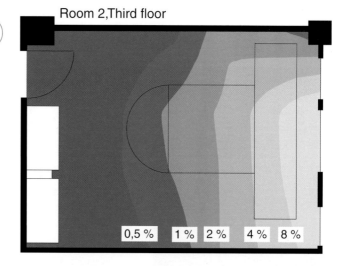

Room 2, Third floor

0,5 % 1 % 2 % 4 % 8 %

Room 3, First floor

4 %
8 % 2 % 1 % 0,5 %

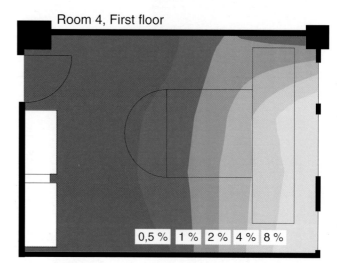

Room 4, First floor

0,5 % 1 % 2 % 4 % 8 %

0   0.5 1.5 1.5m

DIAGNOSTIC ET SIMULATION DES AMBIANCES LUMINEUSES

La qualité de l'éclairage, un challenge pour notre cadre de vie, et plus particulièrement pour notre lieu de travail.

Nous passons aujourd'hui une grande de partie de notre vie à l'intérieur de constructions ou de moyens de transport. Cette évolution n'est pas sans changer notre rapport à la lumière. Ce n'est plus l'homme qui adapte son activité à la lumière mais bien l'inverse. Ainsi, à tout instant, nous exigeons l'éclairage le plus approprié à notre activité, de jour comme de nuit.

Mais que signifie "qualité de l'éclairage" ? Notre groupe juge utile, au-delà des normes et recommandations, d'explorer, par le biais d'enquêtes sur le terrain et de tests en laboratoire, les attentes d'occupants de bâtiments, tout particulièrement dans le cadre de leur travail. Nous complétons les protocoles d'enquêtes et techniques d'analyse des résultats par des mesures lumineuses avec des appareils que nous avons dû développer (photo-luminancemètres, FJ-mètres).

La qualité de l'éclairage, c'est aussi celle de l'éclairage naturel : efficacité lumineuse, contrôle de l'éblouissement et réduction des gènes telles que surchauffes ou impression de froid. Le challenge se trouve ici au niveau du choix des vitrages isolants et des techniques de protections solaires les plus adaptées. Le défi est également architectural, car il s'agit de concevoir des bâtiments capables de tirer le meilleur profit possible de la lumière naturelle disponible sur un site donné.

Pour cette raison, notre groupe développe des outils d'analyse liés à la synthèse d'image et au traitement d'image. Il fournit également des informations essentielles sur le climat lumineux (traitement de données produites par les satellites) et sur les phénomènes optiques se produisant au niveau des prises de jour.

Il n'est donc pas surprenant que nous soyons fortement impliqués dans des activités de R&D avec des industriels de l'enveloppe de bâtiment. Il est également logique que ces travaux débouchent sur des activités d'appui de mission de maîtrise d'œuvre ou d'assistance maîtrise d'ouvrage.

Avec à la clef, notre bien-être.

Marc Fontoynont
Professeur

Groupe Lumière et Rayonnement Electromagétique :

Marc Fontoynont, Dominique Dumortier, Richard Mitanchey,
Pascale Avouac-Bastie, Franz Van Roy, Fawaz Maamari, Laurent Escaffre,
Cyril Chain, Suzanne Escuyer, Catherine Laurentin, Virgile Charton, Yannick Sutter

Luminance: | 2 4 5 8 20 30 40 90 | (cd/m2, log scale)

Analyse de la répartition des luminances dans le champ visuel △ à l'aide d'un appareil photo numérique calibré.

Département Génie Civil et Bâtiment - URA CNRS 1652

Ecole Nationale des Travaux Publics de l'Etat - Rue Maurice Audin, 69518 VAULX-EN-VELIN Cedex - FRANCE
Tel : +33 (0)4 72 04 70 31 - Fax : +33(0)4 72 04 70 41 - E-mail : secretariat.lash@entpe.fr - Internet : www.entpe.fr

ENTPE

△ Description du dispositif de " fausse fenêtre " permettant de simuler une grande variété d'effets lumineux d'aspects naturels ou non, et de mettre en scène des objets.

△ Fenêtre virtuelle de l'ENTPE : exemple d'effet ensoleillé.

◁ Analyse des attentes lumineuses d'occupants de locaux aveugles au moyen d'un système de déclencheur d'expressions utilisant des photos sélectionnées et présentées sur une table lumineuse.

Malgré les progrès réalisés dans les techniques d'éclairage, des critiques continuent à être émises par les occupants, démontrant que la perception de la qualité de l'éclairage nécessite d'intégrer d'autres aspects. Notons en particulier les références visuelles à d'autres lieux, les niveaux d'inconfort thermique, la période de l'année considérée, la couleur de la lumière naturelle, les aspects esthétiques ou encore le contexte sociologique.

Premier outil d'investigation : l'enquête sur le terrain

Il s'agit de déterminer par le biais de questionnaires appuyés par des photographies et des mesures, le décalage qu'il peut y avoir entre des situations d'éclairage vécues au quotidien et les attentes d'une amélioration de ces situations. Quelles sont alors les priorités ? Il apparaît en particulier que la capacité de contrôler soit-même son environnement, et l'absence de gêne, soient les premières préoccupations sur le lieu de travail, bien avant la recherche de quantités élevées de lumière sur le plan de travail. La présence (ou l'absence) de lumière naturelle semble être un facteur déterminant dans les comportements des usagers vis-à-vis de leur éclairage artificiel. Les comportements saisonniers sont également marqués, l'éclairage artificiel étant chargé de compenser plus ou moins le déficit quotidien de lumière naturelle. La couleur de la lumière naturelle modifie également la manière dont les usagers ajustent les niveaux d'éclairage artificiel.

Deuxième outil d'investigation : les salles tests en laboratoire

Nous avons élaboré deux salles tests principales : l'une constituée d'une fausse fenêtre éclairante derrière laquelle les scénarii lumineux peuvent être variés à volonté. Cette cellule nous permet de mieux comprendre la frontière entre une impression de lumière "naturelle" et une impression

◁ Suzanne Escuyer élabore des techniques de commande des éclairages mieux acceptées par les occupants et mieux comprises.

Qualité de l'éclairage : le point de vue des utilisateurs

de lumière "artificielle". On note que des effets de lumière naturelle peuvent être obtenus avec des niveaux lumineux plus de 10 fois inférieurs aux niveaux obtenus dans la réalité. Le dispositif permet également de déterminer les ambiances préférées d'occupants selon les activités envisagées, homogènes pour le travail, contrastées pour le relationnel, suggestives pour les moments de réflexion.

Une autre installation, dite "cellules jumelles" est constituée de deux salles équipées chacune de 3 postes de travail et d'une baie vitrée. Les stores vénitiens sont motorisés. Les éclairages artificiels sont constitués d'éclairages fluorescents encastrés (lèches-murs et encastrés à grille) permettant d'atteindre 1 000 lux sur le plan de travail. Tous les éclairages sont pilotables soit automatiquement, soit par les occupants. Toutes les ambiances lumineuses sont enregistrées par une centrale d'acquisition de données. Par ailleurs la température de l'air peut être réglée plus ou moins 10 degrés au-dessus ou en dessous de la température ambiante du laboratoire. Les principaux résultats portent sur la manière dont les occupants pilotent leurs éclairages selon leur éloignement de la baie vitrée et la couleur de la lumière naturelle.

Troisième outil d'investigation : la réalité virtuelle

Il s'agit d'un système de projection stéréographique permettant la réalisation de scènes lumineuses interactives en relief. Cet outil est destiné à explorer des pistes d'éclairage fictives et de les tester auprès d'observateurs. Les images sont soit recueillies sur des sites donnés, soit produites à l'aide de logiciels d'image de synthèse.

△ *Catherine Laurentin utilise les cellules jumelles pour détecter l'impact de paramètres d'ambiance sur les préférences en matière d'éclairage.*

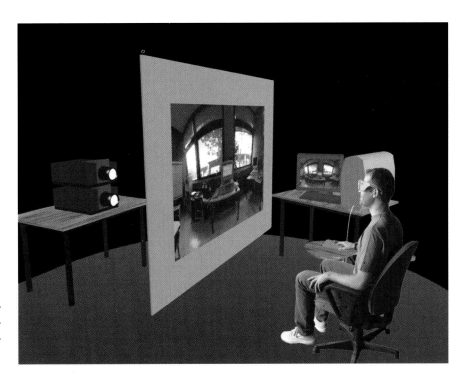

▷ *Le simulateur d'ambiances lumineuses : des possibilités quasi-illimitées pour l'étude des comportements vis-à-vis de la lumière, et l'exploration de nouvelles ambiances lumineuses.*

Le climat lumineux : modélisation des effets lumineux atmosphériques

△ *Dominique Dumortier maintient la station climatique installée sur le toit de l'ENTPE et coordonne le réseau IDMP, comprenant plus de 50 stations réparties dans le monde entier.*

◁ *Cyril Chain effectue régulièrement des mesures spectrales de la voute céleste pour valider ses modèles atmosphériques.*

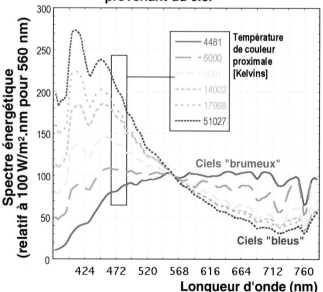
△ *Spectres de lumière naturelle mesurés à Lyon, démontrant la grande dynamique chromatique de la lumière naturelle.*

La station de mesure du climat lumineux située sur le toit de l'ENTPE est opérationnelle depuis 1991 et fournit des données de haute qualité sur le gisement de lumière naturelle dans la région Lyonnaise. Elle fait partie du réseau international IDMP de la Commission Internationale de l'Eclairage (IDMP = International Daylight Measurement Programme). Ce réseau réunissait en 1999, plus d'une cinquantaine de stations. Notre station a participé aux procédures d'étalonnage organisées par l'IDMP, ce qui garantit la cohérence de nos mesures.

La station mesure 13 paramètres en continu et stocke leurs valeurs toutes les cinq minutes, ce qui permet un bon suivi des fluctuations de la lumière naturelle. Ces données sont utilisées pour caractériser le climat lumineux de Lyon et de ses environs. Elles ont aussi été utilisées pour développer et valider des modèles d'efficacité lumineuse (indispensables pour convertir du rayonnement solaire en son équivalent lumineux), et plus récemment pour valider des modèles de calcul de la lumière naturelle à partir d'images satellites.

Depuis 1998, ces mesures ont été complétées par l'acquisition de données directionnelles de spectres de températures de couleur. Ceci a permis l'élaboration d'un modèle permettant de caractériser des points de vue spectral et directionnel la disponibilité de la lumière naturelle. Récemment, un nouveau protocole expérimental permet l'acquisition en continue du gisement de lumière naturelle dans cinq directions privilégiées du ciel. L'objectif est de valider le modèle spectral ainsi que de donner des informations colorimétriques du climat lumineux sur le long terme.

Dans toute l'Europe, il existe moins d'une vingtaine de stations de mesure telles que celle que nous avons mise en place. C'est insuffisant pour pouvoir caractériser correctement les variations du climat lumineux. Les seules autres sources de données relatives à la lumière naturelle ou le rayonnement solaire, sont l'Atlas Solaire Européen (ESRA), Meteonorm v4.0 et l'Atlas Européen de l'Eclairage Naturel (EDA). Cependant, ces ouvrages offrent des données limitées, soit en terme d'information : moyennes journalières mensuelles pour l'ESRA ou Meteonorm, fréquences de dépassement sur des intervalles horaires fixés pour l'EDA, soit en terme de couverture géographique : 6 sites pour l'EDA et environ 700 sites pour l'ESRA ou Meteonorm.

Notre objectif étant d'obtenir des données avec une couverture géographique aussi fine que possible, l'utilisation des images fournies par le satellite METEOSAT s'est vite imposée. En 1996, nous avons lancé le projet de recherche SATEL-LIGHT, un projet de 3 ans financé par l'Union Européenne, réunissant 10 équipes spécialisées dans l'analyse des images satellites et la modélisation du rayonnement solaire.

Traitement d'images satellites pour la caractérisation du climat lumineux

La quantité de rayonnement solaire disponible à la surface de la terre dépend de l'intensité du soleil et de l'opacité de la couverture nuageuse. Plus cette couverture est opaque, plus le rayonnement réfléchi vers le satellite est important. Un point de la terre couvert de nuages opaques sera donc vu par le satellite comme très lumineux. Le principe consiste à calculer à partir de la valeur de chaque pixel de l'image satellite, un indice caractérisant l'opacité de la couverture nuageuse au-dessus de la zone géographique couverte par le pixel. Cet indice est ensuite utilisé pour déterminer les éclairements énergétiques et lumineux. L'ensemble des méthodes utilisées a fait l'objet de nombreuses validations à partir de mesures au sol.

Les images satellites fournies par METEOSAT toutes les 1/2 heures, en 1996 et 1997, ont été utilisées pour construire une base de données (9 Go par année). L'Europe est couverte avec un peu plus de 240 000 pixels. En France, un pixel couvre une étendue d'environ 5 km en longitude par 7 km en latitude.

En collaboration avec la société lyonnaise NCTech et un infographiste, nous avons développé un serveur d'informations utilisant la base de données : www.satel-light.com. Ce serveur permet de générer facilement et rapidement (quelques minutes) des cartes ou des informations spécifiques à un site. Parce qu'il s'appuie sur des données provenant d'images satellites, il produit des cartes d'une précision inégalée sur les variations géographiques de la disponibilité de la lumière naturelle ou du rayonnement solaire. Son importante base de données de noms géographiques (plus de 74 000 pour la France et plus de 750 000 pour toute l'Europe) lui permet de trouver rapidement la ville, le village, le hameau, pour lequel on souhaite des informations.

Les informations disponibles couvrent le soleil : durées de jour moyennes mensuelles, diagrammes solaires (horizontaux et verticaux) utilisant l'heure légale, fréquences de présence du soleil dans certaines zones du ciel, durées d'ensoleillement. Elles couvrent également les éclairements lumineux ou énergétiques, sur des plans horizontaux ou inclinés, en valeurs moyennes mensuelles heure par heure, ou sur la totalité de la tranche horaire, en fréquences heures par heures ou cumulées sur la tranche horaire, en valeurs horaires.

Des modules spécifiques à certaines applications telles que la conception des systèmes d'éclairage naturel ou celles des systèmes photovoltaïques seront progressivement mis en place. En 2001, grâce au projet Européen SODA (http://www-helioserve.cma.fr/soda), la base de données actuelle sera étendue à trois années supplémentaires : 1998, 1999 et 2000.

▷ Le serveur Satel-Light génère des cartes à la demande. Cet exemple montre une carte présentant la fréquence d'observation de ciels ensoleillés dans toute l'Europe sur une année, du lever au coucher du soleil.

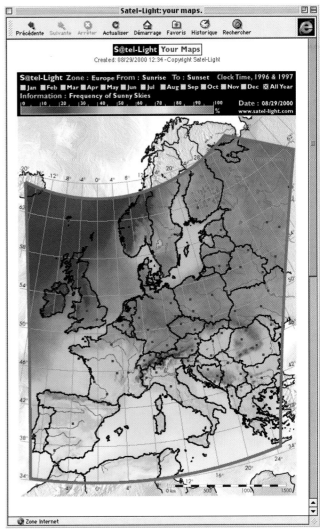

▷ Exemple d'information fournie par Satel-Light pour un site : diagramme solaire donnant dans un plan vertical, la position du soleil à certaines dates en fonction de l'heure de la journée exprimée en heure légale.

◁ Exemple d'information fournie par Satel-Light pour un site : fréquences cumulées de l'éclairement lumineux horizontal global de 9h à 17h.

Simulation d'un poste de travail de jour △

△ Simulation du même poste, la nuit avec un éclairage de type "lèche mur".

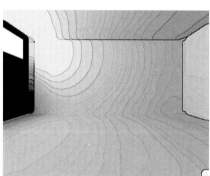

◁ Richard Mitanchey a développé des techniques numériques permettant de traiter les données optiques de vitrages produites par divers goniophotomètres européens afin d'évaluer leur impact sur la répartition de la lumière naturelle dans les locaux.

L'environnement numérique Génélux développé au laboratoire est amélioré en continu afin de permettre une analyse fine des propriétés bidirectionnelles d'éléments de vitrage tels que diffuseurs, films prismatiques et autres produits de cette famille. Les lois optiques doivent intégrer des comportements sensibles à la polarisation de la lumière et aux divers indices de réfraction des matériaux. Un certain nombre de tâches de validation des modèles sont en cours, impliquant le développement de données expérimentales mesurées à l'intérieur de maquettes ou de salles réelles. Ce travail fait l'objet de collaborations internationales par le biais de l'Agence Internationale de l'Energie et de la Commission Internationale de l'Eclairage. Un format international de description de données bidirectionnelles a ainsi pu être proposé de manière à faciliter la communication entre les laboratoires effectuant des mesures bidirectionnelles et les équipes effectuant les simulations numériques des produits verriers.

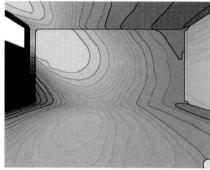

▽ Comparaison de calculs lumineux effectués à l'aide de 6 logiciels.

L'équipe coordonne des actions internationales de validation de logiciels. Elle suit plus particulièrement les progrès des logiciels suivants : Génélux (ENTPE), YART (Ecole des Mines de St Etienne) et Lightscape (Autodesk).

▽ Position des points de comparaison.

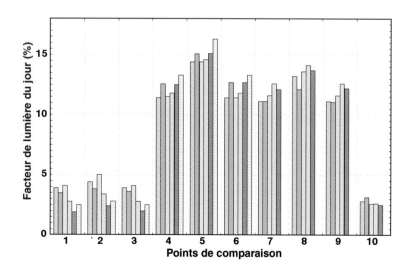

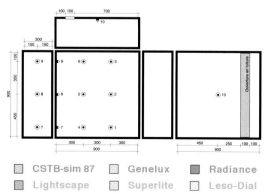

Développement de techniques de diagnostic sur le terrain et d'ingéniérie en éclairage

Toutes les techniques d'éclairage développées par le laboratoire nécessitent d'être évaluées sur le terrain, tant du point de vue de leurs performances qu'au niveau de la satisfaction des usagers. Ainsi le groupe a été amené à développer des protocoles précis d'évaluation permettant de caractériser les performances *in situ* des installations d'éclairage artificiel et des techniques de prises de jour.

Ces techniques portent sur la caractérisation optique des matériaux (verres, revêtements, protections solaires), la caractérisation du site à proximité d'un bâtiment (obstructions, vues), la caractérisation des ambiances lumineuses (répartition des éclairements, des luminances et des températures de couleur), la caractérisation du matériel d'éclairage et de ses performances. Des techniques originales de traitement et de présentation de résultats ont ainsi été élaborées. Elles sont couramment utilisées pour des diagnostics d'établissements scolaires ou d'immeubles de bureaux.

▷ *Visualisation de l'augmentation des apports lumineux de Screen+, par rapport à un screen normal (société Hexcel Fabrics), maquette à l'echelle 1/5ème.*

△ *Yannick Sutter détermine experimentalement des fonctions de transfert lumineux de prise de jour, qu'il applique ensuite aux données lumineuses générées par le serveur Satel-Light.*

◁ *Pascale Avouac Bastie conduisant un diagnostic lumineux à l'aide de divers appareils : luminancemètre, luxmètre, FJ-mètre, chromamètre, appareil photo numérique.*

Laurent Escaffre et l'Architecte Lorenzo Piqueras dans la maquette de la salle des Etats du Louvre pour le réglage des effets lumineux créés par le plafond translucide.

Simulation lumineuse de la salle des Etats du Louvre ▽

▽

Une ouverture au monde professionnel par le développement de serveurs Internet

Trois serveurs ont été développés par le groupe :

• Le serveur " International Daylight Measurement Programme (IDMP)" de la Commission Internationale de l'Eclairage, fournissant une information essentielle sur plus de 50 stations de mesures du climat lumineux à travers le monde.
Adresse : http://idmp.entpe.fr
Coordinateur : Dominique Dumortier, développement Jean-Marc Duport.

• Le serveur Génélux-Web permettant d'offrir des capacités de calculs d'éclairage à distance via Internet, le programme restant sur nos stations de travail Unix.
Adresse : http://genelux.entpe.fr
Coordinateurs : Richard Mitanchey, assisté de Pascale Avouac Bastie et Marc Fontoynont.

• Le serveur Satel-Light offrant en ligne des données de lumière et de rayonnement solaire pour l'Europe de l'Ouest et l'Europe Centrale, les données étant calculées à partir des informations fournies par le satellite METEOSAT.
Adresse : http://www.satel-light.com
Coordinateur : Dominique Dumortier, assistance développement NC Tech, infographie Cédric Pinnedon.

Les chercheurs du groupe prennent des responsabilités dans le cadre de sociétés savantes, de programmes internationaux et d'associations.
Marc Fontoynont est président du Centre Régional Rhône-Alpes de l'Association Française de l'Eclairage depuis avril 1997. Il a été coordinateur Européen du programme Satel-Light (1996-1998). Il a été coordinateur de la campagne de diagnostics en éclairage naturel du programme Européen Daylight Europe (1995-1997). Il est responsable de la conduite des validations de logiciels dans le cadre de la sous-tâche 21C1 de l'Agence Internationale de l'Energie (depuis Mai 1998) et a été élu Directeur de la Division 3 de la Commission Internationale de l'Eclairage (éclairage intérieur) en Mai 1998 pour un mandat de 4 ans débutant en juin 1999. Il est également expert pour le club 3D lumière, chargé de coordonner les efforts Français en matière d'image de synthèse en éclairage. Il fait également partie du Panel Consultatif du Festival Lumière de Lyon

Dominique Dumortier a été élu Vice Directeur pour l'Eclairage Naturel de la Division 3 de la Commission Internationale de l'Eclairage, après avoir assuré le secrétariat de la Division depuis 1996. Il est Chairman du comité technique 3.25 de la CIE en charge de la coordination du réseau IDMP. Il est Chairman du comité technique 3.36 de la CIE en charge d'établir un standard international de calcul de la lumière naturelle à partir d'images satellites. Il est également directeur pour l'éclairage intérieur du Comité National Français de l'Eclairage. Il a reçu la médaille Augustin Fresnel de l'AFE en mars 2000.

Catherine Laurentin a été nommée rapporteur par la Commission Internationale de l'Eclairage pour l'influence des conditions de confort thermique sur la perception des ambiances lumineuses.

Sélection de quelques publications disponibles

BERRUTTO V., FONTOYNONT M., AVOUAC-BASTIE P.
Importance of wall luminance on users satisfaction : pilot study on 73 office workers.
Lux Europa Conference, Amsterdam, Mai. 1997.

BERRUTTO V., FONTOYNONT M., FOURMIGUE J.M.
Effect of temperature and light source type (natural/artificial) on visual comfort appraisal : experimental design and setting.
Conférence Right Light. 1997.

BERRUTTO V., FONTOYNONT M.
Procedure for on-site performance assessment of daylighting systems.
4th European Conf. on Solar Energy in Architecture and Urban Planning, Berlin, mars 1996.

CHAIN C., DUMORTIER D., FONTOYNONT M.
A comprehensive model of luminance, correlated colour temperature and spectral distribution of skylight : comparison with experimental data. Solar Energy 65 (5), pp. 285-295, 1999.

CHAIN C., DUMORTIER D., FONTOYNONT M.
Integration of the Spectral and directional component in sky luminance modelling.
24th Session of the CIE, Varsovie, Pologne, vol.1, pp. 248-252, 1999.

CHAIN C., DUMORTIER D., MITANCHEY R., FONTOYNONT M.
Variation of daylight's colour inside and outside buildings ; experimental and simulated case study.
Conference EPIC, 6 p. Lyon, Novembre 1998.

DUMORTIER D. et al.
SATEL-LIGHT : the European web server providing high quality and solar radiation data based on METEOSAT images (http://satel-light.entpe.fr).
Conférence CIE, Varsovie, Pologne, vol. 1, pp. 277-281, juin 1999.

DUMORTIER D., KOGA Y.
Status of the international daylight measurement programme (IDMP) and its web server (http://idmp.entpe.fr).
Conférence CIE, Varsovie, Pologne, vol. 1, pp. 282-286, juin 1999.

DUMORTIER D.
Evaluation of luminous efficacy models according to sky types and atmospheric conditions. Lux Europa Conference, Amsterdam, 1997.

DUMORTIER D.
European daylighting Atlas, Chapter 2
Commission des Communautés Européennes, pp 9-109, 1996.

ENRECH C., FONTOYNONT M.
Testing of a new method to report lighting quality perception based on semidirected interviews : Results on 40 office workers.
Lighting Quality Conference, pp 92-102, Ottawa, mai 1998.

ENRECH C., FONTOYNONT M.
Simulation of daylight in artificial windows, results of test conducted with 66 participants. Lux Europa Conference, Amsterdam, mai 1997.

ESCUYER S., FONTOYNONT M.
Lighting controls: field study of office worker's reaction
Lighting Research Technology 2000.

ESCUYER S., FONTOYNONT M.
Use of a remotely controlled dimmable lighting system in a two-occupant office. Conférence CIE, Varsovie, Pologne, juin 1999.

FONTOYNONT M.
Daylight performance of buildings.
Edited by James and James, London, UK, 1999.

FONTOYNONT M., BERRUTTO V.
Daylight Europe Case Studies. National Lighting Conference CIBSE, 1998.

FONTOYNONT M., BERRUTTO V.
Daylighting performance of buildings : monitoring procedure.
Daylighting'98 Conference, Ottawa,1998.

FONTOYNONT M.
Prédire et mesurer les ambiances lumineuses en architecture.
Cahiers de la Recherche Architecturale, 1997.

FONTOYNONT M., BERRUTTO V.
Daylighting performance of buildings : monitoring procedure.
Right Light Conference, pp 19-21, Amsterdam, novembre 1997.

FONTOYNONT M., LAFORGUE P., MITANCHEY R.
Influence of the level of precision of sky luminance distribution and site description on the calculated performance of daylighting systems.
Lux Europa Conference, Amsterdam, mai 1997.

FONTOYNONT M., BERRUTTO V.
Eclairage de l'espace de travail : enquêtes et mesures dans les bureaux. Lux 190, pp. II-IV, 1996.

FONTOYNONT M., LAFORGUE P., MITANCHEY R.
Precise daylighting calculations in architecture and city planning
International Daylight Workshop : building with daylight, Energy-efficient design, pp 6-16, Perth, 21 novembre 1996.

LAFORGUE P., SOUYRI B., FONTOYNONT M., ACHARD G.
Simulation of visual and thermal comfort related to daylighting and solar radiation in office buildings. IBPSA'97, Prague, 1997.

LAURENTIN C., FONTOYNONT M.
The interaction of visual and thermal environments on comfort : a review of previous experiments. Conférence CIE, Division 3 – York, juillet 2000.

LAURENTIN C., FONTOYNONT M., BERRUTTO V.
Effect of thermal conditions, season and light source type on visual comfort appraisal.
Lighting Research Technology, 2000.

LAURENTIN C., BERRUTTO V., FONTOYNONT M., GIRAULT P.
Manual control of artificial lighting in a daylit space.
Conférence EPIC, Lyon, Novembre 1998, 6 p. 175-180.

MITANCHEY R., PERIOLE G., FONTOYNONT M.
Numerical simulation of goniophotometric measurements for R & D applications
Lighting Research and Technology, vol 27 (4), p. 189-196, 1996.

Département Génie Civil et Bâtiment
Le DGCB est la réunion de deux laboratoires de l'École Nationale des Travaux Publics de l'État (ENTPE) : le Laboratoire Géomatériaux (LGM), et le Laboratoire des Sciences de l'Habitat (LASH). Il est situé à Vaulx-en-Velin, près de Lyon. Il est financé par le Ministère de l'Équipement, du Logement et des Transports. Composé d'une équipe de 65 membres permanents et d'élèves, il couvre une grande variété de sujets dans le domaine des sciences des matériaux et du bâtiment. Les activités de recherche sont divisées en sous-groupes : les matériaux, les méthodes numériques, les constructions en terre, l'acoustique, la lumière et le rayonnement électromagnétique, ainsi que les systèmes thermiques et aérauliques. Ces trois derniers axes de recherche sont traités par le LASH. Le DGCB est une Unité de Recherche Associée au Centre National de la Recherche Scientifique (CNRS) depuis 1992.

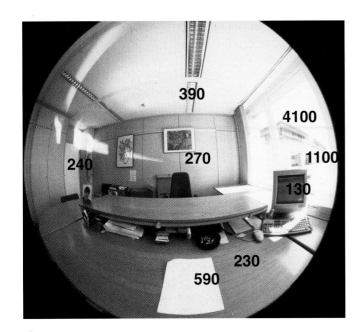
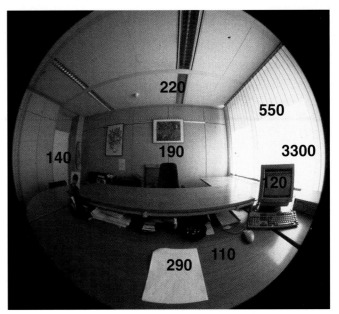

△ Luminances (cd/m²) in the field of view of an occupant during sunny conditions. Left: blinds opened, Right: blinds closed.

The results show that daylight factor values on the work plane fall below 2% at 1.30 metres away from facades on the first floor, and 1.50 metres from the facade on the 3rd floor.

The reduction of obstructions from 38 to 30.5 degrees leads to an improvement of 0.2 metres in the penetration of daylight.

Remark that obstructions also play a role on the SE facade. There is significantly less daylight penetration on the first floor (room 3). This is caused by obstruction due to the building struct-

ure of the main entrance directly in front of the offices.

In summary, work spaces are well daylit if they are located within 1.30 metres of the facade. Due to the modular furnishing of the offices, most of the occupants do their work within this zone.

Sunshades reduce daylight penetration even when removed

Sunshading is provided by Californian blinds made of vertical strips of diffusing material. The colour of the blinds is slightly green, with a measured hemispherical-hemispherical light

transmittance of 22%. The blinds reduce the illuminance on the working surface by a factor of 0.3 to 0.6, depending on the sun's position. Direct sun patches on the working plane disappear and, because of the diffuse properties of the blind, illuminances are more equally spread. This, together with the light-coloured walls, give the shaded room a very clear impression. A major disadvantage is that glare problems may occur due to sun patches on the blinds. This can be seen on the figure showing luminance measurements, taken at 11.30h during summer solstice with an outside horizontal illuminance of 80,000

▽ View of offices under sunny conditions, without blinds.

▽ View of office under sunny conditions, with Californian blinds closed.

lux. While all the luminances in the room are reduced quite equally by a factor between 1.5 and 2, the sun patch has increased luminance around the VDU screen to about 3,300 cd/m², which contrasts strongly with the luminance of the screen which is about 30 times lower (approximately 120 cd/m²). In the situation without shading the contrast between the outdoor environment and the visual task on the screen is much lower because the neighbouring wing is in the field of view.

When moved to the side of the window, the blinds still tend to block a significant amount of daylight: about 8% since they cover ± 0.2m of the 2.60 metre width of the window glazing. This is a common problem with many blinds.

Daylight in an open-plan office

An open-plan drawing room was monitored on the first floor. It is 17.8 metres across, and the ratio of the glazed area to the floor area is 12%. Daylight factors on the work plane across the

room are shown, from the south-east facade to the north-west one.

Daylight factors in the centre drop as low as 0.07% and are still very low (0.5%) near the north-west facade due to obstructions. Daylight can be considered sufficient for only 8% of the work plane. Consequently permanent artificial lighting is required for about 92% of the space.

Daylight monitoring

It was conducted in wing E during three overcast days (10 January, 5 to 8 klux, 19 January, 30 klux and 16 February, 10 to 30 klux) and two sunny days (14 March, 45 to 65 klux and 18 July, 70 to 100 klux).

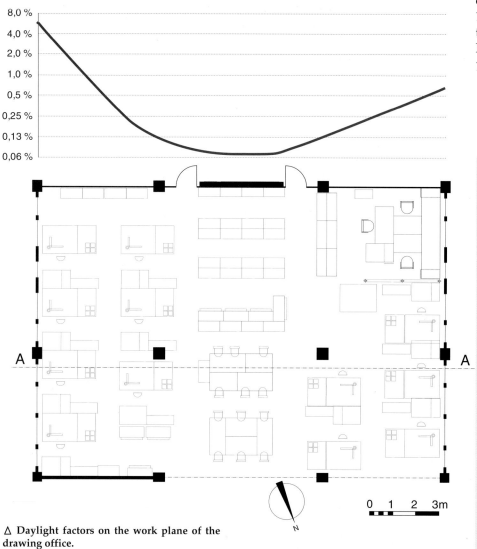

△ Daylight factors on the work plane of the drawing office.

Material properties assessed on site

	Colour	Hemispherical-hemispherical reflectance
Ceiling	white	83%
Wall	light grey	60%
Desk	light oak	32%
Floor	dark grey-blue	11%
		Normal-normal transmittance
Double clear glass		76%
Selective double glass, low E		43%

CREDITS

Building description
Large office building
62,000m² floor area
Built in two phases:
1st phase 'Tractebel': 1988 to 1990
2nd phase: 'Ariane': 1989 to 1991
Occupancy: 2,600 people

Climate
Minimum monthly temperature: 2.4°C (January)
Maximum monthly temperature: 17.1°C (July)
Annual sunshine duration: 1600 hours
Latitude: 50°N, Longitude: 4°E
Altitude: 100m

Client
1st phase 'Tractebel':
Tractebel Engineering SA
Avenue Ariane 7
1200 Brussels
2nd phase: 'Ariane':
Intégral SA
Avenue Ariane 5
1200 Brussels
Belgium

Architect
M. Jaspers & Partners
Raamstraat 13
3500 Hasselt
Tel: + 32-11 22 21 63

Monitoring organisation
BBRI (WTCB-CSTC)
Violetstraat 21-23
1000 Brussels
Belgium
Tel: + 32.2-502 6690
Fax: + 32.2-502 8180

References
Aerial view: Copyright: Airprint

An atrium serves as a daylit link between new and renovated buildings

Sukkertoppen, Valby, DENMARK

The renovation of an old sugar refinery provided an occasion to develop innovative energy conservation techniques, such as a central atrium acting as a buffer space.

A sugar refinery transformed into a multimedia center

'Sukkertoppen' is an old sugar refinery in Valby, an old industrial suburb of Copenhagen, which was renovated in 1992, by Højgaard & Schultz for The Employees' Capital Pension Fund, into a 18,000m^2 multimedia centre. In this retrofit project, a new building was added south of the existing refinery building and the two buildings were connected with a glazed atrium.

Glazed atrium allows larger windows in adjacent facades

The new 84m long, 13m deep office building is located to the south of the old two- and three-storey brick structure on an east-west axis. The new building and the atrium are four storeys high. The atrium, fairly narrow compared to its height (10m wide, 60m long and 19m heigh), was designed and optimized to achieve both reductions of the space heating load and to maintain daylight penetration into both buildings. Other reasons for the atrium were to increase amenity for the building occupants, facilitate circulation and to provide exhibition areas. The site area was constricted and the construction of the atrium permitted the use of larger windows in both buildings, so that the distance between them could be reduced while still meeting building regulation requirements for daylight levels in ground floor rooms.

▽ The glazed atrium connects the renovated sugar refinery (left) with the new office building (right).

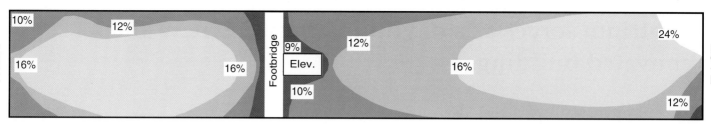

△ Daylight factor distribution on the floor of the atrium.

▽ Section of the building with the luminous flux (Klm) and the daylight factor curves in the monitored rooms (flux values given for a standard overcast sky providing 10,000 lux).

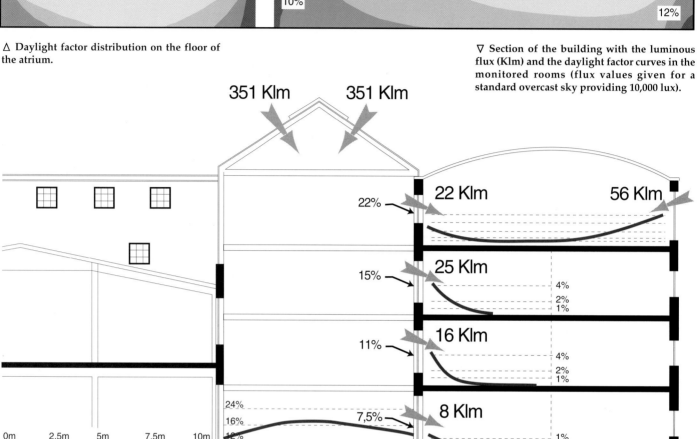

Lower floors with larger windows than upper floors

The exterior of the atrium facades and roof are low-E double glazed. The windows in the office buildings adjacent to the atrium are single-glazed (U-value 6.0 W/m²K), while exterior windows are normally double-glazed (U-value 3.0 W/m²K). A main design consideration regarding the windows in the new building facing the atrium was to maintain daylight penetration at the lower floors, which resulted in increased window sizes towards ground floor (full height). Vertical daylight factors on the planes of the windows vary from 22% for the top floor to 7.5% for the lowest floor. By compensation, glazed areas vary from 45% of the facade at the top to 90% of the facade for the lowest floor.

White facade finishes increase illuminance levels on windows facing atrium

The facade of the new building is white (P=86%) to increase reflected daylight penetration into the old building, while the old building retains its dark red brick facade (P=21%). The atrium floor is paved by pale yellow bricks (P=33%). The old building's dark red brick facade also reduces the daylight factor across the atrium by approximately 2 to 3% near its facade compared to the white facade of the new building. Solar shading of the atrium is provided by automatic internal grey curtains on its south-facing slope (T=60%). The atrium is naturally ventilated through openings in the roof and at 3m above the floor level which are controlled automatically in response to climatic conditions. Artificial lighting in the atrium is supplied by metal halide street lamps.

Some drawbacks related to overheating of the atrium

There have been some complaints about uncomfortable conditions in the office spaces next to the atrium. These are mainly due to overheating in the upper parts of the atrium during sunny conditions which has reduced the possibility for natural ventilation through windows from colder surroundings. But, there is an additional factor: the upper floors of the new building are occupied by a multimedia computer company, with offices containing a lot of computers, leading to large internal gains.

Sunshading moved automatically on the atrium roof

This solution appeared effective for reduction of solar heat gains.

Automatically controlled exterior sunscreens on south-facing windows respond to wind conditions

On the top of the floor of the new building, the open-plan office in the east wing has two full-height exterior south-facing windows, causing several user complaints due to problems with direct sunlight. The windows are shaded by exterior sunscreen curtains (T=8%) and interior 'transparent' glossy reflective

△ Top floor office of the new building with the atrium to the left.

Facade of the renovated sugar refinery, with walls in red brick. ▽

▽ Facade of the new extension, with large window area and bright finishes.

venetian blinds. However, the exterior shading system is also automatically controlled for protection against wind-damage which on windy days results in the curtains being raised. The interior venetian blinds cause glare problems and distracting reflections on the VDUs, particularly during sunny and windy days. Another problem causing over-heating is that the window opens in-wards, which hinders the use of internal blinds.

Daylighting monitoring

The daylight performance of the building was mainly assessed in the atrium and the offices in the new build-ing adjacent to the atrium. In addition the daylight factors were measured on the top floor in the open-plan offices adjacent to the atrium and also exterior windows facing south. Daylight factors were measured on May and June 1996.

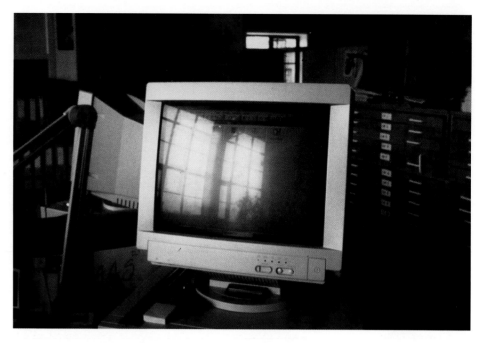

△ Veiling reflection on computer screen due to high luminance of south facing atrium window.

▽ **East facade of the Sukkertoppen building showing the old factory and, right, the new extension.**

Material properties assessed on site

	Colour	Hemispherical-hemispherical reflectance
Floor	yellow bricks	33%
Wall (old building)	red bricks	21%
Wall (new building)	grey (pillar)	36%
Wall (new building)	white	86%
Floor (office)	wood (brown)	33%
Floor (lab.)	grey (brown)	36%
Wall	white	83%
Ceiling	white	82%

	Direct-direct transmittance	Hemispherical-hemispherical transmittance
Single glazing (office atr.)	90%	88%
Double glazing (office ext.)	80%	76%
Double glazing low-E (atrium)	60%	56%

CREDITS

Building
A 18,000m² multimedia centre, developed through the renovation of an old sugar refinery factory in 1992.

Climate
Latitude: 55°40′N, Longitude 12°30′E
The average daily sunshine duration is 0.9 hours in winter, 8.1 hours in summer and 4.9 hours averaged over the year.

Client
Højgaard & Schultz
Jaegersborg Allé 4
2920 Charlottenlund
Denmark

Building owner
The Employees Capital Pension Fund
ATP - huset
Kongens Vaenge 8
3400 Hillerod
Denmark

Architects
Kristian Isager Tegnestue A/S
Kronprinsensgade 32   5000 Odense C
Hjembæk & Præstegård A/S Nyhavn 43
1051 Copenhagen K

Energy and daylighting consultants of the atrium
Esbensen, Consulting Engineers FIDIC
Teknikerbyen 38   2830 Virum, Denmark

Monitoring organisation
Danish Building Research Institute   Energy and Indoor Climate Division, Project Group: Daylight in Buildings P.O. Box 119, 2970 Horsholm, Denmark

References
Kristensen, P. E. 1994. Daylighting Technologies in Non-Domestic Buildings. European Directory of Energy Efficient Building, James & James, Science Publishers Limited, London

Central courtyards compensate for lack of daylight penetration from overshadowed facade windows

Trundholm Town Hall, Trundholm, DENMARK

Fixed external shading on south, east and west facades permanently reduces daylight penetration without providing total protection against sun penetration.

▽ Fixed external shading louvres are fitted to all windows exept the north facing ones.

A single-storey office building built around two courtyards

The Trundholm town hall, constructed in 1970 and extended in 1978, is situated on the outskirts of a small town approximately 100km north-west of Copenhagen. The single-storey 2,500m² building, with a clear views in all directions, is built around two open square courtyards (one 11m² and the other 8m²). Their height is 3.5m. About one half of the floor area houses a single, large open-plan office, while the remaining area consists of individual cellular offices. The daylighting monitoring focused on the luminous behaviour of the former area, daylit from the two courtyards and north and east facade windows.

Daylight penetration under overcast conditions is mainly provided by the north-facing facade and the small central atrium

The open-plan office has a floor area of 917m². Daylight enters the space through the north-facing window (35.7m²), the east-facing window (30.9m²), the window adjacent to the larger courtyard (14.3m² facing west) and the four windows adjacent to the smaller courtyard (four times 22.7m²). The ratio of the glazed area to floor area is 18.7%. The building has a 1m overhang above all windows and all windows have white interior curtains (transmission 45%). In addition, the windows oriented east, south and west including the courtyards are also equipped with fixed

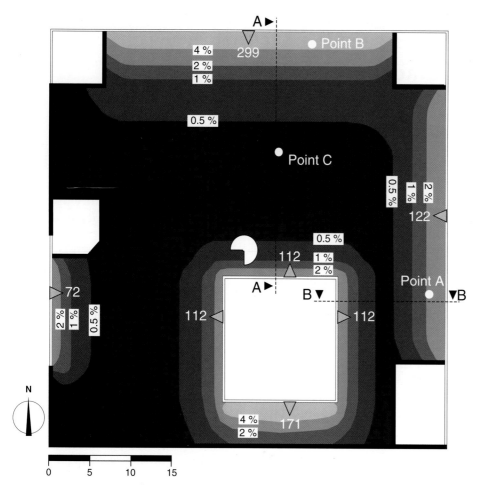

△ General plan of the open-plan office, showing luminous flux penetration (for a total of 1,000 lm penetrating the space).

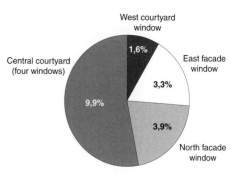

△ Comparison of the sizes of the apertures of the open-plan office.

▽ Origin of the natural light penetration in the space for an overcast day.

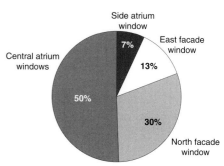

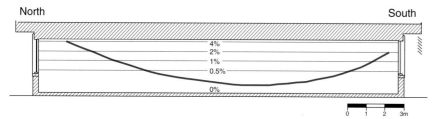

△ Daylight factor variations on the work plane, between the north-facing window and the central courtyard.

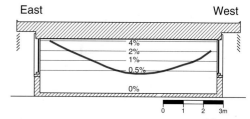

△ Daylight factor variation on the work plane between the east facade and the west facade on the courtyard.

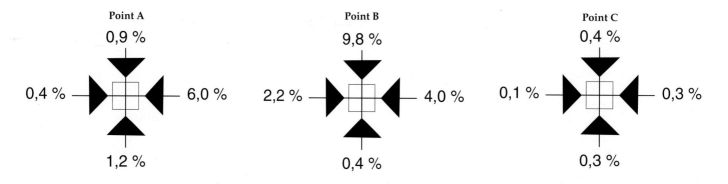

△ Vertical daylight factors at eye level in four directions in the open-plan office. Measurements taken at points A, B, and C.

Windows facing courtyard. △

△ East-facing facade windows with additional curtains.

North-facing facade windows (no external blinds). ▽

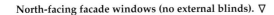

▽ East-facing facade window with fixed external shading louvres.

external sun shading louvres tilted 45° downward.

About 30% of luminaires equipped with automatic dimming in response to daylight

The large glass area at the perimeter of the building and around the two courtyards was the reason for the installation of continuous dimming of the artificial lighting when the lighting system was renovated in 1993. In the open plan office the lighting along each facade and courtyard walls is controlled by individual sensors. The office landscape has 138 luminaries of which 41 are dimmed and controlled in six groups according to the different window orientations. The control sensors are placed 1.4m from window

wall looking at side wall in a distance of 0.4m and tilted 60° from vertical.

A large, central, dark zone requires almost permanent artificial lighting

These zones are located more than 10m from the nearest facade. In these areas, daylight factors fall below 0.25%, 20 times lower than the values of 5% reached next to the windows. The design decision to create these dark deep-plan zones has no doubt been driven by other considerations than daylighting ones. For workplaces where daylight factors fall below 1%, artificial lighting is required almost permanently. The associated area represents roughly 75% of the total area of the room. By comparing the data of daylight factors

and fluxes, it can be said that fixed external blinds reduce the amount of diffuse light penetration to the space by about 40%, and reduce distance of daylight penetration by 1.5m.

Multiple orientation of windows and white curtains affect visibility on VDUs

Everywhere in the space, it appears difficult to avoid light reflections on computer screens due to one of the windows. Furthermore, white curtains lead to extreme luminances when they are exposed to direct sunlight. Luminances of 9,000 cd/m² have been measured for sunny conditions. By comparision, the luminance of the indoor finishes in the window zone is 100 to 500 cd/m² compared to roughly

10 cd/m² when looking into the open plan office, making this latter area appear very dark.

Suggestions for improvement

The analysis suggests that fixed shading tend to significantly reduce daylight penetration, and that a movable system would be more efficient. Care should be given in the selection of shading devices. If their hemipherical-hemispherical transmittance is too high (above 10 to 15%), glare will often occur if they are exposed to direct sunlight. The window frame and the wall thickness were also found to attenuate daylight penetrations.

Daylighting monitoring

The monitoring was conducted on 21 December 1995 and 4 April 1996 (clear sky) and 15 May 1996 (overcast sky).

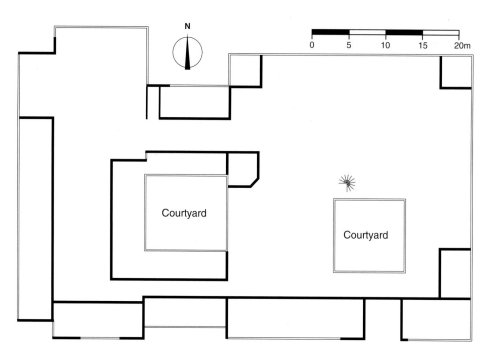

△ Floor plan of Trundholm Town Hall.

◁ **Light reflections on VDU screens.**

Material properties assessed on site

	Colour	Hemispherical-hemispherical reflectance
Walls	blue	19%
Walls	green	43%
Walls	orange	42%
Walls	yelow	59%
Partition wall	orange	23%
Ceiling	white	80%
Furniture	dark green	21%
Floor	dark blue	12%
		Direct-direct transmittance
Curtains	white	51%
		Hemispherical-hemispherical transmittance
Double glazing	77%	81%

CREDITS

Building
Gross area 2,500m²
Area of open plan office: 917m²
Population: 85. Built in 1970.

Climate
Located in Trundholm, Latitude: 55°8'N, Longitude: 11°4'E, Altitude: 30m
Minimum monthly average temperature: 0.6°C. Maximum monthly average temperature 16.7°C. Annual sunshine duration 4.5 hours/day. Global horizontal daily irradiation, from 385 Wh/m² in December to 6,190 Wh/m² in June.

Client
Trundholm Municipality Town Hall
Nyvej 22
4573 Hojby

Architect
Dyck-Madsen & Vesterlund
Slotsgade 19
4760 Vordinborg

Monitoring organisation
Danish Building Research Institute
Energy and Indoor Climate Division,
Group: Daylight in Buildings
P.O. Box 119,
2970 Horsholm,
Denmark.

Daylight from large atrium benefits occupants in surrounding offices

Domino Haus, Reutlingen, GERMANY

This office building displays multiple daylighting features: roof monitors, an atrium and glazed facades. But other aspects such as privacy or the desire to introduce indoor vegetation have led to a reduction in the penetration of daylight.

▽ **General view of the Domino Haus atrium.**

Direct access to the office spaces from the center of the atrium reduces need for light-obstructing balconies

The building is occupied by an architect's office, a number of small investment companies, and law firms. Offices are arranged around a central atrium. Technically, the atrium serves climatic as well as daylighting functions, allowing most working areas to be daylit. The staircase, a glazed elevator, and the gangways are concentrated in the atrium center. This construction does not significantly reduce the daylight available to the interior windows in contrast to designs with gangway balconies directly in front of the atrium facades. The reduction of daylight factors on windows adjacent to the atrium from 11.1% on the top floor to 8% on the first floor down to 4.4% on the ground floor is only due to their deeper position within the atrium.

The flexibility required of office spaces has led to internal zones largely open to daylight

The building design offers great flexibility in the use and possible subdivision of office areas. This concept extends to both the horizontal and vertical grouping of spaces. Movable partitions (like book or storage shelves) tend to offer less obstruction to the penetration of daylight than fixed ones. Some are largely glazed. The

△ Indoor view of top floor.

△ Detail of roof monitor showing obstruction of daylight by plants.

▽ Cross section of the Domino Haus, showing daylight factor variations on work planes and vertical daylight factors in the atrium and on the roof monitors.

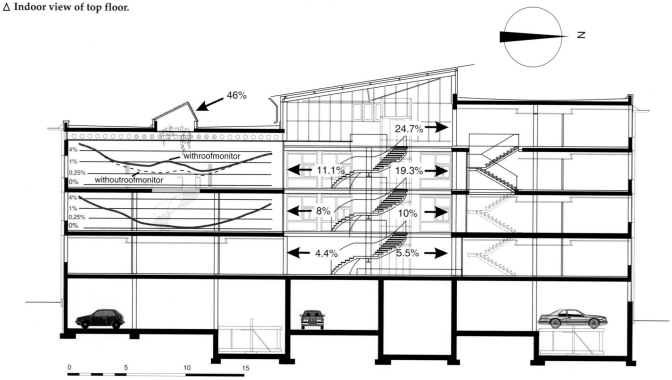

provision of these open volumes should be seen as a complementary strategy to the atrium concept to increase use of daylight.

Secondary daylight is attenuated by curtains for added privacy

Although the areas of secondary light windows are large (typically about 80% on the ground floor and around 60% of the atrium facades on the other floors) relatively little daylight is brought through the atrium on ground floor level. This is due to the extensive use of curtains in front of the glazing towards the atrium to protect the privacy of occupants. Their transmittance is below 50% (estimated). Areas on this floor are thus dependent on artificial lighting for most of the year.

First floor rooms adjacent to the atrium already recieved sufficient amounts of daylight, varying from 3% near windows to 0.1% in the center. Daylight penetration in the centre may be considered too low for tasks such as reading or writing but is generally enough for ambient lighting. Although the actual amount of natural light is very small in the core area it does not appear too confined due to the constant perception of the outdoor environment and the atrium. Rooms on this floor are only separated by glazed walls.

On the southern block of the building, roof monitors take advantage of the open floors to distribute daylight on the upper floor

Three roof monitors are located in the centre of the second floor ceiling of the southern building block. This concept generates a bright and friendly atmosphere which encourages visual communication. Daylight factors below roof monitors reach 1% at places where they should be only 0.3% with light coming only from facades.

Computer screens are positioned to reduce veiling reflections

Almost all work places in the architects' office are equipped with computers. Most of the monitors are placed so that no veiling reflections are possible.

Sunlight penetration is attenuated by external venetian blinds on facades

On the south-facade and on all facades adjacent to the atrium, windows are equipped with external blinds. On the upper floor of the southern building block the clerestory windows had at first been designed without blinds. Direct sunlight penetration has been found to be excessive, leading to the addition of the blinds which are now permanently closed. External venetian blinds efficiently block the incoming sunlight. When they are totally closed they reduce for instance for a sunny spring day direct spots of light on the work desks of about 30,000 lux (and illuminances beyond the sun patch of around 1,000 lux) to an evenly distributed lighting level of around 300 lux over the whole working area.

In addition to the inclined glazing of the atrium roof, there is a significant area of vertical glazing around its perimeter. Thus the atrium roof rises above the roof decks of the parent building admitting light when the sun is at a low angle and increasing the perceived height of the atrium.

Lighting and shading devices may be individually controlled by the occupants through their telephones

The building was designed as a low energy building with a heating demand below 30 kWh/m². The good

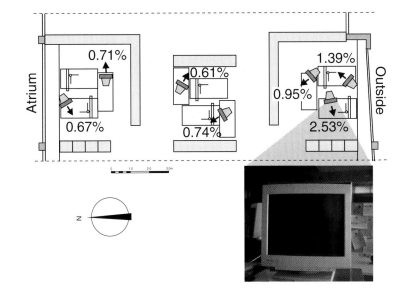

◁ Daylight factors on computer screens. Only one screen is placed critically, with veiling reflections observed.

▽ Indoor space management with open space, glazed partitions and daylight penetration through the staircase.

energy performance is due to a low ratio of the building envelope to its volume and the passive use of solar energy through the atrium glazing.

The operation of artificial lighting as well as shading devices is achieved by telephone dial codes. Depending on the time of day and year lighting is automatically switched off after pre-defined intervals (about every two hours). The user then has to decide whether natural lighting conditions are satifactory or not. The shading system is protected by a weather-dependent control system.

Daylighting monitoring

Monitoring concentrated on the influence of the atrium on lighting conditions in the adjacent office spaces as well as the performance of the roof monitors on the second floor of the southern building block.

Measurements were performed in Jan-uary and December 1996 under overcast skies, as well at the spring equinox under sunny conditions to assess the performance of the shading system.

△ Work spaces near the south facade with venetian blinds.

▽ Illuminance distribution on the work plane as a function of the blind position (sunny conditions).

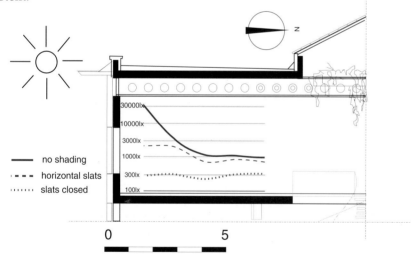

— no shading
- - - horizontal slats
······· slats closed

30000lx
10000lx
3000lx
1000lx
300lx
100lx

0   5

CREDITS

Building description
The building has a total area of 6,800m², and was finished in 1994. On the north side it is four storeys, on the south side it is three storeys high. The basement area accommodates a parking deck.
Area of atrium: 370m²
Ratio of facade area to volume: 0.25m⁻¹
Heating energy consumption below 30 kWh/m² year

Climate
Longitude: 9°2'E, Latitude: 48°5'N.
Reutlingen is located at the foot of the Swabian Alps, 50 kilometers south of Stuttgart in the south-western part of Germany. The climate of Reutlingen is best described by the Würzburg Test Reference Year. The monthly average outdoor temperatures are close to -1.3°C in January and near 18.3° in August.

Client and architect
Riehle and Partner, architects,
Am Echazufer 24
72764 Reutlingen, Germany

Monitoring organisation
Fraunhofer Institute for Building Physics, Nobelstraße 12, 70569 Stuttgart, Germany

Energy and daylighting consultant
Fraunhofer Institute for Building Physics, Nobelstraße 12, 70569 Stuttgart, Germany

References
Um's Atrium herum, Dominohaus, Reutlingen, Deutsche Bauzeitschrift, page 66-69, Sondernummer Büro '95.

Material properties assessed on site

	Colour	Hemispherical-hemispherical reflectances
Floor atrium	wood	47%
Wall offices		71%
Floor office	capel	10%
Desktops		65%
Shelves		14%

	Normal-normal transmittance	Hemispherical-hemispherical transmittance
Glazing, towards outside, south	76%	66%
Glazing, towards atrium	81%	70%
Glazing atrium roof	66%	
Sheer curtains		below 50% (est.)

An open-plan three-storey architects' office provides optimal conditions for occupants

Architects Office, Polydroso, Athens, GREECE

Daylight is intelligently provided to each work space from small side windows, and from roof clerestories for ambient lighting.

A building complex which emphasizes indoor environmental conditions

The Architects Office is part of an office building complex in Polydroso, a northern suburb of Athens. The complex is comprised of three adjoining buildings developed around a common courtyard. To the south, a 17m high linear residential block shades the complex.

As many as possible of the mature olive trees that existed on the site have been saved or transplanted with the result that the landscaping is mature although only recently finished. An important feature of the landscaping is the pond and a sculpture by G. Zongolopoulos and the wooden decks that lead to buildings B and C. The exterior of all buildings is clad with fair-faced cement bricks, which - in combination with the exterior insulation - create a ventilated facade. Building A houses the offices of TEB S.A., a contracting company. Building B houses two engineering companies and building C the offices of the architects.

The Architects Offices: a single open space distributed over three levels

Building C has a net floor area of 615m^2 for some 50 to 60 occupants. The building is long and narrow with interior dimensions of 7.00 x 29.60m oriented along the N to S axis. Except for the basement and area provided for parking, it is virtually one open space, developed on three split level decks, interconnected at two points by two open steel stairs with wooden treads, that have been designed to provide the minimum of visual obstruction.

The ratio of glazing to floor area is 17%

The overall glazed area of the building is 107m^2, 71m^2 of which are windows and 36m^2 clerestories. In relation to the corresponding useful floor area of the building (which is 615m$^{2)}$ the above mentioned values of glazed area

◁ The three floors of the Architects Office with view windows for each work place.

129

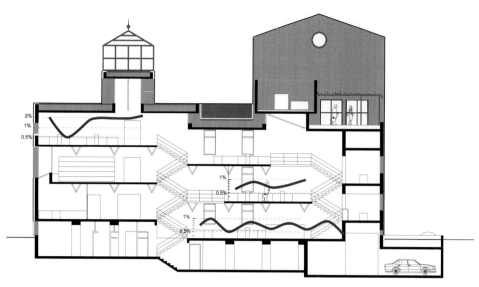

◁Daylight factor contours on the work planes on three different floors.

▽ Daylight factor distribution (ground floor).

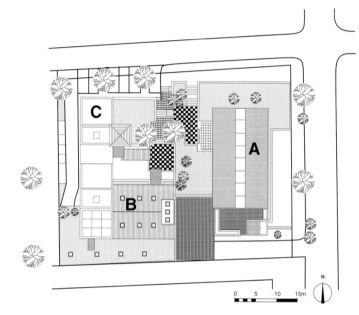

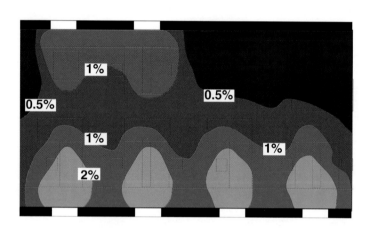

◁ The complex consists of three adjoining buildings A, B, and C, developed around a common courtyard, with a total of 4,000m² of floor area.

correspond to a ratio of glazing per floor area equal to 19%, of which 12.5% is for windows and 6.5% is for clerestories.

Each work place benefits from its own view window

The building, including most of the basement, is naturally lit by means of sill to ceiling windows that are provided on both of the long east- and west-facing facades and clerestories above the two stairwells. All apertures are task- and function-related with one window for each pair of drawing tables, which are perpendicular to the aperture. A third support table is positioned parallel to the exterior wall. Thus most work stations are provided with a direct view outwards. Clerestory lighting with reflecting fabric panels that protect from glare and deflect light downwards are provided above the two stairwells and general circulation areas.

Moderate ambient daylighting is provided by a central clerestory

Clerestory lighting is also provided above the administration area on the ground floor. As all levels are split in half heights and generous voids are provided between levels, the two stairwells are very open and contribute to the airiness, integrity and daylighting of the interior space. Apertures have been deliberately kept small in size so as to provide sufficient, but not excessive, daylighting due to the many days of clear sky conditions, the existence of many VDUs and the need to avoid overheating.

Moderate daylight factors for ambient lighting are adapted to the climate of Athens

Due to the shallowness of the building and the provision of windows on both sides, the lighting environment seems to be relatively homogeneous. Because it is an open space and the interior surfaces have high reflectances, good daylight penetration is ensured. Areas with daylight factors less than 0.5% are used as archives and for photocopy machines. In general, there is a symmetry in the distribution of daylight factors between the different levels. This is because all levels have a similar geometric configuration. Measurements in level 2.1 show the strong influence of the clerestory window on daylighting levels.

◁ The main open staircases, which allow daylight from the clerestory to penetrate to the lower floor.

The clerestory in the northern part of the building above the main stairwell with vertical shading. ▷

▽ The clerestory in the southern part of the building above the secondary stairwell with tilted shading.

High daylight factors near view windows, with strong attenuation from moveable external awnings

Daylight factors near view windows range from 10 to 20% on the work plane within one metre from the window. East- and west-facing apertures are provided with manually controlled vertical electric motorized fabric awnings, positioned approximately 0.15m from the wall, which provide both shading and glare control. This is especially important in relation to computer screens, which are placed perpendicular to the windows. The large clerestory over the main stairwell is provided with a light shelf on the desk near the window, and on the south side.

When the fabric awnings are down, the levels of illumination, away from the sun patches, are reduced on the desk near the window, to a fourth of the original values with direct sun incidence. In the shaded parts of the room, the reduction of light levels is inversely proportional to the distance from the window.

Sun enters the building from the west facing windows after 15:00 LST during summer solstice and after 14:30 LST during winter solstice. The presence of sun patches on working surfaces can be

eliminated by using the shading devices. East-facing windows create a different problem. Because they face towards the common courtyard the sun is blocked during a considerable part of the day. Sun patches on working surfaces can be annoying especially during the summer solstice early in the morning (till 9:00 LST).

Low daylight factors on VDU screens

Vertical daylight factors on VDU screens are moderate, between 0.3% and 1.5%. Problems related to reflections on VDUs are limited. The majority of VDUs are placed perpendicular to the windows. On level 2.1 there are west- and north-facing windows. Axes of computer screens are placed perpendicular to west-facing windows, causing problems to the users in the few cases that have north-facing windows behind

△ Sunshading for facade windows, with awnings 0.15m away from window pane.

them. For this reason, the north-facing windows are equipped with venetian blinds.

Artificial lighting with low power density (6.7 W/m²), but rarely used

Back-up artificial lighting has been little used during the first year of use of the building. The building is usually occupied between 07:00 and 19:00 hours. The main features of the artificial lighting are the fluorescent tube task lighting luminaires provided for each drawing table (which spill some light towards the ceiling), the six metal halide fixtures, which simulate daylighting over the stairwells, and a number of ceiling-mounted fluorescent spotlights provided in the entrance, meeting room and library. All artificial lighting is manually controlled. The installed power for lighting is 6,700 W, leading to a power density of 6.7 W/m², and the monitored power consumption for lighting was only 3.1 Wh/m² for one year (1996). Consumption for computers during the same period was almost eight times higher.

▽ Outdoor landscaping of the project.

Daylighting monitoring

Daylight factors were measured in four rooms of the building during January and March 1996. Additional measurements were conducted under clear sky conditions at 6 July 1996 during summer solstice and equinox.

CREDITS

Building
Building C houses the Architects' Offices. It provides approximately 1,000m² for some 50 to 60 occupants. The complex was built in two phases between 1990 and 1995.

Climate
Athens (Latitude: 37°58'N, Longitude: 23°40'E) is located at an altitude of 107m. Its climate is typically Mediterranean with mean annual dry bulb temperature equal to 18.1°C. Monthly average sunshine duration is 12.42 hours/day in July and 4.1 hours/day in January. Maximum monthly average temperature is 32.5°C in (July) and minimum is 5.6°C in (January).

Architects & Monitoring organisation
Meletitiki - A N Tombazis and Associates Architects, Ltd
Alexandros N Tombazis, project architect
Assisted by: S Paraskevopoulou, J Romanos

Civil engineers
J Mylonas - S Tzivanakis (only buildings B and C)

M/E engineers
LDK - Consultants, Engineers and Planners, Ltd.

Energy consultants
The National and Kapodistrian University of Athens, Group of Building Environmental Studies - Prof. M. Santamouris, physicist

Acoustics
Dr G Schubert

BMS
Digital Control Systems Hellas

Soft Landscaping
Alexandra Tombazis, Sophia Pilavachi

References
'The offices of A N Tombazis and Associates. A bioclimatic approach' by A N Tombazis in European Directory of Sustainable and Energy Efficient Building 1997, James & James 1997, pp. 8-15.

'Office building complex in Polydroso, Athens' in Architecture in Greece 31/1997, pp.104-110.

Material properties assessed on site

	Colour	Hemispherical-hemispherical reflectances
Walls	white	85%
Ceiling	white	85%
Floor	light brown (natural oak)	26%

	Direct-direct transmittance	Hemispherical-hemispherical transmittance
Glazing	87%	80%

Bright atrium maintains neighbour's access to daylight

Beresford Court, Dublin, IRELAND

The Beresford Court building was constructed in 1991 against the facade of an existing office building. The ingenious use of an atrium structure allowed this to be done without a major penalty for its neighbour.

The Beresford Court office building has been attached to the facade of the existing Voluntary Health Insurance

The Beresford Court office building has been constructed on an almost triangular site at the junction of two main streets. One difficulty was that one side of triangle was occupied by the facade of an existing building (Voluntary Health Insurance). The selected design is expressed in the building form in which two 12.5 metre wide wings wrap around two sides of a triangular atrium, the remaining side being the facade of the adjoining (V.H.I.) office building, whose glazing area corresponds approximately to 20% of the facade area. Illuminances on this facade are reduced by about 50% by comparison with the unobstructed situation.

Light-coloured atrium finishes allow high illuminance levels on all facades

The overall light transmittance of the atrium roof for diffuse light is only of about 60%. This value is rather low and is related to the size of the steel structure required to carry the glazed roof on a span of approx 13m. However, light-coloured wall and floor finishes largely compensate for this light reduction, leading to daylight factors on atrium floor of 2.7% (average) and 4.3% maximum. The floor is made of light coloured marble with a reflectance of 57%. The contribution of reflected light from the ground to the daylighting of spaces of the new office on the ground floor has been measured. 85% of the incoming daylight actually comes from the floor.

◁ View of atrium facing entrance.

△ Facade of Voluntary Health Insurance Building, now inside atrium.

▽ Daylight factor distribution on plan of monitored area (4th floor), 0.75m above floor.

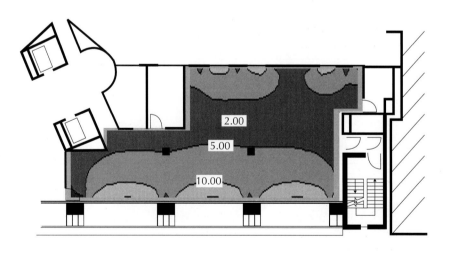

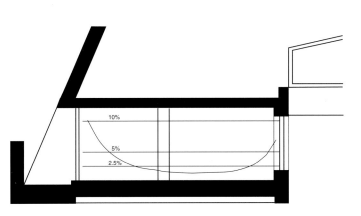

Daylight factor distribution on section of △
monitored area (4th floor), 0.75m above floor.

△ North-facing work station on the fourth floor.

Building section. ▽

▽ Fourth floor work area facing onto atrium.

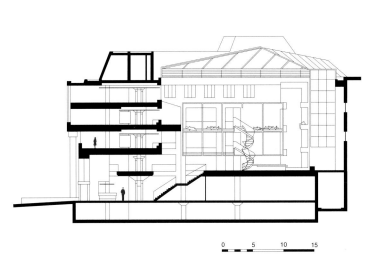

0   5   10   15

Large 'borrowed light' windows compensate for light attenuation caused by atrium

In the new section of the building, the area of the borrowed light windows represents 80% of the facade at the lower floor and 40% at the top floor. This is rather large and leads to a good use of the office space situated within three metres from the atrium facade. Here daylight factors on the work planes of office spaces are found to be higher than 1%, 6m from windows.

However, the building is deep, with a distance between the external facade and the atrium facade of about 12.5m. Fire separation of Beresford Court from its neighbour is achieved by fire and smoke-proof shutters on all windows, operated by sensors. These may also be closed on demand through the Building Management Systems.

In addition to daylight use for ambient lighting, presence detectors afford large lighting energy savings

The lighting system is controlled by presence detectors which automatically turn on the lights. They also sense when a person leaves the space and turn the lights off a short time later. This system operates for all 'public' areas such as stairs, circulation routes, etc. A further refinement of the system allows personal control of individual workstation lighting by the use of 'zappers' similar to car-alarm or television remote controllers. In order to save on peak electricity demand, the building has an 'ice bank' storage system. This uses off-peak night-rate electricity to freeze a large tank of water to ice which is used to cool the building during daytime.

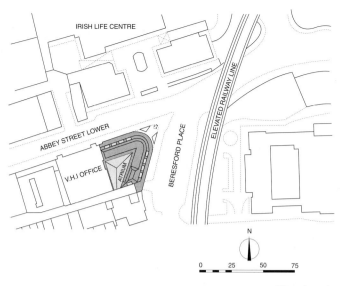

Site plan. △

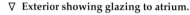

△ Exterior showing curved facade and entrance.

First floor plan. ▽

▽ Exterior showing glazing to atrium.

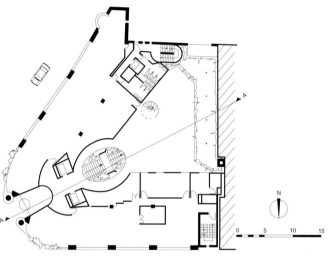
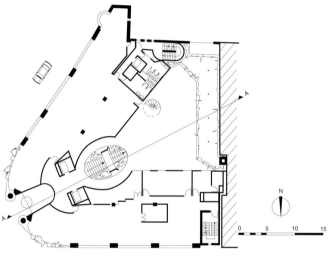

Daylight monitoring

Daylight monitoring was carried out on the fourth floor open plan office on 29 May 1996.

Additional monitoring was carried out on the atrium on 3 October 1996.

Material properties assessed on site

	Colour	Reflectances
Walls	light buff	80%
Ceiling	white	81%
Floor	blue/green	18%
Bench top	grey	39%
Light shelf top	white	71%
Atrium walls	white	80%
Atrium floor	white/brown	57%

	Hemispherical-hemispherical transmittance	Direct-direct transmittance
Double glazing	71%	78%

CREDITS

Building description
Beresford Court, a 6,156m² office building located in central Dublin.
Year built: 1987

Climate
(Latitude: 53°20'N, Longitude: 6°15'W)
Dublin has a temperate coastal climate with mean daily temperature of 4.5° in January and 15.1° in July. Annual mean daily solar radiation is 2.52 kWh/m² (typically 4.66 in June and 0.46 in December). Air pollution levels are low.

Architects & Interior designers
A&D Wejchert Architects,
22 Lower Baggot Street,
Dublin 2

Client
Irish Life Assurances PLC,
Irish Life Centre, Lr Abbey St.,
Dublin 1

Monitoring organisation
Energy Research Group, UCD,
School of Architecture, Richview,
Clonskeagh Drive, Dublin 14

160m of aluminium lightshelves deviate sunlight on one entire facade

EOS Building, Lausanne, SWITZERLAND

The central staircases are daylit from roof openings, and the south-west facades benefit from solar control with lightshelves.

Site constraints led to specific decisions regarding daylighting

The EOS building is built on a slope, giving little opportunity to open windows on the north-east/north-west facade. The division of the building into two separate blocks offers opportunities to admit daylight, particularly on the north-west and the south-east facades above the entrance hall.

Staircases are located in the core of each building, and are daylit from the roof, with areas of about 25m^2 and 35m^2 of double clear glazing.

Most offices are located along the south-west facade and are daylit with continuous windows. Windows are arranged in two horizontal bands, one above each other, accommodating continuous external lightsheves.

▷ View of the lightshelves from the outside, (south-west facade).

▷ Office space on south-west facade, showing sunlight being reflected from the external lightshelf towards the ceiling, as well as the shading effect in the centre of the space.

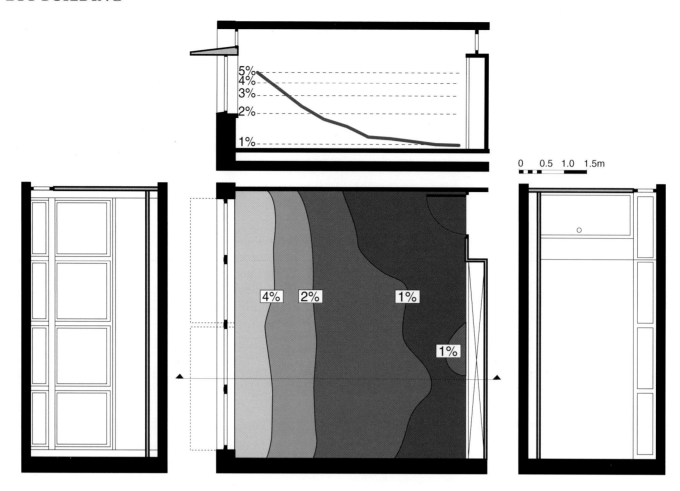

△ The effect of the lightshelves on daylight factor distribution on the work plane.

▽ Plan view of the two building blocks.

▽ Views of the south-west facades of the two buildings, linked by the central entrance hall.

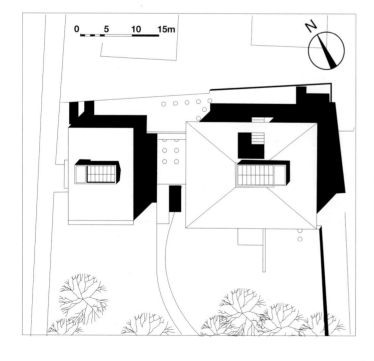

14

334

765

48.5

8

△ Luminance measurements (cd/m²), for a standard overcast sky (10,000 lux) in a room facing south-west.

△ View toward the interior, showing secondary daylighting.

△ View toward the facade.

Aluminium lightshelves redirect surplus daylight towards the ceiling

The ceiling height of offices is quite standard (2.58m), and each office on the south-west facade has a depth of 5.70m. Aluminium lightshelves have been added on the facades at a height of 2m above the floor surface. Their width is 0.8m and they are slightly tilted towards the outside as well as water run-off. They are made of anodized aluminium which offers a reasonable compromise between their reflective properties and durability.

The luminous behaviour of the lightshelf can be described both with respect to sunlight and daylight. For sunlight, a significant fraction of incoming sunlight is intercepted by the lightshelves and reflected towards the ceiling, typically reducing light levels in the first two metres from the facade. Sunshading is also provided for a fraction of the workplane located a few metres away from the facade. It is clear, however, that blinds are still needed since such shading is limited locally.

Regarding diffuse light, the reflective lightshelves lead to a more homogenous daylight distribution, in reducing the illuminance levels in the area of the workplane directly shadowed by them.

For instance, the monitored office has a floor area of 30m², and its glazed area is 4.44m² on the facade (a seventh of the floor area), excluding secondary daylight windows on the hall with glazed area of 1.23m².

Horizontal daylight factors were measured on the work plane, 0.80m above the floor. Vertical daylight factors were measured in the centre of the monitored office, 1.20m above the floor, at eye height of a sitting person. The results are 3.6% facing the window, 0.5% looking away from the window, and about 1% facing the two other walls. The ratio of one to seven suggests that the secondary daylighting windows do not contribute to the daylighting of the space, and that the space remains contrasted even if the walls have bright finishes (reflectance: 0.79%). The daylight factor on the VDU screen is low (0.83%) suggesting limited veiling reflections from diffuse light as long as the image of the window is not seen on the screen.

Luminance measurements conducted on a dark, but not fully overcast day, show that the windows above the lightshelf may contribute to glare as can the windows below the lightshelf, suggesting that shading devices are still useful in such design.

Electric lighting with direct/indirect luminaires

All offices are equipped with one moveable luminaire with three 55W fluorescent lamps. This solution offers an interesting response to the need for flexibility in the space at a low cost, although the global energy efficiency is

lower than solutions based on fixed ceiling mounted luminaires. However, in rooms with large amount of daylight, such solutions become interesting since the indirect lighting may be needed less that 50% of the time the room is occupied. In the EOS building, the controls are manual.

Daylight monitoring

Daylight monitoring was conducted on 26 January 1996 under overcast conditions.

◁ Staircase daylit from the side, leading to the daylit corridors.

▽ Central atrium.

CREDITS

Building description
The building is located in Lausanne, a city on the banks of Lake Geneva, at an elevation of 500m. The construction of this 400m² building was achieved in 1995.

Climate
Latitude: 46°31'N, Longitude: 6°38'E
Minimum monthly temperature is 1.7°C in January.
Maximum monthly temperature is 20.5°C in July.

Client
EOS
Chemin de Mornay 10
CH-1003 Lausanne

Architect
BUREAU D'ARCHITECTURE RICHTER ET DAHL ROCHA
Lausanne
7, avenue Dapples
CH-1006 Lausanne
Tél.: +41.21-617 0424
Fax: +41.21-617 0431

Daylight consultant
SORANE SA,
Lausanne
Route du Châtelard 52
CH-1018 Lausanne
Tel.: +41.21-647 1175
Fax: +41.21-646 8676

HVAC Engineers:
Pierre CHUARD
Lausanne
En Budron A2
1052 Le Mont sur Lausanne
Tel.: +41.21-652 9622
Fax: +41.21-653 5925

Monitoring organisation
SIMOS LIGHTING CONSULTANTS
15, place du Temple
CH-1227 Carouge
Tel.: +41-22.343 5281
Fax: +41-22.343 5880

EPFL/LESO
CH-1015 Ecublens
Tel.: +41.21-693 3394
Fax: +41.21-693 2722

Material properties assessed on site

	Hemispherical-hemispherical reflectances
Wall	79%
Ceiling	82%
Floor	12%
Working table	16%
Lightshelf	64%

	Normal-normal transmittance	Hemispherical-hemispherical transmittance
Glazing of SW facade	69%	65%

Fourteen courtyards and a network of glazed streets distribute daylight thoroughly in a large-scale office building

Reiterstrasse Building, Berne, SWITZERLAND

It is almost impossible in this building to be more than four metres away from a daylight source.

9,500m² of office space distributed over two floors

The Reiterstrasse building has a classical layout of office spaces. The building is flat: the 9,500m² of floor area are distributed on only two floors. Below, two levels of basements are used for storage, services and car parking.

The general layout is the one of a rectangular building (80m x 66m) organized with a regular grid of glazed streets on two levels alternating with square open courtyards. A large, central glazed street, positioned diagonally, is the only major irregularity of the scheme.

Office spaces on the two floors are daylit via 14 square, open courtyards

14 open courtyards are distributed regularly over the floor plane. They are roughly 6m³. Each courtyard distributes daylight to the adjacent office spaces of the two floors through double glazing.

The walls of the courtyard are finished using bright colours. Results in the monitored room show good daylight distribution but very little contribution of secondary daylighting. It also can be observed that the two windows are facing each other, leaving 25% of the

▽ The central glazed street distributes daylight offices and corridors.

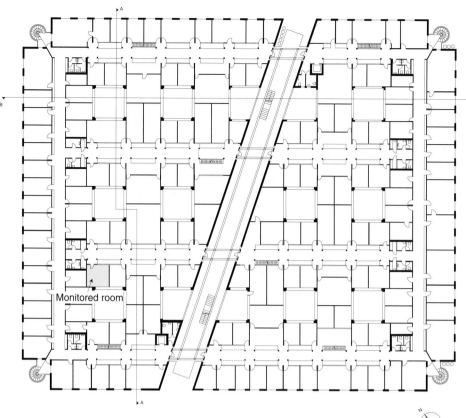

▽ Axonometric view of the building showing location of the courtyards, the central glazed street and the four other secondary glazed street.

Monitored room

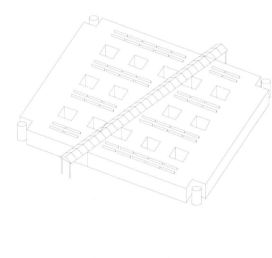

▷ Daylight penetration in an office adjacent to courtyards (monitored room), south-west facade.

work plane with daylight factors below 0.5%. The aperture ratio of the facade glazing is 17% of the floor area. The total light flux entering the room is 8100 lm for a standard overcast sky (corresponding to a horizontal illuminance of 10,000 lux). The secondary glazing has an aperture ratio of half this value.

The central glazed street is 69 metres long, and 6m width.

Daylight monitoring
Daylight factor measurements were conducted on 21 March 1996. The monitored room is located on the first floor (south-west atrium facade).

▷ Daylight factors distribution on the work plane of the monitored office.

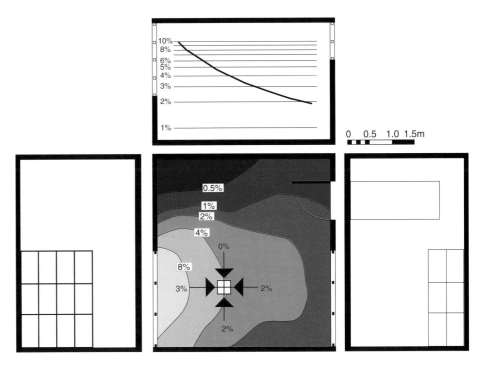

▷ Large overhangs above the secondary daylighting window eliminate the potential for additional daylighting.

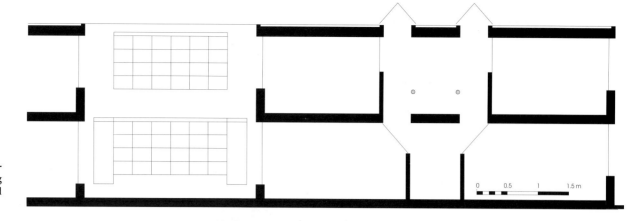

▷ Typical cross-section showing courtyard and glazed street.

△ Luminance distribution within an office under sunny conditions (cd/m²).

▽ Exterior view.

Material properties assessed on site

	Hemispherical-hemispherical reflectances
Wall	74%
Ceiling	76%
Floor	16%

	Hemispherical-hemispherical transmittance
SW facade	65%
Glazed street roof	73%

CREDITS

Building description
Floor area
ground floor: 4,875m²
first floor: 4,706m²
basements (2): 9,700m²
Construction date: 1984 to 1987

Climate
Latitude: 46°57'N, Longitude: 7°26'E
Altitude: 540m above sea level. The minimum monthly average temperature is 0.8°C in January, and the maximum monthly average temperature is 19.6°C in July.

Client
Reiterstrasse 11
CH-3011 BERN

Architect
BUREAU D'ARCHITECTURE
Bern
MATTI, BURGI, RAGAZ
CH-3097 Liebefeld, Bern
Tel.: +41.31-972 0211
Fax: +41.31-972 0605

Electrical Engineer:
Rudolph BRUCKER
Muri Bei - Bern
Thunstrasse 190
CH-3074 Müri Bei - Bern
Tel.: +41.31-951 0346
Fax: +41.31-951 0415

HVAC Engineers:
Hans KUNDIG AG
Bern
Schwarztorstrasse 121
CH-3007 Bern
Tel.: +41.31-381 4927
Fax: +41.31-382 2036

Bauphysik:
Bauphysikalisches Institut AG
Bern

Monitoring organisation
SIMOS LIGHTING CONSULTANTS
15, place du Temple
CH-1227 Carouge
Tel.: +41.22-343 5281
Fax: +41.22-343 5880

EPFL/LESO
CH-1015 Ecublens
Tel.: +41.21-693 3394
Fax: +41.21-693 2722

A renovated office building with automatic lighting control in response to daylight levels

UAP Insurance Building Lausanne, SWITZERLAND

Automatic control of lamps and careful sizing of the lighting installation has led to substantial energy savings.

Advanced lighting controls added during a renovation

The UAP Insurance building in Lausanne has a total floor area of 3,366m² distributed among five floors and a basement level. It was built in 1969 and renovated in 1991. The renovation included new lamps, new partitions and a new facade. Each office is lit with ceiling-mounted luminaires, distributed in three rows over the depth of the room (3.98m). Each luminaire is equipped with a 50W fluorescent tube. The 50W power includes the power consumption of the electronic ballasts.

The controls are performed manually for the luminaires located away from the window and automatically for the two other lamps together, controlled by a sensor located in the ceiling. The sensor (one per office), located in the ceiling, reads illuminance from light reflections on the work plane. Two manual switches are located near the intrance door to permit manual turning on or off each of the two groups of luminaires.

▽ Indoor view of a typical office room.

South facade of the UAP building. ▷

Annual lighting electricity consumption measured at 15 KWh/m² year

The following are figures related to energy consumption of the building during the year.

The building is occupied typically from 7.30 am to 7 pm, five days per week.

Installed power density per floor (561 m²)		Power
Offices (per floor)	12.3 W/m²	4675 W
Corridors, stairs, lifts	8 W/m²	961 W
Mean:	**10 W/m²**	**5636 W**
Mean energy consumption (lighting/year/floor)		
Offices	6545 kWh/year	
Corridors, stairs	1922 kWh/year	
Total: 8467 kWh/year		15 KWh/m² year

Daylighting monitoring

Monitoring was conducted 4 July 1995 and 14 November 1996.

▷ **Daylight factor distribution on the work plane.**

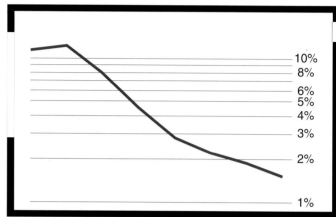

▽ **Detail of the artificial lighting installation, showing location of sensor between the two first array of luminaires.**

Material properties assessed on site

	Hemispherical-hemispherical reflectances
Wall	76%
Ceiling	56%
Floor	12%
Table	42%
	Hemispherical-hemispherical transmittance
Glazing of SW facade	73%

CREDITS

Building description
The building has five floors and a basement level with an area of 561m² each (total 3,366m²). It is located in Lausanne, and was built in 1969 and remodeled in 1991.

Climate
Latitude: 46°31′N, Longitude: 6°38′E
Altitude: 410m above sea level.
The minimum monthly average temperature is 1.7°C in January, and the maximum monthly average temperature is 20.5°C in July.

Client
UAP Building
Avenue de Cour 26
CH-1007 Lausanne

Architect
Bureau d'architecture Danilo Mondada
Chemin de Longeraie 5
CH-1006 Lausanne
Tel.: +41.21-323.70.81
Fax: +41.21-311.01.39

HVAC Engineers:
Bonnard et Gardel
Lausanne
Avenue de Cour 61, CH-1007 Lausanne
Tel.: +41.21-618.11.11
Fax: +41.21-618.11.22

Monitoring organisation
SIMOS Lighting Consultants
15, place du Temple, CH-1227 Carouge
Tel.: +41.22-343 5281
Fax: +41.22-343 5880

EPFL/LESO
CH-1015 Ecublens
Tel.: +41.21-693 3394
Fax: +41.21-693 2722

A large-scale office building built around four courtyards and four atria

Victoria Quay, The Scottish Office, Edinburgh, UNITED KINGDOM

The design strategy aimed at daylight penetration in most office spaces. However, deep plan, dark finishes and indoor partitions tend to reduce the overall performance.

A 35,000m² building for 1,500 personnel

Victoria Quay is a new office block, designed by RMJM Architects, one of the UK's largest multi-disciplinary design practices. The building was completed in 1995 and is home to the Scottish Office which is the UK government department responsible for local affairs in Scotland. The 35,000m², four-storey building has a staff of around 1,500 personnel. It is 250 metres long, 45 metres deep with a total height of about 25 metres.

Courtyards and atria bring additional daylight into the deep core of the building

The deep plan linear building (long axis east-west) is punctuated by a series of four open courtyards and four atria, creating spaces with access to windows on both sides to allow views, natural ventilation and daylight. However, distances between facades remain high (15 metres) except for the two courtyards located at each end of the building. Courtyards and atria are 15 by 20 metres, with an height of 25m.

The atria are designed purely as circulation zones, and, in the interest of energy conservation, these internal unheated spaces are sealed from the ad-

joining offices. These adjoining offices spaces are typically 15 metres across, from the external facade to the facade to the courtyards and atria. The goal of the daylighting measurement was to assess the efficiency of such a solution.

Window sizes and glazing materials have been adapted to needs

The building has four floors in all. The first three floors are of heavyweight construction with around 40% glazing on the external facade. The top floor is of lightweight construction and sits on top of the main structure. This upper floor consists mainly of office suites and is more extensively glazed (around 50% of the facade). The floor plate is narrower than on the lower levels at approximately 13 metres from window to courtyard or atrium compared with 15 metres on the lower floors. Initial impressions suggested that the narrower floor plate, less dense occupancy and variation in interior finishes on the third floor resulted in a brighter space.

Windows on the external facades are triple glazed, consisting of an outer pane of clearfloat glass and an inner double glazed unit with interpane venetian blinds. This is a particularly good choice for Edinburgh's cold climate. Office windows facing into the

▽ Victoria Quay (south elevation).

△ The third floor (looking north) is brighter and appears more open due to lower partitions.

△ The second floor (looking north) appears darker and is more congested with furniture.

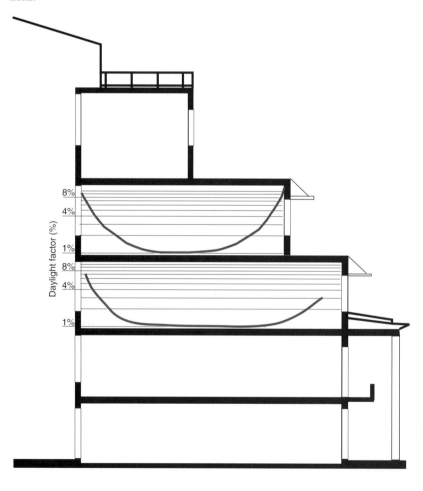

◁ Daylight factor distribution in the linear section looking east.

▽ Plan of the Scottish Office.

N

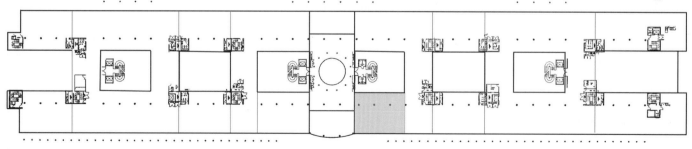

△ Shading on south facade by horizontal louvres, colonnade and mesh screens.

◁ Third floor south-facing offices, triple glazed with between pane blind providing local control.

courtyards are double glazed clear float glass also with mid-pane blinds. Internal windows into the atria are single glazed with clear glass and the fully glazed atrium roof is double glazed with low emissivity glass.

Bilateral daylighting of third floor offices efficiently distribute daylight across the 13 metres depth

Readings were taken at regular intervals on a linear path from north to south. These were extrapolated using a simulation programme when access to some locations of measurements were difficult. In the third-level office area the average horizontal daylight factor ranges from 8.3% on the south side to 0.5% in the middle and almost 9% on the atrium-facing side. The value of 0.5% obtained with bilateral daylighting gives the impression of a brighter space than with single side daylighting solutions. This third floor has a rather open-plan arrangement, low partitioning and moderate density of occupants. This contributes to the good daylighting performance of the space.

Bilateral daylighting of second floor offices barely provides enough daylight across the 16 metres depth

In the second level office area, the average horizontal daylight factors on a working plane height of 0.73m were measured at intervals of 1.5m from the south facade towards the atrium. Daylight factors measured on the working plane ranged from 3.7% on the south side to 0.1% in the middle and 3% on the north/atrium-facing side. The interior furnishings and fittings, particularly the dark blue partitions, substantially suppress the daylight levels. Their removal or replacement would improve daylight distribution. The low reflectance grey finish on the atrium walls may also contribute to poor daylight distribution on the lower floors. The deeper plan form (16 metres across, allows for a higher density of occupation, with a central row of occupants who have no direct access to a window. These occupants are located within the central circulation zone and are afforded privacy by higher partitions than

used on the third floor (1.5m compared with 1.2m).

Wall finishes affect daylight penetration and glare issues

The courtyard and atrium wall finishes are grey (R=32%) to reflect the maritime setting and interior finishes are a mix of white for structural walls with blue-grey, flexible (R=45%), full-height partitioning. The result is a rather sharp decrease in illuminance along the walls of the courtyard and atrium.

However, when sunbeams strike these walls, this rather low reflectance reduces glare from reflections.

Glare issues managed on the external facades, with need of improvement on windows on atria

Extensive use of VDUs makes the issue of glare critical. In this building, glare is tackled by both fixed and locally-controlled shading devices. As the building is oriented north-south, horizontal fixed shades are employed to provide general shading with external louvred overhangs on the south facade and the south-facing courtyard elevations to provide protection from glare and overheating on the first, second and third floors. Ground floor windows are shaded by the colonnade and perforated mesh screens. With the emphasis on elimination of glare, north- and south-facing windows are fitted with interpane venetian blinds providing the occupants with localized control.

The original intention was that blinds should be fitted on all south-facing glazing. However, it was first decided that in the atria, blinds would only be fitted to third floor windows. During sunny days, sunlight is reflected from the south-facing atrium wall across to the north wall which has no shading to provide protection from this source of glare. The occupants, at the time of the monitoring, tried to alleviate the problem by using posters. Now, new blinds have been fitted.

Lighting controls

The building's artificial lighting system is managed centrally by a *'Delmatic'* computerised control system which provides up to 500 lux with heat gains limited to $10\,W/m^2$. Lights are controlled in banks, with daylight sensing on light fittings adjacent to windows and core lighting levels controlled by predicted occupancy levels.

◁ **Use of posters to conteract glare.**

▽ **Effect of glare reflected from south-facing atrium wall.**

Throughout the day, ceiling-mounted photocell controls adjust light levels in accordance with the availability of daylight. Lights can be dimmed to a minimum of 10%. There is an in-built facility to control light switching by infra-red presence detectors, however, at the time of the study this had not yet been implemented. Such a technique would however help considerably, since occupants tend to be often out of their office.

Daylight monitoring

Daylight factors, glazing transmittances and surface reflectances were measured on a number of days between March and May 1996, with internal daylight monitoring occurring on days with the most suitable overcast conditions in the middle of May. Daylight factor assessment of interior spaces was conducted at the working plane, on VDU screens and at the internal pane of windows.

CREDITS

Building description
Size: 35,000m² for 1,500 personnel.
Completed in 1995.

Climate
The building is located at sea level at a latitude of approximately 55°4'N in the Leith Dock area of Edinburgh, on the east coast of Scotland. The site is flat, open and subjected to very little overshading. Monthly average outdoor temperatures are 4.5°C in winter and 16°C in summer. The average daily sunshine duration on the site is 5.2 hours in summer, 1.5 hours in winter and 3.5 hours averaged over the year.

Client
The Scottish Office
Victoria Quay
Leith, Edinburgh, Scotland

Architect
RMJM Architects
RMJM Scotland Ltd
10 Bells Brae
Edinburgh EH43BJ

Monitoring organisation
ESRU, University of Strathclyde, Glasgow, Scotland
BRE, Building Research Establishment, Watford, UK

References
Clarke J, Hand J, Johnstone C, McElroy L - Daylight Monitoring, Victoria Quay, Leith,

Material properties assessed on site

	Colour	Hemispherical-hemispherical reflectances
Atrium walls	grey	32%
Window frames		39%
Internal walls	white	82%
Desks		34%
Partition walls	blue-grey	45%
Movable partitions	blue	13%
Atrium floor		08%
External sandstone walls		51%

	Normal-normal transmittances
Triple glazed window	64%
Double glazed window	79%
Single glazed window on atria	94%

Sunlight plays on room surfaces

National Observatory of Athens, Athens, GREECE

Nothing special about the daylight penetration inside the NOA building, apart from some variable light patterns in this building built in 1865 by the architect T.C. Hanssen.

A building in which two long-term thermal and luminous monitoring projects have been undertaken

This building houses a research team which has conducted various long-term assessments of heat and luminous fluxes in their own working environment. This building was included as a case study in the extended monitoring campaign which was carried out within the frame of PASCOOL research project.

A statistical approach to glare

The photographs show how sun patches cover during one day an area much larger than covered at any instant. This shows that sunlighting analyses should be conducted using frequencies of occurrence, in preference to values or average values over the space. For instance, the glare issue in relation to direct sunlight could be expressed as the fraction of the time, or the number of hours per year, per month or per day in which the occupants will experience glare.

Daylighting monitoring

It was performed in 7 December 1995 for overcast conditions. Pictures were taken in 10 February 1996 for sunny conditions.

10:00 - East window

10:00 - East window
reflection on the window pane

12:00 - East window

15:00 - South window

◁　Movement of sun patches on the floor, during the day.

151

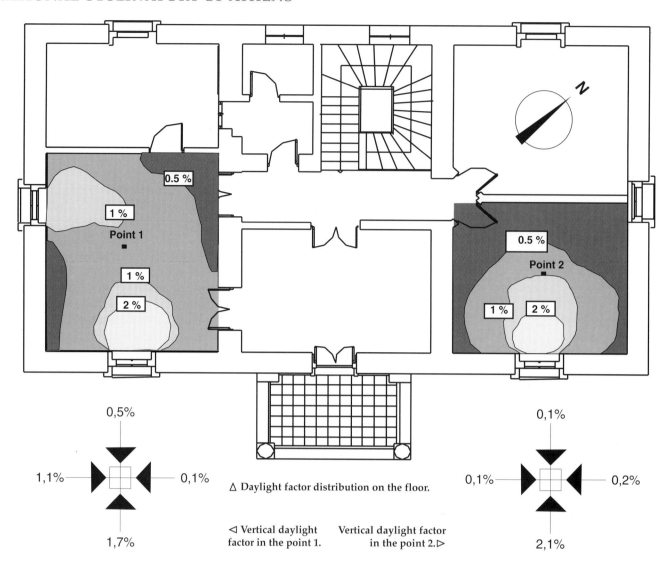

0,5%

1,1% ← → 0,1%

1,7%

△ Daylight factor distribution on the floor.

◁ Vertical daylight factor in the point 1.

Vertical daylight factor in the point 2. ▷

0,1%

0,1% ← → 0,2%

2,1%

◁ Exterior view.

Material properties assessed on site

	Colour	Hemispherical-hemispherical reflectances
Wall	dark beige	35%
Ceiling	dark beige	35%
Floor	wood	10%
	Normal-normal transmittance	Hemispherical-hemispherical transmittance
Glazing	90%	82%

CREDITS

Building
Three levels of 137m² each.
Aperture ratio: 13% of the floor area.
Built in 1865.

Climate
Athens has a Mediterranean climate. Latitude: 37°97'N, Longitude:23°72'E, Altitude: 107m. The monthly average temperature is 22.5°C while the minimum one is 13.8°C. Heating degree days (base 18°C) are 1,110 through the year and the cooling degrees days (base 26°C) are 122. Compared with northern Europe, Greece has a high sunshine duration and enjoys higher values of incident radiation. The maximum value is in July, with 12.4 hours/day. The least sunny days occur in January with 4.1 hours/day. Sunshine in winter depends mainly on cloudiness which is a function of the weather systems influencing the town.

Architect
T.C. Haussen

Monitoring organization
National Observatory of Athens, Aris Tsangrassoulis
P.O. Box 20048
11810 Thisio, Athens - Greece.

How to control shading devices?
Results of experience in an office complex

Statoil research centre, Trondheim, NORWAY

The performance of automatic control of blinds is compared with manual control. Occupant response teaches us useful lessons.

A large office building designed with concern for security

Statoil is the government-owned Norwegian petroleum company responsible for exploration, development and marketing of Norway's abundant offshore oil and gas reserves. The company's main operations are based in Stavanger and Bergen, but because of the concentration of technology research in Trondheim, it was decided to locate the research centre here.

The first stage of the research centre was completed in 1993, it consists of 29,500m^2 of laboratory and office facilities, with a staff of around 400 scientists and support personnel. The site is a field sloping slightly northwards to the fjord shoreline, with a magnificent view of the fjord and the mountain range on the distant northern shore.

The main features of this research centre are an office and administration building, and a compact laboratory building, separated from the offices for safety reasons. The offices are located in three wings, extending in a fanshaped fashion from the semi-circular central lobby and circulation area, with a restaurant area inserted between two of the office wings. This layout has been likened to a typical US prison layout, as all entry/

▽ Facade windows with external venetian blinds.

▽ Typical office in one of the office blocks.

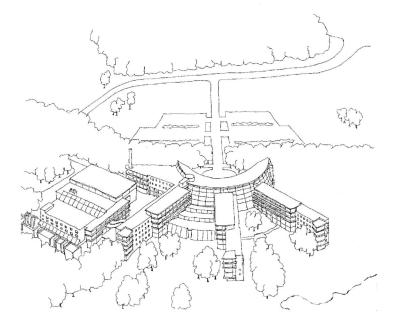

△ Perspective drawing showing the central hub and the three office blocks.

▽ The 10m² office space with the 1.08m² window glazing.

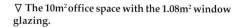

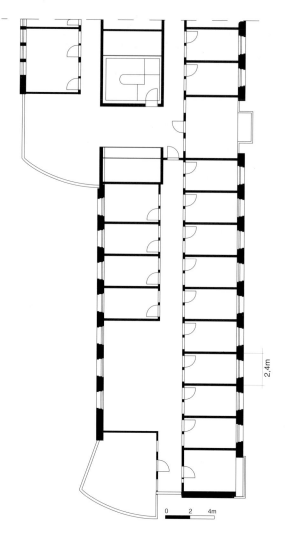

△ Office space distribution in a typical wing.

▽ Typical cross-section of an office block, with vertical daylight factors.

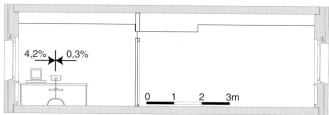

exit points are through the central security controlled hub.

The central hub is raised higher than the extending office wings, and has a large expanse of inclined glass, both on the south and the north side, giving the restaurant area good daylighting and a commanding view across the fjord.

The main axes of the three blocks of offices are oriented at about 45° ang-

ular distance apart, covering the sector from almost due west to due north. Future extensions have been planned allowing another office block in a south-westerly direction to be built later. The office blocks have partly three, partly four storeys, and about half of each floor is laid out conventionally with a central corridor with one-person office rooms on either side. The rest has a double corridor layout, where the core area is used for support functions.

Small windows with significant light obstruction due to wall thickness

The office rooms are 2.3m wide and 4.2m deep and are daylit with a square window in the centre of the external wall. The dimensions of the glass pane are 1.04m².

It consists in double sealed glazing with a low-e coating. The resulting glazing-to-floor area ratio is 11.2%, which is

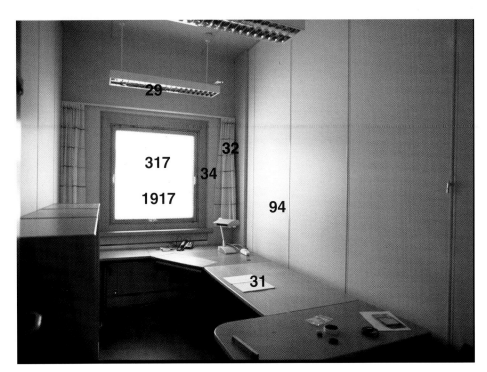

△ Luminance distribution on an standard overcast day (cd/m²).

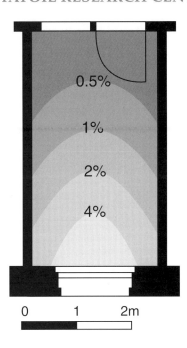

△ Daylight factor distribution on the work plane of an office in the southern block (block III, level 2).

rather low in comparison with common practice, even at such a latitude.

The daylight factors on the work plane hardly exceed 4%, and vertical daylight factors are below 0.6% for all directions except the one facing the window (4.2%). Such measurements were done 1.5 metres from the window and 1.3 metres from the floor. Occupants typically place their computers near the windows, and the resulting daylight factors on the screens were found equal to 6%.

The external brick facing extends into the projected opening in such a manner that it partly obstructs the glazing, probably to give protection to the venetian blinds. Another factor is the small size of the room, consequently, a large percentage of the wall surfaces and the floor is covered by bookshelves, posters, calenders, furniture etc. This increases light absorption by the room.

External venetian blinds operated with motors in several modes

All blinds on one facade are motor-controlled by a roof-mounted light sensor. A wind speed-controlled override allows the blinds to be raised when wind speed becomes excessive. This system was later modified by installing a manually switched override for each

floor, later modified by installation of localized manual switching for every pair of offices. Each electric motor serves two windows, preventing users from operating their blind individually.

Long-term monitoring shows the difficulty of adapting automatic controls to occupant needs

Long-term monitoring has been conducted in 26 office rooms, located on the second and third floor of the east facade of the office block extending northwards, and on the south facade of the block extending westwards. The monitoring programme included the recording of many parameters: illuminance measurements in two zones, occupancy, window opening, lighting electricity consumption, equipment energy, temperatures of inlet and exhaust air, and status of the daylight-responsive lighting control system. Different lighting systems and control systems have been tested.

The control of the blinds has created a lot of problems. All of the office occupants use computer screens extensively and experience visually disabling reflections in the glass surface if sunshine is allowed into the room, even if they close the light interior curtains. Therefore the central blind control system is set to operate as soon as the

vertical light level indicates sunshine. But at the same time many offices may be shaded by the building in front (high latitudes = low solar altitudes!), and with blinds pulled down the offices appear very dark. Therefore, the control system was later modified by floor and individual room pair manual override functions. Even one switch for two room has created some controversies about the use of blinds, suggesting a very high sensitivity of occupants to the control of their shading devices.

When sunblinds are automatically controlled, energy saving potential of lighting control is small

The two ceiling luminaires in each room were fitted with individual, daylight-based control systems. Two types of systems were used: on-off and continuous dimming. All systems were calibrated to provide minimum 450 lux in the normal working plane of the room. The results show only small differences between the offices in the same block, but a systematic difference between the offices facing south and those facing east. The energy consumption savings, using automatic lighting controls, were on average 7% for the south facing offices and 2% for the east facing. These low values are mainly a result from the use of the automatic blinds combined with

△ Sunlight on the entire facade of the office block.

△ Shadowing of the office facade by the neighbouring block.

manually operated curtains. The diagrams show results for one typical office on each facade. Room 1.2.112 is facing east, while room 3.3.096 is facing south. The energy saving diagrams show the monthly savings in lighting electricity in comparison with situation with artificial lighting on during the whole working period (8 am to 4 pm).

Clearly, the electric lighting energy saving potential in this type of office building, using automatic sun blinds, is very small.

Daylighting monitoring

Daylight factors and brightness distribution have been assessed on the basis of measurements conducted.

△ Annual lighting energy savings (1996) room n°1.2.12.

▽ Annual lighting energy savings (1996) room n°3.3.096.

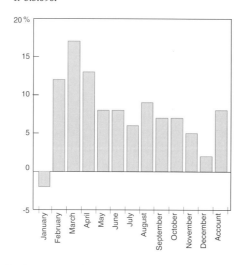

CREDITS

Building descriptions
First stage of a research centre which will be developed in the future. It consists of 29,500m² of laboratory and office facilities, for a staff of around 400 scientists. Completed in 1993.

Climate
Latitude: 63°5'N
Longitude: 11°0'E
Hours of sunshine: 1352 h/a
Typical day duration in December: 4:30h and June: 20h

Client
STATOIL Research Centre
Address: Arkitekt Ebellsvei 10 N-7053 Ranheim, Norway
Tel: +47.73-584 011
Fax: +47.73-967 286

Architect
KS Per Knutsen Architectoffice AS with Siv. arch. Per Fossen.
Address: Fjordgt. 7. N-707010 Trondheim,
Tel: +47.73-529 130
Fax: +47.73-529 638

Daylight consultant
Øyvind Aschehoug. Professor at Dept. of Building Technology.

Monitoring organisation
Professor Øyvind Aschehoug and Siv. arch. Dr.ing. student Barbara Matusiak at Dept. of Building Technology, Faculty of Architecture, Planning and Fine Art. Norwegian University of Science and Technology
Address: N-7034 Trondheim, Norway
Tel: +47.73-595 040
Fax: +47.73-595 045

M. Sc Heidi Arnesen and Siv. arch. Dr.ing Anne Gunnarshaug Lien at SINTEF Civil and Environmental Engineering, Architecture and Building Technology.
Address: N-7034 Trondheim, Norrway
Tel: +47.73-592 620
Fax: +47.73-598 285

Material properties assessed on site

	Colour	Hemispherical-hemispherical reflectances
Walls and ceiling	white	89%
Floor	bluish-colored	18%
Working desk	pine-colored	41%
	Normal-normal transmittances	Hemispherical-hemispherical transmittances
Double glazing	83%	75%

More than half the windows of the building use secondary daylight for energy conservation

Kristallen office building, Uppsala, SWEDEN

Although compact in shape, this building optimizes the collection of daylight through tilted glazing on the atrium facade.

A building with ambitious goals regarding daylighting and energy conservation

The Kristallen (the Crystal) office building in Uppsala is probably the first and only Swedish office building where daylighting analyses have been made during the design phase. Unfortunately much of the intended lighting/daylighting systems have not been realised in the building due to bankruptcy of the original building owner following the crash of the Swedish market for commercial buildings just when the building owner was starting to search for tenants.

The original idea was to create a very high quality office building that also included services for the people working in it. The quality of the indoor climate in terms of thermal and lighting conditions, as well as indoor air quality, has been designed to reflect the prestige of the building. The present tenants are mainly high-tech companies in the information technology sector, which is in accordance with the developer's original intentions.

A narrow atrium in the centre, and a large atrium with the shape of a crown

The Kristallen building has in principle a square footprint (75m^3) with a large central glazed atrium with a maximum height of 20m. However, there is a

∇ View toward the south-east corner of the atrium, showing a small part of the central building to the extreme left and the external glazed wall of the east facade on the right.

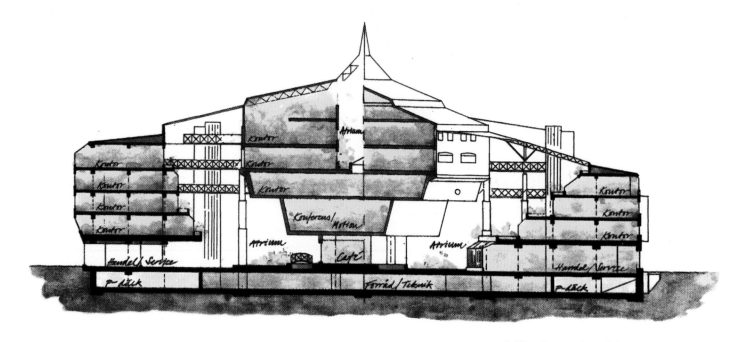

△ West-East section of the Kristallen building (original drawing by Kristensen and Nordfelt).

◁ Floor plan of the Kristallen building with daylight factors on atrium floor.

▽ Cross-section of monitored rooms, south facade, upper floors.

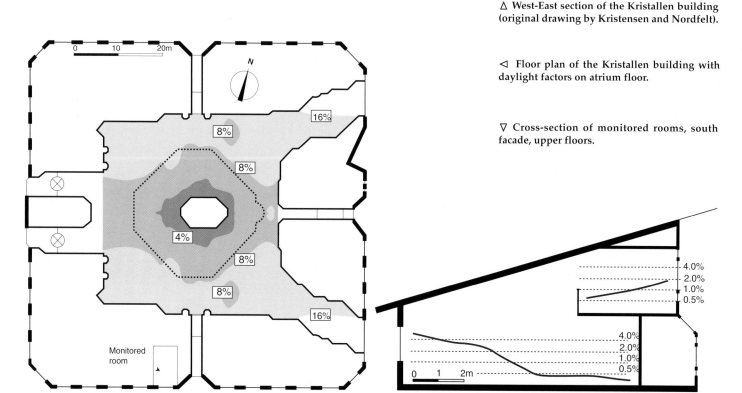

central building (maximum 27m³) in the middle of the atrium, with its own narrow atrium covered with an emerging glass cover (in the shape of a crystal).

The eastern facade of the perimeter building is opened by two large vertical 'windows' covering the whole height of this facade (four floors), located at the north and south sides of the atrium, respectively.

On the upper three floors, footbridges connect each stairwell with the central building in the atrium. The flower boxes contain many plants, e.g. hanging plants that partly cover the windows of the floor below, particularly the 45° tilted roof windows that are intended to increase the daylight penetration on the floor below. The floors of the eastern perimeter building is more stepped back from the atrium than the floors of the other buildings. This eastern part of the perimeter building was originally intended to contain a restaurant and a day care centre on the ground floor, but these areas are now general offices.

The floor width of the perimeter buildings changes from a wide two-corridor floor plan with a large dark core on the ground floor, to a narrow one-corridor floor plan on the top floor.

The very varying design of the facades towards the atrium give a lively impression together with the restful, mainly light brown (perforated maple plywood) or light grey (wood wool plates), colours of the walls as well as the large amount of plants, both on the atrium floor and the balconies. These features also give the atrium good sound absorption qualities and it is experienced as quiet even during busy lunch hours.

Atrium facades with tilted glazing to increase daylight collection. Plants cover some of the tilted glazing.▷

Atrium facades are largely glazed and tilted glazing increases daylight penetration in offices

The area of the windows towards the atrium is slightly increased from the top floor towards the ground floor to give more or less uniform daylight penetration on each floor. One special daylighting feature is the 45° tilted skylight window on the atrium facades. However, many of these windows are now covered by hanging plants. Due to fire regulations (the windows must withstand hot smoke for 30 minutes) all windows towards the atrium have a single pane of steel-wired armoured glass and are not easily openable.

Outside windows are equipped with fixed external sunshading

The windows on the outside facades are somewhat higher than typically. External solar shades are in place on all facades, except the north facade. On the top floor, the roof overhang works as a somewhat shorter solar shade. The shades are made of red-painted aluminium profiles (tilted approximatly 30°) and are therefore not totally opaque. Consequently, some light from the sky may penetrate but this is probably very limited. At the winter solstice, the max-imum solar altitude above the horizon is 6.8° at solar noon. Consequently, the angle will be even lower on the east and west facades compared with the south facade, which is the one the photo shows. At the summer solstice, the solar shading will, of course, not be total on the east and west facades, in contrast to the south facade at solar noon, because of the path of the sun.

A moderatly bright atrium

Most of the light reaching the floor of the atrium comes from the roof glazing. Its overall transmittance is reduced by the metallic structure and the fact that triple glazing is used for thermal insulation. The resulting daylight factors on the floor of the atrium are in the range of 4 to 8%. Only in the shade under the lowest part of the central building is the daylight factor between 2 to 4. The large east facing windows contribute with a high daylight factor (>16%) up to 15m from the facade.

Winter sunlight penetration generates glare

As sunshading is not provided for all spaces at all times, some glare situations can be found at work places, particularly when computer screens are used. Furthermore, unwanted reflections on VDU screens were also observed with the same cause.

Daylight monitoring

The daylight factors (0.8m above the floor) in the main atrium and the office rooms were measured on 27 April 1996 with overcast conditions and additional measurements and photos taken on clear days at the winter solstice (15 and

△ Fixed solar protection on the south facade. The photo is taken at noon (solar time) on the winter solstice.

16 December 1995), the spring equinox (16 March 1996) and the summer solstice (19 June 1996). In addition photographs were taken at occasions both before and after these monitoring visits. The monitoring team was not given access to the areas used by the tenants for security reasons, which means that the only accessible offices rooms were those used by the building owner.

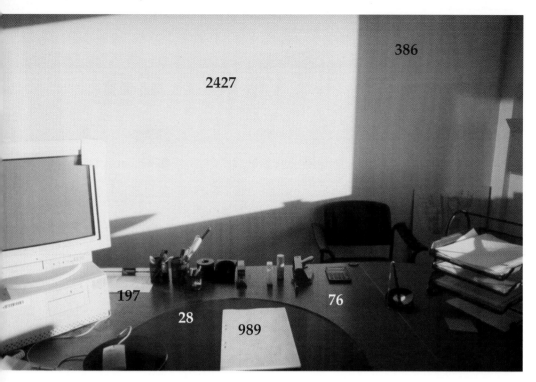

△ Solar penetration at winter solstice, (mid-day) in the monitored room, showing that luminance of the sun patch on the wall reaches three times that of the paper on the table and 10 times that of the desk surface (values in Cd/m^2).

△ Exterior view of the building (west facade) before the installation of the solar shades. Window width varies as a function of the distance to ground.

Material properties assessed on site

	Colour	Hemispherical-hemispherical reflectances
Maple plywood walls	light brown	47%
Wood wool wall panels	light grey	41%
Fire painted steel columns	white	81%
Painted walls	light yellow	90%
Stone footings	grey	36%
Polished stone floor	grey, brown decor lines	too specular
Walls in office rooms	white	87%
Ceiling in office rooms	white	87%

		Hemispherical-hemispherical transmittances
Atrium facade window	(2-glass)	79%
Atrium roof glazing	(3-glass)	70%
Windows towards atrium	(1-glass)	80%
Windows towards the outside	(2-glass)	79%

CREDITS

Building description
Constructed: January 1990 to October 1991
Floor area: 14,955m^2, mainly cellular offices in 12m to 19m wide floors around the main atrium. Distributed over seven floors, including one basement of 810m^2 with 130 parking places.

Climate
Uppsala, Sweden, Latitude: 59°87'N, Longitude: 17°60'E, Altitude: 18m.
Uppsala is located near the Swedish Baltic coast, about 65 km north of Stockholm. The climate is of the temperate north European coastal type, although more continental than the Swedish west coast climate. The monthly average temperature is around -4°C in winter and around 16°C in summer. During October to February there are on the average 15 to 21 totally cloudy days per month, whereas during the rest of the year there are on average 8 to 13 totally cloudy days per month. The clear days are maximum during March to July with an average of about 5 to 7 clear days per month. During November and December there are only about 2 clear days per month.

Client
Donald Ericsson Fastigheter KB
Uppsala, Sweden
Present owner: Kristallen Fastighets AB, a subsidiary company to Castellum AB, which is the real estate subsidiary company to the state-owned PK Banken.

Architect
Jan Nygren, Contekton Arkitekter AB
Helsingborg, Sweden

Daylighting study
Esbensen Consulting Engineers F.R.I.
Copenhagen, Denmark

Monitoring organisation
Chalmers University of Technology
Department of Building Services Engineering
The Monitoring Centre for Energy Research
S-412 96 GÖTEBORG, Sweden

Acknowledgements
National funding for the monitoring from the Department of Energy Efficiency (DOEE) at the Swedish National Administration of Technical and Industrial Development (NUTEK) and from the Swedish Council for Building Research (BFR) is gratefully acknowledged.

References
Kristensen, P.E. and G. Nordfelt. 1990. *Årsta - Kristallen in Uppsala*. Nordic Energy and Environment Seminar, Danish Technical University, Lyngby. 27 to 28 August 1990. 5 pages. (in Danish).
Diös & Esbensen. 1992. *Kristallen - An Atrium Building with Utilization of Natural Daylight. Design Study*. Diös Properties AB, Uppsala and Esbensen Consulting Engineers, Copenhagen. October 1992, Uppsala, Sweden. 39 pages. (available from ByggDok, Stockholm, #900104-3).
Kristallen - A Living Environment. Ljuskultur 2:1991, pp 24-28. Ljuskultur förlag, Stockholm, Sweden. (in Swedish).
Green, L. 1991. *Refined Play with the Light in Uppsala*. ERA 6-7:1991, pp 40-41. Elektricitetens Rationella Användning, Stockholm, Sweden (in Swedish).

Prismatic external panels in double skin can be tilted to deflect sunbeams to desired angle

CNA - SUVA Building, Basle, SWITZERLAND

This building has been retrofitted with a new double skin using original light deviating systems.

A double skin facade designed for energy savings and natural ventilation control

This building is located in a urban area of Basle. In 1993, it was retrofitted for office spaces and extended to provide appartments. The designers selected a double skin system for facade renovation.

This double skin can reduce heat losses in winter and filter heat gains in summer, through optical control of sunlight and natural evacuation of hot air through the double skin.

▷ The tilting glazing panels of the double skin, and, above the prismatic element, north-east facade.

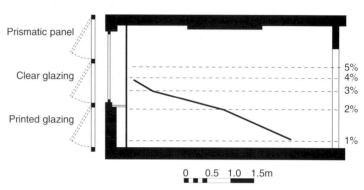

Construction detail of the double skin. △

△ Daylight factors on the work plane as a function of the distance to the center of the facade.

Principle of the prismatic panel allowing deviation of transmitted light (Doc. Siemens). ▽

▽ Daylight factor distribution on the work plane.

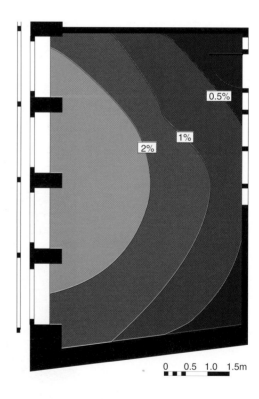

The double skin uses three types of glazing assemblies

At each floor level the double-skin facade consists of three horizontal arrays of glazing, constiting of glazing panels of 1.70 metre in width and 1 metre in height. Each of them can be opened remotely and individually. The glazing panel tilts forward, when hinging arround the top edge of the panel.

The upper panel is made of insulating glass with integrated prismatic panels which is automatically adjusted as a function of the angular altitude of the sun. It can reflect sunlight toward the outside, and admit some skylight into the room.

The glazing band at window level is made of clear insulating glass and is manually controlled by the user during daytime. The third glazing array is designed to perform as a passive solar system. It is automatically controlled to stay closed when solar gains and thermal insulation are desired, and opened when heat needs to be expelled.

Reasonably unobtrusive presence of prismatic panels

From the interior, the prismatic panels in the upper part of the facade appear rather bright. In overcast conditions, the luminance of the prismatic component is typically twice as high as that of the sky, and 50 to 100 times higher than the luminance of indoor finishes.

Behaviour of the double skin under sunlight. ◁

Indoor view of the office space. ▷

The prismatic panels totally block the vision to the outside, and appear a little bit like bright, thin venetian blinds. The horizontal lines are spaced every 15mm.

Reduction of daylight penetration compensated for by a better sunlight protection

Daylight factor values on the work plane appear rather low, with values below 1% achieved about three meters away from the facade. This is due to the small area of the glazing of the first skin: 2.59m² for 30.45m² of floor (8%). The double skin also partly diminishes the penetration of daylight, due to the additional framing.

Daylighting monitoring

The monitoring was conducted on 21 January 1997 under overcast conditions. The monitored room is located on the 3rd floor (south-west backyard facade). The room dimensions are 4.35m x 7m x 2.57m, and the facade faces south-west.

CNA - SUVA BUILDING

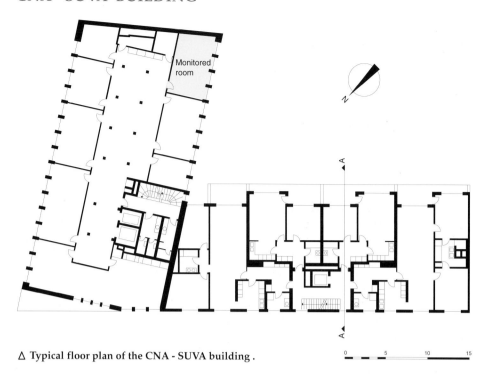

△ Typical floor plan of the CNA - SUVA building .

△ The windows and the prismatic panels seen from outside, north-east facade.

Material properties assessed on site

	Colour	Hemispherical-hemispherical reflectances
Wall		75%
Ceiling		65%
Floor		12%
Working table		65%

	Normal-normal transmittance	Hemispherical-hemispherical transmittance
Prismatic	—	72%
Clear glass	86%	68%

CREDITS

Building description
Area 3,150m², in six floors and one basement of 450m² each.
It houses for 90 people.
It was refurbished in 1993.

Climate
Latitude: 47°56'N, Longitude: 7°59'E,
Altitude: 270m.

Client
CNA SUVA
St Jakobstrasse 24,
CH-4002 Basle

Architect
Herzog and De Meuron
Rheinschanze 6
CH-4056 Basle
Tel.: +41.61-322 5737
Fax: +41.61-322 4515

Facade engineering
SCHMIDLIN AG
CH-4147 Aech/Basle
Tel.: +41.61-799 9111
Fax: +41.61-751 3688

Electrical engineers
SELMONI AG
CH-4006 Basle
Tel.: +41.61-287 4420
Fax: +41.61-287 4434

HVAC engineers
WALDHAUSER HAUSTECHNIK
CH-4142 Münchenstein
Tel.: +41.61-411 5100
Fax: +41.61-411 5233

Bauphysik
GYSIN & EHRSAM AG
Pratteln

Prismatic elements
Siemens AG
Lighting Systems Division
Ohmstraβe 50, D-8225 Traunreut.

Monitoring organisation
SIMOS LIGHTING CONSULTANTS
15, place du Temple
CH-1227 Carouge
Tel.: +41.22-343 5281
Fax: +41.22-343 5880

EPFL/LESO
CH-1015 Ecublens
Tel.: +41.21-693 4545
Fax: +41.21-693 2722

Photos by S. Simos

South-facing clerestory brings sunlight into atrium on winter days

Gothenburg Law Courts Annex, Gothenburg, SWEDEN

This design by architect E. Gunnar Asplund in 1937 shows a very advanced approach to daylighting. The partition-free space combines daylight from facades and a clerestory.

▽ Daylight penetration from the clerestory above the atrium. Most of the daylight falls on the two balconies on the north side of the atrium.

A modern design from the 1930s

The Gothenburg Law Court Annex, des-igned by the architect Gunnar Asplund in 1934 to 37, is a functional extension of the old Town Hall of Gothenburg. Generally controversial when new, today this is an often inter-nationally quoted example of first-rate extension design. The Great Hall, which rises through the three stories of the Annex and the courtrooms on the first floor, are among the best examples of room form and design produced by Asplund in the tradition of Swedish functionalism.

The Annex is concentrated around the rounded forms of the Great Hall, in which the first and second floor cantile-vered balconies seem to float, partic-ularly in the evening when the lighting from below (by an early version of track lighting) is particularly bright. All vertical surfaces are covered with Oregon pine, the floors with oak par-quet, and the ceilings are painted white. The southern part of the first floor contains four courtrooms and a waiting area for witnesses. The second floor and the attic floor contain offices, and originally the ground floor also contained offices, but these were later changed to courtrooms.

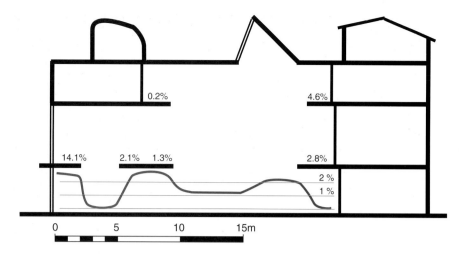

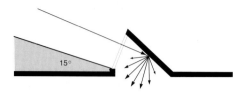

▽ Optical principle of the clerestory above the atrium (15° is angle of obstruction).

◁ Section through the Gothenburg Law Courts Annex showing daylight factors along a N to S line under the middle of the stairs.

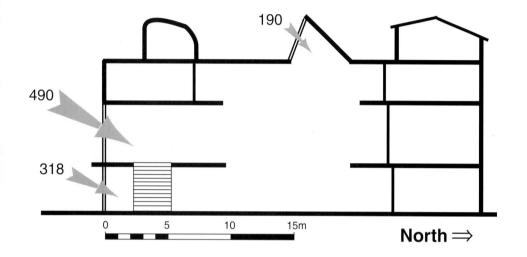

North ⇒

◁ Section through the Gothenburg Law Courts Annex showing luminous flows (in klm, for 10 klux external luminance) entering the Great Hall through the clerestory windows and through the south-facing windows at the ground floor and at the first floor facing the courtyard.

▽ Daylight factor distribution on the floor of the Gothenburg Law Courts Annex.

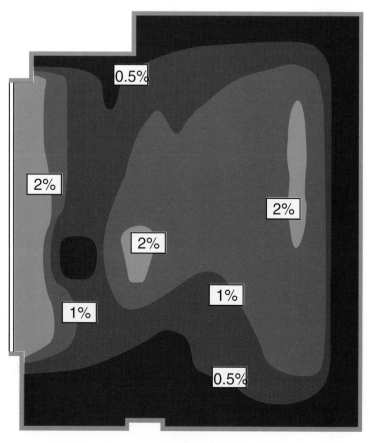

Facade window and roof clerestory bring complementary daylight into a large volume free of partitions

The south facade of the ground and first floors is more-or-less fully glazed with three-pane windows. However, the windows at the ground floor have a limited view of the sky, mainly because this facade faces the old courtyard and thus the old building 20 metres away, but also due to the rather narrow balcony on the first floor. The outdoor obstruction angle is approximately 30°. For the windows on the first floor, the obstruction angle is approximately 20° which means that the floor of the witnesses waiting area between the windows and the open part of the Great Hall offers a view of the sky. The courtyard is covered with a rather light coloured stone and the walls of the surrounding buildings are a whiteish yellow.

A south-facing clerestory provides top-lighting to the Great Hall of the Annex.

△ The stair and the first-floor balcony from near the north-east corner of the ground floor of the Great Hall looking towards the south-facing windows.

The south-facing windows of the clerestory are tilted to a 75° angle and the light is redirected and diffused by the north facing ceiling of the clerestory, inclined at 40°, and by the structural beams in the clerestory opening. The windows of the clerestory have three panes with the inner pane of wired cast glass and were at the time of measurements rather dirty. The roof of the attic floor south of the clerestory gives a 15° horizon screening. The daylight through the clerestory is further reduced by the low reflectance of the black roofing material in front of the windows.

The daylighting systems achieve high luminous uniformity and allow a large amount of sunlight penetration during winter days

The light in the Great Hall is experienced as far more uniform than the daylight factor curves imply. The electrical lighting fixtures serve more to emphasise the shape of the room, particularly through indirect lighting of walls and ceilings, than to provide any great amount of extra luminance. The

waiting area on the first floor between the windows and the opening is well daylit, and witnesses can comfortably read books and papers while waiting to be called into court.

The large horizon screening (20° to 40°) of the south-facing windows by the old building opposite the courtyard provides good protection against direct glare during sunny winter days as the sun rises to a maximum of 9° to 32° above the horizon between the autumn and spring equinoxes in Gothenburg.

The area of the first floor facing the windows is very well daylit and the daylight factor remains above 1% even close to the open balcony railing. The area of the ground floor between the stair and the windows is also well daylit, despite the fact that the windows have a rather limited view of the sky. The large stairwell gives a substantial increase in daylighting on the ground floor north of the stairs.

The tilted clerestory combines direct daylighting and daylighting from reflections on diffusing surfaces

The clerestory windows gives a rather local increase in the daylighting on the ground floor of the Great Hall. The daylight factor is above 2% for a small area directly under the clerestory. This is due to the fact that the reflectance of the atrium walls is rather low. However, the clerestory contributes to good daylighting of the north balconies on the first and second floors. This atrium cannot be considered as a light box distributing daylight to other spaces. It is more a daylit space of its own, with reasonable amounts of daylight to facilitate circulation, meeting and waiting.

It is interesting to note that the area of the clerestory window is 58.7m^2, which is 11% of the atrium floor area. Clearly the architect feared excessive heat losses as well as solar heat gains in summer through windows and selected a moderate glazed area. Hence the rather low daylight factor values on the atrium floor.

△ Facade of the Gothenburg Law Courts Annex facing the old courtyard.

Lack of controls limits potential for energy savings

Large south-facing windows and south-facing clerestories could lead to savings in heating energy requirements if night insulation was employed. Since the building is rather old, no automatic lighting controls which respond to natural light were planned. Therefore, it cannot be said that the Gothenburg Law Courts Annex saves large amounts of lighting electricity through daylighting.

Daylight monitoring

The performance of the daylighting features was assessed mainly on the ground floor of the Great Hall and the part of the first floor close to the south-facing windows. In addition, the daylighting factors were measured on the balconies of the first and second floors in the Great Hall. The measurements were carried out in October 1995.

CREDITS

Building
The Gothenburg Law Courts Annex was designed by the Swedish architect E. Gunnar Asplund during 1935 to 1937. The Annex makes up the northern part of the Town Hall of Gothenburg. The east, main building and the south wing are from 1672; in 1817 a third floor was added and the facade remodelled to the present classical style; in 1835 a north wing was built. The courtyard was created by the erection of a west wing in 1869. The old north wing was demolished when the Annex was built in 1935 to 1937.
Area roof windows: 58.7m²
Area entire atrium floor: 548m²
Area opening in the lower balcony: 198m²

Climate
Gothenburg is located at the Skagerrak on the west coast of Sweden, with a temperate north European coastal climate. The monthly average temperature is around -1°C in winter and around 17°C in summer. During October to February, there are on average 15 to 20 totally cloudy days per month whereas during the rest of the year there are on average 10 to 15 totally cloudy days per month. The clear days are at a maximum from March to May with an average of about seven clear days per month. During November and December there are only about two clear days per month.

Architect
E. Gunnar Asplund (1885 to 1940)

Building owner
KIGAB - Kulturfastigheter i Göteborg AB
P.O. Box 5104
S-402 23 GOTHENBURG, Sweden

Monitoring organisation
Chalmers University of Technology
Department of Building Services Engineering and
The Monitoring Centre for Energy Research
S-412 96 GOTHENBURG, Sweden.

References
Wrede, S. 1980. 'The Architecture of Erik Gunnar Asplund - A Book'. The MIT Press, Cambridge, Massachusetts, and London, England. ISBN 0-262-23095-X.

Caldenby, C & O. Hultin (Editors) 1985. 'Asplund - A Book'. Arkitektur Förlag, Stockholm, Sweden.

Acknowledgements
National funding for the monitoring from the Department of Energy Efficiency (DOEE) at the Swedish National Administration of Technical and Industrial Development (NUTEK) and from the Swedish Council for Building Research (BFR) is gratefully acknowledged.

Material properties assessed on site

	Hemispherical-hemispherical reflectances
Wood wall panels in atrium	32%
Stone bottom floor atrium	38%
Wood floor (1st floor)	23%
White paint walls 2nd floor and roof	84%

	Normal-normal transmittance
Roof windows (3 glass)	58%
Other windows (2 glass)	72%

Fixed awnings and movable blinds for low maintenance

LNEC Main Building, Lisbon, PORTUGAL

Fixed external awnings are moved twice yearly according to the season, but occupants can manually control indoor venetian blinds.

An example of Portuguese Modernist architecture

LNEC is a public institution devoted to research in civil engineering. It occupies a large campus in the northern part of Lisbon, close to the airport, in a dense urban environment. The campus consists of several buildings of different types of architecture and ages.

The LNEC main building was built in 1950 and is one of the most representative examples of the extension of Portuguese Modernism: long symmetric facade, high doors and ceilings, etc.

P. Pardal Monteiro, the architect, was one of the most important architects of

the Portuguese Modernist Architecture. His work, mainly in the region of Lisbon, and dating from the second quarter of this century, was generally formal and essentially devoted to large public buildings. Although his work had not always been appreciated (he used to be considered an architect of the regime), nowadays there is a tendency to regard his work in a different and more positive light.

The building has three storeys, and consists of rooms facing south (main facade), rooms facing north, and central corridors. There are also west- and east-facing wings. Obstructions in front of the south facade are minor.

▽ **Eight of the 72 tilted yellow awnings on the south facade. They are used during the summer season and removed in winter. Internal, manually controlled blinds, provide the necessary solar control.**

LNEC MAIN BUILDING

▷ Daylight factor distribution in a cross-section of the building. The daylight factor was measured in four different situations: with shading devices OFF, with awnings ON; with internal venetian blinds ON (slats at 0°) and with internal venetian blinds ON (slats at 45°). The figure also shows flux penetration under standard overcast sky conditions, corresponding to a horizontal external illuminance of 10,000 lux.

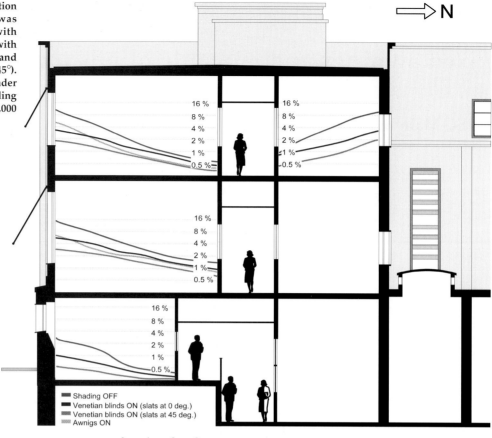

▷ Distribution of daylight factors in two south-facing rooms and three north-facing rooms, with no awnings or venetian blinds. Vertical daylight factors were measured in the centre of each room.

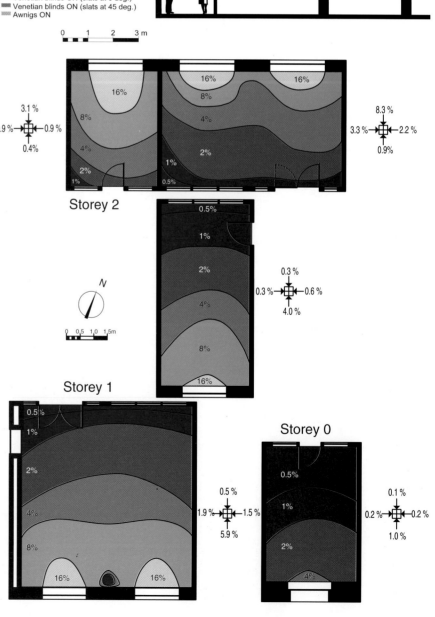

A main facade oriented south, with external awnings moved twice a year

LNEC Main Building has traditional daylighting solutions, with high vertical windows in the south facade, and horizontal ones in the north facade. The building has been retrofitted recently. The retrofitting included the installation of yellow external awnings on the South facade, which can be put in a tilted position with respect to the plane of the facade. This was aimed at reducing solar penetration. Indoor wall surfaces were painted with light-coloured finishes and lighting fixtures were replaced with more efficient ones. The awnings are manually operated by LNEC's maintenance division twice a year: they are retracted at the beginning of the cold season, and deployed at the end of that season. The attenuation of diffuse skylight of the awnings is about 70% (hemispherical-hemispherical transmittance equal to 18%).

Complementary indoor manually controlled venetian blinds

Occupants can control their daylight conditions by manipulation of internal venetian blinds. Such control helps in preventing sunlight penetration when sunbeams can penetrate from the open spaces on the sides of the external awnings. On overcast days, they provide an additional attenuation of daylight penetration (about 40% when the slats are tilted at 45°).

△ North-facing windows are not equipped with external awnings.

▷ Luminance distribution around the computer screen with reflection of daylight from the unshaded window. The luminances shown were readjusted for a standard overcast sky leading to a horizontal illuminance of 10,000 lux.

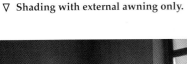

▽ Shading with external awning only.

▽ Additional attenuation with indoor venetian blinds.

Daylight monitoring

The daylight monitoring of the LNEC Main Building was performed between December 1996 and January 1997 (overcast sky conditions) and between June and July 1996 (clear sky conditions). The measurements were made in three rooms on the third floor, one room on the second floor and one room on the first floor.

Outdoor illuminance levels varied from 5 klux to 20 klux (overcast sky measurements) and typically above 100 klux under clear sky. The outdoor illuminance meter was placed on the roof of the building (near the Daylight Measurement Station existing in LNEC) with no relevant obstructions.

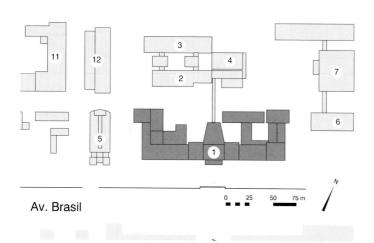

Av. Brasil

△ Site plan of LNEC campus including the Main Building (1).

◁ General view of the south facade with the 72 awnings.

Material properties assessed on site

	Colour	Hemispherical-hemispherical reflectances
Walls	white	85%
Walls	light-grey	75%
Walls (circulation areas)	medium light-grey	67%
Ceilings	white	87%
Wooden floors	dark wooden-coloured	21%
Window frames	dark olive-green	20%
Window marble sills	dark-grey	19%
Working desks	light grey	48%
Working desks	dark wooden-coloured	9%
Drawing desks	light wooden-coloured	31%
Drawing desks	light green	37%

(drawing office 2nd storey east)

	Hemispherical-hemispherical transmittance	Normal-normal transmittance
Single glazing (windows)	81%	88%
Yellow awnings	55%	
Glass tiles (dome)	70%	80%

CREDITS

Building
Total gross floor area: 7,000m²
Year built: 1950

Climate
The LNEC Main Building is located in LNEC's Campus in the north part of Lisbon. Latitude: 38°46'N, Longitude: 09°08'W, Altitude: 100m. The average temperature in January is 10.5°C and in July 22.6°C. The average maximum temperature in January is 13.9°C and in July 22.6°C. The average minimum temperature in January is 7.0°C and in July 17.4°C.

The average cloud amount (in tenths) is six in January and three in July. The average sunshine duration is 143.1 hours in January (48%) and 321.3 hours in July (72%). The average relative humidity in January is 79% and 62% in July. The average total precipitation is 95.3 mm in January and 5.5mm in July.
(Source: Portuguese Institute of Meteorology: Data for Lisbon, Climatic Normals 1961 -1990)

Architect
Porfírio Pardal Monteiro

Building owner
Laboratório Nacional de Engenharia Civil (National Laboratory of Civil Engineering)
Av. do Brasil, 101
1799 Lisboa Codex - Portugal

Monitoring organisation
LNEC - Laboratório Nacional de Engenharia Civil
Av. Brasil, 101
1799 Lisboa Codex, Portugal
Tel: +351.1-848 2131
Fax: +351.1-840 1581

References
"Daylight Monitoring of The LNEC Main Building", Lisbon, LNEC, 1997.

"Guia da Arquitectura de Lisboa". 1994. Ed. Assoc. Arquitectos e Lisboa, Capital Europeia da Cultura, Lisboa, 1994. Architectural Guide of Lisbon.1994 Ed. The Architects Assoc. and Lisbon European Cultural Capital, Lisbon, 1994. (In Portuguese and English)

The monitoring organisation wish to acknowledge the following for their contribution:
The Director of LNEC, Prof E R de Arantes e Oliveira, for the authorization of the monitoring of the building.

The Heads of the Building and Structures Departments of LNEC for allowing monitoring in their departments.

Open-plan offices with daylighting from four sides

Irish Energy Centre, Dublin, IRELAND

The form of the Irish Energy Centre offices maximizes daylighting for occupants through various features: borrowed light from a glazed atrium and daylighting from all walls.

The Irish Energy Centre on the north side of Dublin is surrounded by about twenty buildings of various ages, sizes and shapes

The site is a former carpark in the centre of the Forbairt campus bounded to the east by an established route between Administration and the Canteen (two of the largest existing buildings), to the south by a work yard, and a green space to the north.

The building provides office accommodation for thirty people together with exhibition space and ancillary spaces in a total area of approximately 410m². The accommodation is arranged on two floors.

Innovative use of standard construction materials and technologies was a design objective

The intention was to create a building which was architecturally responsive to climate, context and function, while using proven energy-efficient strategies to satisfy heating, lighting and ventilation requirements, thus placing minimal demand on non-renewable energy sources.

The narrow, elongated plan allows for light on all four sides of open plan offices

Four open-plan offices are grouped around a small double-height atrium space which is used for entrance, exhibition and meeting areas, and

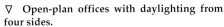
▽ **Open-plan offices with daylighting from four sides.**

Entrance space is a double-height atrium △
with south-facing roof glazing.

△ Exterior showing courtyard with white,
reflective gravel.

View of atrium showing north-facing window. ▽

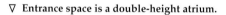

▽ Entrance space is a double-height atrium.

contributes to the natural lighting and the ventilation of the adjoining office areas. The overall transmittance of the atrium roof is 76%.

Cellular accommodation, vertical circulation and services are organised along a corridor attached to the open plan office areas. The plan size of this flat-roofed services block is smaller than that of the offices and thus all of the open-plan offices have windows on four sides which results in optimum daylight and views for all of the occupants. Daylight distribution in the space is relatively uniform except for two areas where daylight is obstructed by external objects (extended gable wall to comply with five regulations and entrance lobby in atrium). The slightly smaller office on the opposite side of atrium is not affected in this way and has even daylight distribution.

The open-plan office areas look onto small planted courtyards at the east and west ends of the building. The ground surface is of light-coloured gravel for maximum reflectance.

The atrium is a 'light box' distributing daylight to other spaces

The section of the building is used to bring light deep into the building through the atrium roof glazing which in turn is "borrowed" by the adjoining offices and circulation corridor.

Each open plan office has an area of $60m^2$, and is lit by three windows of $2.7m^2$ each, plus windows in the gable wall of $8m^2$ and in the atrium timber screen of $6m^2$.

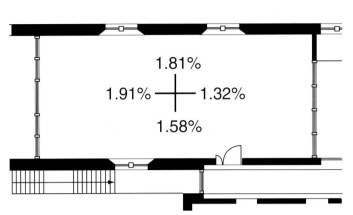

△ Vertical daylight factors at eye level in four directions.

△ North-facing workstation on first floor.

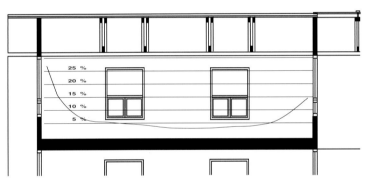

△ Daylight factors across the space along a east-west axis.

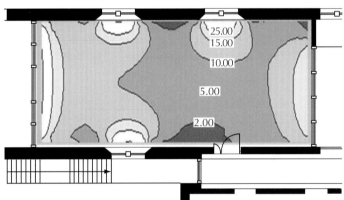

△ Daylight factor distributions on work plane.

Window design and light coloured finishes allow high illuminance levels

Irish-fabricated, Scandinavian timber-framed argon-filled double-glazed windows with low-emissivity coating were specified. The design, with large fixed glazing at high level, maximizes daylight penetration with smaller opening sections at occupant level for ventilation. The masonry window reveals are splayed to increase natural light and reduce glare. White painted surfaces reflect the light within the open-plan offices. Highly reflectant wall surfaces together with the glazed areas lead to daylight factors on the work plane in the first floor office varying typically from 5% to 10%.

Adjustable shading provides protection against glare

Metallic venetian blinds provide protection against the immediate effects of sunlight and glare. It is estimated that reflective blinds reduce incoming light fluxes by a factor of 6 compared with normal internal blinds.

Natural shade from summer sunshine

Deciduous trees have been planted in the courtyards which will in future screen the sun in summer and filter light in winter in order to reduce glare and heat gain.

In addition to the use of daylight, presence and light level detectors assist with energy savings

Detectors are provided throughout the building to control the electric lighting system. On detecting movement in space and when illuminance from daylight is judged insufficient the lights are turned on automatically. When the sensors detect that the space is no longer occupied, the lights are turned off. Daylight sensors prompt switching or dimming of artificial lighting in response to daylight levels. When illuminance lev-

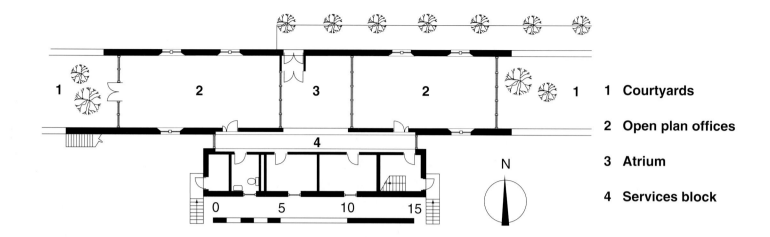

1 Courtyards

2 Open plan offices

3 Atrium

4 Services block

els fall below 300 lux, the artificial light comes on automatically. Task lighting is controlled manually by the occupant. Energy-efficient lamps and luminaires are used throughout and all fluorescent lights are high frequency.

The occupant of each workspace can control his or her own environment

A critical factor in the design was that the occupant of each workspace should be able to control his or her own environment: each has opening windows for ventilation and view; thermostatically controlled radiators; and task lighting. The workspaces are defined by movable screens, each 1.5m high, which provide visual and acoustic privacy when seated, but do not block light from the windows which are 2.6m high.

Daylight monitoring

Daylight monitoring was carried out on the first floor open plan office and atrium on 13 August 1996 under overcast conditions.

CREDITS

Building
The total floor area is 410m², for a working population of 30 people.
It was built in 1995 to 1996.

Climate
(Latitude: 53°20′N, Longitude: 6°15′W)
Dublin has a temperature coastal climate with mean daily tempetature of 4.5° in January and 15.1° in July. Annual mean daily solar radiation is 2.52 kWh/m² (typically 4.66 in June and 0.46 in December). Air pollution levels are low.

Architects
Energy Research Group,
University College Dublin

Client
Irish Energy Centre,
Glasnevin,
Dublin 9

Monitoring organisation
Energy Research Group, UCD,
School of Architecture, Richview,
Clonskeagh Drive, Dublin 14

▽ **Section along an east-west axis.**

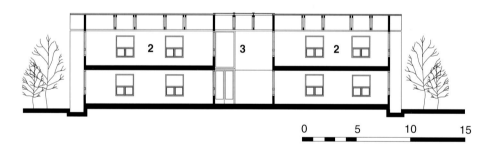

Material properties assessed on site

Opaque surfaces	Colour	Reflectances
Walls	white	81%
Ceiling	white	81%
Floor	grey	39%
Bench top	timber	18%
Atrium walls	white	81%

Glazing	Hemispherical-hemispherical transmittance	Direct-direct transmittance
Double glazing	-	78%

Classrooms are best lit from the left side, due to the large majority of right-handed students, but any supply of light from the other side will benefit the students located away from the facade window, by increasing the minimum daylight factor from a value which may be as low as 0.25% to more than 1%. The result is a more uniformly lit space, with fewer veiling reflections on the blackboard. This also facilitates the control of artificial light in response to daylight penetration. Moveable shading devices are important, particularly in the vicinity of the blackboard, to reduce disturbing reflections. Shading devices with transmittance values as low as 5% may have to be chosen if slide projectors or video displays are often used. Specific artificial lighting on the blackboard may, however, still be necessary during daylight hours to facilitate students located at the back of the room.

Glazed streets 450 metres long bring daylight deep into a university building

Dragvoll University Center, Trondheim, NORWAY

Glazed street forms are the spinal column of the building, providing communication, daylight and amenity to the users.

Almost 50,000m² of floor area in a severe climate

The Dragvoll University Centre comprises the campus for the humanities and the social sciences faculties of the Norwegian University of Science and Technology (NTNU) in Trondheim. The architectural concept of the centre is based on the winning design by the Danish architect Henning Larsen in a Nordic competition conducted in 1968 to 1969.

The site is an open stretch of farmland on the outskirts of the city, on a plateau in the hills to the southeast. The site is quite open, with only minimal, distant obstructions to the south.

The university centre consists of a complex of offices and classrooms/auditoria buildings, connected by glazed streets, based on a 100m² orthogonal network, much like the regular city matrix in Trondheim. The current centre was built in two stages, 24,900m² completed in 1978 and 20,800m² completed in 1993.

Most of the building has five stories, two being below the glazed street and used for services and circulation areas, and three adjacent to the glazed streets. The glazed streets are 8.4m wide, and

▽ View of one of the glazed streets.

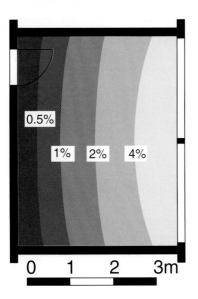

◁ Daylight factors distribution on the work plane of an office on the second floor.

0.5%
1% 2% 4%

0 1 2 3m

▽ Cross section of the Dragvoll building (original drawing by architect Henning Larsen).

▷ Daylight factors distribution on the work plane of a seminar room on the first floor.

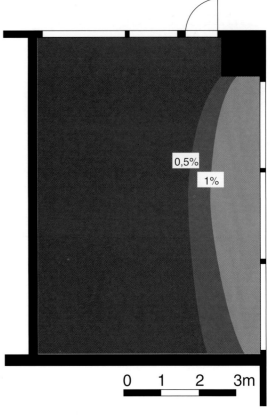

0,5%
1%

0 1 2 3m

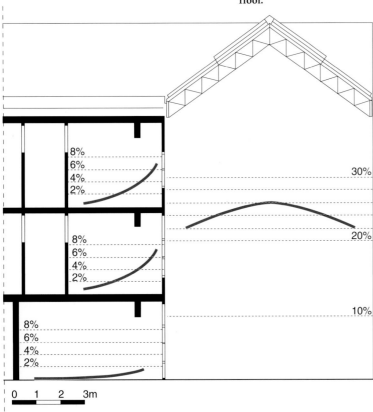

8%
6%
4%
2%

30%

8%
6%
4%
2%

20%

10%

8%
6%
4%
2%

0 1 2 3m

Directions	Daylight factor [%]
east (window)	4.2
north (VDT-screen)	0.3
north (bookshelf)	1.5
west (bookshelf)	0.8
on VDT-screen	0.7

△ Vertical daylight factors at eye level (A) in four directions in the second floor office.

▽ Vertical daylight factors at eye level (B) in four directions. Measurement taken in the centre of the Seminar room.

Directions	Daylight factor [%]
south (teacher)	0.3
east (windows)	0.5
north (door)	0.1
west (wall)	0.1

the height below the top of the glazed roof is 12m. The campus blocks are penetrated by large open courtyards that provide daylight in addition to the glazed streets.

The streets themselves are used mainly for circulation and rest areas for students between lectures. Elevators, stairways, and footbridges provide communication between floors and buildings. Service functions - lobby, bookstore, bank, market etc. - and auditoria are located on the ground floor of the streets, while offices, meeting and seminar rooms etc are found mainly on the upper two floors.

The buildings surrounding the streets are laid out with a central spine corridor, leaving half of the rooms with daylight from the glazed streets only. The other half are oriented towards courtyards or the perimeter of the campus complex.

Window areas are larger where daylight is less abundant

The building blocks along the glazed streets are three stories high. The window area is smallest on the top floor, increasing towards the ground floor. This scheme leaves room for opaque white-painted areas on the upper parts of the facades that improve the daylighting by reflection to rooms at the lower floors and to the street itself. Based on the measurement of daylight factors behind the windows used for secondary daylighting, the amount of light was assessed for a reference overcast sky (equivalent to horizontal outdoor horizontal illuminance of 10,000 lux).

▷ Classroom windows facing a glazed street with and without awnings.

The windows facing the bottom (ground) floor are thus totally glazed, necessary glazing bars giving only a 10% obstruction. The upper part of the windows on the second floor have rough-cast semi-diffusing glass, all other windows have clear glazing, double glazed except for some rooms with sound invitation requirements which are triple glazed. The external windows and the street overhead glaz-

ing have double sealed glazing in phase one. In the second building phase, a low-e coating was incorporated.

Good daylight penetration in offices located on the second floor

Daylight factors on the work plane of offices on the second floor were found to vary from more than 4% near the window to about 0.5% about 4 metres away. Such values are comparable to the

ones obtained with facades directly connected to the outdoor. Assessment of vertical daylight factors in the centre of the office show a ratio of about ten between the illuminance facing the window and the illuminance away from window. This is typical for standard spaces with windows on facades and limited obstructions outside. It suggests that the light reflection on the walls of the glazed street is significant.

△ Exterior view.

▽ Seminar room, First floor.

Material properties assessed on site

	Colour	Hemispherical-hemispherical reflectances
Marble tile (wall)	marble	53%
Brick (wall)	tile colour	20%
Concrete pillar	grey	36%
Grille on concrete pillar	dark brown/black	11%
Acoustic panel (wall)	white	81%
Brick tile (floor)	red	14%
Brick tile (floor)	yellow/brown	26%

CREDITS

Building description
The whole building consists of 46,000m² of teaching rooms, auditoria, office facilities, glazed streets, and service functions for a staff of around 3,800 students and 400 employees. Completed in 1993.

Climate
Latitude: 63°5′N, Longitude: 11°0′E
Hours of sunshine: 1352 h/a
Typical day duration in December: 4:30h and June: 20h

Client
NTNU
Norwegian University of Science and Thecnology, Trondheim
Address: NTNU, N-7034 Trondheim, Norway
Tel: +47.73-595 000
Fax: +47.73-598 090

Architect
1. stage:
Henning Larsen, Denmark
2. stage:
KS Per Knutsen Architectoffice AS with Siv. arch. Per Fossen.
Address: Fjordgt. 7. N-707010 Trondheim, Norway.
Tel: +47.73-529 130
Fax: +47.73-529 638

Daylight consultant
Øyvind Aschehoug. Professor at Dept. of Building Technology.

Monitoring organisation
Professor Øyvind Aschehoug and
Siv. arch. Dr.ing. student Barbara Matusiak
Dept. of Building Technology, Faculty of Architecture, Planning and Fine Art. Norwegian University of Science and Technology
Address: N-7034 Trondheim, Norway
Tel: +47.73-595 040
Fax: +47.73-595 045

M. Sc Heidi Arnesen and
Siv. arch. Dr.ing Anne Gunnarshaug Lien at SINTEF Civil and Environmental Engineering, Architecture and Building Technology.
Address: N-7034 Trondheim, Norway
Tel: +47.73-592 620
Fax: +47.73-598 285

Filtering sunlight: a challenge for daylighting design in southern Europe

Pharmacy Faculty, West Wing, Universidade Técnica, Lisbon, PORTUGAL

This building shows how a strong reduction of daylight penetration with sunshading techniques can be compensated for by bright indoor finishes, an excellent design option for sunny climates.

▽ One of the two central atria daylit with glass tile blocks, moderating sunlight penetration, and leading to reasonable daylight levels.

Classrooms and office spaces are organized around a central atrium
The Pharmacy Faculty is located in the northern part of Lisbon in a university campus which also includes several other faculties, schools, research institutes and the university sports centre complex.

The Pharmacy Faculty complex includes several buildings. The West Wing which is presented here, was finished in 1995 and its occupancy started in mid 1997. It shape is almost rectangular and its main facades are oriented toward east and west. To the west and north trees create some obstructions, but they also provide useful shading in summer-

time. In front of the east facade, the Central Wing also creates some obstruction. The building has four storeys. Storey 0 is a car parking area. Storey 1 includes technical, maintenance and storage areas as well as the Janitor's house. Storey 2 (main entrance level) includes spaces for administration, general services and offices for the teaching staff. Storey 3 includes classrooms, two amphitheatres (each with capacity for 100 people) and offices for the teaching staff. Central corridors throughout storeys 2 and 3 give access to the classrooms and offices. There is a total of 60 classrooms in storeys 2 and 3. The maximum number of occupants in the West Wing is about 550.

◁ Indoor view of the facade elements, composed of four windows each. The glazing ratio of the facade is equal to 28%.

△ Outdoor view of the facade. Shading is partly provided by the thickness of the masonary walls (about 0.50m). Only the largest window is equipped with an exterior venetian blind.

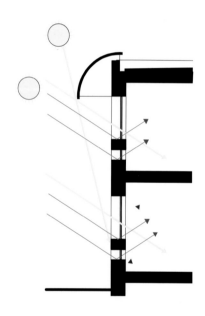

◁ Detail of the facade wall design, showing overghang above the upper floor, and thickness of masonry wall, providing additional shading, as well as sunlight reflections.

Repetitive facade elements composed of four windows

Facade windows are split into four parts, creating an interesting and repetitive architectural pattern. The glazing on the windows is recessed inwards in relation to the wall structure, which acts both as overhang and vertical fins, providing additional shading. Windows are made of single glazing. External venetian blinds are used to deviate direct sunlight and provide shading. Internal surfaces are white coloured and compensate for the strong attenuation of daylight through the facade. On the top floor of both east and west facades two long rounded overhangs provide additional shading. However, the shading effect is limited due to the orientation of the facades. The glazing to floor ratio is 19% for the offices and 13% for the classrooms. The building transparency co-efficient (facade glazing area/facade surface area) is 28% for the west facade and 26% for the east facade. The largest windows of the facade elements are equipped with exterior blinds with orientable horizontal slats (80mm wide made of white-coated aluminium). The blinds can be moved up and down, and the slats oriented by occupants from the inside.

Hundreds of small apertures distributed over two vaults

The circulation areas inside the building are daylit by sets of small rooflight apertures distributed over two domes. They consist of glass tile blocks (0.20m x 0.20m x 0.08m). The largest dome has 126, and the smallest 70. They provide enough daylight in the circulation areas (daylight factors 1.70m above floor were found to vary between 0.5 and 1%), but not enough to provide any secondary daylighting. They also generate spectacular lighting effects under sunny conditions.

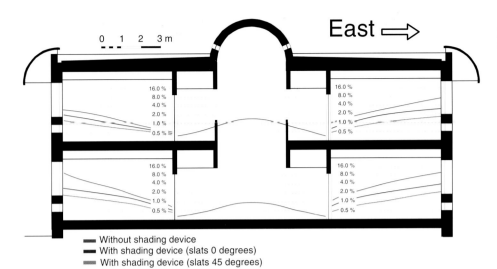

0 1 2 3 m

East ⇒

16.0 %
8.0 %
4.0 %
2.0 %
1.0 %
0.5 %

16.0 %
8.0 %
4.0 %
2.0 %
1.0 %
0.5 %

16.0 %
8.0 %
4.0 %
2.0 %
1.0 %
0.5 %

16.0 %
8.0 %
4.0 %
2.0 %
1.0 %
0.5 %

■ Without shading device
■ With shading device (slats 0 degrees)
■ With shading device (slats 45 degrees)

◁ Daylight factor variations in offices for three positions of the venetian blinds: open, closed, and closed with a 45° slant angle.

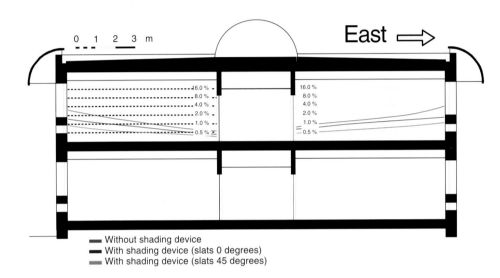

0 1 2 3 m

East ⇒

16.0 %
8.0 %
4.0 %
2.0 %
1.0 %
0.5 %

16.0 %
8.0 %
4.0 %
2.0 %
1.0 %
0.5 %

■ Without shading device
■ With shading device (slats 0 degrees)
■ With shading device (slats 45 degrees)

◁ Daylight factor variations in classrooms for three positions of the venetian blinds: open, closed, and closed with a 45° slant angle.

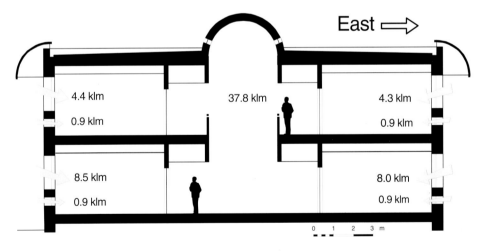

East ⇒

4.4 klm

37.8 klm

4.3 klm

0.9 klm

0.9 klm

8.5 klm

8.0 klm

0.9 klm

0.9 klm

0 1 2 3 m

28%
14%

51%
15%

△ Penetration of luminous flux for standard overcast conditions, external horizontal illuminance equal to 10,000 lux, (each glass tile lets 0.3 Klm in).

△ Oudoor daylight factors near facade, horizontal value, facing upward and down ward.

East and west overhangs reduce daylight penetration from the sky vault by 50%

Measurements of horizontal daylight factors near the facade (facing upward and downward) show that the overhangs significantly reduce the amount of daylight from the sky vault which penetrates the rooms. The value of this reduction is equal to about 50%. Fortunately, it appears that ground reflections partly compensate for this loss. The bright gravel outside reflects enough light so that, under overcast conditions, it contributes half the daylight penetrating through the windows of the upper floor, and one third of natural light penetrating the windows of the lower floor.

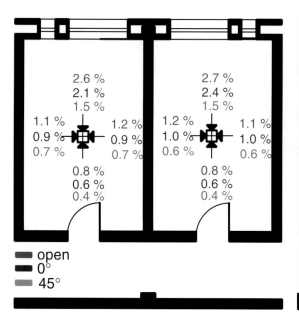

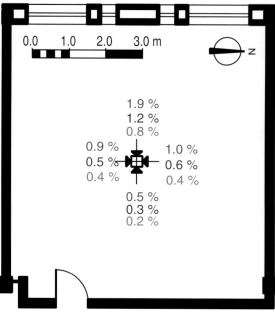

◁ Vertical daylight factors in the classroom for the three positions of the external venetian blinds (open, closed with 0° angle, and closed with a 45° slant angle).

open
0°
45°

△ Vertical daylight factors in the offices for the three positions of the external venetian blinds (open, closed with 0° angle, and closed with a 45° slant angle).

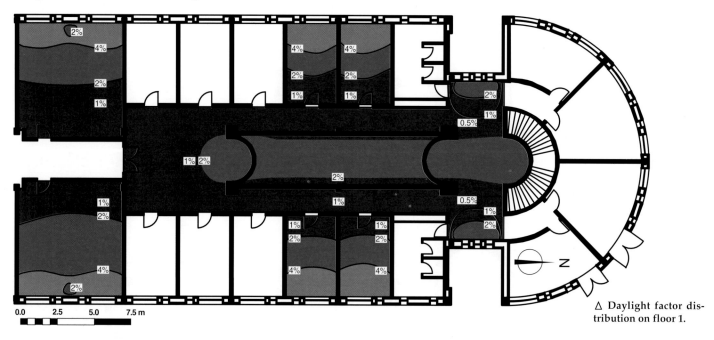

△ Daylight factor distribution on floor 1.

▽ Daylight factor distribution on floor 2.

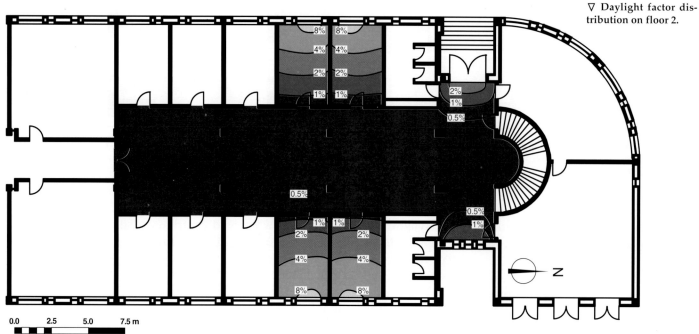

▷ Luminance distribution (in cd/m²) in one classroom for standard overcast sky conditions (corresponding to a horizontal illuminance of 10,000 lux).

▷ One of the two domes, on the roof of the atria, showing the distribution of the glass tile blocks.

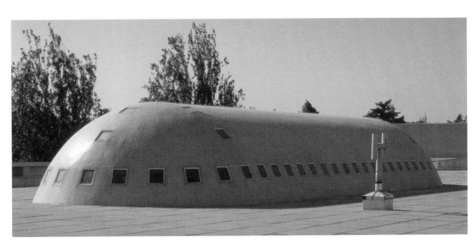

▽ Pattern of the glass tile blocks, seen from below.

△ Patterns of sunlight penetration through the facade elements with venetian blind up (left) or down (right).

▽ Patterns of daylight penetration, showing the effect of sunlight reflected from the bright gravelled ground outside.

▷ View of one atrium, from the upper floor, under sunny conditions, showing the aspect of the light patches due to the transmission of sunlight through the glass tile blocks.

△ Variations of the patterns of daylight penetration through the facades on a sunny day. Vertical axis shows the effects for four different times: 9:00, 9:30, 10:00 and 10:30 . Horizontal axis corresponds to three configurations: no blinds, blinds tilted 45°, blinds closed, in September 1996.

Daylight monitoring

The bulk of the daylight monitoring of the Pharmacy Faculty was performed in January 1997 and April 1997 (overcast sky conditions) and July 1996 and May 1997 (clear sky conditions). The measurements were made in two classrooms on the second floor and in eight office rooms on the first and second floors. Measurements were also made in the circulation areas under the daylit dome. Outdoor illuminances varied from 5 klux to 25 klux (overcast sky measurements) and typically above 100 klux under clear sky conditions.

△ West facade of the pharmacy faculty. Note the vertical concrete fins near the entrance which provide solar protection.

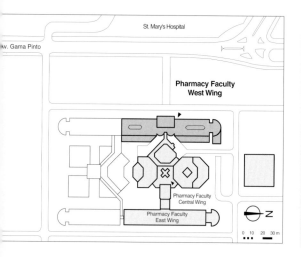

△ Pharmacy Faculty - site plan.

△ Artificial lighting of the atria.

CREDITS

Building
The West Wing of the Pharmacy Faculty was finished by mid 1995, and its occupancy started in mid 1997. The West wing has an approximate gross area of 8,500m², with an average area per storey of about 2,100m². The classrooms have an area of 51.1m², and the offices for the staff 17.5m².

Climate
The Pharmacy Faculty is located in the northern part of Lisbon (Latitude: 38°46'N; Longitude: 9°08'W; Altitude: 100m. Lisbon has a unique variant of the typical Mediterranean climate due to its closeness to the Atlantic Ocean. The winters are mild and the summers relatively mild.

The average temperature in January is 10.5°C and in July 22.6°C. The average sunshine duration is 143.1 hours in January (48%) and 321.3 hours in July (72%).
(Source: Portuguese Institute of Meteorology: Data for Lisbon, Climatic Normals 1961 to 1990)

Architect
R. Hestnes Ferreira
Largo da Graça 82, 2° E-F
1170 Lisboa, Portugal

Building owner
Faculdade de Farmácia da Universidade Técnica de Lisboa
Av. das Forças Armadas
1600 Lisboa, Portugal
Tel : +351.1-848 2131
Fax : +351.1-840 1581

Monitoring organisation
LNEC - Laboratório Nacional de Engenharia Civil
Av. Brasil, 101
1799 Lisboa Codex, Portugal
Tel: +351.1-848 2131
Fax: +351.1-840 1581

References
"Daylight Monitoring of The Pharmacy Faculty-West Wing", Lisbon, LNEC, final report 1997.

Acknowledgements
The monitoring organisation wishes to acknowledge the following persons/ institutions for their contribution:
the President of the Direction of the Pharmacy Faculty for the authorisation for the monitoring of the building; and

Architects R Hestnes Ferreira and Victor Ennes for their availability and collaboration in providing the elements requested.

Material properties assessed on site

	Colour	Hemispherical-hemispherical reflectances
Walls and ceilings	white	94%
Wooden & cork floors	pine-coloured	32%
Window frames	white	79%
Window marble sills	white	73%
Working tables	blue-grey	14%
Marble-tile floors	marble white	44%
Concrete walls and pillars	light-grey	69%
Walls (circulation areas)	white	92%

	Hemispherical-hemispherical transmittance	Normal-normal transmittance
Single glazing (windows)	77%	86%
Shading system with slats 0°	41%	-
Shading system with slats 45°	18%	-
Shading system with slats 90°	4%	-
Glass tiles (dome)	70%	80%

Direct bilateral daylighting leads to uniform luminous environment of engineering laboratories

Queen's Building, De Montfort University, Leicester, UNITED KINGDOM

Each level of this laboratory building is daylit from both sides: the street facades offer a very small glazed area, and the courtyard facades use a combination of large lightshelf windows on top of narrow view windows.

▽ Section through the northern wing showing measured daylight factors. The values are lower below the lightshelf and reach higher values at places where the lightshelf window is visible.

The shallow depth of the laboratory, in combination with direct bilateral lighting, leads to uniformly daylit spaces

Each wing contains shallow plan laboratories on four floors and the two wings are separated by a small courtyard with white cladding to increase external reflection. Each laboratory is lit mainly from two sides with some additional glazing in the end wall. The courtyard side is fitted with a low internal light shelf, the design of which differs from one floor to another. Daylight factor measurements show a high uniformity of light distribution in spaces. The short distance from facade to facade (all less than 6.4 meters from wall to wall) avoids the presence of a darker area in the center.

The amount of daylight is higher in rooms on upper floors

The daylit appearance of the laboratories varies from floor to floor. The top two floors appear attractively daylit; the lower two, particularly the ground floor are less well lit. Daylight factors throughout are fairly low, but the uniformity of lighting from both sides compensates for this. In each case the lowest daylight levels are under the light shelves on the courtyard side.

On the ground floor, daylight factors are low everywhere (average 0.8%) and the space as a whole looks gloomy without electric lighting. Daylight factors near the external/street walls are reduced by racks of equipment. The first floor has an average daylight factor of 1%. It has an intermediate daylit appearance: on sunny days daylight could be sufficient but most of the time supplementary electric lighting is required. The second floor laboratory has the best daylighting (average daylight factor 1.4%). Here, the light shelf results in an area of significantly lower daylight factor. But the space as a whole is well lit. The third floor with its high, sloping ceilings has particularly uniform, well balanced daylight.

The light flux distribution reveals a different pattern of light admission on the different floors. On the ground floor the Mill Lane side admits more than the courtyard side; a significant amount (6,900 lumens) comes through the end wall, increasing light levels in this part of the laboratory. On the first and second floors the large windows facing the courtyard provide most of the incoming light. On the third floor these windows are smaller and the windows facing Mill Lane dominate.

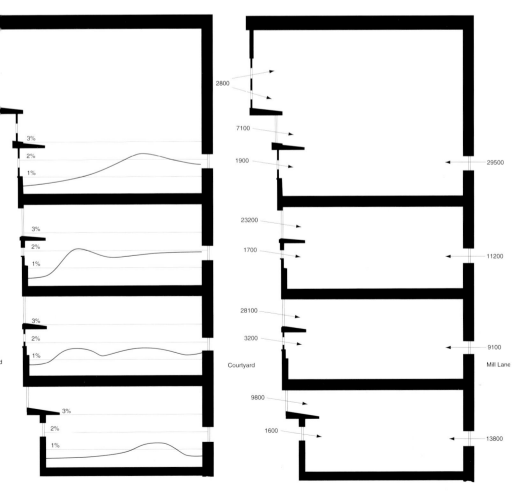

◁ Section through the northern wing showing incoming light fluxes in lumens under a reference overcast sky (external illuminance 10,000 lux).

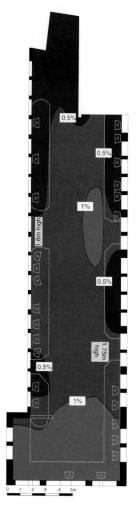

△ Daylight factor contours on the ground floor.

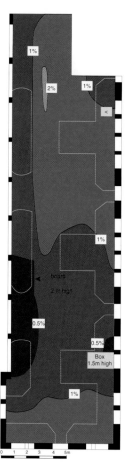

△ Daylight factor contours on the first floor.

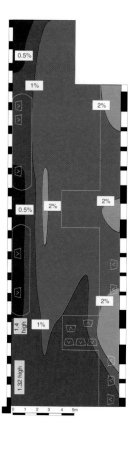

△ Daylight factor contours on the second floor.

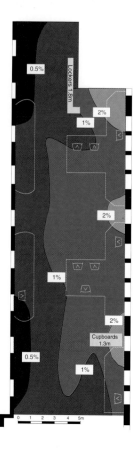

△ Daylight factor contours on the third floor.

View of the courtyard separating the two wings of electrical laboratories. Note the two families of windows: large lightshelf ▽ windows and small square windows below.

▽ View of the first floor laboratory.

The second floor laboratory has the highest daylight levels with an average daylight factor of 1.4%.▷

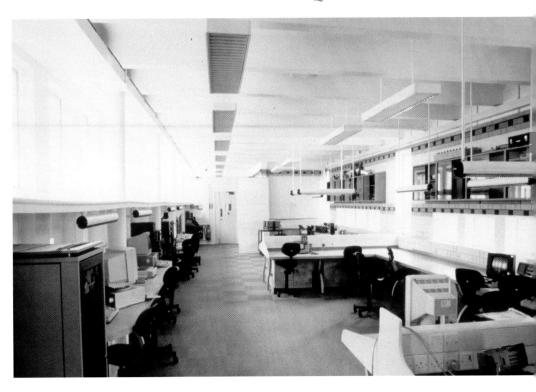

The upper floor laboratory also benefits from reasonable daylight penetration, leading to average daylight factors above 1%. With bilateral lighting, this value is largely sufficient for the type of activity in the building.▷

Lightshelves on courtyard facade provide an area of shade near computer screens

The laboratories contain many computers and VDU lighting is therefore important. Reflections of bright windows on the screens are common, and a number of occupants have complained of glare from the sun. The light shelves provide an area of shade close to the courtyard window wall, but do not shade other areas in the space.

The small windows above the second light shelf on the third floor provide little light and are a source of unwanted reflections on VDU screens. Fewer, larger windows in a horizontal strip close to this second shelf would have been more appropriate.

Adjustable shading devices could have reduced reflexions on computer screens

Since daylight is extremely variable, it is often difficult to design daylighting systems which are satisfactory for every climatic condition. The light shelves of the Queen's Building are such an example. Adjustable shading devices would have improved the luminous environment in glare conditions.

Light reflections on computer screens due to light coming from opposite lightshelf windows. ▷

▽ Principle of lightshelf on ground floor.

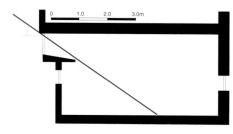

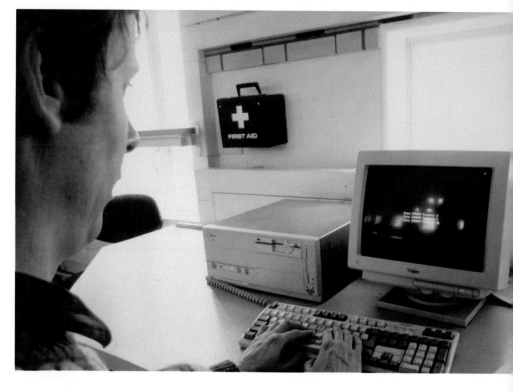

Task lighting provides a good complement to ambient daylight in lighting working areas, though it also causes reflections on computer screens.▷

▽ Principle of lightshelf on first floor.

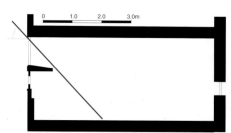

Occupants are satisfied by their illumined environment, but frustrated by the small size of the view window below the lightshelves

A survey of the occupants indicated that over half of them would prefer bigger windows to provide more daylight and better views out. Views through the small low level windows are limited.

The laboratories contain a variety of computer equipment which is exten-sively used. The lack of adjustable shading devices mean that reflections of windows can often be seen on display screens. Out of 52 VDUs in the northern wing, 31 contained reflections of bright windows when viewed from a normal sitting position. Surprisingly, only 4% of occupants found these very disturbing; another 11% found them moderately disturbing.

Screen reflections could have been re-duced by altering the benching so that it ran perpendicular to the windows rather than parallel to them. The elect-ric lighting also caused glare for VDU users, over 40% saying they often or sometimes were bothered by it.

Improved energy performance is mainly due to lighting electricity savings

The laboratories are fitted with back-ground lighting, switched at the en-trance, and localized lighting with individual pull cords. Initial results

Exterior view of courtyard △
facade of laboratory.

△ Interior view of courtyard facade
seen from the third floor laboratory.

Exterior view of courtyard ▽
facade of laboratory.

Interior view of courtyard facade seen
▽ from the ground floor laboratory.

◁ Street facade of the Queen's Building.

indicate that users are selective about which lighting they switch on, giving savings over an automatically switched installation.

Numerous simulations of the energy flows through the Queen's Building show that electric power consumption is signficantly reduced by comparison with a reference building in the same location. Thermal and visual comfort are improved, but there is no effect on maximum heating load.

Daylight monitoring

Monitoring was carried out in the northern wing of the electrical laboratories. Daylight factors were measured in January 1996. From January to June 1996 external illuminances, lighting use occupancy, and internal and external temperatures were all continuously recorded. A survey of occupant reaction to the building was carried out in December 1995.

CREDITS

Building description
The Queens Building houses De Montfort University's School of Engineering. The overall floor area is 10,000m², and it has up to 2,000 occupants during university term time. The Electrical Laboratories occupy 1,200m² at the west end of the building. The building was completed in 1993.

Climate
The Queens Building is situated in the centre of Leicester (Latitude: 52°6'N, Longitude: 1°0'W, Altitude: 75m), a large urban area in the East Midlands region of England, around 150km north of London. The climate is mild; January is the coldest month (3°C average) and July the warmest (16°C). Sunshine varies from 1.4 hours per day on average in December, to 6.5 hours/day on average in June.

Architects
Short Ford Associates
15 Prescott Place, London SW4

Client
De Montfort University
The Gateway, Leicester LE1 9BH

Daylight consultants
Max Fordham and Partners,
43 Gloucester Crescent, London NW1
ECADAP Group, De Montfort University

Monitoring organisation
BRE/De Montfort University

References
P J Littlefair and M E Aizlewood, "Measuring daylight in real buildings" Proc CIBSE National Lighting Conf, Bath, 1996.

R Asbridge and R Cohen, "PROBE 4- Queens Building" Building Services v18 (4) 35-38, (March) 1996.

P J Littlefair "Daylighting under the microscope" same issue, pp 45-46.

Material properties assessed on site

	Colour	Hemispherical-hemispherical reflectances
Walls	light buff	80%
Ceiling	white	81%
Floor	blue/green	18%
Bench top	grey	39%
Light shelf top	white	71%
Cladding courtyard	white	80%
	Direct-direct transmittance	Hemispherical-hemispherical transmittance
Double glazing	71%	78%

Circular clerestories create a uniform and glare-free environment for an anatomical theatre

Anatomical Lecture Theatre, Uppsala, SWEDEN

Olof Rudbeck designed and built this anatomical theatre in 1662 to 1663. The octagonal room is day-lit with two circular arrays of clerestories which admit moderate quantities of glare-free daylight, except when sunbeams penetrate and animate the space.

A unique building designed by its main user

The Anatomical Theatre in the Gustavianum, the former main building of Uppsala University, is one of only three remaining 17th century anatomical theatres in Europe. It was designed and built in 1662 to 63 by Olof Rudbeck, professor of medicine and a universal genius.

The anatomical theatre was given the form of an octagon and the interior design had an educational intent, since it was furnished with stylistic elements from antiquity that an educated young man should be aware of. The interior of the theatre consists of an upper part (crowned by the dome) which is shaped like the round Ionic temple of Plato's description; and a lower part, the theatre itself, which resembles a Roman amphitheatre described by Vitrivus. In an architectural sense the Anatomical Theatre can be seen as a temple to our knowledge of Man and Nature.

The anatomical theatre itself can accommodate about two hundred standing spectators on five levels. The arrangement of these five viewing levels is, like that of the Coliseum, decorated with the classical column forms. Starting at the lower level and moving up the pilasters, painted in grey marble imitation, are the Tuscan, Doric, Ionic, Corinthian and

The octagonal ceiling with the two arrays of ▷ clerestories photographed from the dissection table.

▽ The clerestories seen on a sunny day.

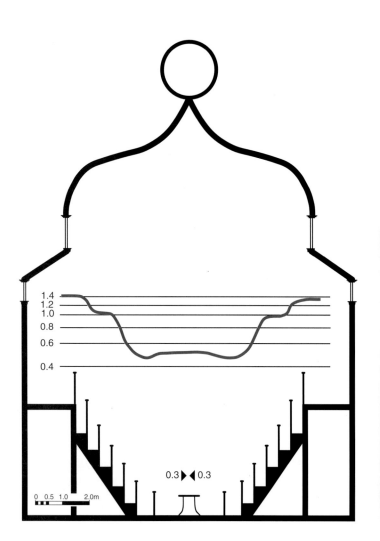

△ Daylight factors on desks and on the dissection table.

△ Exterior view showing the two rows of clerestories.

Composite orders. Between the pilasters are fields painted with red marble imitation.

Daylighting replaces light from fires

The double row of clerestory windows was Rudbeck's own idea. He sought to eliminate the need for open fires as a source of light for the theatre, which was the case in Leiden. Olof Rudbeck also designed every detail of the interior himself and personally took part in the carpentry work, for example he carved the capitals of the columns. The upper and lower window rows have nearly the same height, (about 1m, including frames) and cover the whole circumference of the octagon. The cross-section of the upper level of the room is 11.5m

in width while that of the upper spectator level is 8.3m, and that of the inner spectator level is only 3.7m in cross-section. Daylight factors were measured on the desks of the spectators and on the dissection table. They vary from 1.4% at the upper level down to 0.5% at the lower level, this value being the same as on the dissection table. On this table vertical values are equal to 0.28% in all directions. These values are low by comparison with the visual requirements of anatomical demonstrations. In fact, it appears that the ratio of glazed area to total window area is low (66%) with large obstructions to the penetration of daylight.

However, the fact that wall finishes are rather dark (reflectance lower than 20%)

leads to the feeling that daylight is beamed to the dissection table.

In overcast conditions, and for an outdoor illuminance of 10,000 lux, the total flux entering the room is equal to 50,000 lm, and is equivalent to the light produced by luminaires equipped with about thirty 36 W fluorescent tubes.

Daylight monitoring

The measurements were carried out at the end of the months of April and June 1996. The reference exterior sensor was placed on the roof of the Main Building of the University, on slightly higher ground, about 150m west of the Gustavianum.

Δ Pictures of sunbeam penetration taken at one hour
intervals, on 27 May 1997.

13:00

14:00

15:00

△ Pictures of sunbeam penetration taken at one hour intervals, on 27 May 1997.

Material properties assessed on site

	Hemispherical-hemispherical Reflectances
Grey painted walls	35%
Painted grey marble imitations	18%
Painted red marble imitations	18%
	Hemispherical-hemispherical Transmittance
Window	72%

CREDITS

Building description
Built in 1663.
Glass area/Floor area: 0.40% - Diameter: 12m
Height floor at dissection table - inner roof 14m
Number of standing spectators - about 200.

Climate
Uppsala is located near the Swedish Baltic coast, about 65 km north of Stockholm. Latitude: 59°87'N, Longitude: 17°60'E, Altitude: 18m.

The climate is of the temperate north European coastal type, although more continental than the Swedish west coast climate. The monthly average temperature is around -4°C in winter and around 16°C in summer. During October to February there are on average 15 to 21 totally cloudy days per month, whereas during the rest of the year there are on average eight to 13 totally cloudy days per month. Clear days are at a maximum during March to July with an average of about five to seven clear days per month. During November and December there are only about two clear days per month.

Client
The Swedish National Board of Public Buildings (Statens Fastighetsverk),
P.O. Box 2263, S-103 16 STOCKHOLM, Sweden. The building is managed by Academic Buildings Uppsala (Statliga Akademiska Hus i Uppsala AB).

Architect
Olof Rudbeck (1630 to 1702). Professor of medicine at Uppsala University; Discoverer of the lymphatic system. Author of the glorification of Sweden's Age of Greatness, the massive, confusing, at times intellectually grotesque, four-volume work *Atland eller Manheim* (the *Atlantica*). Rudbeck here claimed that Sweden, and particularly Uppsala and environs, was identical to Plato's submerged Atlantica and consequently the ancestral home of all earthly culture and knowledge.

Monitoring organisation
Chalmers University of Technology
Department of Building Services Engineering and
The Monitoring Centre for Energy Research
S-412 96 GÖTEBORG, Sweden

References
- Andersson, H.O. and F. Bedoire. 1986. *Swedish Architecture - Drawings 1640 - 1970.* Byggförlaget. Stockholm, Sweden.
- Building Project Group. 1995. *A Short Compilation of the Building History - Gustavianum C50:2, Uppsala.* (in Swedish). Statens Fastighetsverk, Uppsala, Sweden.
- Engström, J. 1983, 1986. *The Anatomical Theatre.* Information Office, Uppsala University. Uppsala, Sweden.
- Sörbom, P. 1995. «Renaissance Man or Pseudo-Intellectual Fanatic?» *Griffin* 1-95, pp 54-64. SAAB Information Office. Linköping, Sweden.

Acknowledgements
National funding for the monitoring from the Department of Energy Efficiency (DOEE) at the Swedish National Administration of Technical and Industrial Development (NUTEK) and from the Swedish Council for Building Research (BFR) is gratefully acknowledged.

Two levels of gangways distribute daylight along a school 220 metres long

Collège de la Terre Sainte, Coppet, SWITZERLAND

The 24 classrooms of this rectangular three-storey building are organized along a central atrium used for circulation.

A linear atrium brings access and daylight to 24 classrooms

The linear form of this school is typical of school buildings in Switzerland, with a 9.5m wide and 149m long large glazed central atrium and classrooms located on each side. In theory, this creates opportunities to bring additional daylight to all classrooms through the central atrium. However, the building has three storeys, and the central atrium has to accommodate circulation on three levels. The consequence is large obstructions. The central atrium operates more as a series of light wells than as a central light box.

Obstruction in atrium and small area of secondary daylighting windows reduce potential of daylighting

Vertical illuminance on the glazing of secondary windows facing the central atrium reaches only few hundred lux during the day due to three factors:
- obstructions in the atrium
- high angle of incidence of incoming daylight
- shadowing effect of masonry and indoor furniture next to the aperture.

In addition to factors regarding incident light, the glazed area of the windows (6.18m²) is barely a third of the facade

▽ Intermediate floor gangway showing light wells on each side.

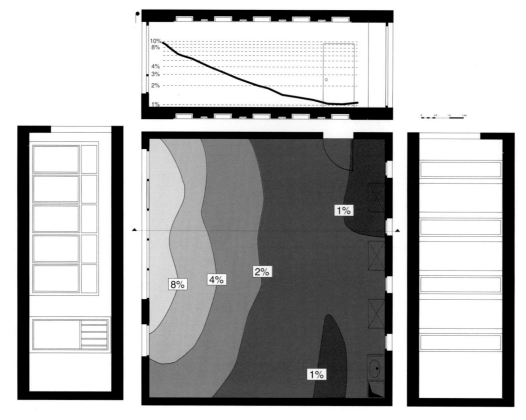

△ Daylight factor distribtion in monitored classroom.

◁ Cross section.

▽ Location of the monitored room.

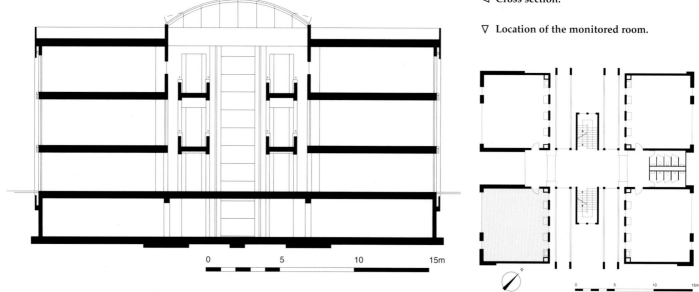

area of the classrooms. Each of the four windows is 2.34m high and 0.66 wide and represents 8.4% of the floor area. By comparison, the 11.6m² of the facade window represents 15.8% of the same floor area.

Finally, the glazing material which was selected is diffusing, for privacy reasons, leading to lower luminous transmission than clear glass. The result is a contribution to the daylight entering the classrooms (see daylight factor values on graph).

Low energy consumption

The organization of the building along a central atrium also has some interesting consequences regarding energy consumption.

The consumption of the building has been assessed and compared with the average consumption of schools throughout Switzerland. The typical occupancy is from 8 am to 5 pm, and the building is not used during the months of July and August.

It should be noted also that all facade windows are equiped with electrically

	College La Terre Sainte	Surin college (mean)
Total energy consumption	246 MJ/m².yr	730 MJ/m².yr
Lighting consumption	62 MJ/m².yr	85 MJ/m².yr

Secondary daylighting windows △
in monitored classroom.

△ Facade windows in monitored classroom.

Luminance measurements inside
classroom for standard overcast
sky conditions (cd/m²). ▷

Lower floor gangway. ▽

driven external aluminium venetian blinds, leading to efficient and adaptable solar protection.

Globally, it seems that both students and teachers are happy with the general quality of daylighting, regarding visual comfort and amenity.

The daylight factor measurements show that the translucent glazing in the wall opposite the windows has an insignificant contribution to the daylight factor distribution.

Installation of artificial lighting

Four rows of four recessed fluorescent fittings (1 x 36 W) are used in each classroom, leading to a electric lighting power density of less than 10 W/m².

It is possible to switch the artificial lighting in a row of four luminaries near the blackboard, two rows near the windows or the room near the corridor.

The three light switches are situated by the door. No automatic regulation is provided.

△ **Glazing cover of the atrium.**

Daylight monitoring

The monitored classroom is located on the first floor (south-west facade). The monitoring was conducted on 16 December 1995 and on 11 December 1996, under overcast sky conditions.

▽ **South-west facade.**

Material properties assessed on site

	Hemispherical-hemispherical refectance
Wall	83%

	Hemispherical-hemispherical transmittance
Facade and atrium glazing (double)	70%
Secondary daylighting windows	48%

CREDITS

Building description
College de la Terre Sainte is located in Coppet, Switzerland (Latitude: 46°316'N, Longitude: -6°19'E, Altitude: 370m).
Building floor area: 4,155m² (27.7m x 150m).
Floors: three+ basement
Construction date: 1991

Climate
Minimum monthly temperature is 2.2°C in January.
Maximum monthly temperature is 20.3°C in July.

Architect
ATELIER D'ARCHITECTURE SYNTHESE SA
Patrick CHICHE
23, avenue Dapples, CH-1006 Lausanne
Tel.: + 41.21-617 5060
Fax.: +41.21-617 5025

Daylight consultant
SORANE SA, Lausanne
Route du Châtelard 52, CH-1018 Lausanne
Tel.: +41.21-647 1175
Fax.: +41.21-646 8676

HVAC Engineers
PERRIN ET SPAETH SA
43, rue Louis-Favre, CH-1201 Genève
Tel.: +41.22-734 6878
Fax.: +41.22-734 8173

Monitoring organisation
Simos Lighting Consultants
15, place du Temple, CH-1227 Carouge
Tel.: +41.22-343 5281
Fax.: +41.22-343 5880
Email: simos@eig.unige.ch

EPFL/LESO - PB
CH-1015 Ecublens
Tel.: +41.21-693 4545
Fax.: +41.21-693 2722

Inclined glazing on borrowed light windows improves recovery of light from the atrium

Collège La Vanoise, Modane, France

Each classroom of this school receives daylight entering from both sides: from the facade and through the atrium. This reduces differences in the visual environment between students, causes fewer veiling reflections, and allows working at lower lighting levels.

▽ Indoor view of one of the three atria showing the borrowed light systems on each side and each floor. The roof opening is made of frameless, self-supporting, triple layer polycarbonate panels.

Severe winter conditions led the architect to provide large buffer spaces

The college is located in Maurienne valley at an altitude of 1,000 metres in the French Alps near the Italian border. The monthly average outdoor temperatures are close to 0°C in winter and 17°C during summer. This led the architect to offer large unheated buffer spaces where winter temperatures will be more comfortable than those outside.

The 33 classrooms of the college are organized around three atria, which act as light boxes

Each atrium also works as a light box. Daylight penetrates from the roof of the atrium through triple layer poly-carbonate glazing. Then, secondary daylight glazing admits a fraction of the transmitted daylight to bring it in the classrooms. The secondary daylight systems use inclined glazing panels to improve the collection of light penetrating from the roof. The lower level windows are angled forward to collect more light. The yellow colour of the wall surfaces (R=70%) prevents the atrium from appearing gloomy in winter. The rest of the atrium is painted white (R=75%).

Luminance on tilted surfaces is greatly increased by comparison with vertical glazing

Daylight penetrates the atrium mostly through the roof opening, whose aspect is towards the sky zenith. Vertical

◁ View of classroom on an overcast day. Bilateral lighting increases uniformity of daylighting.

▽ East facade of the college showing the three main blocks of the building surrounding three atria acting as buffer spaces.

▽ The inclined glazing is made of armoured glass for fire safety reasons.

glazing could not collect such a quantity (and quality) of light and transfer it into the classrooms. Hence the concept of presenting tilted glazing to the incoming daylight. Such a strategy increases the luminous flux on indoor surfaces by 50% on the north side of the atrium and ten-fold on the south side.

Even at the lower floor levels, the amount of transmitted daylight is significant

At the lower floor level, daylight entering from the atrium allows the daylight factors to exceed 1.5% at the back of north-facing classrooms, and 3% for south-facing ones. Without internal windows, daylight factors would have been less than 0.5% at the back of ground-floor classrooms.

Internal windows are best positioned in first-floor, north-facing classrooms where they provide a more evenly distributed light: this is due to a better angle of incoming daylight. In these areas, dependence on electric lighting is reduced from 500% to less than 50% of the time rooms are occupied.

The internal windows do not provide more light on the blackboard but they increase by 70% the amount of daylight falling on the rear wall, improving the illuminance ratio between walls (0.9 as against 0.5) as well as the ratio between the rear wall illuminance and the work-plane illuminance (0.45 as against 0.29).

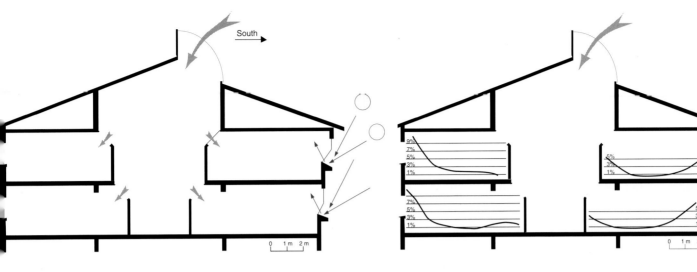

Daylighting strategy of Collège La Vanoise: △ combination of core and facade daylighting.

△ Daylight factor distribution in four typical classrooms.

Distribution of incoming daylight flux on ▽ overcast days, per 1,000 lumen of incoming flux in each classroom.

▽ Daylight factor distribution in lower classrooms showing secondary daylight glazing obstructed and un-obstructed.

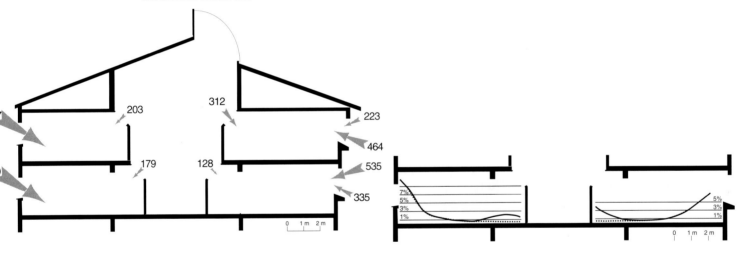

Facade systems with inclined reflectors deflects sunlight to the ceiling in winter and reflects it back to the outside in summer

Southern facades are equipped with forward-tilted glazing and stainless steel external light-shelves originally intended to reduce glare and heat gain in summer and to reflect sunlight onto the classroom ceiling in winter. Stainless steel was selected in preference to aluminium, glass or chromium for maintenance reasons as well as cost. However the operating specular reflectance does not exceed 50%. Glass is tilted forward to reduce sunlight penetration through the reduced, projected glazed area and the higher incidence angle of incoming light beams. Sunlight reflections to outside observers are comparable in direction and intensity to those from standard vertical glazing.

Bilateral daylighting tends to decrease glare, but upper windows on the south facades tend to be glare sources

The overall luminance of walls is increased by bilateral lighting, reducing contrasts between the luminance of glare sources and background luminance. However, the facade concept does not reduce the brightness of the top window of the facade through which the sky can be seen. This particular window deserves a glare attenuation device such as a venetian blind, interpane horizontal louvred blinds, or screen-printed glass. The lower window facing the opposite facade tends to cause less glare since it shows less of the sky.

Large savings in lighting electricity are achieved with no major changes in heating requirements

The Modane school's energy performance was simulated and compared to that of a base case model with the same geometry but without lightshelves and internal windows. Based on simulations, it can be concluded that the Modane school offers:

- no significant reduction in maximum heating load and therefore plant capital cost.

△ Detail of south facade lightshelf concept.

▷ Daylight factor distribution on the work plane of southern classrooms:

A first floor.
B ground floor.
C ground floor without internal windows.

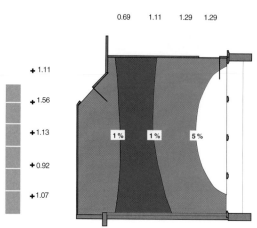

0.69   1.11   1.29   1.29

+ 1.11
+ 1.56
+ 1.13
+ 0.92
+ 1.07

1 %   1 %   5 %

▽ Principle of the south facade design showing a combination of external forward-tilted light shelf and inclined glazing.

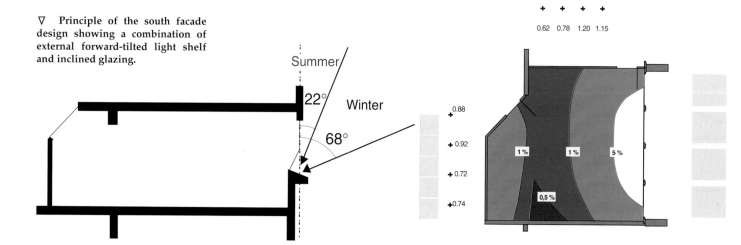

Summer

22°   Winter

68°

0.62   0.78   1.20   1.15

+ 0.88
+ 0.92
+ 0.72
+ 0.74

1 %   1 %   5 %

0,5 %

▽ External view of facade.

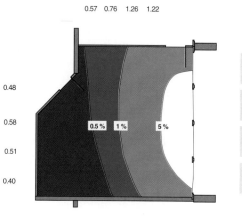

0.57   0.76   1.26   1.22

0.48
0.58
0.51
0.40

0.5 %   1 %   5 %

◁ The classroom without borrowed light.

◁ The classroom with borrowed light.

△ Penetration of direct sunlight on the ceiling and sections of the facade allowing vision toward the sky.

▽ Sunlight penetration in north classrooms through the central atrium.

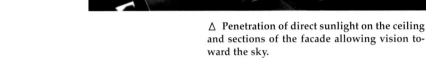

◁ Fish-eye lens photograph of the south facade of the classrooms showing sunbeams redirected toward the ceiling.

◁ Fish-eye display of calculated luminances allowing identification of the glare sources in the upper windows on the south facade.

- A significant lighting energy reduction: the total heating requirement for the building is similar to that of the base case model but the artificial lighting electricity consumption is 40% lower.

- Slightly improved performance with respect to thermal comfort, with a reduced number of hours where the resultant temperature is above 26°C.

Daylight monitoring

The performance of the Modane school daylighting features was assessed in four classrooms of the central building (Building B). Two rooms face north and two face south. Daylight factors were measured in December 1994 and April 1995. Additional measurements were conducted under clear sky conditions at the equinoxes and solstices.

COLLÈGE LA VANOISE

◁ View of the atrium.

▷ **Plan of first floor.**

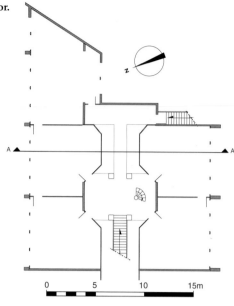

▽ **Site plan of the Collège La Vanoise.**

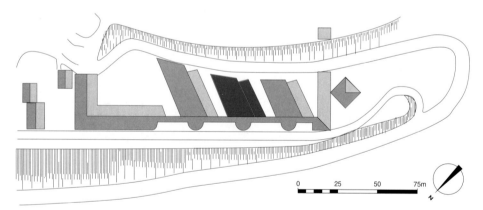

Material properties assessed on site

	Colour	Hemispherical-hemispherical reflectance
Walls atrium & classrooms	white	70%
Walls exterior of classrooms	yellow	75%
Ceiling of classrooms	white	90%
Floor	grey	40%

	Direct-direct reflectance	Hemispherical-hemispherical reflectance
Double glazing	80%	76%
Simple glazing		78%
Everlite (rooflight)	65 to 70%	74%

CREDITS

Building description
8,000m² building accommodating 600 students, including housing. Completed in 1989.

Climate
Latitude: 45°3'N, Longitude: 6°6'E, Altitude: 1,000m. Minimum monthly average is -3°C in January . Maximum monthly average is 18°C in July.Annual sunshine duration is 2,200 hours.

Client
Syndicat Intercommunal de Modane
90 rue Polset
F-73500 Modane

Architect
Philippe Barbeyer
Agence Barbeyer & Dupuis
21 rue de Boigne
F-73000 Chambéry

Daylighting consultants
M. Fontoynont and C. Badinier
ENTPE/DGCB
Rue Audin
F-69518 Vaulx-en-Velin Cedex

Monitoring organisation
ENTPE/DGCB

References
Fontoynont M., Badinier C., Barbeyer P. "Technique de contrôle des ambiances lumineuses dans le collège de Modane". Conférence Internationale du Bâtiment 92, Montréal, 18-22 Mai 1992, 4p.

Ward G., The Radiance 2.3. Synthetic Imaging System, Lawrence Berkeley Laboratory, 1993.

The luminous impact of retrofitting for energy conservation

Berthold Brecht School, Dresden, GERMANY

Transforming open courtyards into glazed atria is an efficient way of decreasing energy consumption and gaining space, but it also has some lighting drawbacks.

A typical school building from the seventies retrofitted in 1995

The Berthold Brecht school is one of the so called 'typical schools' built with a modular concept (Plattenbauweise) in the former German Democratic Republic in the 1960 to 70's. In the Dresden area alone, about 180 schools of this type exist. It was originally constructed in the seventies as a poly-technical school. The building core consists of two rectangular east-west aligned three-storey blocks connected by three staircase wells. Retrofitted as a representative example for this type of school in 1993 to 1995 it shows the energy saving potential and possible improvements in the social-cultural features of schools. Nowadays it is used as secondary school.

Two courtyards transformed into two covered atria, air flows managed according to season

Besides standard measures such as improving the thermal insulation of the facades, the retrofitting process concentrated on transforming the courtyards into covered atria, thus incorporating these spaces into the thermal as well as social-cultural life of the school. The atria are the heart of the ventilation concept, allowing for night ventilation during summertime, drawing the colder air from the outside classroom facades through the classrooms into the atrium and in winter time using the opposite direction by ventilating pre-conditioned air from the atria into the classrooms. Beside this, transmission losses towards the former, open court-

▽ One of the two new atria, converted from open courtyards.

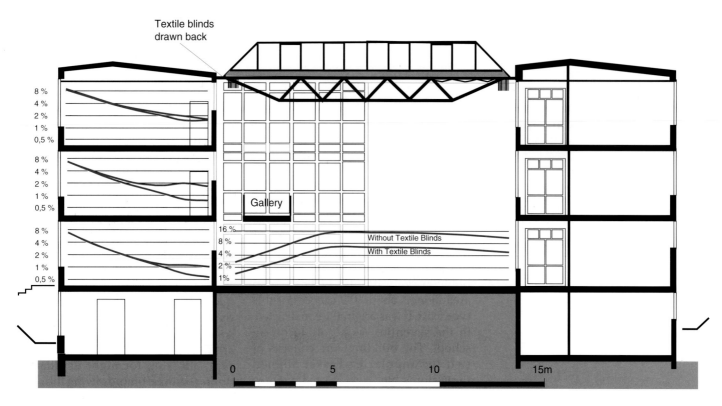

Textile blinds
drawn back

Gallery

16 %
8 %
4 %
2 %
1%

Without Textile Blinds
With Textile Blinds

0   5   10   15m

△ Daylight factor distribution on the workplane of the classrooms and in one of the two atria.

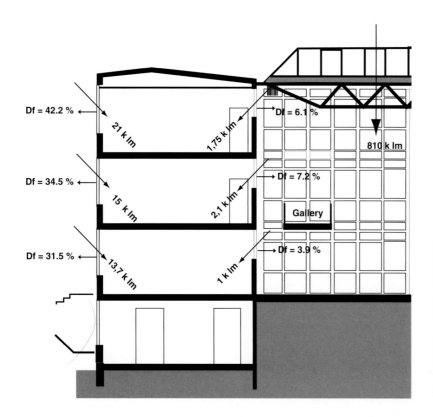

Df = 42.2 %   Df = 6.1 %

21 k lm   1,75 k lm   810 k lm

Df = 34.5 %   Df = 7.2 %

15 k lm   2,1 k lm   Gallery

Df = 31.5 %   Df = 3.9 %

13,7 k lm   1 k lm

◁ Light flux entering classrooms for standard overcast sky conditions (10,000 lux).

▽ The textile solar protection below the roof of an atrium.

yards are reduced nowadays by the generally higher temperature levels within the atria. Additional usable floor area of about 400m² has been gained which is now used as schoolyard, auditorium and reading space. To gain more classroom spaces a western three-storey block has been added in the course of retrofitting.

Atrium roof reduces the luminous flux which used to penetrate in the courtyard to one third

Due to the original floor plan layout around two central courtyards, most classrooms receive daylight from two sides. By transforming the courtyards into glazed atria light penetration into these core areas and thereby into the

adjacent classrooms has been reduced. Structural elements of the atria roofs reduce daylight penetration by about 45% compared to an open courtyard, and the addition of a new glazing layer, tilted to 45° and with a hemispherical glazing transmisssion of 67%, further reduces daylight penetration. Globally, illuminance in the atria is about one

Daylighting of classrooms throughthe external facades. △

△ Daylighting of a classroom through the windows facing an atrium.

Description of artificial lighting installations in the two ▽ two classrooms where long-term monitoring was conducted.

▽ Location of the two classrooms where long-term monitoring was conducted.

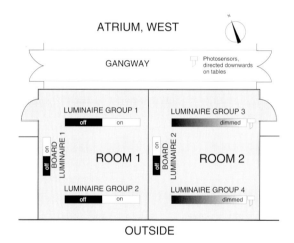

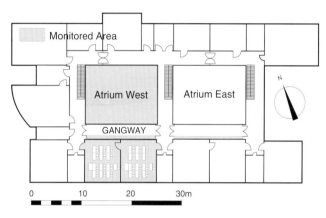

third of the value reached when the courtyards were open. On the atrium floor, the maximum daylight factor has been reduced from 50% to 15%.

The total luminous flux entering each of the atria (for a reference external illuminance of 10,000 lux) has decreased from around 2,000 klm for the old courtyard to about 800 klm. To reduce summer overheating risks, the atrium is equipped with a textile blind shading system with a diffuse light attenuation of 55%.

Secondary daylighting of classrooms is also affected

In addition, transfer of daylight to the classrooms adjacent to the atrium was also significantly reduced: standard double glazing was changed to lower glazing with lower light transmission coefficients; ventilation equipment was added in the atria, near the windows,

leading to new daylight obstructions; and balconies were constructed to serve as gangways on the first floor level in the southern atrium, blocking light penetration into ground floor classrooms. Finally, when the textile shading covering the atrium is pulled back, it forms a temporary overhang above the classrooms of the southern building block on the upper level.

Globally, daylight levels reduced by about 50% in areas of classrooms near atria

Before the retrofitting, daylight factors reached typical levels of 3% in the middle of the classrooms and up to 5% close to the courtyard facades (these data were obtained from measurements in scale models). Nowadays, the contribution of secondary daylighting has declined, resulting in typical levels of 2% in the middle of the classrooms and average values of 1.5% toward the atria

sides. Nevertheless secondary light still contributes above 50% to total illumination in the deeper room areas of the ground and second floor, compared to a contribution of around 80% before retrofitting. Ground floor daylight factor levels in the back of the rooms are about 50% lower than on the other floors due to the gangways. On the second floor, the contribution from the atrium is significantly lower than one might expect. This is a result of the location of structural elements of the atrium roof and the drawn back textile blinds, forming a low transparent overhang above the windows.

Daylighting monitoring

General measurements were undertaken in February '97. Detailed monitoring of the lighting system was performed in the framework of an overall energy monitoring program of the whole school from November '96 to June '97.

213

BERTHOLD BRECHT SCHOOL

Dimming controls permit smoothing of illuminance variations throughout the day and a reduction of lighting energy consumption of 50% by comparison with manual switching

In both rooms the two arrays of luminaires parallel to the window front are connected to seperate circuits. With continuous dimming in room 2, artificial lighting only provides the difference of illuminance between the one provided with daylight and the target value of 500 lux. In contrast the manually controlled system in room 1, allowing only on/off switching (i.e. either full or non output from the luminaires) adds onto the base level of natural illumination, thus exceeding the target value of 500 lux significantly. For a typical day in November the power consumption of the automatic system is thus on average

half the consumption of the manually-controlled luminaires. For the entire monitored period (from November 1996 to May 1997) the automatic system consumed even less, only about one third of the manually operated luminaires.

△ View of the Berthold Brecht school in Dresden.

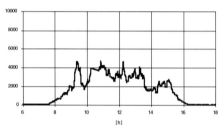

External diffuse horizontal illuminance on an △ overcast day at the end of November 1996.

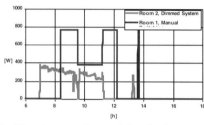

△ Direct comparison of luminaire power consumption for the two arrays of luminaires in the test rooms.

Typical indoor illuminance variations record-▽ ed in test room 1, showing that a combination of daylight and artificial light occasionally leads to illuminances above the 500 lux.

▽ On the same day, the dimming system tends to maintain illuminance levels at 500 lux, with lamps operating at half their maximum power.

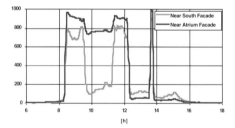

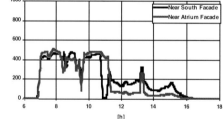

Material Properties assessed on site

	Hemispherical-hemispherical Reflectances
Blackboard	5%
Desk	42%
Wall	72%
Floor	28%
Floor	17%
Wall	59%

	Hemispherical-hemispherical Transmittance
Glazing	67%

(outside facades, atrium facade, atrium roofing)

CREDITS

Building
A school building, with a total floor area of 3,800m² before retrofitting; 4,500m² after retrofitting. Formerly used as polytechnical school, after retrofitting as secondary school. The exact year of construction cannot be obtained. It was retrofitted from 1993 to 1995.

Site and climate
The Berthold Brecht School is located in the urban environment of the city of Dresden, the capital of the state of Saxony, in the Eastern part of Germany at Latitude: 51°N, Longitude: 13°4'E, Altitude: 106m. The monthly average outdoor temperatures ranges from a minimum of -1.2°C in January and a maximum of 18.1°C in July.

Acknowledgements
Retrofitting of the school was a joint venture by four institutes, funded by the German government.

Architects
IBUS, Institut für Bau- Umwelt- und Solarforschung,
Casper-Theiss-Straße 14a,
14193 Berlin.

Daylighting
Technical University of Berlin, Fachgebiet klimagerechtes und energiesparendes Bauen, Straße des 17. Juni,
10623 Berlin

Building Physics and Monitoring organisation
Technical University of Dresden, Institut für Bauklimatik, Mommsenstraße 13,
01069 Dresden (coordinator)
and Fraunhofer Institute of Building Physics, Nobelstraße 12,
70569 Stuttgart

References
Energetische Sanierung und energieökonomische Erweiterung unter Verbesserung des sozial-kulturellen und des pädagogisch-funktionellen Niveaus von Typenschulbauten, Bericht zur Phase 1, Berlin, Dresden, Stuttgart, April 1994.

Sunlight protection and bright-coloured wall finishes inprove benefits from daylight under sunny conditions

Training Centre-Agricultural Bank of Greece, Athens, GREECE

Roof and facades equipped with a solar protection system contribute to the "softness" of the indoor luminous environment.

A large building, partly buried underground, to fit into a residential area

The building is intended to serve as a Training Centre for 340 staff of the Agricultural Bank of Greece. The overall size of the site is approximately 1,500m², while the total floor area of the new building, including the basement garage, is approximately 9,200m².

The building is on three levels and has 30 teaching rooms. It consists of three teaching units in which classrooms are grouped on either side of a two-storey space on two levels and four other units that house an amphitheatre, the en-

trance and administration, the library and sleeping accommodation. All units are separated and lit by open atria and are linked by corridors.

The whole building is built underground with only one floor level protruding higher than the imaginary line of the natural slope of the terrain. This approach, influenced by bioclimatic considerations, was chosen because the area is residential and it was the designers; wish that the considerable volume of the new building should make its presence felt as little as possible. Thus the dominant features are the volume of the old hotel and present trainees' accommodation.

▽ The barrel vaults and roof monitors above the halls provide filtered indirect light and act as a protection against direct sunlight penetration.

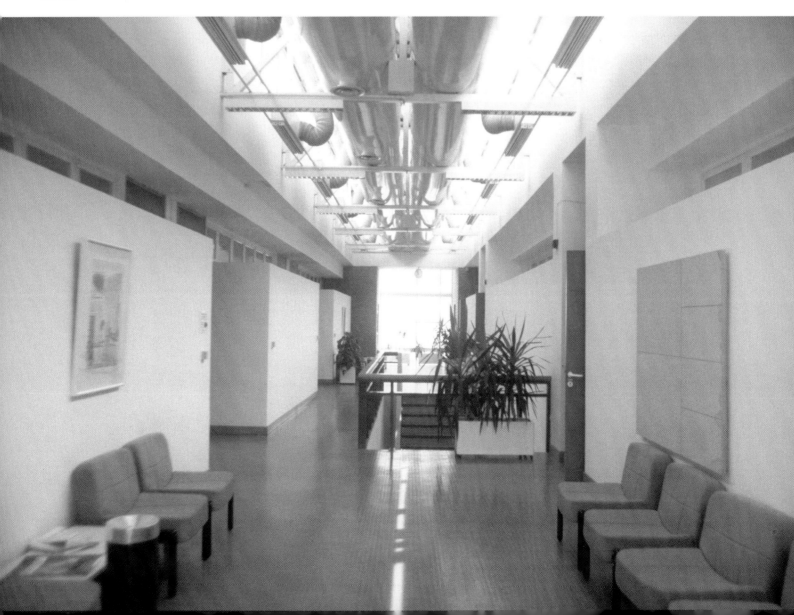

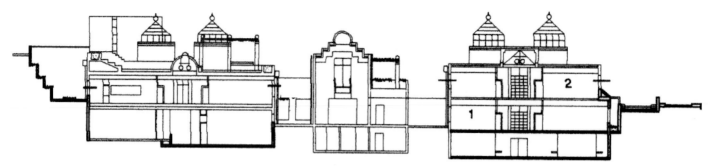

△ Section of the building across SE-NW axis, showing different daylighting systems. Measurements took place in the rooms with the numbers.

Indoor view of a teaching room △ on the north-west facade.

Indoor view of a teaching room ▽ on a south-east facade.

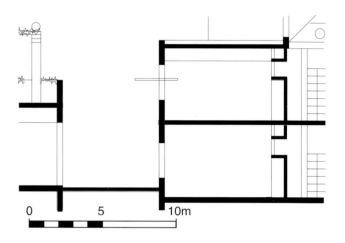

△ Detail of a lightshelf on the north-west facade.

▽ Detail of a lightshelf on another south-east facade.

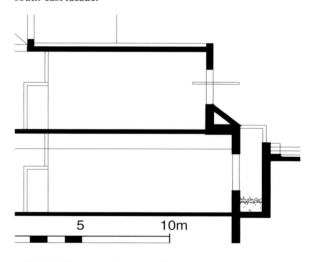

◁ View of the north-west facade, showing lightshelves.

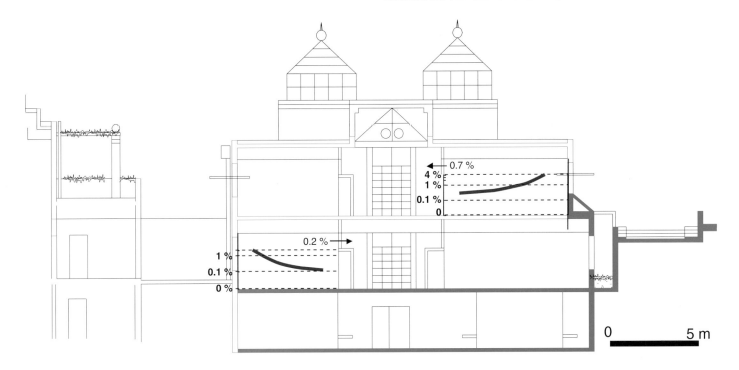

△ Daylight factor distribution in rooms 1 and 2.

◁ The hall of the cafeteria.

The same bricks together with exposed aggregate paving have been used as exterior paving materials. The choice of materials, colours and shapes allude to the history of the surroundings and reflect a certain romanticism. White natural ash wood, bright colors, white walls and exposed services were used for the interiors.

South-east and north-west facing windows equipped with large lightshelves

Natural lighting was a determining design parameter. Since a large fraction of the building is below ground level, various windows face courtyards and lightwells. Windows above the ground level have been designed with large lightshelves. For instance, a typical room used for training has a ceiling height of 3.10 metres and a depth of 7.0 metres. The lightshelf is located 2.40 metres above the floor level. It is 1.50 metres wide (0.90m outside - 0.60m inside the window) and made of steel sheet painted white. Its upper surface has a reflectance of 0.80.

Light shelves significantly reduce daylight penetration and lead to a more homogeneous luminous environment

In room 1 (facing south-east) the average daylight factor was found equal to only 0.58% with a minimum value of 0.11% and a maximum one equal to 2%. Apparently, external obstructions significantly contribute to the reduction of daylight penetration.

Room 2 (facing north-west) has a higher average daylight factor of 1% with minimum value equal to 0.12% and maximum of 4.1%. The values are higher due to the absence of major obstructions.

Secondary daylighting contributes to the amenity of the space, but provides a very small amount of additional daylight

Both rooms have one main facade window and a second one on the back wall running its whole length and facing the central hall to increase the levels of daylight (via secondary daylighting) at the back of the rooms. Results of measurements conducted

217

with and without shading of the secondary daylighting window show very few changes in the daylight factors, values, suggesting that the additional contribution of daylight is limited. In fact measurements of daylight factor in the hall showed that the floor of the halls receives a very smalll amount of light (Daylight factor=1%). For this reason, secondary daylighting solutions should generally be seen as features contributing mainly to the amenity of the space.

Californian blinds decrease illuminance levels near the window and increase illuminance levels away from it

The measurements of horizontal illuminance took place to investigate the influence of the shading device on the distribution of daylight.

There is an increase in illuminance at the back of the room and a sharp decrease near the window, leading to a more homogeneous luminous environment. However, the brightness of the Californian blind is significantly increased, leading to glare problems.

In room 2, during winter solstice, the sun enters at 13:48 LST. The geometry of the light shelf causes the whole of the lower window to be shaded until 14:58 LST. The sun patch on the ceiling is limited to an area near the window. After 14:58 LST this area starts to expand due to the lower altitude of the sun. Direct glare is experienced, although there are some external obstructions (trees etc.).

During the spring equinox (19 March) the sun appears at 14:35 LST and during

△ **View of scale model of Training Centre-Agricultural Bank.**

the summer solstice at 15:40 LST. Direct glare is experienced in these cases as well.

Light in both monitored rooms comes completely from one side. As a consequence, occupants perceive a very bright area (the window) in an otherwise much darker environment.

Daylighting monitoring

Daylight factors were measured in two rooms of the building during 13 December 1995. Additional measurements were conducted and photographs were taken under clear sky conditions during the winter and summer solstice and the equinoxes.

CREDITS

Building description
Total building floor area: 9,200m²
built on a 1,500m² site, for a population of 340 people.
Built in 1989.

Climate
Its climate is typically Mediterranean with mean annual dry bulb temperature equal to 18.1°C. Annual maximum temperature is 22.5°C while the minimum one is 13.8°C. Heating degree days (base: 18°C) are 1,110 through the year and the cooling degree days (base: 26°C) are 122. Compared to northern Europe, Greece has a high sunshine duration and enjoys higher values of incident radiation. The maximum value is in July, with 12.42 hours/day. The least sunny days occur in January with 4.1 hours/day. Sunshine in winter depends mainly on cloudiness which is a function of the weather systems influencing the town.

Client
Training Centre-Agricultural Bank of Greece, El. Veniselou str 106 Kastri-Athens GR 146

Architect
Meletitiki - A.N. Tombazis and Associates
27 Monemvasias str, Polydroso
Athens GR 151 25

Monitoring organisation
Aris Tsangrassoulis
National Observatory , Athens

References
Design + Art in Greece, 24/1993
Monographs II: Alexandros Tombazis, p.46-47.
Revista 3, Revista de Teoma, Historia y Critica de la Arquitectura, March/April 1994, p.44-45.

Material properties assessed on site

	Colour	Hemispherical-hemispherical reflectances
Walls	white	82%
Ceiling	wood	28%
Floor	light green	16%
	Direct-direct transmittance	Hemispherical-hemispherical transmittance
Glazing	71%	85%

Sunlight protection with high daylight penetration: a solution for southern Europe

Teacher Training College, Setbal, PORTUGAL

Most of the solar protection is provided by fixed overhangs, and reductions in daylight penetration are compensated by light reflections from the light-coloured concrete slab in front of the windows.

▽ **View of the central courtyard, showing open gangways in front of classrooms, with large overhangs, and bright ground cover.**

An award winning building
Setbal Teacher Training College is located on the outer periphery of the city of Setbal (50km south of Lisbon). The building houses the higher School of Education of Setbal, and was inaugurated in 1993. The architect Ivaro Siza Vieira was awarded the Portuguese National Architecture Prize for this project.

This H-shaped building faces southwest in a long platform, slightly elevated in relation to the surrounding farmland. The building is located in an open area of cork trees, and the only obstructions are related to shading of aisles by others.

Its H-shaped plan has two open courtyards. Around the larger courtyard are wings with two levels of classrooms, with large walkways protected by overhangs. Attached to the north facade is a sports hall, daylit with south-east facing clerestories.

Classrooms with bilateral daylighting
Classrooms are located between two walkways: one open to the outside and one enclosed but providing secondary daylighting through upper windows and glazed doors. Thanks to the bright indoor finishes, the daylight penetration is satisfactory, with daylight factors between 1 and 8% on the work plane.

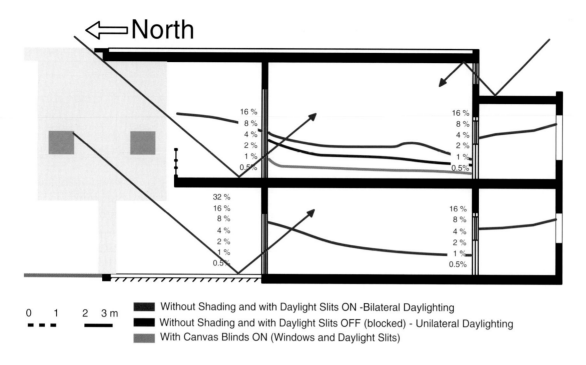

⟸ North

0 1 2 3 m

███ Without Shading and with Daylight Slits ON -Bilateral Daylighting
███ Without Shading and with Daylight Slits OFF (blocked) - Unilateral Daylighting
███ With Canvas Blinds ON (Windows and Daylight Slits)

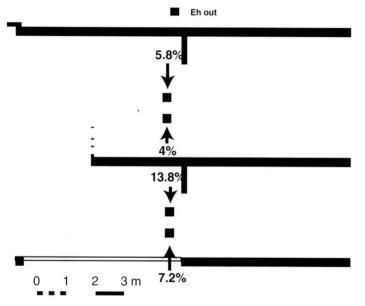

■ Eh out

5.8%

4%

13.8%

0 1 2 3 m   7.2%

△ Daylight factor distribution on the work plane (height 0.72m) in two classrooms on the first floor and second floor. The three curves correspond to 1) all blinds and awnings retracted, 2) awnings on secondary daylighting windows only, 3) all blinds and awnings deployed.

◁ Daylight factor values in front of windows, facing up and down, showing that reflection from external ground accounts for more than 30% of incoming daylight.

▽ Daylight factor variations in the Gymnasium. The internal illuminances were measured on a horizontal plane 1.7m above the floor level.

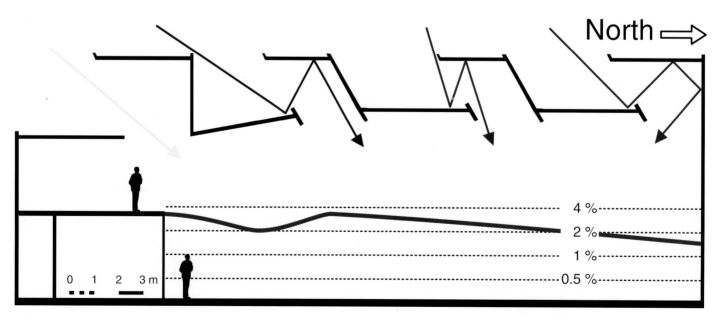

North ⟹

4 %
2 %
1 %
0.5 %

0 1 2 3 m

▷ The bright Portuguese pavement in front of the classrooms windows reflects significant amounts of daylight.

▷ Luminance distribution (cd/m²) in a classroom on the first floor, under standard overcast sky conditions (external illuminance equal to 10,000 lux).

▷ Indoor view of the gymnasium with the roof monitors.

△ Construction detail of the roof monitors on the roof of the gymnasium.

When shading is deployed on both sides, daylight factors become uniform and as low as 0.5%, a value suitable for bright summer days. Horizontal daylight factor measurements in front of windows shows that the contribution of external ground reflectance is high, contributing about 34 to 40% of incoming light under overcast days.

Roof monitors with overhangs and forward tilted window panes

The gymnasium is daylit through three roof monitors, facing south-east. They are shaded from sunlight with overhangs and side protections. Such a shading is efficient, but not total over the year and sunpatches can be observed on the gymnasium floor. The window panes are tilted forward and the light reflection from the bright gravel on the roof cover is partly compensated for by a reduction in daylight penetration. Resulting daylight factors on the floor of the gymnasium are equal to 2%. A reasonable value, which could benefit from being higher since users of the gymnasium appreciate illuminances in the range of 500 to 1,000 lux.

Daylight monitoring

The daylight monitoring was performed during January and February 1997 (overcast sky conditions) and during July to September 1996 and May 1997 (clear sky conditions). The measurements were made in two classrooms (one in each storey) in the northern courtyard wing, and in the Gymnasium. Measurements were also made in circulation areas. Outdoor illuminances varied from 15 klux to 30 klux (overcast sky measurements) and above 100 klux under clear sky. The outdoor illuminance meter was placed in the roof of the building with no relevant obstructions.

Material properties assessed on site

	Colour	Hemispherical-hemispherical reflectances
Walls and ceilings	white	88%
Wood panels	beige	21%
Cork floors (cork tiles)	beige	30%
Working desks	beige	79%
Interior marble-tile floors	white	44%
Exterior marble-tile floors	light pink	37%
Portuguese pavement	white	40%

	Hemispherical-hemispherical transmittance	Normal-normal transmittance
Double glazing (exterior)	75%	82%
Single glazing (interior)	90%	96%
Interior shading (perforated canvas blinds)	18%	-

CREDITS

Building description
Building size: 7,100m² of floor distributed over two storeys. Built in 1993.

Climate
Setbal is located 50 km south of Lisbon. Latitude: 38°31'N, Longitude: 09°80'W, Altitude: 50m. The climate in Setbal is very similar to the one of Lisbon, with the difference that winters are colder and wetter, and summers are hotter and drier) but it can also be considered a variant of the typical Mediterranean climate. The average temperature in January is 10.3°C and in July 22.1°C. The average maximum temperature in January is 15.0°C and in July 28.6°C. The average minimum temperature in January is 5.6°C and in July 15.6°C.

The average cloud amount (in tenths) is six in January and two in July. The average sunshine duration is 136.4 hours in January (46%) and 359.7 hours in July (81%).
(Source: Portuguese Institute of Meteorology: Data for Lisbon, Climatic Normals 1951 to 1980)

Architect
lvaro Siza Vieira
Rua da Alegria 399-A, 2Ĵ
4000 Porto - Portugal

Building owner
Escola Superior de Educacion de Setbal (Setbal Teachers Training College)
Rua Vale de Chaves
Lugar de Estefanilha
2910 Setbal - Portugal

Monitoring organisation
LNEC - Laboratório Nacional de Engenharia Civil
Av. Brasil, 101
1799 Lisboa Codex - Portugal
Tel: +351.1-848 2131
Fax: +351.1-840 1581

References
"Daylight Monitoring of The Teachers Training College", LNEC, 1997
lvaro Siza, 1986-1995. Blau, Lisboa, 1995. (Portuguese and English)
lvaro Siza, Obras e Projectos. Exhibition catalogue. Electa/Fundacion das Descoberta/Centro Cultural de Belem, Lisboa, 1996. (Portuguese and English)
lvaro Siza. 1958-1994. El Croquis 68/69. El Croquis Editorial, Madrid, 1994. (Spanish and English)

Acknowledgements
The monitoring organisation wishes to acknowledge the following persons/institutions for their contribution:
The Direction of the Teachers Training College and in particular Prof. Ana Maria Bettencourt, for the authorisation of the monitoring of the building and for all the availability and collaboration in providing elements of the building; and

Architect lvaro Sizaís office for the collaboration in providing additional elements of the building.

Libraries

Libraries are spaces used mainly for the consultation of books, writing and book storage, and increasingly for the retrieval of information using VDUs, microfiche readers and slide viewers. Daylight should clearly be attenuated in the storage area for the conservation of documents (as is the case in museums for artwork). Consultation of books, particularly if the lettering is small, requires illuminances from 500 lux to 1,000 lux. This can be achieved either with task lamps or in the vicinity of windows. In the latter case daylight factors of 4% and above may be desirable.

As more and more computers are used in libraries, the relevant areas require careful control of glare and unwanted reflections.

Peripheral daylighting of a 25 metre wide cylindrical library hall

Stockholm Public Library, Stockholm, SWEDEN

Peripheral windows located high above the floor create an homogeneous and glare-free illuminated environment, but the resulting lighting is low, more adapted for the conservation of books than reading.

A cylindrical shape preferred to a dome for economical reasons

This building is generally considered as Gunnar Asplund's great masterpiece in the neo-Classical style, which was popular in Sweden during the 1910s and 1920s. The Stockholm Public Library had a long design and construction process, between 1918 to 1927. Based on layouts from American libraries, a perimeter zone of reading rooms forms a square, open courtyard almost entirely filled by the tall, cylindrical central lending hall. The hall is lined with three tiers of bookshelves stepped back to accommodate access passages. However, the fourth wing to the west that completes the square was not built until the 1940s. The shape of the lending hall was changed during

the design work. The idea in 1921 was to surmount the hall with a spherical space by covering it with a dome. The dome had skylights laid out in a pattern not dissimilar to the coffers of the Pantheon. The original floor has a pattern also inspired by the floor of the Pantheon. For structural and formal reasons the dome was changed to a tall cylinder. The dome would not only have been difficult and expensive to built, it would also have been hardly perceptible from the exterior, given that the site of the building lies on a slope when seen from the main entrance side towards Sveavägen towards the east. One advantage of this design change from a daylight point of view, was that the skylights of dim raw-glass were replaced by twenty tall windows (with

▽ **Lending hall of the Stockholm Public library.**

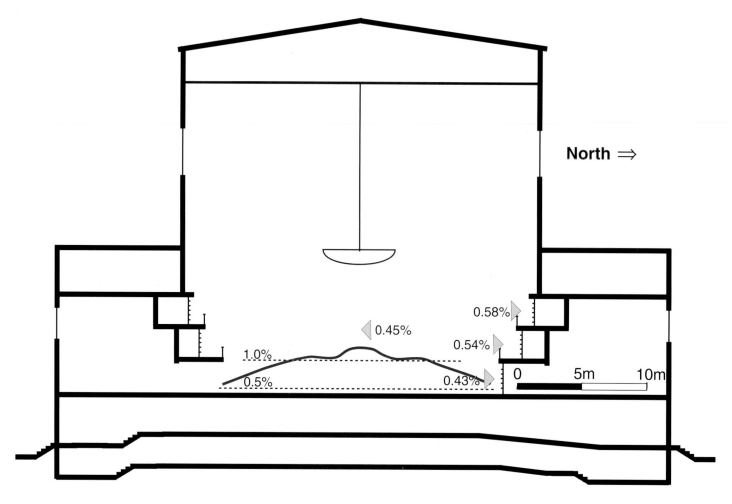

North ⇒

0.58%
0.45%
0.54%
1.0%
0.5%
0.43%

0   5m   10m

△ Section of the Stockholm Public Library
with measured daylight factors.

clear double-glazing, replaced by triple-glazing in the early 1980s) in the upper third of the cylinder.

Dark entrance hall covered with black stucco creates the transition between the outdoor and the indoor spaces

Starting at the street one enters a slightly sloping stair, surrounded by walls that slowly drop away, towards the Egyptian-like portal (like the other two portals inspired by those of the Thorvaldsen's Museum in Copenhagen) in the main facade. Once inside, the walls of polished black stucco of the tall (8.5m) and proportionally narrow (5.5m) entrance hall are daylit by the all-glassed high portal. The rather long walking distance from outside into the lending hall means that the eyes have time to adopt to the changing light levels.

Dark bookshelves below bright wall finishes, and a large central chandelier collecting and distributing light

When entering the straight, narrow stair up towards the central lending hall one floor above, the main object seen is the huge, bow-like chandelier, concave upward, of white opalescent glass in the centre of the hall. This chandelier captures daylight (and sometimes sunlight) from above and takes on an almost magically intense glow and becomes the focal point as one ascends from below into the lending hall. During the ascent the large volume of the lending hall slowly makes itself known.

When reaching the top of the stairs one enters the lending hall in front of the main lending desk. Above the beautifully detailed three tiers of wooden, dark bookcases, and in contrast to them, rise the sheer, rough very white plaster

walls of the cylinder, bathed in the light of the high clerestory windows.

Low values of daylight factors, with a rather large glazing ratio

The clerestory windows are equipped with triple glazing. The glazing ratio of glazed area to floor area is about 15%. The total glazed area of the clerestory windows is 74.4m². Their hemispherical transmittance being 45%, they provide about 170klm of light for standard overcast sky conditions. The resulting daylight factors are low: on a horizontal plane 1.5m above the floor of the lending hall, the values range between 0.5 and 1.2%, and appear to be small in relation to the glazed area (20% of the floor area). The hall appears however rather bright, probably due to the location of the windows outside the field of view, leading to an adaptation of the eye to the dark indoor surfaces. The vertical daylight factor in the

△ Artificial lighting provided from the central luminaire and a hidden 'gutter' above the shelves. Books are illuminated with hidden fluorescent tubes.

middle of the hall (1.5m above the floor) is about 0.45% regardless of the orientation. The lending hall gets a very small contribution of side lighting from the rather large openings (4.4m² each) towards the reading halls at the north and south sides.

Artificial lighting required during all opening hours for task requirements

These rather low daylight factors mean that the electrical lighting in the lending hall is always turned on when the library is open, even on sunny days in the summer. The light is typically switched on and off manually by the staff in the morning and the evening. However, the large chandelier can be seen as a task light for the main lending desk, which is located in centre of the hall. Above each tier of bookshelves there is a row of fluorescent tubes illuminating the backs of the books. The row on the top

tier also have uplighters for illuminating the rough white plaster walls of the cylinder. This uplight contributes to the experience of the volume of the space, it can be considered as pure ambient lighting.

Clerestories are efficient for glare control except when sunlight penetrates the reading area

Glare is generally not a problem since the clerestory windows are placed very high above the floor of the lending hall. However, a couple of VDUs at the central desk get direct sunlight on sunny summer days, which was not a problem when the building was designed. Some years this problem was dealt with by covering the clerestory window that let in sunlight with black plastic. The access to the clerestory windows is very troublesome: entering by climbing a vertical ladder from the roof of the reading halls to a small access hatch and

then the need to use a small carriage to move around the perimeter of the cylinder at the bottom level of the windows.

Daylight monitoring

The illuminance measurements were done in the cylindrical lending hall, mainly 1.5m above the floor. Since the roof of the lending hall was not accessible, the external reference was placed on the Observatory Hill to the southwest, on a lawn with fairly free horizons. The surrounding trees were all leafless. The measurements took place on 11 November 1995. The external illuminance varied between 2,000 lux to 3,000 lux and rose slowly during the meas-urements. The sky luminances was checked every 15 minute at the four compass points. The average zenith luminance was $1051cd/m^2$ and the average luminance 15° above the horizon was $565cd/m^2$, i.e. the ratio between the luminances was 54%.

STOCKHOLM PUBLIC LIBRARY

△ East elevation.

◁ Detail of the main entrance.

CREDITS

Building description
The building is located at the north side of the Observatory Park with the tall Observatory Hill with the Royal Observatory to the south-west. It was buit in 1927.

Site
Stockholm (Latitude: 59°21'N, Longitude: 18°04'E) is located on the Swedish Baltic coast, which means that the climate is somewhat more continental than the temperate north European coastal type. The monthly average temperature is around -3°C in winter and around 17°C in summer. During October to February there are on average 15 to 20 totally cloudy days per month whereas during the rest of the year there are on average eight to 12 totally cloudy days per month. The clear days are maximum during March to August with an average of five to seven clear days per month. During November and December there are only about two clear days per month.

Client
The City of Stockholm
The City Hall
S-105 35 STOCKHOLM

Architect
E. Gunnar Asplund 1885 to 1940

Monitoring organisation
Chalmers University of Technology
Department of Building Services Engineering
and
The Monitoring Centre for Energy Research
S-412 96 GÖTEBORG, Sweden

Acknowledgements
We would like to thank Mr Lars Lindberg at the Stockholm Public Library who allowed access to the building during a weekend and with his valued help during the measurements. The monitoring was conducted with contribution from the Department of Energy Efficiency (DOEE) at the Swedish National Adminis-tration of Technical and Industrial Develop-ment (NUTEK) and from the Swedish Council for Building Research (BFR).

References
Wrede, S. 1980. *The Architecture of Erik Gunnar Asplund.* The MIT Press, Cambridge, Massachusetts, and London, England. ISBN 0-262-23095-X.

Caldenby, C & O. Hultin (Editors) 1985. *Asplund - A Book.* Arkitektur Förlag, Stockholm, Sweden.

Material properties assessed on site

	Hemispherical-hemispherical reflectance
White plaster walls	88%
Wood on bookshelves	21%
Backs of books (average)	15%

	Hemispherical-hemispherical transmittance
Clerestory windows (triple glass)	45%

228

View and glare versus seclusion and visual comfort

Darwin College Library, Cambridge, UNITED KINGDOM

Users of this library appear to prefer working in the vicinity of windows, without shading devices, than deeper in the room.

A bright space daylit from large south-facing windows, south-facing clerestories and north-facing strip windows

Darwin College Study Centre is one of the modern examples of library buildings in Cambridge. A combination of oak and brick, it gives the impression of a boat house as viewed from the south and riverside. It occupies a long six-metre deep site squeezed between the river and one of the principal tourist routes into the city centre. It is not a conventional library in the sense that it combines access to both books and computers, as well as a seminar room and a residential apartment. After entering from the east, one passes through a top-lit vestibule into a double

height-reading space. The building is enclosed by a curved wall with high clerestories on the road side, while opening on the south to the river Cam.

The upper level on this side consists of four highly glazed bays of study area which are situated above the computer rooms on the ground level. The latter has very low daylight levels due to the small openings towards the river, which avoid glare on VDUs. Light in the remaining space is reflected from the south clerestories above the bays onto the fan-shaped white and oak ceiling. This light blends with the northern light from the clerestories along the curved bookcases and thus allows satisfactory daylight

▽ The second-floor reading room with the south-facing window on the left.

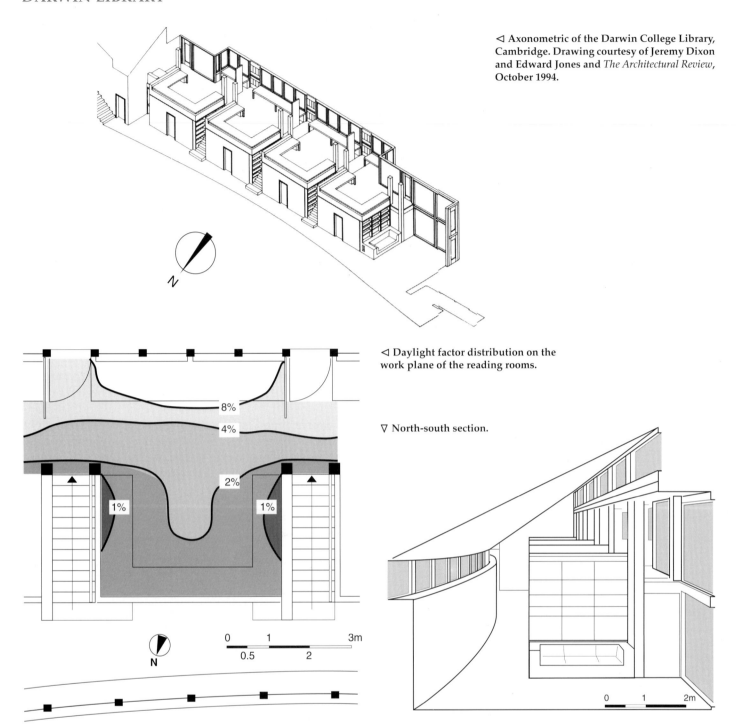

◁ Axonometric of the Darwin College Library, Cambridge. Drawing courtesy of Jeremy Dixon and Edward Jones and *The Architectural Review*, October 1994.

◁ Daylight factor distribution on the work plane of the reading rooms.

▽ North-south section.

levels along the narrow walkway outside the computer rooms.

The study centre gives an immediate impression of light and space. Due to the large area of openings, the occupant has ample day lighting in which to work. There is however a glare problem on the south-facing tables which overlook the river, due to the absence of shading devices. It is quite interesting that the readers actually prefer those workspaces, possibly due to the view.

Moderate daylight penetration on the ground floor

On the ground floor, the measurements taken in the corridor along the curved

wall indicated consistent illuminance levels, with daylight factor varying roughly from 0.8% to 0.5%. The measurements on the vertical plane of the bookcases indicated an average level of 1% on the top and 0.5% on the lower part (500mm from the ground), due to the daylight entering form the clerestories above and reflected on the opposite wall.

Extreme variation in daylight levels near the south facade, but balanced luminous environment deeper in the reading room

Light levels are extremely high close to the south-facing windows (11 to 8.8%)

due to the large glazing area. The levels drop abruptly as we move to the north side (2%). Only at the desks facing the north clerestories do we witness higher levels (average of 3%) due to the windows and the clerestories above which bounce light to the ceiling and down to the working plane.

Glare conditions for occupants facing windows emphasized by dark, glossy finish of desks, and the absence of shading devices

The whole daylighting performance of the space is adequate in order to reduce the use of artificial light as much as possible. The best lit reading areas are

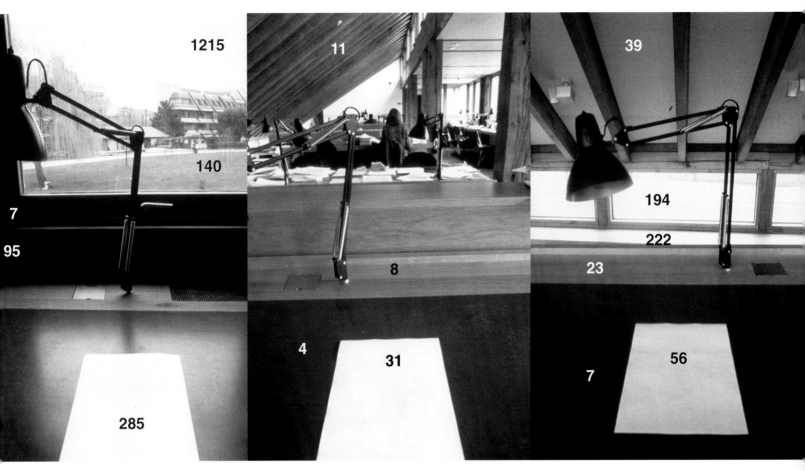

△ Three work spaces monitored under daylight only, with a standard overcast sky. Luminance values are in cd/m². The luminous environment is well balanced, except for work spaces facing the south window with high reflectances on the desk.

▽ The northern corridor daylit from clerestories above the bookshelves.

those facing north and those adjacent to them in the bays. A significant problem appears on the south-facing desks, which suffer from glare due to the very large glazing areas. On clear days, sunlight reflecting on the tables increases the glare even more. This is worsened by the fact that the user has no way to control the daylight, since there are no shading devices. The fact that the students prefer those workspaces is due, most probably, to the magnificent view outside.

Daylighting monitoring

The performance was assessed along the ground floor corridor, on a vertical grid on the curved bookcases and on the top floor in detail for one bay, on the 4 March 1996, at 0.85m above the floor. Reflectance and transmittance measurements were taken on the 23 February 1996 and the remaining ones were taken on the 26 March 1996.

△ South-facing clerestory and windows.   ▽ South facade to the river Cam.

CREDITS

Building
The study centre has an area of approximately 550m². It was completed in 1992.

Site and Climate
The Darwin College Study Centre is located in Cambridge (Latitude:52°12'N, Longitude: 00°08'E). The site is severely compressed between the river Cam to the south east and Silver Street to the northwest. The climate in Cambridge has a monthly average outdoor temperature close to 5.43°C in winter and near 14.9°C during summer. The average daily sunshine duration is 4.18 hours.

Acknowledgements
We would like to thank the Master of Darwin College, Professor G E R Lloyd and the bursar, Mr A Thompson for approving the monitoring of the library. Furthermore we would like to thank Jeremy Dixon and Edward Jones and *The Architectural Review* for giving us permission to reproduce their drawings of the building.

Client
Darwin College, University of Cambridge Silver Street,
Cambridge CB3 9EU, U.K.

Architect
Jeremy Dixon, Edward Jones
41 Shelton Street,
London WC2H 9HJ, U.K.

Monitoring organisation
The Martin Centre for Architectural and Urban Studies, Department of Architecture, University of Cambridge,
6 Chaucer Road
Cambridge CB2 2EB, U.K.

Bibliography
Carolin, P., "Natural selection: Jeremy Dixon in Cambridge", *Architecture Today*, No. 49, June 1994, pp. 24-29.

Davey, P., "Heart of oak", *The Architectural Review*, Vol. CXCVI, No. 1172, October 1994, pp. 50-53.

Jayatillaka, S., *Darwin College Study Centre - An Investigation into its Environmental Performance*, Unpublished, Essay for the M.Phil. in Environmental Design in Architecture, Department of Architecture, University of Cambridge, 1995.

Material properties assessed on site

	Colour	Hemispherical-hemispherical reflectances
Floor carpet	dark grey	7%
Floor tiles	almost white	57%
Timber	brown	28%
Working plane	dark green	15%
Ceiling	white	87%

	Direct-direct transmittance	Hemispherical-hemispherical transmittance
South glazing	75%	69%

Nine occuli of four metres diameter designed to balance the luminous environment

Bibliothèque Nationale de France, Paris, FRANCE

Circular ceiling openings located below roof lanterns contribute to the magnificence of the Main Prints Room but fail to provide the light quantities required by modern standards.

▽ General view close to what the visitor sees when entering the Main Prints Room.

Grandiosity impression

Designed by Henri Labrouste and completed in 1875, the Grande Salle des Imprimés (Main Prints Room) of the National Library of France covers a 1,300m² area mostly dedicated to book reading. At the time of its construction, gaslight was prohibited for fear of fires and only natural light was used.

Daylight enters partly through three large semicircular north-facing vertical windows, but the most remarkable daylighting features are the nine innovative circular skylights centred on spherical vaults and supported by a slender metal structure. They were de-signed in response to space constraints and the need to store a large amount of books, but it was also felt that such a system would tend to provide uniform daylight distribution on reading tables and would convey an "impression of grandiose simplicity" as Labrouste said. No doubt visitors are impressed by the splendour of the library when first passing through the entrance located in the north wall. The vertical windows are not immediately visible and all of the daylight seems to fall from skylights. A question remains however regarding the actual contribution of these zenithal features to lighting in the library.

◁ Roof lanterns above the Main Prints Room.

△ Circular lay light below the lantern, showing construction detail of the occuli.

△ Cross section of the roof lighting system. The aperture ratio of the occuli is 12.5%.

◁ Occuli seen from below.

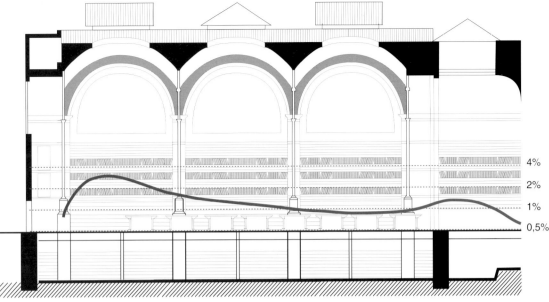

▷ Daylight factors on the reading tables as a function of the distance from the facade windows.

△ Reading space showing the task lighting introduced in the 1930s, and glare potential from the facade windows.

△ Daylight factor distribution over the reading plane.

The skylight optical efficiency has deteriorated with time

Each skylight consists of a protecting roof lantern on top of a circular opening (diameter: 4 metres). This opening is made of translucent glass pieces arranged according to an eight-point star pattern. A visit to the technical space between the lanterns and the circular glazing shows that these elements have significantly deteriorated through age and have become less and less efficient in terms of daylight admission. The same observation can be made for the much larger semicircular skylight which illuminates the back of the room (so-called 'Hemicycle'). The transmittance of its different glass pieces has decreased.

Facade windows, high above the floor, are the major contributors to the space daylighting

The average horizontal daylight factor on reading tables is around 1% which means that, on average and based on Paris daylight availability data, 400 lux is likely to be exceeded more than 15% of the time during one year between 9.00 and 17.00. The maximum measured daylight factor value is 2.5% and it is located at the room entrance.

The north windows' sills being several metres high, horizontal daylight factors are at a maximum a few metres away from the north wall. The best lit illuminated reading places are on the second and third rows (from the entrance). Then, daylight factors decrease smoothly when moving deeper inside the room till one enters the 'hemicycle' and receive additional daylight from the semicircular skylight. There, levels can exceed 1%.

Despite the token task lighting few ergonomic problems remain

In the 30s, task lights were introduced in the Prints room to supplement daylighting. Consisting of incandescent bulbs under green diffusing glazing, they have become emblems of the library and, together with recently added task lights, have significantly improved illuminance levels on reading tables. However, a few ergonomic problems remain such as glare from the facade windows. These problems depend on whether the visitor is facing north or south.

Window reflections on glossy material on reading tables can reduce the contrast for north-facing readers' and, more often, constitute a secondary glare source because of the shiny black table covers. Facade windows are high above the floor and oriented north, thus direct glare chances are minimized. However, north-facing readers seated at the back of the room can experience similar problems because (unshaded) windows are closer to their horizontal line of sight, and surrounding vertical surfaces (e.g. bookshelves, wood joineries, paintings) are quite dark, and occuli fail to compensate for decreasing daylight deep into the room. As for south-facing readers, the luminance distribution within their field of view is more homogeneous but vertical windows can make them cast a disturbing shadow on their visual task (and add veiling reflections on portable computer screens).

Daylighting monitoring

It was performed on 28/29 April 1995 when the library was closed to the public. External illuminances were measured at the highest accessible location on the roof which offered an unobstructed view of the sky, which was overcast during the measurements.

▷ Facade windows seen from outside.

Material properties assessed on site

	Hemispherical-hemispherical reflectance
Floor	30%

	Hemispherical-hemispherical transmittance
Roof lantern glazing	40%
Occulus glazing	30%

CREDITS

Building description
Build in 1854 to 1875.
Size of the reading room: 31.5 x 31.5m
Capacity: 345 sitting and 70 standing
40,000 books over three levels of balcony.

Site
Paris: 2°C in January and 18°C in July.
Rains fall: more than 5mm per day, 35 days a year.
Foggy days: 50 days
Latitude: 48°8'N Longitude: 2°3'E.

Architect
Henri Labrouste (1801 to 1875)

Monitoring organisation
ENTPE-DGCB
Light and Radiation Group
rue Maurice Audin, 69518 Vaulx-en-Velin
Cedex, France

Efficient bilateral daylighting achieved with a clerestorey above bookshelves in a 17th century building

Trinity College Library, Cambridge, UNITED KINGDOM

The daylighting design of the Wren library of the Trinity College is very innovative for a 17th century construction: reading booths are efficiently lit without generating significant glare.

▽ The library consists of a central corridor 6m in width by 60m in length with 14 projecting bookcases on each side creating 26 reading booths.

A high ceiling and bilateral openings generate a luminous space well suited to library activities

Two of the most important buildings in the architecture of Cambridge University are the chapel and the library. At Trinity College, the renowned 17th century library designed by Sir Christopher Wren is exemplary in its ingenious manipulation of light. This ingenuity is evident in the architect's decision to lift the windows above the bookcases, thus retaining valuable wall space for bookshelves while allowing a series of roomy bays to be created.

Conventional 17th century library architecture often had the windows positioned between bookshelves which projected from the walls. Light was thus constricted in the small bays, allowing only low levels of light along the corridor.

The Wren library has its main axis running from north to south and is located on the first floor above an undercroft. At ground level it is supported along its centre by a single row of Tuscan columns with an open arcade along the Neville's Court side. One enters by a rectangular staircase at the north end. The library consists of one large space with a long corridor in the centre. It has panelling on the end walls and fourteen projecting oak bookcases

◁ All windows are located 0.6m above the bookcases. Cornices prevent daylight from entering the area just below the windows.

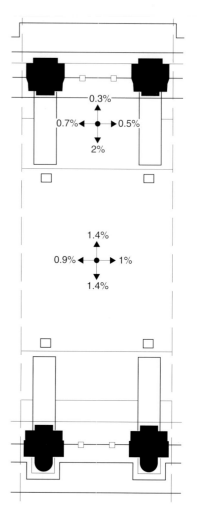

△ An original drawing by Sir Christopher Wren of the Trinity Library floor plan. The grey area indic-ates where daylight measurements where taken.

▷ Daylight factors on vertical planes. Light is perfectly isotropic in the centre of the corridor. In the reading booths, light coming from the opposite windows is six times more intense than light coming from the window above.

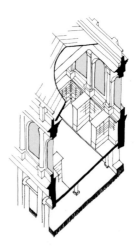

△ Axonometric sketch.

on the east and west sides which rise to about 0.6m below window sill level. The broad central aisle or 'middle alley' is paved with black and white marble squares while the bays or 'cells' have timber floor boards. The side walls are divided into thirteen bays by the bookcases.

Each reading booth is lit by the opposite window

The lower edges of the windows are located 0.6m above the bookcases. Cornices prevent light from falling directly onto the shelves and tables below. The result is that most of the light penetrating the reading booths comes from the opposite windows.

Efficient daylighting in reading booths

Raising the windows above the bookshelves allows light to enter both from above and the side. It results in a homogeneous luminous environment suitable for reading and consulting documents.

Daylight factor measurements were taken along the corridor and on a grid in one of the central bays. The daylight factor levels are very uniform along the 'middle alley' as was expected, due to the repetition of identical bays and windows, and to the bilateral origin of daylight. Light levels are high (daylight factor values 0.8m above floor: 1.7% to 3%) due to the addition of equivalent amounts of light from both directions, with little obstruction. A high floor reflectance (41%) enhances the feeling of brightness: floor luminances in the centre are more than 10 times those in the bays.

In the bays, light levels are slightly lower (0.8% to 1.8% at floor level) due to the low surface reflectances (book-cases: 8% and timber floor:

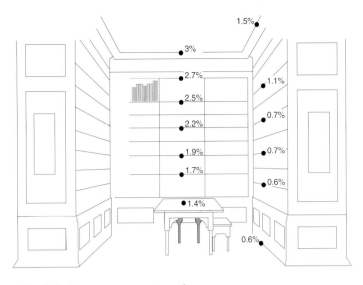

Study area in the centre of the △
reading booths.

△ Daylight factor measurements on the
bookshelves and table.

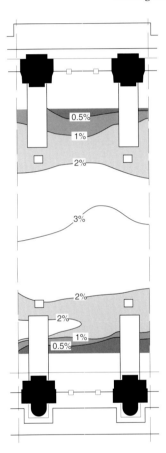

◁ Plan of a bay area of the Wren Library showing daylight factor contours.

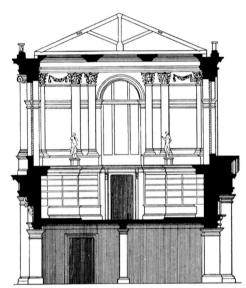

A cross section of the Wren Library, based on ▷
an original drawing by Sir Christopher Wren,
showing the large opposing windows above the
bookshelves.

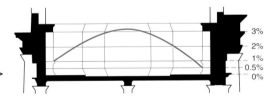

Daylight factors 0.8m above floor level along ▷
a cross section of the library.

10%); the height of the bookcases and the positions of the windows. The value on the reading table is comfortable (3.3%) and well suited to reading. Glare is not significant since most of the windows are not in the main field of vision.

Low transmittance of windows and obstruction by cornices attenuate daylight penetration

Even though one would expect high daylight factors in the space due to the very large areas of glazing, the daylight factors do not rise above 3%. The light transmittance of the glass was found to be 44% partly due to its thickness and large percentage in iron, and partly to the large number of lead glazing bars dividing the sheets into small rectangular panes. The window frame and glazing bars were estimated to block about 35% of the incoming light.

Today, VDU screens are used in the bays, and little complaint is made regarding unpleasant light reflections on the screens. This is probably due to the low luminances of the bookshelves surrounding the VDUs.

Field measurements

The performance was assessed along the corridor and in one of the central bays on a grid defined by the marble tiles, on 7 March 1996, at a height of 0.85m above floor level. Reflectance measurements were taken on the same day and transmittance measurements were taken on 26 March 1996.

TRINITY COLLEGE LIBRARY

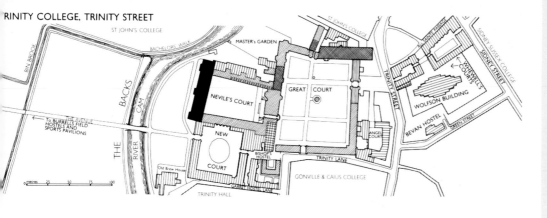

△ Location of the Wren Library, Trinity College.
Drawing by Tim Rawle, 1985.

▽ East facade of the library facing Neville's
Court.

Material properties assessed on site

	Colour	Hemispherical-hemispherical reflectances
Floor black tile	black	17%
Floor white tile	white	70%
Wooden reading table	dark brown	6%
Bookcases	dark brown	5%
Wooden profile of bookcases	dark brown	8%
Wooden floor in bays	dark brown	10%
		Direct-direct transmittance
Green glass		44%

CREDITS

Site and climate
The Trinity College (Wren) library is located in Cambridge (Latitude: 52°12'N, Longitude: 00°08'E). The site is on the west side of Neville's Court, facing the river. The climate in Cambridge has a monthly average outdoor temperature of 14°C in winter and 27.7°C during summer. The average daily sunshine duration is 4.18 hours.

Building
The library was designed by Sir Christopher Wren and constructed from 1676 to 1695. This building has a floor area of approximately 900m² including the entrance staircase out of which 660m² are used for the library.

Architect
Sir Christopher Wren

Client
Trinity College, University of Cambridge, Cambridge CB2 1TQ, U.K.

Monitoring organisation
The Martin Centre for Architectural and Urban Studies, Department of Architecture, University of Cambridge,
6 Chaucer Road
Cambridge CB2 2EB, U.K.

Acknowledgements
We would like to thank the Master of Trinity College, Sir M Atiyah, the Librarian, Mr D J McKitterick, and the Sub-Librarian, Mrs A Sproston for approving the monitoring of the library. Finally we would like to thank Mr Tim Rawle, for allowing us to reproduce his site plan drawing of the college.

References
Fletcher, Sir B, A History of Architecture, 19th Edition, Butterworths, London, 1987.

McKitterick, D, The Making of the Wren Library, Cambridge University Press, Cambridge, 1995.

Rawle, T, Cambridge Architecture, Trefoil Books, London, 1985.

Royal Commission on the Historical Monuments of England, City of Cambridge, Part II, Her Majesty's Stationery Office, London, 1959.

Willis, R, Clark, J W, The Architectural History of the University of Cambridge, Vol. 2, Cambridge University Press, Cambridge, 1988.

A four-storey library lit from a central atrium and facade windows with semi-mirrored indoor lightshelves

APU Learning Resource Centre, Chelmsford, Essex, UNITED KINGDOM

Semi-transparent indoor light-shelves are more successful in blocking daylight than redirecting it deeply into the space.

A design strategy aimed at introducing daylighting and natural ventilation

The new Anglia Polytechnic University occupies a site on the outskirts of Chelmsford and is the first major building constructed on site by ECD Architects. The clients' brief was for an environmentally conscious, low-energy building. The main strategic features are:

- good insulation and draught sealing to reduce winter heat loads
- increased use of daylight, and artificial light responding to daylight availability

- controlled natural ventilation, driven by stack effect
- limiting high summer temperatures by window shading, by exposed thermal mass, by cooling this mass at night and by high ventilation rates
- integrated control through a building management system (BMS)
- low energy plant
- acomfort range from 20°C minimum to 27°C maximum.

A typical floor has a 3.60m outer zone of desks on all sides except for the entrance side and an inner zone of bookcases around the central atrium, (7.50 x 10.30m and a height of 21.50m).

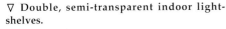

▽ Double, semi-transparent indoor lightshelves.

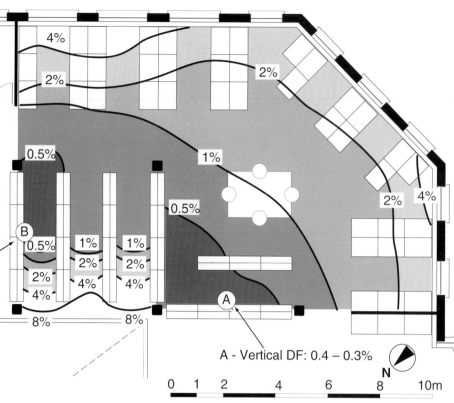

A - Vertical DF: 0.4 – 0.3%

0 1 2   4   6   8   10m

▽ A north-east facing window with double louvered projection, coloured black.

△ Daylight factor distribution in the north-west part of the centre, on the 2nd floor.

▷ Detail of the indoor semi-mirrored lightshelf design (Source: ECD Architects).

▽ Bookcases seen from the study area.

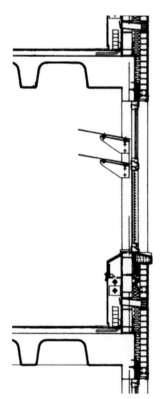

A building with sophisticated window design

The windows are the most elaborate part of the building's design. They cover a maximum of 40% of the wall area and accounted for 8.7% of the total building cost. Their design was required to combine the functions of light transmission, glare control, solar shading, insulation, to provide a route for ventilation air, and to be more precisely controlled than in conventional designs. A typical window size is 2.05m high by 1.8m wide, narrowing to 1.5m on the south west facade and 1.2m on the south facade to reduce solar gain (see south facade drawing).

The main lower part of the window combines a sealed, argon-filled double-glazed unit with a low-emissivity inner pane. On the outside of this unit there are venetian blinds and another single pane. These blinds are manually

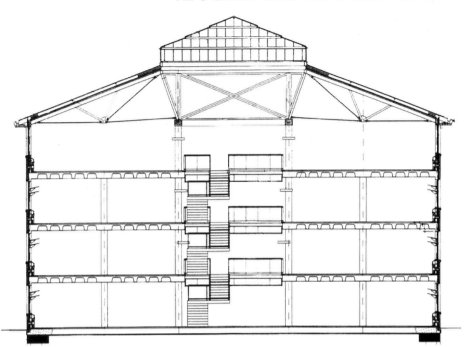

△ Central atrium showing white fabric lightshelves at each floor and diffusing white sails below the roof.

△ Cross-section of the centre (Source: ECD Architects).

▽ Bookcases are located around the atrium.

▽ The top floor benefits from a higher ceiling and from large amounts of daylight from the atrium, through diffusing white sails.

operated and they are perforated (13% transmittance).

Above this fixed part there is an openable clerestory (centrally pivoted on a horizontal axis) which consists of a triple-glazed argon-filled unit with a low-e coating. At the bottom of the clerestory windows there are double, internal, 700mm inclined lightshelves which have semi-mirrored surfaces. These were incorporated in order to cut out direct radiation and glare on the desks. Low evening sun or winter sun penetrates beyond the desk space to the bookshelf areas.

Externally, the building has no shading devices except on part of the north-east facade on the first and second floor, where there is a double louvred projection, coloured black.

Bookshelves obstruct daylight penetration from the atrium

The daylight factor on the south-east part of the facade varies from 8% close to the atrium to 0.5% in the bookshelf area. It is interesting to note that, due to the high reflectances of the atrium and its clear glazing, the daylight factor (8%) on that side is much higher than

in the 5m deep zone adjacent to the windows (4%). The light from the atrium is greatly obstructed by the bookshelves as was expected and so its contribution to the reading space lighting is quite small. The horizontal daylight factor in the bookshelf area drops abruptly from 8% to 0.5% and on the vertical plane it is equally low, varying from 0.6% at the highest shelf to 0.2% on the lowest.

The lightshelves are probably more successful in cutting out the light than redirecting it deeper into the space. Due to the fact that a lot of VDU users prefer

243

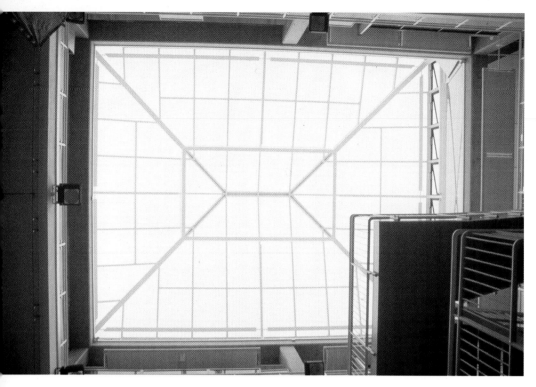

△ Elevation seen from the east.

◁ Double glazing (clear glass) covering the central atrium.

to shut the blinds completely, the daylight which finally penetrates that space is very low. The low daylight levels are also due to the fact that the ceiling is coffered.

Daylight from the atrium is diffused by sails and redirected with white fabric lightshelves

All the remaining features found in the floor below are also found for upper floors. An important addition in the upper space are the sails positioned on all sides of the atrium which are very successful in shading and eliminating glare due to the direct view of the sun and the bright sky. Furthermore they reflect light down to the lower floors. These sails are white and slightly perforated and are successful in terms of lowering the brightness ratio between the sails and the very brightly lit atrium. The daylighting environment on the top floor of the library was felt to be very agreeable by the permanent staff working there on one of the days the monitoring took place (29 May 1996).

On the atrium side, there are white fabric lightshelves which are parallel to the ceiling and which bounce the light from the atrium deeper into the stack area while at the same time shading direct sunlight. Due to the obstructions by bookshelves, it appears that the re-direction of daylight is poor, but that lightshelves contribute to the protection of the books.

Daylighting monitoring

Daylight factor measurements were taken 0.75m above the floor, on 4 March 1997. Reflectance measurements and transmittance measurements were taken on 29 May 1996.

Material properties assessed on site

	Colour	Hemispherical-hemispherical reflectances
Computer desk	brown	34%
Desk	grey	43%
Carpet	grey	30%
Concrete	grey	40%
Wall	brown	44%
Ceiling	white	82%

	Direct-direct transmittances	Hemispherical-hemispherical transmittances
Sails	5%	-
Triple glazing	70%	66%
Mirrored lightshelf	-	14%

CREDITS

Building description
The building was designed by ECD Architects and completed in August 1994. It incorporates a library that can seat 700 students. The library has four storeys. The ground floor has reading areas, bookstacks and the reception, the next two floors up include reading areas and bookstacks and the 4th floor includes offices for the staff.

Climate
The APU Learning Resource Centre is situated in Chelmsford, Essex (Latitude: 51°7'N, Longitude: 01°00'E). The site is flat as is most of the Essex countryside. The climate can be described by the Cambridge one due to their proximity. Thus, the monthly average outdoor temperature is close to 5°C in winter and near 14°C during summer.

Client
Anglia Polytechnic University Development, APU, Chelmsford, Essex, UK.

Architects
ECD Architects: David Turrent, John Doggart, Juliet Wood,
11-15 Emerald Street, London, WC1N 3QL, U.K.

Monitoring organisation
The Martin Centre for Architectural and Urban Studies, Department of Architecture, University of Cambridge, 6 Chaucer Road Cambridge CB2 2EB, U.K.

References
Evans B., "Integrating fabric and function", *The Architects' Journal*, Vol. 197, No. 22, 2 June 1993, pp. 44-48.

Wood, J., "Architect's report", *Building*, Vol. 260, No. 7876 (3), 20 January 1995, pp. 39-46.

Acknowledgements
We would like to thank Mr Ian Frame of the Department of Built Environment, Ms Nicky Kershaw, the University Librarian for approving the monitoring of the library and the BPRU for providing us with the results of their monitoring. Finally we would like to thank ECD Architects for allowing us to reproduce their drawings.

While access to daylight, amenity of the space and efficient solar protection are important, a house is primarily a living space allowing large contrasts in daylight penetration and lighting conditions. It is a space which responds mainly to the type of occupation and, therefore, it may be dangerous to specify lighting standards too rigidly, except for minimum window sizing and efficient sunlight protection.

High daylight factor values (2 to 4%) may be helpful in reading areas, or on work surfaces in the kitchen. Most of the space may look bright with daylight factors values in the range of 0.25 to 1%. It is only the presence of totally obscured areas which may lead to the feeling of a dark house. On the contrary, sunspaces near large glazed areas can lead to daylight factors above 10%. These are sensitive spaces which require efficient shading solutions.

An example of multidirectionality of daylight penetration

La Roche House, Paris, FRANCE

The natural lighting of this dwelling enriches Le Corbusier's architectural promenade with harmonious light compositions.

▽ The balanced light composition within the monochromatic triple height entry hall is due to the inter-penetration of surfaces and to the multiplicity of daylight sources.

Harmonious light compositions

Designed by Le Corbusier in 1925, this dwelling is divided into one semi-public part (including one gallery) and one private part. It invites the visitor to what the architect called an architectural promenade. "Provided with his two eyes and looking in front of him, our man walks, moves about, reading his surroundings, registering the unfolding sequence of architectural events appearing one after the other, feeling emotion, the fruit of these successive surprises".

According to Le Corbusier, "when you enter, the architectural spectacle" is taken in at a glance. You follow an itinerary and the perspectives unfold with much variety; one plays with the effects of light on the walls making pools of light or shadow. Often in the villa these pools are harmoniously balanced in the space and, since Le Corbusier is known to have aspired all his life to a synthesis of arts, a correspondence can be seen here between light compositions along the promenade and the influential modern paintings of that time.

A bright gallery

The villa was designed to provide a gallery to display the owner's collection of modern art. This gallery is lit by natural light coming mainly from two one-metre high window bands opposite each other, running the full length of the

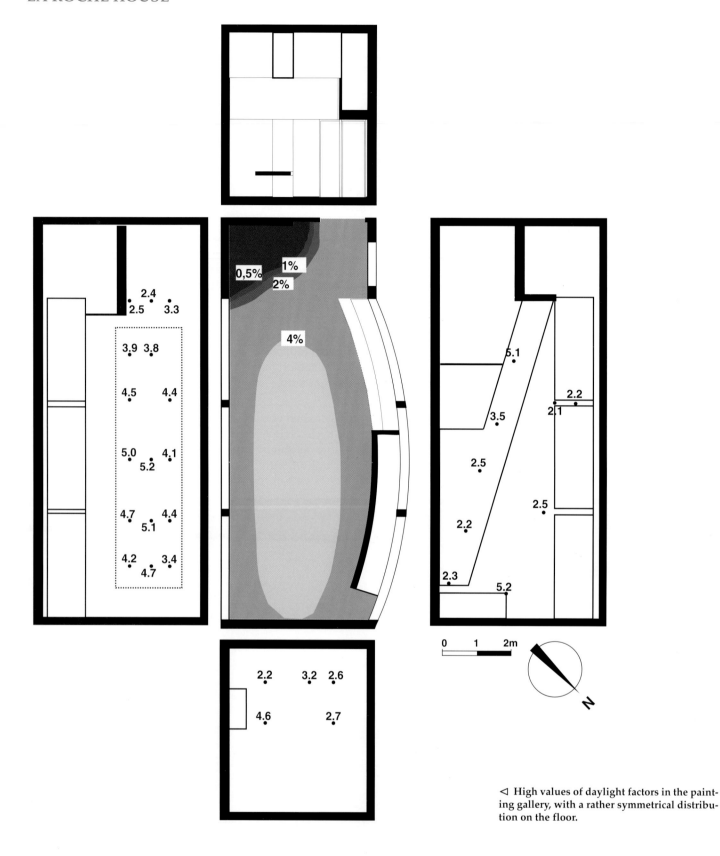

◁ High values of daylight factors in the painting gallery, with a rather symmetrical distribution on the floor.

lenght of the double height space. Located right below the ceiling, these strip windows maximize the exhibition surface, focus the attention on paintings, and minimize reflection problems. Horizontal daylight factors are relatively high (around 5% on average and up to 8%) and symmetrically distributed along the longitudinal room axis. In the same symmetrical manner, the adapta-

tion luminance is identical whether one is looking toward the north wall or toward the south wall.

Vertical daylight factors on walls are high compared to current protective recommendations for galleries. For example, on the straight longitudinal wall opposite the ramp, the actual surface used for exhibition has homogeneous

daylight factors close to 4.5% on average, higher than typical values which should be in the range of 0.5% to 2%.

A peculiar shading luminaire

After the villa was completed, the owner's main apprehension was the problem of direct sunlight penetration: "When the sun shines it strikes fair and square on several of my paintings, and

Surfaces within the gallery are painted △ ▽ with colours borrowed from purism: burnt earth, light blue, yellow, white and black.

△ The strip window of the gallery (on the left) recalls the one on the first level (on the right). To ensure the curvature, they are made of adjoining glazed panels.

◁△ **The shading luminaire which was added by Le Corbusier, following complaints from the owner.**

whatever Le Corbusier may say, I must admit to some anxiety, especially because of the Picassos and Braques which, I fear, were not executed in pigments which can stand up to such tests". Le Corbusier's response was a peculiar shading luminaire added in 1928 when the villa was renovated and which served also as a glare protection. However, some tests carried out with a mock-up placed under a movable simulated sun (a 'heliodon') show that this feature is not very effective in providing the required protection from sunlight.

Daylighting monitoring
The monitoring was conducted on 23 February 1995 and on 7 March 1996.

CREDITS

Building description
Le Corbusier said that La Roche House had an 'exploded' type of plan. The gallery and La Roche's dwelling spaces are connected by a triple height entry hall. The gallery occupies about 50m² and has a maximum indoor height of 4.5m.

Climate
La Roche villa is located in downtown Paris (Latitude: 48°52′N, Longitude: 2°20′E, Altitude: 25m). The monthly average outdoor temperature ranges from about 3°C in January to 19°C in July.

Client
M. La Roche
8 square du Docteur Blanche F-75016 Paris.

Architect
Le Corbusier

Monitoring organisation
ENTPE/DGCB
Rue Maurice Audin
69518 Vaulx-en-Velin- France

References
Benton, T. "Les villas de le Corbusier 1920-1930", Philipe Sers Editeur, Paris, 1984, p.224.

Curtis W.J. "Le Corbusier", Phaidon Press Ltd, London, 1992, p.736.

Material properties assessed on site

	Colour	Hemispherical-hemispherical reflectance
Floor		38%
Wall (south-east)	grey	35%
Wall (north-west)	grey	26%
Wall (north-east)	yellow	55%
		Normal-normal transmittance
Glazing		86%

A bright terraced house with daylighting techniques adapted to each space

Architect's House, Kifissia, Athens, GREECE

Daylight and sunlight animates the interior of this private house through a variety of openings.

A house built as a sequence of spaces looking towards a courtyard

This 350m² house is part of a 17-house complex, developed along three streets and around a common interior courtyard with mature pine trees. It is located in a northern suburb of Athens. The narrow, long layout contributes to the contact with the outdoor gardens. The Architect's House is developed as a sequence of spaces on two levels and a basement along a N to S axis. Opening onto the courtyard is the main feature of the house: a double height sunspace tilled with a plants. The sunspace incorporates the main stairs and a steel and wooden bridge that connects the master and childrens' bedrooms pro-

vides light and heating from the greenhouse and a feeling of exterior space. The house is surrounded by tall pine trees which provide shading, except for the south elevation, during most of the year. The absence of west-oriented windows protects the house from overheating during summer months.

Transparency between indoor spaces is provided by open planning and internal windows

The main daylighting strategy is to provide light in a selective and individual way to brightly each space. The sunspace is the most lit space, shaded

▽ **Sunspace daylit with east- and south-facing openings.**

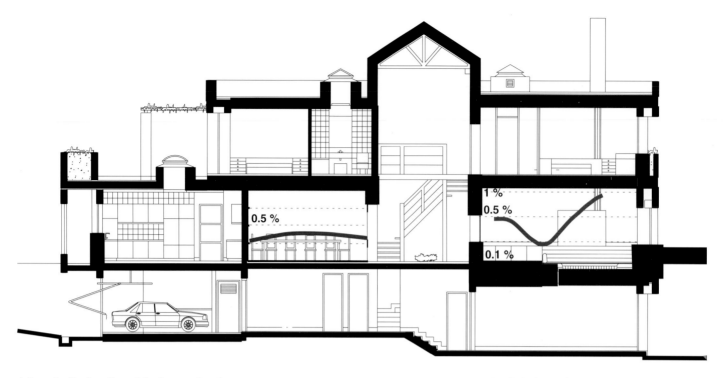

△ Longitudinal section of the house, showing daylight factor distribution in the dining and sitting rooms.

Daylight factor distribution 0.8 metres from the floor in the sitting room, the sunspace and the dining room. ▽

▽ △ Workplace daylit with borrowed light through a circular aperture (providing 270 lux on the desk under standard overcast sky conditions).

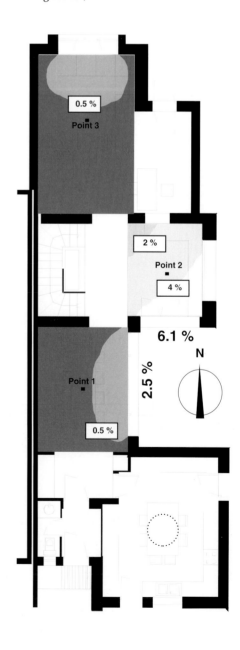

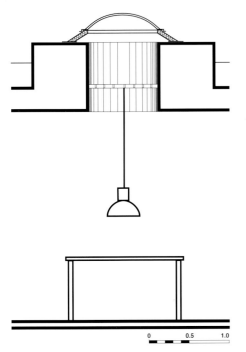

△ Section through kitchen skylight.

South-facing kitchen, with skylight ◁
(providing 2,267 lumen under standard overcast
sky conditions).

East-facing dining room. ▷

shaded by a fabric awning driven by an electric motor. It provides secondary daylighting to the adjacent spaces facing onto it.

Most doors are either glazed or provided, as in the bedrooms, with a top glazed panel in order to provide a high level of continuity of space and secondary light to the spaces behind. The basement sitting and work room is provided with a transparent insulation clerestory. The material used is a panel

of 'transparent insulation', a double glazed unit filled with a transluscent capillary material.

Spaces with high range of daylight factors, partly attenuated by light-colored finishes

The total window area is 62m^2, which represents 27% of the ground and first floor area. This area is large, but exterior obstructions cause a severe reduction of sky view and consequently a reduction in daylight levels.

The sitting room receives daylight mainly from a north-oriented recessed window. The mean daylight factor is 0.4% which is rather low. The contrast with the very bright sunspace next to it gives a darker appearance than would be expected. However, the area of the desk is well lit from the circular aperture toward the sunspace providing 290 lux on an overcast day (with horizontal external illuminance of 10,000 lux).

△ Scale model of house, seen from a south-east direction.

◁ North elevation, in the evening.

The luminance ratio between the window and surrounding walls is above 7.5 making the window a potential glare source. The daylight effect caused by the sunspace is significant. The daylight factors achieved are quite high, varying from a minimum value of 2% to a maximum of 4.3%. Despite the large amount of light reaching this room, light does not penetrate very deeply into the neighbouring spaces.

The east-oriented window is totally covered by external obstructions while the south one permits diffuse light to enter the space.

The dining room has a large window on the east side extending the whole width of the wall. Despite its large size, the measured daylight factors are quite low, due to external obstructions (walls, trees etc.), reaching a maximum value of 0.6%.

In the sunspace, the size of the glazed area permits a view of a large portion of the sky. Due to the narrowness of the room, the daylight levels observed give a rather bright outlook without distracting glare problems.

Daylighting monitoring

The measurements took place on 15 March 1996. Three rooms of the ground floor were monitored.

CREDITS

Building description
The suburb of Kifissia is located 15km north of downtown Athens. Seventeen terraced houses have been grouped in five separate clusters along the three open sides of a building block. Sizes of the houses vary from 150 to 350m^2, each with a basement including a private garage, a ground floor with living areas and an upper level with bedrooms The monitored house has an area of 350m^2, and was built in 1992.

Climate
Latitude: 37°58'N, Longitude: 23°40'E.
Its climate is typically Mediterranean with mean annual dry bulb temperature equal to 18.1°C. The maximum monthly average temperature is 22.5°C while the minimum is 13.8°C. The heating degree days (base: 18°C) are 1110 through the year and the cooling degree days (base: 26°C) are 122. Sunshine duration: maximum in July (12.42 hours/day, minimum in January (4.1 hours/day).

Client
Alexandros and Alexandra Tombazis

Architect
Meletitiki - A. N. Tombazis and Associates Architects, Ltd
Design by Alexandros N. Tombazis, assisted by N. Fletoridis
Monemvasias str, Polydroso Athens GR 151 25.

Monitoring organisation
Aris Tsangrassoulis
National Observatory, Athens

References
Design + Art in Greece 24/1993, Monographs II: Alexandros Tombazis, p48-49.

Material properties assessed on site

	Colour	Hemispherical-hemispherical reflectances
Wall finishes	white	85%
Ceiling	white	85%
Wooden floor (oak)	brown	30%

	Normal-normal transmittance	Hemispherical-hemispherical transmittance
Double glazing	82%	70%
Kitchen skylight		18%

Sunlit house on a sunken urban site

Casa Serra, Barcelona, SPAIN

Clerestories collect winter sun-light and bring it deep into the interior of this house which was renovated in 1992 by Architects Professor Rafael Serra, Helena Coch & Xavier Solsoria.

A building extension covering the former house

Over an old, small house built in 1890 on a narrow site giving onto a street without winter sun in an old district of the city, a new private house was constructed that sought to catch winter sun through clerestories in the roof and interior mirrors reflecting sunlight throughout the indoor spaces.

The former facade was preserved, within the new building. The creation of a new roof above the existing building, with vertical east-facing clerestories, allows daylight to be distributed from above.

Most of the rooms benefit from bilateral daylighting

The 240 square metres of new construction re-use the existing ground floor, above which three mezzanines have been inserted at intermediate levels. The first of these, housing the kitchen-dining-living room, occupies the former flat roof of the original house. The second, featuring a bedroom, studios and a bathroom, projects towards the street facade, covering the entrance space, which extends to the former facade. Finally, the third is located on top of the first, and includes the library, a bedroom and a bathroom.

The first and third floors open on one side onto the rear garden and on the other onto the central, covered courtyard. The second opens on one side onto the street and on the other onto the courtyard. Thus practically all the spaces have two openings, allowing lighting from two sides, cross-ventilation and great freedom in the internal layout.

Mirrors direct winter sunbeams deep into the building interior

Sunlight reaches the core of the building through three large south-east-facing clerestories in the sloping roof. The clerestories capture the morning sun in winter and reflect it, by means of sloping plastic mirrors, towards the various lower parts of the house. Thus, on the mornings of the colder months, the sun

◁ Shower of sunbeams in the office.

▽ Daylight factor distribution 0.80m above the floor levels.

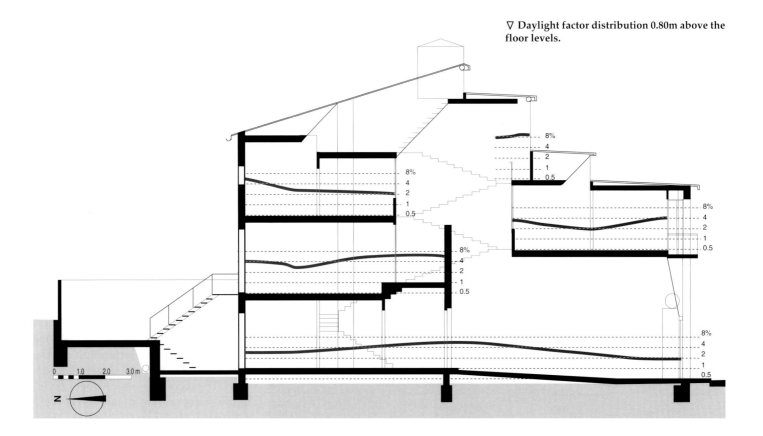

sun reaches the rooms on the northwest facade, giving life to rooms that would otherwise be dark and gloomy. At the same time, through the central space, the original facade is bathed in a magical light recalling the history of the house.

The same reflections that illuminate the innermost parts of the building provide lighting for the interior of the built-in wardrobes and, by means of a shaft lined with mirrors, the inner zone of the kitchen. The walls and finishings, for the most part in light tones, also enable light to be distributed to all the surfaces of the spaces.

During the summer season, roof openings contribute to cooling through natural ventilation, and filter daylight and solar heat with external blinds

In summer mode, the behaviour of the house with respect to light and heat changes substantially. The openings in the roof are protected with adjustable blinds allowing simultaneous ventilation and the entry of a low but sufficient amount of diffuse light to obtain a visual field with low uniform luminances. The glazed walls of the various facades are openable and permit the through-ventilation of all the spaces,

favoured by the openings in the roof for temperature circulation. The intermediate spaces without thermal protection, which are not used in winter, are incorporated into the house as living areas.

These strategies ensure that the house is operational all year round. In the intermediate seasons, when the Mediterranean climate is equally likely to produce hot weather as cold, the flexibility of the systems employed enables the behaviour of the building to adapt to the prevailing weather conditions.

Street facade. △

△ Main entrance.

The old facade, seen from the entrance in the new facade. ▽

▽ Clerestory above the stair well.

Luminous sequence enhances character of the living areas and transitional zones

It is worth describing the lighting sequence offered to the visitor walking from the street to the back garden. The first light sequence is related to the access from the street (bright light), which leads through the entrance space (shade) to the former facade illuminated from above (light). Then comes the original entrance hall (shade), from which we can choose either to go upstairs (light) or to continue into the back garden (light), which we glimpse through the glass doors. In this way a rhythm is established that can be perceived from the street, with a glimpse of the back garden through the glazed doors of the new facade, the old one, the internal partition wall and the rear facade.

Upstairs, we enter the communication area between the various levels, which are connected by shallow flights of stairs across the central courtyard, illuminated by the large clerestory. A variegated visual pattern is established between these levels, and at the same time the transparency between each of them provides views of the exterior beyond the space opposite us.

Daylighting monitoring

The measurements were taken at hourly intervals on 21 June, 21 December and 24 September with a data logger that takes eight simultaneous cells, and the exterior.

△ Tilted mirror above the former facade.

▽ Exterior view of the clerestories.

Material properties assessed on site

	Colour	Hemispherical-hemispherical reflectances
Walls	white	78%
House floor	grey-pink	25%
Atrium floor	grey	25%
	Normal-normal transmittance	Hemispherical-hemispherical transmittance
Window glazing	80%	70%

CREDITS

Building
The building is located at 14 Carrer Francolí, in Barcelona, (Latitude of 41°3′N, Longitude 2°1′E). As it is in an area of old buildings, the street is only 8 metres wide, and the houses are terraced, with frontages of irregular height. The renovation was conducted in 1992. Total floor area: 160m².

Climate
The climate of Barcelona is of the coastal Mediterranean type, with warm winters, relatively dry, hot summers with high humidity but little rain, and intermediate seasons with variable conditions and frequent torrential rain. The mean annual temperature is around 16°C and the winter and summer monthly averages are 8°C and 22°C respectively.

Client (owner)
Rafael Serra and Helena Coch

Architects
Rafael Serra, Helena Coch and Xavier Solsona

Monitoring organisation
Team from the School of Architecture of Barcelona (UPC)
Av. Diagonal 649
08028 Barcelona
Tel: +34.3-401 6421
Fax: +31.3-401 6426

A variety of south-facing facade and roof apertures provide daylight to a home with site constraints

Hawkes' House, Cambridge, UNITED KINGDOM

This small house with a simple layout is daylit through a variety of unusual apertures which animate the space. The window features include large south-facing glazing, and various south-facing clerestories and lightwells operating in combination with white diffusing surfaces.

▽ View of the south facade of the building seen from inside.

A variety of light levels is experienced as one moves through the indoor spaces

This case study was chosen to illustrate an ingenious response to a restricted site. The architect-owner has carefully worked with the constraints of size and orientation producing a 'simple box' washed with light. It runs east-west with its windowless back turned to the houses behind and its more open south and west side embracing a sunny private garden. The lighting design in this house is based on a series of transitional spaces. One enters from the west side into a dark entrance enhanced by the matt-black quarry tiles and the coloured walls. On the opposite side, abundant daylight penetrating the south-facing glazing invites us into the spatially complex living room. As Dean Hawkes says: "...*the section becomes more elaborate as you move through...*". Daylight in the living room penetrates from the south facade and the bay window with its clerestory. The light from the latter penetrates a square opening near the ceiling and is reflected downwards by the curved ceiling to the back of the seating area. The ceiling changes shape and height depending on the use of the space below and in order to create varying spatial qualities, as in the case of the dining area and the circulation route along the south side.

HAWKES' HOUSE

▷ View of the kitchen showing daylight from the clerestory.

▷ Daylight factors along a cross-section of the house, showing daylighting systems in kitchen and bathroom.

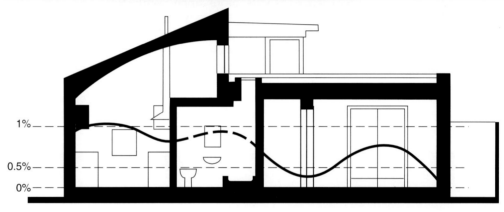

1%

0.5%

0%

0   2   5m

◁ Daylight factor contours on a plane 0.85m above floor.

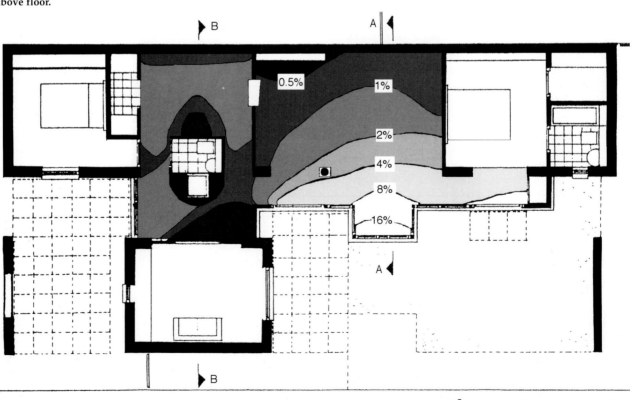

B

A

0.5%

1%

2%

4%

8%

16%

A

B

0   2   5m

1

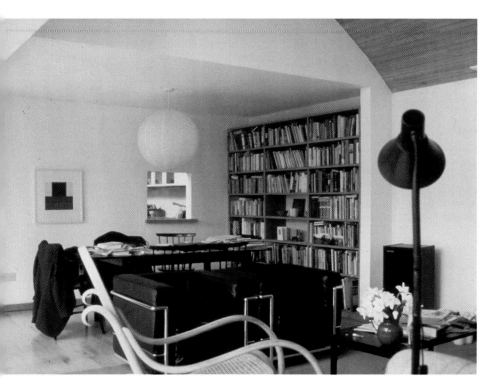

◁ View of the main room with the south-facing window and the clerestory enhancing sunlight and daylight penetration.

▽ Daylight factors along a cross-section of the main room.

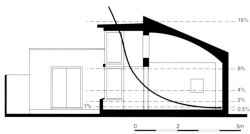

A south-facing clerestory in the kitchen

Another interesting space from a daylight point of view is the kitchen, which is lit by a clerestory facing south and, indirectly, from the openings connecting it to the surrounding spaces (entrance, dining area). Daylight bounces off the brightly coloured surfaces and the specular granite worktops, giving a feeling of a brightly lit space. Its south-facing orientation allows sunlight to penetrate this room located on the north side of the building.

Large fluctuations in daylight factor characterize contrasted spaces

The house design uses materials, colour, window design and space height in order to create different environments in a small overall volume. The visitor moves through different spaces which are differentiated by varying light levels. The windows are double glazed and use indoor roller blinds to provide insulation and shading. The house benefits from the south-facing series of openings which produce useful gains from the low winter sun.

Finally the lowered ceiling, indicating the passageway, protects the seating area from the high angle summer sun.

Daylight factors 0.8m above the floor vary from 1.5% to 0.5%. Even though the daylight factors are not very high, the space seems bright due to the high reflectances of the materials used: the wall has a reflectance of 86% and the granite surface, 32%. Finally, from the vertical daylight factor measurements, the even distribution of light can be clearly seen on the isolux contour figure: north, south, east and west have a daylight factor of 0.6%.

Bright finishes homogenize the light which enters only from the south

The main living room of the house has south facing double glazing and floods the adjoining corridor with light. Thus the daylight factors near the window vary from 5% to 18%. The room is not as dramatic as might be expected due to the small size of the interior wall opening. Thus the rate at which the daylight factor drops as we move towards the north wall is not

seriously affected. According to the architect, this effect was deliberate since the idea was to create a variety of conditions with moderate levels of light for relaxation, listening to music and reading. This effect is enhanced by the low reflectances of the furniture and the floor (13%). This is also obvious from the cross section showing the dramatic drop in daylight levels from south to north. Finally, even though there is a strong directional light entering from the south-facing glazing, this effect is diminished in the carpeted area of the living room. The light there seems diffused and this is shown by the vertical daylight factor measurements taken in the centre of the carpeted area where the south-facing factor is 1.5% and the north-facing factor is a third of this value: 0.5%.

Field measurements

The daylighting performance was assessed in the living room, kitchen and entrance area and along the cross section of the latter into the study. Daylight factors were measured at 0.85m from the floor on 22 March 1996.

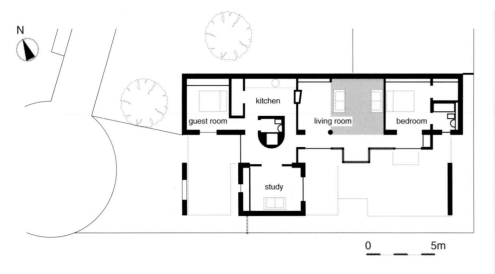

△ Hawkes' House floor plan. (Source: Dean Hawkes and *The Architects' Journal*).

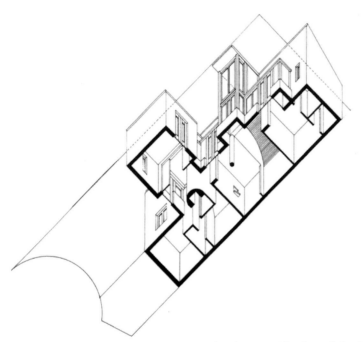

▽ Axonometric view of the house. (Source: Dean Hawkes and *The Architects' Journal*).

CREDITS

Site and climate

The Hawkes house is located in Cambridge (Latitude: 52°12′N, Longitude: 00°08′E). The site is bounded on the north side by a series of private gardens, and has a total area of just over 250m². The climate in Cambridge has monthly average outdoor temperatures close to 5.4°C in winter and 14.9°C during summer. The average daily sunshine duration is 4.18 hours.

Building

The 110m² house was designed by the owner, Prof. Dean Hawkes in 1991. It is a single-storey space entered from the west. Moving from west to east the spaces are: a guest room with a single south-facing window, an entrance hall with a guest bathroom, a kitchen on the north side and a study on the south side. Moving towards the east we enter the living room and at the end of the corridor we reach the master bedroom with ensuite bathroom.

Architects

Stephen Greenberg & Dean Hawkes: Dean Hawkes

Client

Christine Hawkes

Monitoring organisation

The Martin Centre for Architectural and Urban Studies, Department of Architecture, University of Cambridge,
6 Chaucer Road
Cambridge CB2 2EB, U.K.

Acknowledgements

We would like to thank Professor Dean Hawkes and Mrs Hawkes for approving the monitoring of their house. Furthermore we are grateful to the architects, Stephen Greenberg & Dean Hawkes and *The Architects' Journal* for providing us with the drawings of the residence and Prof. Dean Hawkes for offering some of his slides.

References

Banovic, M, *Environmental Aspects of the Hawkes' House, Cambridge*, Unpublished, Essay for the M.Phil. in Environmental Design in Architecture, Department of Architecture, University of Cambridge, 1995.

Field, M, 'Discreet, simple box has a richness born of experience', *The Architects' Journal*, Vol. 203, No. 9, 7 March 1996, pp. 37-41.

Kennedy, J, 'Cambridge blue', *Architecture Today*, No. 37, April 1993, p. 32.

Materials properties assessed on site

	Colour	Hemispherical-hemispherical reflectances
Floor - carpet	blue	13%
Floor - timber boards	brown	45%
Floor - quarry tiles	dark grey	6%
Wall	white	86%
Window frame	grey	31%
Granite kitchen surface	grey	32%
	Direct-direct transmittance	Hemispherical-hemispherical transmittance
Living rm.sth. glazing	86%	63%

Demonstration projects

In this section we present buildings which have a research or energy technology demonstration function and contain some interesting daylighting features.

Daylight smoothes over rectangular components and rooms

1929 World Fair, German Pavilion, Barcelona, SPAIN

In this avant-garde 1929 construction by architect Mies Van der Rohe, daylight penetrates freely through transparent or translucent walls.

▽ Transparent walls join floor and ceiling, leading to a maximum penetration of daylight, but large overhangs prevent direct sunlight penetration.

An elegant architectural landmark built in 1929

The German pavilion was built on the occasion of the 1929 World Fair in Barcelona. It was reconstructed in 1986. The architect, Mies Van der Rohe, proposed this restrained elegant pavillon. It can be seen as an assembly of rectangular panels, either opaque, translucent or transparent. It is largely open to the exterior, but large overhangs protect it from direct sunlight. So much has been written on this landmark building, often seen as the architectural expression of Cubism, that it would be pretentious to give another analysis of the pavilion. The comments therefore concentrate on its general optical behaviour, with respect to shapes and materials.

No windows, just transparent walls, for a very bright building

Transparent and translucent walls stretch from floor to ceiling, providing large amounts of daylight deep in the interior. Daylight penetrates only from the facades, but from all four orientations. Minimum daylight factors are high: 2% except for a small passageway between two partitions. Most of the floor has daylight factors in excess of 4%. In cross-section, the ratio of building width to ceiling height is three to one, and ratio of building length to height is eight to one.

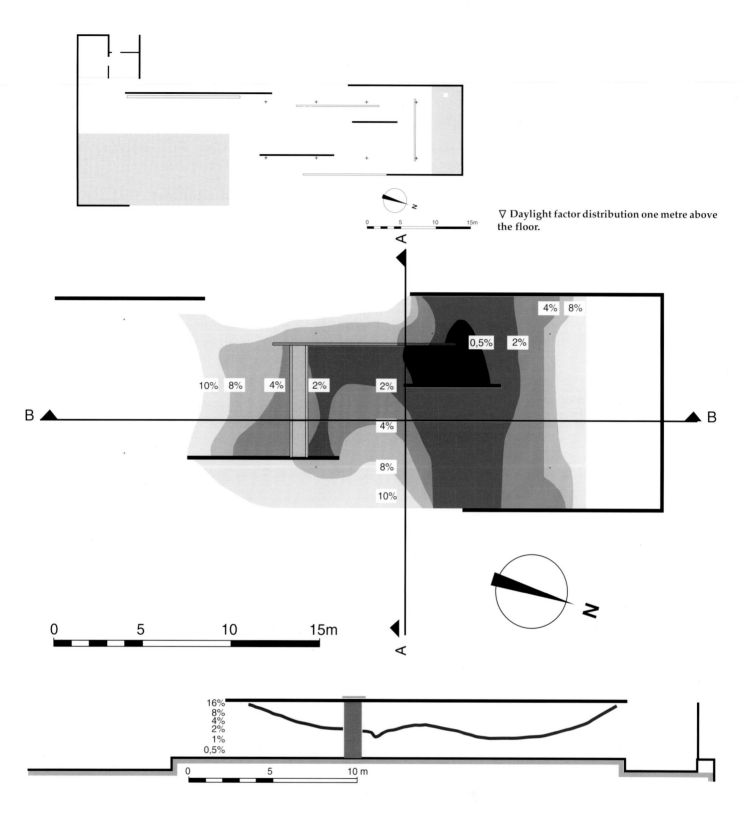

◁ General plan of the German Pavilion.

▽ Daylight factor distribution one metre above the floor.

△ Daylight factor distribution along a north-south axis (BB).

▽ Daylight factor distribution along an east-west axis (AA).

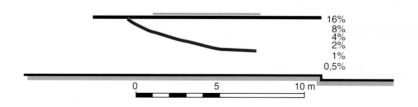

△ Indoor space management showing the translucent wall, the marble wall, the stone floor and the supporting column.

◁ Central room with sunlight striking the exterior black marble.

◁ Central room, with external walls in shade.

▷ The black marble wall, and the light coloured floor extending beyond the glazed door.

Mineral or wooden walls are displayed like art work

Opaque walls are made of Larissa green marble, onyx and wood. They are dark, enhancing the effects of direct daylight penetration versus the internal reflections. In the centre is a translucent glazed wall. Optically, one can say that the white ceilings and the light-coloured floor reflect daylight to each other, but that partitions and walls tend to absorb light. Overhangs spread way over the external walls, up to five metres on the north side. The design is clearly adapted to a sunny climate: shading from overhangs, use of ground-reflected sunlight.

Daylighting monitoring

Daylighting monitoring was conducted in April 1996.

△ Detail of the indoor glazed partition.

∇ Overhangs block sunlight, floor extensions reflect it, marble walls absorb it.

CREDITS

Building
Built in 1929. Demolished then rebuilt between 1981 and 1986.

Climate
The climate of Barcelona is of the coastal Mediterranean type, with warm winters, relatively dry, hot summers with high humidity but little rain, and intermediate seasons with variable conditions and frequent torrential rain. The mean annual temperature is around 16°C and the winter and summer monthly averages are 8°C and 22°C respectively.

Architect
Mies Van der Rohe

Monitoring organization
ENTPE, Rue Audin
F 69120 Vaulx en Velin
Tel: +33.4-72 04 70 27
Fax: +33.4-72 04 70 41

References
Juan Pablo Bonta, "Anatomie de l'interprétation en Architecture. Etude sémiotique de la critique du Pavillon de Barcelone de Mies Van der Rohe", ed. Gustavo Gili, Barcelone, 1975, p. 29.

José Quetglas, "Imagenes del Pabellon de Alemania", "Der Gläserne Scherecken", 1991.

Nicolau M. Rubio, Cahiers d'Art VIII-XI, 1929.

Publication de la Fondation Publique du Pavillon Allemand de Barcelone de Mies Van der Rohe, Ajuntament Barcelone 1987.

Material properties assessed on site

	Colour	Hemispherical-hemispherical reflectances
Wall		36%
Ceiling	white	70%
Floor	marble	45%
Exterior wall	marble	45%
Exterior wall	green marble	24%
		Hemispherical-hemispherical transmittance
Glazing		86%

Four window systems compared in the same building give useful data concerning lighting control strategies

Conphoebus Office Building, Catania, Sicily, ITALY

This experimental building is equiped with various window systems, allowing simultaneous comparison of their performance under identical climatic conditions.

Windows systems designed for Mediterranean climate

The Conphoebus office building is located in Catania's southern industrial zone, on a flat site at 7 meters above sea level. The 1650 square meters of office space are distributed over three floors in a rectangular 12m wide, 42m long building. The two major facades face north and south. The entire ground floor is a service area without offices and it has full-height windows provied with slatted, horizontal, over-hanging shades on the South facade. The two upper floors are divided into four vertical modules.

All northern modules have exactly the same facade component consisting of a reinforced-concrete precast panel, splayed outside, and provided with a central double pane window.

The facade of the southern modules is characterized by four different bio-climatic strategies, one for each module. They allow different levels of solar gain and daylight penetration, and are named as follows:

- module A south: 'smart windows'
- module B south: 'total shading grid'
- module C south: 'self-shaded windows'
- module D south: 'solar integrated components'

▽ **Indoor views of the four test rooms.**

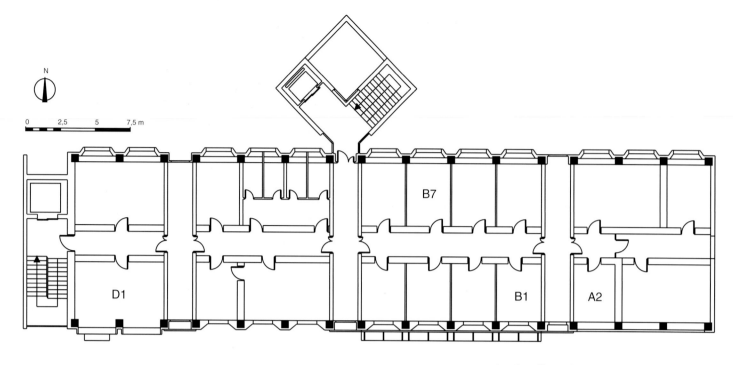

△ First floor plan of the Conphoebus office building.

Room D1 (south - solar integrated component)

Room D1 is a large office room with dimensions 4.3m x 6.3m. There is a clerestory window at the upper part and a larger flat window aligned to the facade at the lower part; the other unit differentiates only in the lower portion which is designed as a bay window protruding from the facade. The windows have low conductivity double glazing (6/12/6). The clerestory window has a 350mm air cavity and is provided with vents that permit the communication with solar chimneys on the side. The clerestory is made of single glass (6mm) and is partially obscured at the top by the horizontal concrete beam of the building structure, which reduces the daylighting performance of the component (see section).

The shading devices are a light roller blind located in the clerestory window, close to the external glazing, and a light-coloured retractable venetian blind placed on the flat and bay windows, 25cm from the external glazing. The roller as well as venetian blinds are motorized and can be lowered or raised by manual operation. Also, the tilt of venetian slats can be controlled by the user. The horizontal position is very effective to cut out the high sun angles and to shade the window seat.

The external light-shelf is made of tilted aluminium sheets reflecting daylight

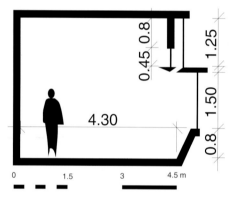

Principle of window system D1. △

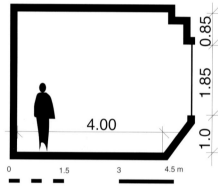

△ Principle of window system B7.

Principle of window system B1. ▽

▽ Principle of window system A2.

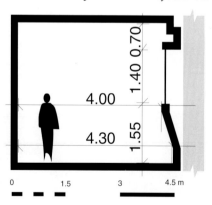

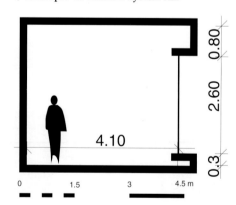

deeper into the room through the upper cavity window when the roller blind is raised. The internal light-shelf shades the area of the room close to window and reduces the glare by redirecting daylight to the back of the room.

270

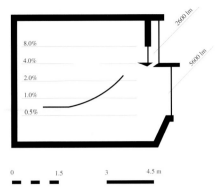

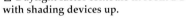

Section of room D1 showing daylight factor profile △ and incoming light flux under overcast sky.

Section of room B7 showing daylight factor profile ▽ and incoming light flux under overcast sky.

△ Daylight factor contours in room D1 with shading devices up.

▽ Daylight factor contours in room B7 with venetian blind up.

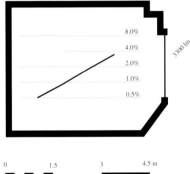

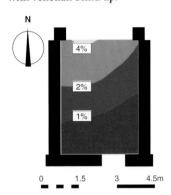

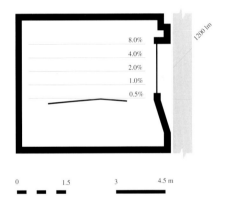

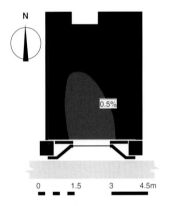

Section of room B1 showing daylight factor profile △ and incoming light flux under overcast sky.

Section of room A2 showing daylight factor profile ▽ and incoming light flux under overcast sky.

△ Daylight factor contours in room B1.

▽ Daylight factor contours in room A2 with venetian blind up.

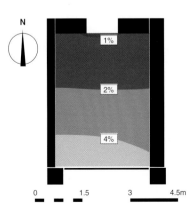

271

△ External view of the four window systems.

The results of measurements show that daylight penetration is rather low, although the glazed area is large (6m²) by comparison with the floor area (26m²). The concrete beam blocks most of the daylight coming from the light-shelf. When the venetian blinds are pulled down, with blades in the horizontal position, the values are decreased by roughly 20%.

Room B7 - (north - module B)

Room B7 is located at the first floor of the building in the North module B. The room dimensions are 3.2m x 3.9m and the window is 1.4m x 1.5m (same dimensions as in room B1). The main difference consists of the facade panel splaying to collect more daylight from the environment. The window, located at the centre of panel, is equipped with an internal venetian blind (plastic material, bright colour). Except for the north wall, the other walls are of built-in furniture. More than half the workplane has a daylight factor higher than 1%, for a glazing ratio of 0.12 (1.5m² of glazing devided by 12.5m² of floor area).

Daylight factor contours in room B7 show a pronounced asymmetry due to the V-shape form of the external stairs which shades the east zone of the room. This asymetry disappears in north-facing rooms located far from the stairs as demonstrated by additional daylight factor measurements.

Room A2 (south - smart windows)

Room A2 is an office room with dimensions of 2.9m x 3.9m. North and east walls consist of furniture whereas the West one is a traditional brick wall. In the south wall there is a large double pane window (dimensions 2.4 x 2.5m) starting 0.5m above the floor and recessed 0.5m from the outer face of the building. Externally to the window there is a box containing two automatic motor-driven retractable venetian blinds with horizontal metallic slats. During the vertical displacement, the angular position of the slats is adapted: partially closed during lowering and totally open during raising. The rotation of the slats is allowed only when the vertical movement is stopped. The overhang together with the external blind box provide adequate sun shading in summer, while the external blinds prevent sun penetration in winter.

This room happens to be the brightest of all, with daylight factors ranging from 1 to 6%.

Room B1 (south - total shading grid)

Room B1 is a typical office room located in the south module B and has dimensions of 3.2 x 3.9m (see room B7). North and west walls are made of furniture, the east one is a traditional brick wall. On the south wall a 1.4m x 1.5m window is fixed to the innerface of a reinforced-concrete cladding panel, which provides approximately 0.1m of overhang to window head and sides. This window-and-panel arrangement is shaded by a fixed reinforced-concrete brise-soleil. This is 0.6m deep, and the angle and pitch of its blades provide total shading during the summer and partial shading in the mid-seasons.

Daylight factor measurements show that the brise-soleil significantly reduces the amount of daylight inside, with daylight factors barely reaching 0.5%.

Daylight factor values are strongly reduced by protection against solar penetration

The former results show clearly the loss on diffuse light penetration when significant solar protections are added. However, designs with solar protections made of a simple overhang above the window perform best. Such systems do not block too much the light penetrating deeply inside the rooms, since such light originates from areas of the sky vault located close from the horizon. This trend is however different for buildings surrounded by other constructions.

Occupancy pattern and human behaviour are key criteria in performance of lighting control strategies

In room A2, the behaviour of two control strategies were tested: one dealing with the control of venetian blinds and the other with operation of automatic/manual lighting system. The artificial lighting could be controlled either automatically or manually.

In the automatic mode, control was based on measurement of illuminance on the work plane, and vertical internal illuminance near the window. Continuous measurement of climatic data was

undertaken, as well as the recording of the electricity consumption of the luminaires.

The monitoring showed the modulation of venetian blinds as a function of the sun position and external illuminance conditions. On clear days in winter, the modulation effect of the automatic lighting control occurs and the behaviour of power lamps follows the occupancy. On very cloudy winter days, because of insufficient daylighting levels inside the room, the maximum power of lamps is required for the entire occupancy period.

The performance of the automatic lighting system in terms of energy saving was estimated in case of the venetian blinds being raised, by comparing two daily periods in which the sky was cloudy and the room occupancy was the same. The corrresponding graph shows the hourly lighting consumption on the two days, for mean occupancy equal to 30%. Lighting energy consumption was only 2870 kJ due to automatic operation, increasing to 4500 kJ with manual control, resulting about 50% in energy saving.

Another interesting result is that there is a rather good correlation between the vertical global illuminance on the facade of the building and the indoor illuminance, suggesting that electric lighting control systems and blind control systems can be operated on the basis of external vertical values. This could be preferred to indoor illuminance measurements which are influenced by the light attenuation of the blinds.

Daylighting monitoring

The monitoring was performed in four rooms of the first floor and in two rooms of the second floor. In the rooms A1 and D1 a long-term monitoring was performed, while in the other rooms only spot measurements of daylighting availability were carried out.

Daylight factors and penetrating luminous fluxes were measured in several months: January 1996 (room B7), April and May 1996 (room B1), and September 1996 (rooms A2 and D1).

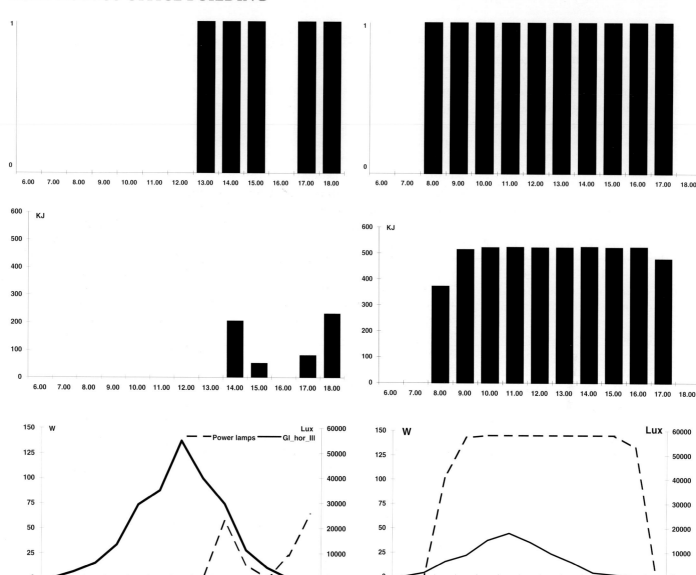

△ Room A2: occupancy pattern on a fairly clear day (30 January 1996).

▽ Room A2: occupancy pattern on a cloudy day (1 Febuary 1996).

Room A2: energy consumption due to lamps (30 January 1996).

Room A2: energy consumption due to lamps (1 Febuary 1996).

Room A2: lighting power and global horizontal illuminance (30 January 1996).

Room A2: lighting power and global horizontal illuminance (1 Febuary 1996).

CREDITS

Building description
1,650m² of office space distributed over three floors in a rectangular building, 12m in width, 42m in length. It is used for research purposes and houses 48 people. It was built in 1987.

Climate
Latitude: 37°28'N, Longitude: 15°04'E, Altitude: 7m.
Average ambient temperatures: 10.7°C in January and 26.5°C in July.
Annual sunshine duration: 2,492 hrs/yr

Client
Conphoebus Scrl
Passo Martino
95030 Piano d'Arci, Catania (Italy)

Architect
Sergio Los
Synergia Progetti
c/da Boschetto, 9
36061 Bassano del Grappa, Vicenza (Italy)
tel. +39.424-503 098

Monitoring organisation
Conphoebus
Energy in Buildings dept.
Catania, Sicily.

Material properties assessed on site

	Colour	Hemispherical-hemispherical reflectance
Walls and ceiling	white	72%
Beam	grey	47%
Floor	light brown	52%
Furniture walls	walnut	31%
Desk	brown	11%

	Hemispherical-hemispherical transmittance	Normal-normal transmittance
Double glazing (room B7)	75%	83%

Daylight and sunlight redirected to reflective ceiling for deeper daylight penetration

Brundtland Centre, Toftlund, DENMARK

The south facade of the Brundtland centre is equipped with a sophisticated optical system combining fixed and movable reflective blinds, and built-in luminaires, all of them beaming light to a reflective ceiling.

▽ **Indoor view of a meeting room, showing the reflective ceiling and the luminaires in front of teh window (Photograph by KHR A/S Architects).**

A building aimed at demonstrating energy-efficient solutions

The overall design concept of the Brundtland Centre is based on a further development of the principles of the winning project in the European Commission's competition 'Working in the City', won by Esbensen Consulting Engineers, KHR Architects and ISLEF entrepreneurs. The 1,800m² Brundtland Centre, located in Toftlund in southern Jutland, was built in 1994, and has become an important exhibition building in Denmark, showing new energy efficient strategies for office buildings embodied in an extraordinary architectural design. The Centre has been built in the context of the Brundtland town project in Toftlund, where a significant attempt has been made to respond to the aims of the Brundtland Commission in achieving sustainable development within the fields of energy and the environment. The Brundtland Centre is used for exhibition and educational activities, in energy related topics and disseminating results from energy saving activities; while the building itself serves as an energy efficient demonstration project.

The project has been subsidized by the Solar House programme of the European Commission DG XII as part of its JOULE II research and developments programme for low-energy buildings. Additional support was supplied by the

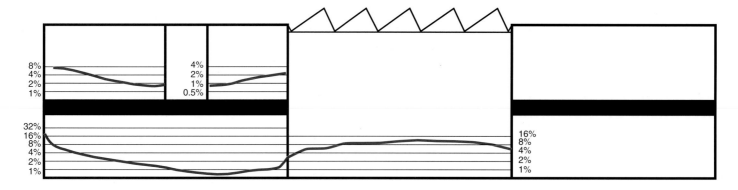

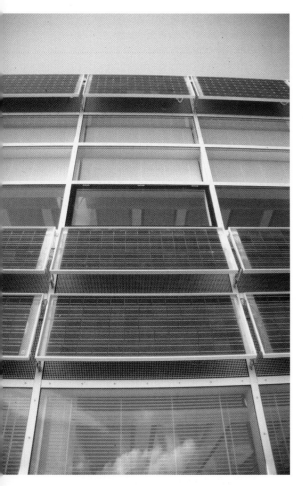

△ External view of the south facade, showing windows with built-in blinds and PV panels (Photograph by KHR A/S Architects).

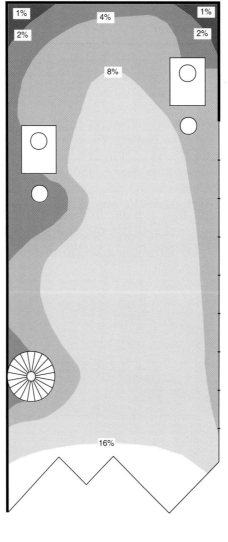

△ Daylight factor variations on the work plane of the offices and in atrium.

◁ Daylight factor distribution on the floor of the atrium.

Southern Jutland County, Nørre Rangstrup Municipality, and the Danish Energy Council. The building will go through comprehensive monitoring and dissemination phases, addressing decision makers, consultants and architects throughout Europe.

An atrium covered with photovoltaic cells, contributing to daylighting and natural ventilation

The basis of the scheme is a large circular plan, recessed in the south sloping terrain. Within this circular form there is a three-winged composition of two-storey, rectangular buildings that surround a glass-roofed atrium. The general building design strategy has been to use passive solar energy and natural ventilation techniques and to minimize use of mechanical air treatment in the building. Active cooling has been completely avoided. The whole building, except for the office spaces, is ventilated using the atrium as a pre-heating buffer for fresh air. An exhaust air system maintains an underpressure in the building and fresh air flows naturally from the atrium through openings into the adjacent spaces. The building has a large atrium oriented to the south-west at the centre of the building. The atrium is fully glazed on its south-west facade with integrated PV-elements in the south-facing glazed atrium saw-tooth roof to demonstrate architectural integration of PV-elements which has been the one of the main themes in the energy design of the building. Lecture halls and classrooms are located towards south-east, while offices are located either adjacent to the atrium or facing south. South-east facing offices adjacent to the exterior facade have decentralized ventilation systems incorporating local heat exchangers with integrated double fans, where presence detectors control the unit, so only occupied offices are ventilated. The efficiency of the heat exchangers is about 60%. The south-east facade has 46m² of standard PV-elements integrated in the facade.

Facades deviate daylight and sunlight and integrated lamps are dimmed according to daylight penetrations

The daylighting design with innovative daylight systems demonstrate the exploitation of daylight as a major design parameter. Two new venetian blind systems, integrated in sealed double glazing have been developed by Lichtplanung Christian Bartenbach (Austria). The main function of the systems is to redirect diffuse daylight up to a reflective anodized aluminium ceiling from where the daylight is to be reflected to the working surfaces at the back of the room. The window is divided into three parts. The upper daylight window, consists of numerous, equally spaced specular louvres in between the glazed unit permitting daylight and sunlight to enter the room while remaining opaque to the view-out side. In front of the louvre system, between the glazed

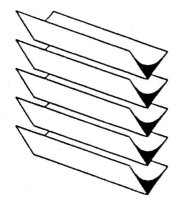

Reflection above 0°

0°

No glare within this area

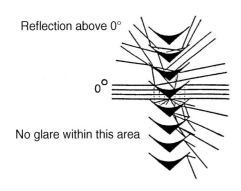

△ The blinds are integrated with the daylight windows and reflect light onto the ceiling and from here, by way of reflectors, deeper into the building.

units, direct sunlight is controlled by a thin roller blind to reduce glare problems and visual discomfort caused by direct sunlight projected onto the system. The middle view windows, where the upper edge of the window corresponds to the eye height of a standing person, have thin, inverted specular venetian blinds, which allow visual contact with the outside while redirecting daylight to the ceiling. The lower window is a normal, openable window with manual, specular venetian blinds.

The artificial lighting is automatically controlled by a daylight-responsive lighting control system located in the centre of the window facade above the daylight window pointing towards the interior. The lighting control system dims the interior lighting according to the daylight level, but the user can override the control manually. In each office, specially designed luminaires with four tubular fluorescent light sources of 55 W (HF-ballast) are located in the window facade between the daylight window and view window. The indirect lighting system radiates light up to the specular reflective ceiling giving a work plane illuminance level of 600 to 1000 lux.

Atrium PV-roof transmit about 20% of incoming light

The atrium has low-E double glazing with a U-value of 1.6 W/m²K. In the south-facing glazed atrium roof, solar shading is provided by circular PV-elements integrated in the incident sealed glazing unit permitting 20% of light to enter the atrium. Since some shading will occur within the roof itself, only the upper half of the south facing parts have PV-elements. The remainder being 'dummy' PV cells which appear to be identical to the real ones. Measurements along the centre of the atrium towards the south-west glazed facade show an increasing daylight factor distribution varying from 4 to 16%, while daylight factors near the facade are roughly 19% over a distance 0 to 2m from the facade. The south-east red brick facade also reduces the daylight factor across the atrium by approximately 2% near its facade compared to the glazed facade in the office wing. However fairly uniform well-daylit conditions are experienced in the atrium when the sky is overcast.

Large glazed areas on atrium facade lead to reasonable daylight penetration in rooms adjacent to atrium

The exhibition space on the ground floor is well daylit since daylight is received from the atrium and from the full height exterior, south-facing windows. The internal full height window towards the atrium gives daylight factors of approximately 2 to 3%. Near the exterior facade, measurements show that the daylight factors varies varies from 7% near the window to 1% in the middle of the room (6m). The fairly low daylight factors near the window are caused by the shading effect of the artificial lighting system possitioned in the window, by the exterior PV-elements and by the window frames. In the offices on the second floor, measurements on the work plane show that the daylight factor of 2%, occurs at a distance of approximately 1 m from the window. The daylight factor distribution is altogether fairly uniform with daylight factors no less than 0.8% at the back of the room.

Facade system increases daylight penetration

Offices with exterior south-facing windows have daylight factors of about 2% measured at a distance of 4.5m from the window, which is higher than with standard window configurations. The artificial lighting system in the window, the window frame and the exterior PV-elements reduce the daylight factor penetration close to the window to 7%. As for the offices adjacent to the atrium, the daylight illuminance distribution is uniform and the offices are perceived to be well daylit due to the large windows and the reflective anodized aluminium ceiling. However, the VDUs can suffer from veiling reflections and occupants may experience glare problems since most of the light from the window and the lighting system is radiated upwards increasing the luminance of the reflective ceiling.

The indirect artificial lighting system together with the daylighting system reverses the typical spatial light distribution of a normal office as the ceiling is of higher luminance than the working plane. Even though the light distribution is uniform, such a lighting scheme may cause the interior to lose character due to the diffuse light distribution.

However, all offices have local task lighting which will minimize these effects.

General satisfaction of occupants but with some concerns about the aesthetics of the lighting patterns

The offices receives favourable comments from the occupants, but the daylighting systems may cause distracting, distorted patterns on the ceiling when reflected sunlight is projected onto the interior surfaces, since the daylighting systems may reflect bands of light at particular spatial frequencies on the ceiling and adjacent wall.

Field measurements

The daylight performance of the building was mainly assessed in the atrium and the offices in the building adjacent to the atrium. In addition, the daylight factors were measured at the top floor in the open-plan offices adjacent to the atrium also facing south. Daylight factors were measured in December 1996. Typical outdoor illuminance were around 5,000 lux.

△ Scale model of the Brundtland centre with the roof opened, showing the orientation of the saw-tooth roof with respect to the atrium shape (Photograph by KHR A/S Architects).

Material properties assessed on site

	Colour	Hemispherical-hemispherical reflectance
Wall	yellow bricks	30%
Wall	grey	45%
Floor	red bricks	20%
Wall	white	30%
Ceiling	aluminium	95%
Ceiling	white	89%
Floor	wood block	42%

	Direct-direct transmittance	Hemispherical-hemispherical transmittance
Double glazing	79%	73%
Atrium PV-GLAS		20%

CREDITS

Building description
The building is built in 1994 with a gross area of 1,800m².

Site and climate
The minimum average temperature is -1.1°C in February and the maximum average temperature is 16.7 in July. The minimum global radiation on a horizontal is 384 Wh/m²day in December and the maximum global radiation on horizontal is 6188 Wh/m²day in June.

Client
Norre-Rangstrup
Manicipality
6520 Toftlund, Denmark

Contractor
Hojgaard & Schultz
Jaegersborg Allé 4
2920 Charlottenlund, Denmark

Architect
KHR A/S Architects
Teknikerbyen 7, 2830 Virum, Denmark

Building owner
Brundtland Centre Denmark
Brundtland Parken 4
6520 Toftlund, Denmark

Engineers, energy concept and design
Esbensen Consulting Engineers FIDIC
Teknikerbyen 38, 2830 Virum, Denmark

Daylighting and special uplight design
Bartenbach LichtLabor
Rinnerstasse 14, 6071 Aldrans, Austria

Design tools and evaluation
The Martin Centre
Univeristy of Cambridge
6, Chaucer Rd., Cambridge CB2 2EB,
United Kingdom

Monitoring organisation
Danish Building Research Institute
Energy and Indoor Climate Division, Project Group: Daylight in Buildings
P.O. Box 119, 2970 Hørsholm, Denmark

References
Kristensen, P. E. 1994. *Daylighting Technologies in Non-Domestic Buildings*. European Directory of Energy Efficient Building, James & James, Science Publishers Limited, London

Madsen, C. E., Sørensen, H. 1994. *BrundtlandCentre in Toftlund Denmark - Focus 21*. North Sun 94: Solar energy at high latitudes (Editors: MacGregor K., Porteous C.), James & James, Science Publishers Limited, London

Esbensen, T., Madsen, C. E., Sørensen, H., Givskov K. 1996. *BrundtlandCentre Denmark - Focus 21: EU Joule House demonstation project on energy efficient office buildings*. 4th European Conference on Architecture (Edited: Stephens H. S.), Berlin, Germany

Other notable buildings

The buildings included in this section could not be classified under a generic title. They house daylight patterns which are worth detailed descriptions.

A 19th century conservatory with a lightweight supporting structure

The Palm House, Royal Botanic Gardens, Kew, London, UNITED KINGDOM

This structure, built in 1847, offers very little obtruction to daylight which helps to compensate for the reduction in glazing transmittance inherent in such conservatories due to deposits of algae inside and dirt outside.

"The Greatest Glasshouse"

Although smaller than other glasshouses at Kew, the Palm House is often described as "the greatest glasshouse" in response to its elegant, economical structure and the quality of its exhibition space. It is the largest surviving curvilinear Victorian glasshouse and represents the first use of

wrought iron to span such widths without obstructive supporting columns. The Palm House is not a building in the traditional sense of the word but rather an engineering structure. It contains 7,500 sheets of wrought and cast iron, of which about 20% are structural, the remainder being purely decorative. It is a perfectly symetrical fully glazed white-painted iron structure with its long axis running north-south and has two spiral staircases which lead to a walkway at the top of the raised central part of the glass house.

◁ Exterior view of the Palm House.

▽ Interior view of the central body of the conservatory.

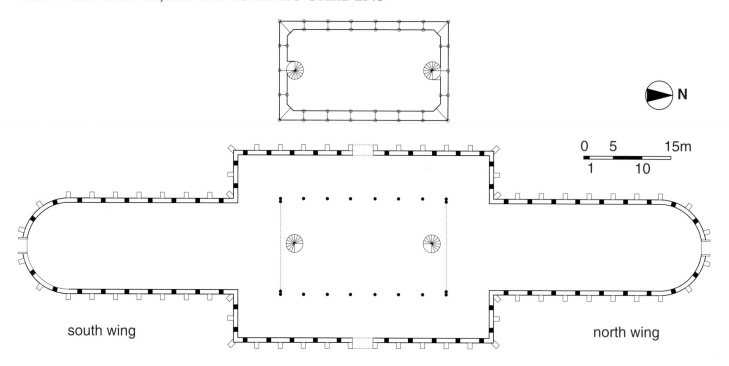

N

0 5 15m
1 10

south wing

north wing

△ Ground floor and gallery plan.

▽ Ground floor walkway.

Algae and dirt reduce the luminous transmittance of the glazing

Light is filtered down through the dense and impressively high foliage, which represents a tropical rainforest. The original glazing was renovated in 1985 to 88. Initially, it seemed that polycarbonate would have been the ideal replacement glazing material, since it is shatterproof and easy to bend. However, as polycarbonate glazing materials are susceptible to damage from hailstones and must be imported, curved, toughened glass was used instead to ensure safety and reduce maintenance costs. Individual templates were provided and cut on site. The upper edge of each lap was sealed with clear silicone, for heat retention and to avoid trapping algae.

The general appearance of the building's interior is less bright than expected due to the enormous plants and the significant degree of dirt on the glazing caused by algae growth on the interior side and air pollution on the exterior side.

Lightweight, elegant supporting structure minimizes obstruction of daylight

The glazing is not uniformly dirty and thus measurements on cleaner, newly

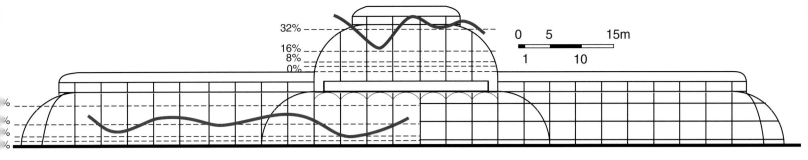

△ Daylight factors along a longitudinal section, based on an original drawing by Postford Duvivier.

▽ Daylight factors along a cross-section, based on an original drawing by Postford Duvivier.

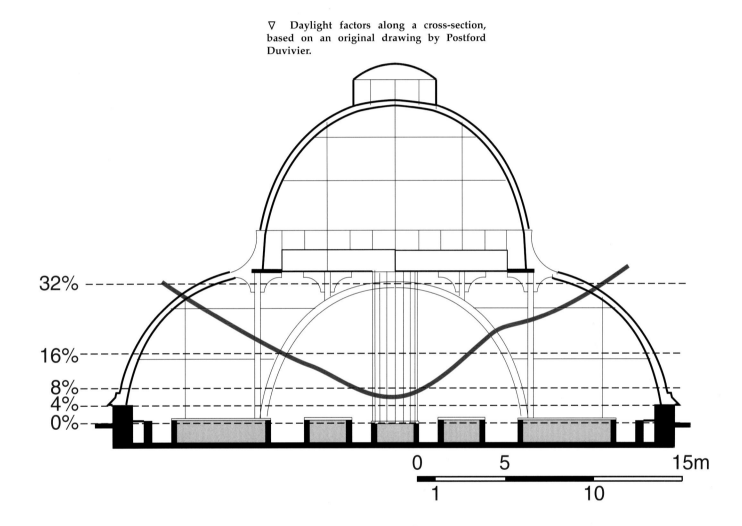

replaced parts indicate a transmittance of 75% compared with 61% on dirtier parts. The internal finishes, due to the white colour, have high reflectances (88%) while the floor, as expected due to its dark grey colour and the density of plants has a reflectance of only 10%.

Daylight measurements could only be performed in parts of the conservatory, along the corridors and walkways, thus no isoline contours can be drawn. It should be noted that differences in daylight factor levels are often due to obstructions from dense foliage. As shown on the longitudinal section, the daylight factor varies from a maximum value of 24.5% to a minimum of 11.8% (average daylight factor: 18%). In the taller middle space, the average daylight factor increases to 20%, while on the top part of the main space the average is 34%.

Light, in general, is evenly distributed and the levels are quite high because of the nature of the space. However, these levels would be much higher if the glazing was cleaner. If we were to estimate the daylight factor levels without the presence of the plants, then it would be: glazing transmittance x structural obstructions x 100% = (0.57 x 0.80) x 100% = 46%.

Field measurements

The daylighting performance was assessed along the longitudinal corridor of the west side of the conservatory, along the middle cross section and on the east and west sides of the top floor corridor. Daylight factors were measured at a height of 1.20m from the ground level on the 12 March 1996.

THE PALM HOUSE, ROYAL BOTANIC GARDENS

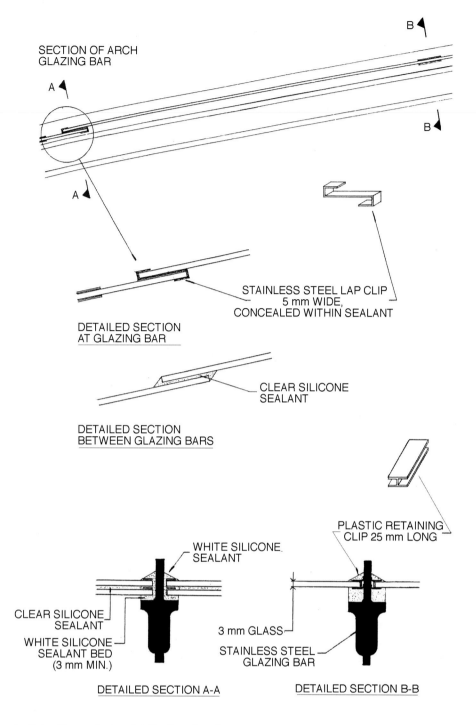

SECTION OF ARCH
GLAZING BAR

A

B

B

A

A

STAINLESS STEEL LAP CLIP
5 mm WIDE,
CONCEALED WITHIN SEALANT

DETAILED SECTION
AT GLAZING BAR

CLEAR SILICONE
SEALANT

DETAILED SECTION
BETWEEN GLAZING BARS

PLASTIC RETAINING
CLIP 25 mm LONG

WHITE SILICONE
SEALANT

CLEAR SILICONE
SEALANT

WHITE SILICONE
SEALANT BED
(3 mm MIN.)

3 mm GLASS

STAINLESS STEEL
GLAZING BAR

DETAILED SECTION A-A   DETAILED SECTION B-B

△ Palm House glazing details. Drawings by
Postford Duvivier.

CREDITS

Site and climate
The Palm House is located at the Royal
Botanic Gardens, in Kew, U.K. (Latitude:
51°28'N, Longitude: 00°19'W). The climate
at Kew has a monthly average outdoor temperature of 5.43°C in winter and 14.9°C during summer. The average daily sunshine
duration is 4.18 hours.

Building
The Palm House is a conservatory designed
by Decimus Burton and Richard Turner and
was completed in 1847. The building is
109.7m long, spans 32m and at its centre
rises to a height of 19.8m. Its floor area is
2,173.8m². The structure is an ingenious
combination of wrought and cast iron supporting 16,000 panes of toughened glass. It
was restored in 1955 to 57 and again in 1985
to 88, when it was modified to house samples of the tropical rain forest and the coral
reef.

Architects
Decimus Burton and Richard Turner

Client
Commissioners of Woods and Forests
Royal Botanic Gardens
Kew, U.K.

Monitoring organisation
The Martin Centre for Architectural and
Urban Studies, Department of Architecture,
University of Cambridge,
6 Chaucer Road
Cambridge CB2 2EB, U.K.

Acknowledgements
We would like to thank the Enquiry Unit of
the Royal Botanic Gardens for approving the
monitoring of the Palm House. Furthermore
we would like to thank Mr T Bailey from the
Building and Maintenance Department of
the Royal Botanic Gardens and Mr C R
Jones, the Divisional Director of Postford
Duvivier for providing us with the drawings
of the building.

References
Fletcher, Sir B., *A History of Architecture*, 19th
Ed., Butterworths, London,1987, p.1110.

Minter, S., *The Greatest Glass House, The
Rainforests Recreated*, HMSO, London, 1990.

Material properties assessed on site

	Colour	Hemispherical-hemispherical reflectances
Iron structure	white	88%
Floor	grey	10%

	Direct-direct transmittance	Hemispherical-hemispherical transmittance
Dirty glazing	58%	66%
Clear glazing	65%	89%

Factory with early curtain wall facade

Fagus-Werk, Alfeld an der Leine, GERMANY

This factory, designed in 1911, anticipated modern facade techniques with its early curtain wall, but at this time insulating glass and efficient shading devices were not yet developed. As a result, there are some indoor environmental problems.

An architectural landmark
The factory represents in its clear and simple layout the pioneering work of architectural rationalism. The most significant part is the administration building. The historical importance of the building is principally due to its steel and glazed facade, the so-called 'curtain wall', an innovative and trail-blazing construction technique at the time.

Originally designed by Walter Gropius (1883 to 1969)
The architect Walter Gropius focused on the design of the building's core and outer appearance, i.e. the design of the facades. Reflecting his sensitivity to the social structures in his company, the client Karl Benscheidt wrote: "Unser Reichtum sind nicht Maschinen und Gebäude, sondern das Wissen und Können und die Einsatzbereitschaft unserer Mitarbeiter", ("Our capital is not the machines or buildings, but the knowledge and skills and motivation of our workers"). The glazed skin covering the whole room width and extending almost from floor to ceiling lifted for the first time the then rigid separation between the outward 'architectural' representation of the building and its daily, inner working realities. This transparency was what Benscheidt was looking for.

An advanced curtain wall design, to enhance communication with the outside
Gropius used five different types of steel-glazing constructions for the complex. The elements are suspended

▽ **Inside view of the monitored office in the north-eastern building corner.**

◁ View down one of the corridors showing the transparent open connection to the office spaces which provide secondary light.

▽ Daylight factor distribution in a single glazed corner room and an adjacent double glazed office.

from each of the separate floor ceilings. The facade corners are reduced to slim steel-glazing elements; the supporting piers have been drawn away from the corners, making the building appear more transparent, opening it to the outside. The glazing systems in the administration building are characterized by non-structural steel frames, using prefabricated industrial profiles. The areas in between the steel frames have either been tilled by single glazing or with sheet steel, where transparency was not required.

Large amounts of daylight as a result of the highly glazed facade (65%)

The transparent appearence is expressed in the 65% ratio of window to facade area. Interrupted only by the supporting piers, the office spaces are almost totally glazed horizontally. Vertically, the facade only blocks light in relatively narrow areas covered by sheet steel. The offices thus receive large amounts of daylight.

Illumination levels in both monitored rooms are very high and even in the deeper room parts (at 5.6m) daylight factors are still well above 1%. This results from the big window/facade ratio of around 65% and the small structural window frame elements. In particular, the corner room is flooded with light, due to light penetration from two sides and the higher transmittance of the single glazed windows.

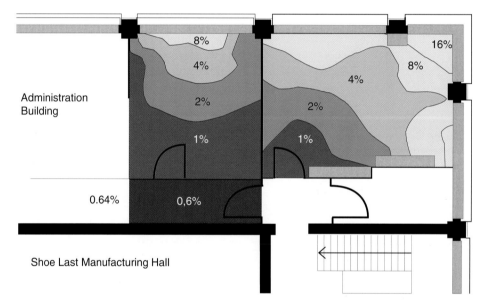

Administration Building

8%
4%
16%
2%
4%
8%
1%
2%
1%

0.64%   0,6%

Shoe Last Manufacturing Hall

Few partitions and indoor walls to block daylight

Little was allowed to reduce light penetration into the building core area. Gropius constructed the office space without supporting walls. Structural forces are led into the supporting piers. Many internal walls are highly glazed thus contributing to the above mentioned impression of transparency in the building. The corridors receive significant amounts of borrowed light (daylight factor of about 0.6%) from the glazed office partitions.

Daylight as a safety feature in the shoe last manufacturing hall

The roof of the shoe last manufacturing area was largely daylit via a rooflight construction giving very high illumination levels for that time directly at the work spaces. This concept was employed to increase work safety. It proved to be very effective, since it reduced accidents at the machines by 65% compared to other factories in the same business. Daylighting thus became part of Benscheidt's overall approach to the welfare of his employees.

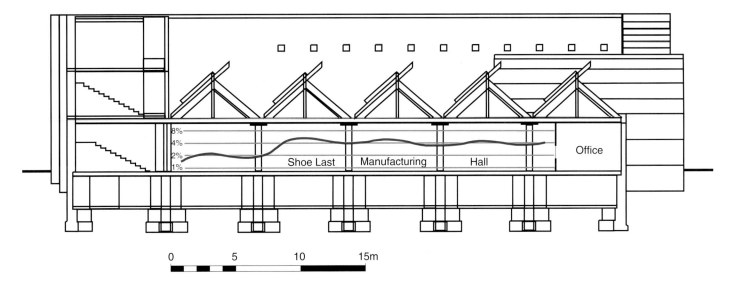

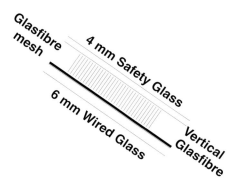

△ Daylight factor distribution on a cross-section through the shoe last manufacturing hall daylit with rooflights.

△ Rooflight detail. Multiple layer structure.

View of the shoe last manufacturing hall, daylit with an early rooflighting concept. ▷

A manufacturing hall with a glazed area equal to 25% of the floor area

On an axis perpendicular to the rooflights, the daylight factors were measured from the deep end adjacent to the administration building to the north, up to an office at the southern end. In the northern hall area, daylight factors are fairly low for a rooflit construction, around 2%. They then gradually reach a constant level of around 5% (corresponding to 500 lux for a 10 klux overcast day). The low value below the rooflight furthest to the north is mainly due to obstruction by the administration building. The ratio of rooflight glazing to floor area of 25% is high by current standards. Nevertheless daylight factors are satisfactory but not as high as one might expect with such big openings. The levels obtained nowadays are mainly a result of the retrofitting proc-

ess, where the architects responded to the excessively high illumination levels and poor acceptance of these levels by the workers (the roof glazing was painted to reduce light penetration). Nowadays, the rooflights are glazed with a diffusing four-layer construction with an overall luminous transmission estimated to be below 50%.

Thermal comfort issues raised by excessive glazed area

Due to the glazing and frame technology at the time of construction, high maintenance and usage costs accumulated over the years. Energy performance and thermal comfort conditions fell way behind improving standards. No changes were made to the facade elements.

Recent retroffitting for energy conservation

Retrofitting had to fullfill two criteria. Since the factory is a national building monument of high architectural value, the appearance of the facade had to be left unchanged. On the other hand the factory is still in use, and is not a museum, and the functional use of the building had to be maintained for commercial reasons. The challenge was to update the construction to modern standards, of thermal, comfort and lighting performance.

The old facades in standard office rooms were double-glazed with heat insulating framing in order to help fulfill the energy requirements. In preference to other glazing CLIMAPLUS was selected as a thermally acceptable glazing on a test facade, coming closest

△ Gropius curtain wall, 65% glazed.

△ Exterior view.

in the colour rendering, reflection, and transmission properties to the original glazing. The width of the original steelframe profiles has been kept, although the construct-ion has been carried out with state-of-the-art profiles and technology. For building spaces with lower thermal and comfort boundary conditions, such as staircases and occasionally used convention rooms, the old facade has simply been renewed (in these spaces).

Textile awnings on the first floor have been carefully reconstructed. Nevertheless, no additional awnings have been added. For glare protection, most offices are nowadays equipped with sheer curtains.

Daylighting monitoring

Performed in two office spaces and the old manufacturing hall. Measurements were performed in December 1996.

CREDITS

Building description
Built in 1911, retrofitted in the 1980s. The size of the manufacturing hall is about 1,400m², of the administration building 1,700m².

Climate
Alfeld an der Leine is located 50 kilometers south of Hanover in the state of Lower Saxony (Latitude: 52°N, Longitude: 10°E). It's climatic conditions are best described by the Trier Test Reference Year, coldest month: January with a mean of 0.4°C, warmest mo-nth: August with a mean of 17.7°C.

Client
Karl Benscheidt(1858 to 1947). Owner and founder of the Fagus Factory. Today's client: Fagus GreCon GmbH

Architect
Walter Gropius (1883 to 1969). The Fagus Factory was his first project. He later founded the Bauhaus and became an American professor at Harvard University after his emmigration in 1937 to the United States.

Monitoring organisation
Fraunhofer Institute for Building Physics, Nobelstraße 12, 70569 Stuttgart, Germany

References
"Walter Gropius und Carl Benscheidt, Aus dem Alltag der Bauzeit des Fagus-Werkes". Prof. Dr.-Ing. Dr. H.c. Helmut Weber, Deutsche Bauzeitung 35 (1987), Journal Nr. 5

"Industriebau-Sanierung - eine Herausforderung der Denkmalpflege", Der Rolladen-Jalousiebauer 6/89

"Restaurierung des Fagus-Werk in Alfeld an der Leine", Glasforum Nr. 5, 1986

"Zur Restaurierung des Fagus-Werkes in Alfeld (Leine), Werkoriginalität kontra optimierte Nutzungstauglichkeit", Dieter Rentschler-Weißmann, Jörn Behnsen, Berichte zur Denkmalpflege in Niedersachsen 6 (1986), Heft Nr. 1

Material properties assessed on site

	Colour	Hemispherical-hemispherical reflectance
Manufacturing building		
Floor	grey concrete	18%
Walls	white	85%
Administration building		
Floor	black carpet	5%
Walls	white	74%

	Normal-normal transmittance	Hemispherical-hemispherical transmittance (estimated)
Sheds		50%
Double glazing (facade)	81%	74%
Single glazing (facade)	87%	82%
Single glazing (indoor partitions)	93%	86%

A stylish, totally daylit furniture showroom

Paustian House, Copenhagen, DENMARK

The architects of this furniture showroom sought to re-create the luminous atmosphere of a Danish beech forest. They created a unique space, where daylight contributes to the quality of the displays.

▽ **The centre hall of the furniture showroom, with a height of 13 metres.**

Long white columns widen near the roof

The Paustian House, designed by Utzon Associates, is located on the Copenhagen waterfront. The building, a furniture store and showroom, was built in 1986 to 87 by H. Hoffmann & Sønner for Paustian A/S. Utzon's own sketches reveal that his inspiration was found in the Danish beech forests with their long, straight smooth trunks from which the lowest branches spread to form a horizontal canopy, while the upper ones reach up in open triangular forms towards the sky. However, in spite of the poetic purpose of the building design, the architect's main theme was to give the visitor a familiar spatial experience.

Together with its clear and modern structure, the building has maintained its contemporary link with a relationship to the waterfront surroundings of ships, docks, cranes and warehouses.

The building consists of a simple, columned space with open, split-level balconies. A structure of prefabricated concrete columns and beams runs throughout the building, resulting in a variety of heights, spans and rhythms. The decks are prestressed, double-tee beams and all surfaces are painted white.

A naturalistic theme

The architect, Christian Norberg-

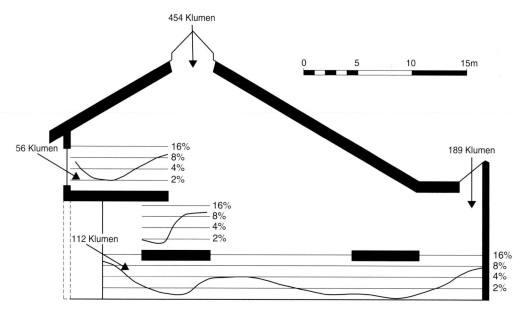

454 Klumen

0 5 10 15m

56 Klumen
16%
8%
4%
2%

189 Klumen

112 Klumen
16%
8%
4%
2%

16%
8%
4%
2%

▽ Distribution of the glazed area.

4 %
13%
North Skylight
South
45 % West Facade
Central Roof Skylight
38 %

The central North-South oriented skylight ▷ aperture above pierced balconies.

Daylight factor distribution on the first floor and vertical values in the centre. ▽

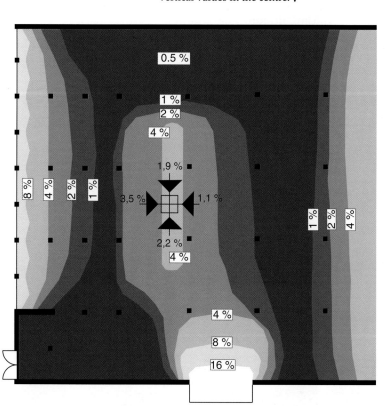

0.5 %
1 %
2 %
4 %
1,9 %
3,5 % 1,1 %
8 % 4 % 2 % 1 %
1 %
2 %
4 %
2,2 %
4 %
4 %
8 %
16 %

Schulz stated that "on the facade, the columns are gathered in a row, like the edges of the forrest surrounding a Danish meadow. When we enter, we admidst the trees. A low balcony creates a sense of intimacy, a feeling of being 'under', and then the space suddenly opens and the slim columns shoot upward toward the light that reflects from their triangular capitals. A truly fascinating interior! Although my description can seem somewhat too 'naturalistic' I should emphasize the fact that the forest metaphor is not obtrusive. One's primary experience is that of a modern space that simply suits its situation" (Norberg-Schulz 1989).

Roof lights for daylighting, up-lighting metal halide projectors for artificial lighting

In the centre of the building, daylight is mainly recieved from the north-south oriented skylights while a smaller sky-light admits daylight to the transition area between the new exhibition building and the existing warehouse. A two-storey high glass facade is also located in the end wall facing south which improves daylight penetration to the exhibition building's ground floor. In the centre of the building, uplighters (high pressure mercury lamps), provide the general artificial lighting level, while spotlights (incandescent and low voltage halogen lamps) are used primarily

△ Deep daylight penetration from the central skylight.

△ Daylight penetration below the north roof aperture.

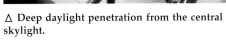

▽ One of the balconies surrounding the central hall.

to accentuate the design of the furniture, its shape and texture. Measurements with only the artificial lighting system on gives an illuminance level of 50 to 175 lux throughout the building. The artificial lighting is manually controlled and the lights are on throughout the day for the display of the furniture.

Apertures through intermediate floors bring daylight to the lowest floor

The admission of daylight from the skylights to the centre of the ground floor is achieved by piercing the open, split-level balconies with a type of a light well. Below the skylight, large white baffles prevent direct sunlight reaching down to the exhibition areas, but reflect diffuse light to the ground floor and the adjacent balconies. On the ground floor below the skylight, measurement of the horizontal daylight factors are shown that the skylight and reflected light from the west- and south-facing windows result in a fairly well-daylit area varying from 4% in the middle to 1% near the balconies. The extended roof and the exterior columns and beams represent an architectural solution within the theme of the building, but reduce daylight penetration through the west facade while providing

no shading of direct sunlight. However, measured horizontal daylight factors show fairly high illuminance levels, with daylight factor varying from 8% near the window to 1% at a distance approximately 5m from the window. The inclined glass facade towards the south increases the illuminance level below the balcony on the first floor mainly by reflecting skylight from the room's interior surfaces, especially the floor. The north-south oriented skylight (light well) in the transition area between the new exhibition building and the existing warehouse gives a well daylit zone with daylight factors from 1 to 4%, highest below the skylight.

The total glazed area divided by the total floor area is 17%. Most of the glazing is facade glazing, but most of the contribution to daylighting appears to be from the roof apertures.

Daylight on the balconies is mainly received from the skylight and the windows in the west facade. Measurements on the first floor show low daylight factors between 1 to 2% near the west facade, since the balcony is recessed from the facade and the balcony on second floor acts as a large overhang. Below the

skylight, daylight factors increase to 10%. The balcony on the second floor receives more daylight near the facade but the extended roof and the exterior columns and beams reduce daylight penetration significantly. However, measured daylight factors are fairly high, varying from 2% in the middle to 6% near the facade and 10% below the skylight.

Very little lighting energy savings achieved, due to manual control and commercial concerns

The artificial lighting of the Paustian House is manually controlled. But lights tend to stay on throughout the day to enhance the displays and bring customers to the showroom. This is unfortunate, since illuminance levels from daylight are quite sufficient to display the furniture. This suggests that in such stores an approach including a balance between energy conservation objectives and the need to light product displays to attract potential customers has to be found.

Field measurements

The daylight performance of the building was assessed on the ground and first floor in the exhibition building. Daylight factors were measured on November 1996.

▽ **South facade of the Paustian House, on Copenhagen waterfront.**

Material properties assessed on site

	Colour	Hemispherical-hemispherical reflectances
Tile floor (ground floor)	light grey/white	52%
Floor (second floor)	brown carpet	28%
Wall	white	86%
Ceiling	white	86%
	Direct-direct transmittance	Hemispherical-hemispherical transmittance
Double glazing	66%	64%

CREDITS

Building
A 1,750m² exhibition area built in 1987 on the Copenhagen waterfront.

Climate
Latitude: 55°40′N, Longitude: 12°30′E, Altitude: 3m.
The average daily sunshine duration is 0.9 hours in winter, 8.1 hours in summer and 4.9 hours averaged over the year. Monthly average air temperatures range from -0.6C in January to 16.7 in August, and global horizontal daily average radiation ranges from 384 Wh/m² in December to 6,188 Wh/m² in June.

Client and building owner
Paustian A/S
Kalkbrænderiløbskaj 2
2100 Copenhagen East

Architect
Utzon Associates
Odinshojvej 21, 3140 Aalsgaarde, Denmark

Monitoring organisation
Danish Building Research Institute
Energy and Indoor Climate Division, Project Group: Daylight in Buildings
P.O. Box 119
2970 Horsholm, Denmark

References
Norberg-Schulz, C. 1989.
Paustian House.
Arkitektur DK, No. 8

Daylight performance: daylight quality and control of energy consumption

The Daylight Europe simulation team has undertaken detailed performance appraisals of seven of the monitored buildings. This section describes the simulation procedure adopted and some of the major results obtained.

Seven buildings selected for detailed energy simulations

Simulation was applied to seven existing buildings incorporating different daylight utilization technologies. For each case studied, performance has been assessed in terms of HVAC and electrical system capacities, fuel consumption, environmental emissions, thermal and visual comfort and glare sources.

Simulation was preferred to energetic monitoring for reasons of costs, but also because it offers the possibility to compare long-term performances of various options.

Combined thermal/lighting simulation was used in the project to critically examine the performance of seven case study buildings as identified in the following table.

A well defined simulation procedure shared by all members of the simulation group

Each of these seven buildings have been extensively monitored so that data is available to facilitate model calibration before the integrated appraisal exercise commences. A group of laboratories have conducted the simulation tasks (see list at the end of this chapter).

The premise underlying the DL-E performance assessment method (PAM) is that the impact of daylight utilization can best be determined by systematically removing relevant technologies and comparing the performance to result with some base case representation of the existing design. The method consists of several steps; listed in Table 2. The intention is that such a PAM may be attributed with alternative know-

Buildings selected for simulation ▷

DL-E PAM: actions underlined, know-▷
ledge entities in *italics*.

Case study building	Daylight technology
Collège La Vanoise, Modane, France	External, sloped, low level light shelves, borrowed light from atrium and lighting system control.
Victoria Quay, Edinburgh, United Kingdom	Mix of open plan and cellular offices with configurable lighting control and borrowed light from atria.
Queen's Building, Leicester, United Kingdom	Electronics laboratory with bilateral lighting and internal light shelves.
Brundtland Centre, Toftlund, Denmark	Light directing blinds, reflective ceiling, linked control of blinds and luminaires, borrowed light from atrium, atrium light diffused by PV modules.
Town Hall, Trundholm, Denmark	Lighting control and fixed external solar shading.
Architects Office, Athens, Greece	First floor offices use borrowed light from upper zones. Ground floor lighting via a light well in north facade. Indirect lighting and high efficiency fixtures.
EOS Office, Lausanne, Switzerland	Light shelves and special optical coatings.

Step	Description
1	Establish computer representation corresponding to a *base case design*.
2	Calibrate model using *reliable techniques*.
3	Locate representative boundary conditions of *appropriate severity*.
4	Undertake integrated simulations using *suitable applications*.
5	Express multi-variate performance in terms of suitable *criteria*.
6	Identify problem areas as a function of *criteria acceptability*.
7	Analyse simulation results to identify *cause of problems*.
8	Postulate remedies by associating problem causes with *appropriate design options*.
9	For each postulate, establish a reference model to a *justifiable level of resolution*.
10	Iterate from step 4 until overall performance is *satisfactory*.
11	Repeat from step 3 to establish replicability for other *climate zones*.
12	Archive models for possible future use in other *contexts*.

ledge instances depending on the user's viewpoint and simulation program capabilities.

Some of the essential steps within the PAM are elaborated here.

Step 1: A base case computer model is formed for the target building to a level of resolution which is sympathetic to the particular technical system. For example, a light shelf would require a detailed representation of sky and sun reflections, an illuminance-based switching system would require that the characteristics of the photocell be included, while an atrium used for 'borrowed light' would require a rigourous treatment of geometry and inter-reflections. Clearly, for a daylighting focus, some aspects of the model can be abstracted: e.g. the operational characteristics of the heating system or the control applied to the ventilation system.

Step 2: The results from simulations using this model are compared with experimental data and, if required, judicious adjustments made to the model until its performance is satisfactory.

Step 4: Simulations are then carried out using detailed thermal/lighting simulation programs and the outputs collated in the form of an integrated performance view or IPV (see Figures 2 and 3) which quantifies overall performance in terms of a range of relevant criteria.

Step 9: A corresponding reference model is then developed by removing the particular daylight capture/control device(s) and adjusting the design as required. Results from the base case model can then be compared with this reference in order to quantify the benefits (or otherwise) of the daylighting features. Where a building incorporates several features, these may be systematically removed by the creation of several reference models.

Step 10: As required, new models can be established in order to 'optimize' the performance of specific design features which have merit on the basis of IPV comparison.

Step 11: Replication studies can be undertaken to establish the sensitivity of a design to location.

Step 12: Finally, the base case and reference models, along with their IPVs, are contained within an electronic 'model manager' which allows 3D browsing, model exporting to CAD, and further exploratory thermal/lighting analysis.

A procedure using a whole set of simulation tools

Within the DL-E project, the ESP-r system [3] was used to create and manipulate the models and map these to the thermal and lighting simulation programs. ESP-r provides access to databases of material properties, climate, plant components, etc. and supports the attachment of constructional and operational attributes to geometrical models created internally or imported from CAD packages. The simulation tools used within the project include RADIANCE [14] for room luminance/illuminance distribution computation, JINDEX [1] for visual comfort assessment, and ESP-r [9] and TSBI3 [5] for building/plant energy simulation.

Lighting tools linked to energetic tools

The modelling of daylight-responsive luminaires requires the prediction of the time-varying internal illuminance distribution to accommodate the various *climate-building-systems-occupant* interactions (e.g. blind actuation). The approach used offers:

- high frequency variation of the sky luminance
- fully 3D, variable building geometry to accommodate movable and light redirecting systems
- comprehensive treatment of light transfer by multiple reflections and transmissions
- accurate representation of artificial lighting control
- full integration of the approach within the overall building/ HVAC energy simulation.

The approach is based on the conflation of the ESP-r [3] and RADIANCE [14] systems, within a *UNIX* platform, and

with the former system providing the overall supervisory control at simulation time as shown in the figure below.

At each simulation time-step, ESP-r's luminaire control algorithm initiates the daylight simulation. RADIANCE is then driven by ESP-r to carry out several tasks as follows: (1) transfer of data defining current solar position, solar irradiance and building state; (2) generation of sky model; (3) re-building of scene model; (4) calculation of internal illuminance for defined sensor locations; (5) transfer back of illuminance data to luminaire controller. The returned data are then used to determine, as a function of the active control algorithm, the luminaire status and hence the casual gain associated with lights at the current time-step.

In essence, ESP-r supports luminaire and shading device control on the basis of the value of any model parameter (although some combinations may not be available because they are unrealistic or too esoteric). For example, window blind control may be achieved on the basis of the internal zone air temperature, the ambient air temperature or the prevailing irradiance level on a specified facade, while luminaire control may be based on the illuminance at a given point or averaged across several points. Likewise, control parameters may be imposed in terms of aspects such as photocell position, vision angle, controller set-point, switch-off lux level, switch-off delay time and minimum stop.

Studied issues cover topics such dealing with building envelope design as well as interior design
By applying this simulation method, in

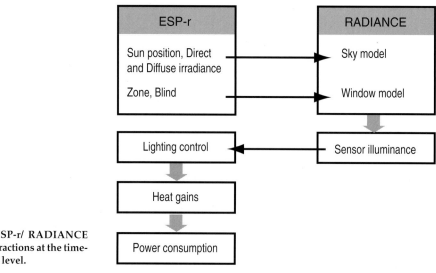

▷ **ESP-r/ RADIANCE Interactions at the time-step level.**

conjunction with the previously described PAM, to the case study buildings listed in Table 1, it proved possible to explore several issues as summarized in the following table.

From the outcome, the following conclusions were drawn in relation to several daylight utilization technologies.

Light shelves appear to be more efficient in rejecting sunlight than displacing diffuse light deep in the interior. Major energetic impact should be seen in increase of thermal comfort in summmer

Light shelves are intended to modify daylight distribution by reducing the sky component and increasing reflection from the ceiling resulting in a more uniform daylight distribution.

Compared to a standard window:
- with an overcast sky, daylight decreases at perimeter but sustained at core
- with a clear sky and low sun (winter) there is an enhancement of the internal illuminance over the entire room depth
- with a clear sky and high sun (summer) there is an enhancement of the internal illuminance, but only close to the perimeter for the case of a conventional light shelf
- the low level light shelf in Collège La Vanoise provides a global reduction of the internal illuminance
- specular light shelves generally provide a higher internal illuminance than diffusing light shelves (this is especially noticeable with clear, low sun, winter skies).

The Collège La Vanoise light shelves are not effective in increasing core illuminance under overcast skies. They increase glare under clear skies (because of reflections) and make no significant contribution to energy saving. Light shelves could be used within the Victoria Quay building to prevent glare from the atrium, maintain core daylight penetration and diminish the perimeter daylight levels. They are significantly more effective than blinds.

- Within the Queen's Building light shelves are effective in providing a glare-free environment for VDU users but they give rise to no energy saving. Blinds would be even less effective.

Case study building	Issue studied
Collège La Vanoise, Modane, France	Light shelf removal; borrowed light removal; proportional dimming control; comparison of as-built with conventional light shelf.
Victoria Quay, Edinburgh, UK	Effect of interior design (finish colour and partition heights); use of atrium light shelf to control glare; luminaire control strategy.
Queen's Building, Leicester, UK	Use of local light shelf to control glare; geometry and finish of courtyard.
Brundtland Centre, Toftlund, Denmark	Impact of redirecting blind and control; impact of PV shading on discomfort glare and illuminance in offices adjacent to an atrium.
Town Hall, Trundholm, Denmark	Effect of fixed external shades and lighting control
Architects Office, Athens, Greece	Effect of borrowed daylight
EOS Office, Lausanne, Switzerland	Effect of light shelf removal.

△ Table 3: The DL-E parametric simulation set.

▽ Light shelf issues.

Overcast sky and specular light shelf

| Light shelf | As-is light shelf | Conventional light shelf |

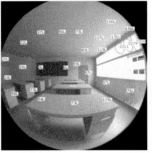  

Daylight Availability under overcast sky conditions for specular light shelf

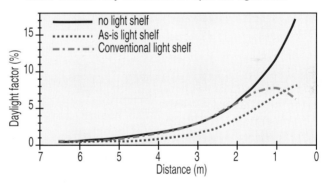

- Conventional notions of required lighting levels might underestimate the viability of daylighting. For example, a detailed study within the Queen's Building showed that the natural lighting levels with light shelves can be compatible with VDU work, where daylight factor contours did not indicate this to be the case.
- Light directing systems can often be used in place of light shelves.

In general, it can be said that the impact of lightshelves on heating peak capacity and energy consumption is marginal, but that they tend to improve summer thermal comfort by decreasing the number of hours (e.g. by up to 40%)

with high operative temperatures. Clearly, if the building is air conditioned, this will have a significant impact on cooling peak capacity and energy consumption.

Recommendations on light shelf design could be stated as follows:
- ensure that they do not exclude winter passive solar gains.
- ensure that they achieve effective-shading in summer. This may require an integrated approach using also movable shading devices and/or solar control glazing.

Reflective blinds offer good control of glare, solar protection and if the ceiling is bright, may maintain reasonable light levels inside

- Light redirecting (towards ceiling) blinds showed higher levels of daylight availability in the perimeter (up to 2m from the facade) and maintenance of light levels further from the facade, when compared to open conventional blinds.
- Redirecting blinds which allowed no direct transmittance ('fish' blinds) result in a higher level of daylight availability in the perimeter with little degradation of daylight levels further from the facade, when compared to conventional blinds.
- Special 'fish' redirecting blinds improve visual comfort when evaluated by state-of-the-art discomfort glare indices. They produce relatively low directional luminance (towards the occupant), while maintaining background luminance.
- In the Brundtland Centre, daylight factor indices were found to underpredict the benefits of light directing systems. It was also found that, where incident radiation is predominantly diffuse (as in a PV shaded atrium), light directing systems provide little benefit.

It has been found that the impact of reflective blinds on heating peak capacity and energy consumption is marginal. However summer thermal comfort tends to improve by decreasing high operative temperatures (e.g. by up to 4°C). Clearly, if the building is air conditioned, this will have a significant impact on cooling peak capacity and energy consumption.

Analysis of results of simulations lead to the following recommandations on reflective blinds design:
- ensure blind is effective in reflecting light towards reflective ceiling (e.g. consider shape factors and possibility of different upper and lower blind coatings).
- ensure that blind management system is implemented to control levels of visible and solar penetration.

Control of artificial lighting needs to be simple, reliable, and well adapted to the needs of the occupants.
The simple control strategy used in Collège La Vanoise is effective (i.e. hourly switch off).

**Brundtland Centre
Redirecting blind system**

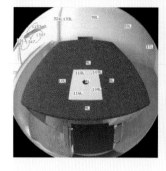  

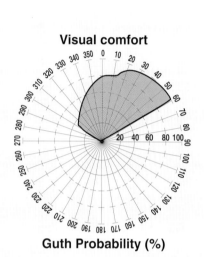

Visual comfort

Guth Probability (%)

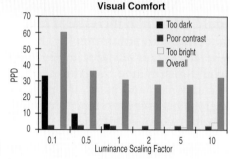

Visual Comfort

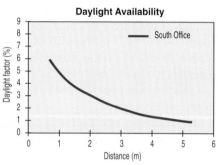

Daylight Availability

△ **Light redirecting blind issues.**

The proportional dimming system within Victoria Quay produces significant energy savings but requires careful photocell zoning and set-point/field of view setting.

The best energy performance is achieved from closed-loop proportional control with appropriate sensor field of view and shielding from direct light.

Within the Queen's Building there is an enhanced level of core daylight but reliance on manual switching results in no energy saving.

Local luminaire/task lighting control offers the best solution for deep plan buildings. Algorithms are required for managed blind systems.

More precisely, here are some figures concerning the energetic impact of lighting controls:
- lighting control will slightly increase heating consumption (e.g. by 5% to 10%) by reducing heat gains from lights.
- lighting control will significantly decrease the number of hours with higher operative temperatures (e.g. by up to 40%).
- simple lighting control (e.g. automatic switch-off) will significantly reduce artificial lighting energy consumption (e.g by up to 40%).
- sophisticated automatic light dimming will significantly reduce artificial lighting energy consumption (e.g by up to 70%).

Hence few recommendations on lighting control:
- simple control strategies (e.g. timed off) will result in significant energy savings.
- daylight linked dimming control is relatively complicated to implement and calibrate. If effectively implemented it has the potential to deliver substantial energy savings.

Atria can contribute to reduce heat losses, but their daylighting efficiency depends on the brightness of their walls and shading on windows should not be forgotten

- Within Victoria Quay and Collège La Vanoise atria provide the principal contribution to enhanced daylight factors and energy savings.
- Within the Victoria Quay building, the atrium is a source of excessive glare because of direct sky access and intra-reflections.
- Within the Brundtland Centre, the application of PV glazing panels on the south atrium roof improves the visual comfort and helps to achieve an adequate internal illuminance.

It seems that the following recommendations can be stated regarding atrium design:

- diffusing/redirecting roof glazing is required to reduce glare and maintain daylight penetration. Non-specular, highly reflective finishes will help to ensure daylight penetration to the atrium base
- care should be taken to avoid glare and overheating problems
- attention to detail is necessary to ensure the beneficial penetration of daylight to adjoining spaces.

Regarding the enegetic impact of atrium, it can be said that borrowed daylight from atria has a major impact on artificial lighting consumption, with savings of the order of 40%.

Deep plan depth rapidly leads to permanent artificial lighting

- in Victoria Quay the deep plan causes glare problems due to limited daylight penetration causing maximum contrast. An inappropriate solution is to use artificial lighting to balance contrasts and therefore reduced energy savings
- victoria Quay has non-optimum finishes and partitioning heights, which cause poor daylight factor distribution
- within the Queen's Building, the VDUs/trunking obstruct daylight penetration. The importance of task orientation in the relation to light source is also highlighted.

In general, within the core of deep plan buildings, artificial lighting will give rise to a cooling load but cannot con-

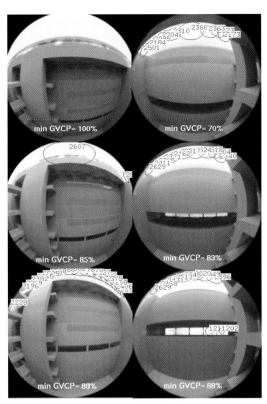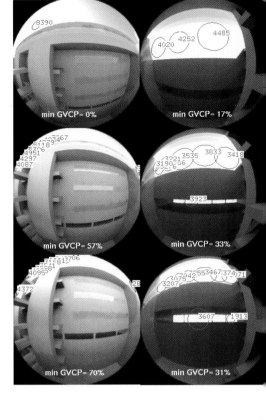

△ **Atria design issues – visual comfort under advanced diffusing (left) vs. normal (right) roof glazing system.**

tribute to a reduction in the heating load since there is no heat loss. Core daylight penetration will therefore result in a cooling and lighting energy consumption decrease with no corresponding increase in the heating load because of the reduced lighting heat gain.

Large lighting electricity costs could be saved with optimized daylighting solutions, but designers need to be aware of associated risks of daylighting strategies

- between 40% and 70% of the energy consumption associated with artificial lighting can be saved if daylight capture technologies are implemented together with automatic lighting control
- careful attention to detail is required to ensure that the negative impacts on heating (through reduced casual gain), on cooling (through increased solar gain) and on comfort (through excessive glare or space temperatures) are avoided.

Within the project, it has been observed that enhanced daylight performance has often resulted in reduced thermal performance. Effective design solutions will require supervisory level control algorithms by which designers can balance the visual and thermal aspects.

Also, the use of daylight factors has been shown to have limitations, especially in the case of light directing components and advanced control systems. The direct, real-time coupling of thermal and lighting simulation offers a new level of information to the design process [20].

A methodology has been developed for the combined thermal and lighting appraisal of buildings and applied to existing buildings in support of design guideline production within the EC's Daylight-Europe project. The method includes the notion of an integrated performance view by which the benefits associated with a particular set of daylighting features can be ascertained across a range of criteria. The method has been applied to six existing buildings in order to determine the performance of specific daylight utilization approaches and the impact of selected design changes on this performance.

List of members of the simulation team

From ESRU, University of Strathclyde, Scotland:
Joe Clarke (co-ordinator)
Jon Hand
Milan Janak
Iain MacDonald

From Danish Building Research Institute:
Kjeld Johnsen, SBI
Kim Wittchen, SBI

From Esbensen Consulting Engineers, Denmark:
Christina Madsen

From LESO-PD, Ecole Polytechnique Federale de Lausanne, Switzerland:
Stephane Citherlet

References and bibliography

1. Compagnon R (1996) 'The JINDEX visual discomfort analysis program' *Daylight Europe Project Report*, LESO-PB, EPFL.
2. Clarke J A, Hand J W, Janak M, Macdonald I (1997) 'Performance Assessment of Selected Case Study Buildings', *Daylight-Europe Project Final Report*, ESRU, University of Strathclyde, Glasgow.
3. ESRU (1997) *ESP-r Version 9 Series Users' Guide*, ESRU, University of Strathclyde, Glasgow.
4. Fontoynont M (1997) ?, *Proc. Right-Light 4*, Copenhagen.
5. Johnsen K and Grau K (1994) *TSBi3 Users' Guide*, Danish Building Research Institute.
6. Kristensen P E (1996) 'Daylight Europe', *Proc. 4th European Confer ence on Solar Energy in Architecture and Urban Planning*, Berlin.
7. Clarke J A, Compagnon R, Hand J W, Johnsen K, Janak M, Macdonald I, Madsen C, Wittchen K (1996) 'Performance Assessment Method for DL-E Case Study Simulations' *Report of the Daylight-Europe Simulation Team* University of Strathclyde, Glasgow.
8. Private communication.
9. Clarke J A (1985) *Energy Simulation in Building Design* Adam Hilger Ltd., Bristol.
10. Winkelmann F C, Selkowitz S (1985) 'Daylighting Simulation in the DOE-2 Building Energy Analysis Program' *Energy and Buildings 8*, pp271 - 286.
11. Szerman M (1994) 'Auswirkung der Tageslichtnutzung auf das energetische Verhalten von Burogebauden' *Doctoral thesis*, Stuttgart.
12. Littlefair P J (1992) 'Modelling Day light Illuminance in Building Environmental Performance Analysis' *Journal of the Illuminating Engineering Society*, pp25 - 34.
13. Rubinstein F, Ward G, Verderber R (1989) 'Improving the Performance of Photo-Electrically Controlled Lighting Systems' *Journal of the Iluminating Engineering Society*, pp70 – 94.
14. Ward G J (1993) 'The Radiance Lighting Simulation System' *Global Illumination, Siggraph '92 Course Notes*.
15. Perez R, Seals R, Michalsky J (1993) 'All-Weather Model for Sky Luminance Distribution-Preliminary Configuration and Validation' *Solar Energy Vol 50 No 3*, pp235 – 243.
16. Skartveit A, Olseth J A (1992) 'The Probability Density and Autocorrelation of Short-Term Global and Beam Irradiance' *Solar Energy Vol 49 No 6*, pp477 – 487.
17. Janak M, Hraska J, Darula S (1996) 'Modelling Lighting Control in Bratislava Luminous Climate' *International Conference on Energy and Mass Flow in Life Cycle of Buildings*, Vienna.
18. Littlefair P J (1992) 'Daylight Coefficients for Practical Computation of Internal Illuminance' *Lighting Research and Technology. 24 (3)*, pp127 – 135.
19. Herkel S, Jankowski S, Pasquay T, Sick F (1995) 'New Procedure for Dynamic Lighting Simulation of Buildings' *Achievements and Results, Annual Report. Fraunhofer Institute Solare Energiesysteme*.
20. Janak M (1997) 'Coupling Building Energy and Lighting Simulation' *Building Simulation '97*, Prague.
21. JOU2-CT 920144 CIPD-CT 925033 (1995) 'Availability of Daylighting – Design of a European Daylighting Atlas. Luminous Climate in Central Europe' *Final report, ICA SAS Bratislava*.
22. Teregenza P R (1980) 'The daylight factors and actual illuminance ratios' *Lighting Research and Technology Vol 12 No 2*, pp64 - 68.

The detail results of the simulation concerning the seven buildings can be obtained in contacting Professor Joe Clark, ESRU, University of Strathclyde, James Weir Building, 75 Montrose Street, Glasgow G1 1XJ, Scotland, UK
Fax: +44 141 552 8513.

User evaluation of visual comfort through Post Occupancy Evaluation (POE)

Staffan Hygge and Hans Allan Löfberg from KTH, Centre for Built Environment, Gävle, Sweden, have coordinated a task of Post Occupancy Evaluation for a few projects. They have put forward a questionnaire which has been used by the teams involved in the task of user evaluation. Background, method and some results are presented.

Satisfaction of occupants, a goal for energy efficient lighting solutions

In looking for energy-efficient lighting scenarios, technically good solutions may become unsuccessful if the user of the building is not satisfied. User evaluations, so called post-occupancy evaluations (POEs), have been tried out in some of the buildings to evaluate how successful the chosen system is.

A questionnaire with 37 questions

The questionnaire proposed for the project is the result of a survey of reports from POEs and similar studies. It is to a large extent based on a questionnaire used in POEs of government buildings in the USA constructed by Elder et al (1979) and also reported by Collins et al (1989).

The questionnaire consisted of 37 questions that cover the attitude to the building as a whole, the work station, lighting and other environmental factors such as thermal and acoustical conditions, privacy, view etc. The major part was of course on lighting, both daylight and artificial light. There were questions about how the workplace is lit, if the windows created problems, the attitude to windows as such with advantages and disadvantages of windows. The worker's position in relation to the nearest window was recorded as well as the orientation of the windows. Data concerning age etc of the respondent and how long (s)he has been working in the building were also collected.

As daylight constantly varies with weather, time of day and year the user was asked to give an opinion on how the conditions are experienced over time and to say when problems arose.

The identity of the user was not revealed but an identification code was asked for to enable comparisons of evaluations made at different occasions, for instance after some change in the lighting system.

For each building additional questions were allowed if there were some special features of interest to evaluate. Some questions might on the other hand have been irrelevant for the special building and should have been then been removed from the form. If questions were deleted or added the numbering of the basic questions should have been kept to facilitate comparison between results from different buildings. New questions should have been given numbers outside the ones used in the basic questionnaire.

Details of the questionnaire, requirements on number of persons to fill in the form and other guidance on how to perform a POE are found in the Daylighting Design Guidelines Book.

Formal and informal POEs

Out of all the buildings in the project seven were evaluated in some way by a questionnaire. Only two of the buildings, all offices, had enough occupants to form a good basis for a formal POE. In one university laboratory a slightly different questionnaire was used at an early stage. Possible buildings dropped out late in the project or the POE was drastically delayed due to problems in changing the daylighting system and/or getting the employer's permission to carry out the survey.

Some observations and results

One observation is that you must get good cooperation from the employer and from the users to be able to carry out a POE. The effort has been to introduce some change in the daylighting system in a building to be able to compare the situations. As both situations must be experienced for a relatively long period to allow for changes in weather conditions and time of the year the study takes a long time, often too long to allow for a proper evaluation within the present project time.

As problems were delayed or prevented POEs, statistical analysis and results can not be presented here. The following list shows in which buildings some POE were undertaken.

However, for the EOS-office results are available. The figures below show how physical features are rated in making a work place pleasant to work in and the satisfaction the occupants actually had with the work place.

Good light, windows and view out are rated the most important daylight-related features in a work place. The reported satisfaction with the work place was highest for window size and view. That is, the EOS-office was successful in providing the daylighting features that were most in demand by the occupants.

References

Collins, B.L. et al (1989) "Post-occupancy Evaluation of Several U.S. Government Buildings", NISTIR 89-4175, U.S. Dept. of Commerce, NIST, Gaithersburg.

Hygge, S., Löfberg, H.A., Poulton, K. (1996) "A manual for post-occupancy evaluation (POE)", KTH - Centre for Built Environment, Gävle, Sweden

Elder, J., Turner, G.E. & Rubin, A.I. (1979) "Post-occupancy evaluation: A case study of the evaluation process", Center for Building Technology, National Engineering Laboratory, NBS, (NBSIR 79-1780).

Queens´s Building:	Informal POE with different questionnaire. No changes in lighting introduced. Leicester, UK Some 50 students and 10 staff.
Beresford Court:	Informal POE. Effort was made to change switching system. Dublin, IR 25 occupants
Domino Haus:	Informal POE. Effort was made to change lighting system. Reutlingen, GE 38 occupants.
Architects´ Office:	Informal POE. New survey after blocking sky-lights for 3 weeks. Athens, GR About 40 occupants
E.O.S. Office:	Informal POE. Lausanne, CH About 30 occupants
LNEC Building:	Formal POE Change in external awnings. Lisbon, PT About 80 occupants.
Scottish Office:	Formal POE One POE wave Edinburgh, UK About 1,200 occupants

EOS Building

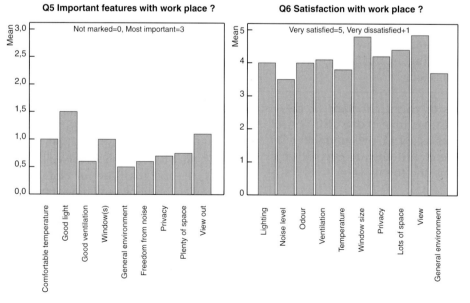

Q5 Important features with work place ?

Q6 Satisfaction with work place ?

JOULE II Daylight Europe
Monitoring Subtask
Survey of Portable Light Measuring Instruments

manufacturer	photo	model	luminance meter	illuminance meter	chromameter	output range min	output range max	acceptance angle	optional measures w/ interchangeable sensors	V(λ) match (fl')	size (mm)	weight (kg)	apx. cost (ECU) (tax not incl.)	comments
GRASEBY Optronics (ex UDT) 12151 Research Parkway, Orlando, FL 32826-3207 USA Phone: +1 407 282 1408 Fax: +1 407 273 9046		GO 352 (main unit) + GO 268 P (detector)		●		10^{-3} lux	10^5 lux		Power in W Luminance of CRTs	3%	157x84x30	0.23	1208	
HAGNER B. Hagner AB Box 2256 S-171 02 Solna Sweden Phone: +46 8 839 357 Fax: +46 8 836 150		EC 1 & EC1-X		●		10^{-1} lux	2.10^5 lux				135x75x35	0.19	450 (EC1) 630 (EC1-X)	EC1-X is same as EC1 but with a 2 m cable between the remote sensor and the readout. 4 ranges (manual)
		E2 & E2-X		●		10^{-2} lux	2.10^5 lux		Special Detectors: Ec,Esc,E2π, L of CRTs,IR,UV,etc. (E2-X only)		180x100x25	0.45	1320 (E2) 1400 (E2-X)	E2-X is same as E2 but with a 2 m cable between the remote sensor and the readout. 5 ranges (manual)
		S3	●	●		10^{-2} lux or cd/m²	2.10^5 lux or cd/m²		with all Hagner Special Detectors: Ec,Esc,E2π, L of CRTs,IR,UV,etc.		270x130x70	1.4	3800	illuminance is measured with an external detector (incl. in the cost). 5 ranges (manual). Analog display through the view finder
LI-COR P.O. Box 4425 Lincoln, Nebraska 68504 USA Phone: +1 402 467 3576 Fax: +1 402 467 2819		LI-189 (main unit) + LI-210SA (detector)		●		10^{-2} lux	2.10^5 lux		Global solar radiation	5%	140x77x38	0.26	1900	

manufacturer	photo	model	luminance meter	illuminance meter	chromameter	output range min	output range max	acceptance angle	optional measures w/ interchangeable sensors	V(λ) match (f_1')	size (mm)	weight (kg)	apx. cost (ECU) (tax not incl.)	comments
LMT Helmholtzstraße 9 D-10587 Berlin Germany Phone:+49 30 393 40 28 Fax: +49 30 391 80 01		Pocket-lux A & Pocket-lux B		●		10^{-1} lux	2.10^5 lux		model B only : Ec,Esc	3%	135x80x40	0.35	1120 (A) 1150 (B)	Ranging automatic. B is same as A with a 2 m cable between the remote sensor and the readout.
		B 360 E		●		10^{-2} lux	6.10^5 lux		model B only : Ec,Esc	1.5%	175x114x58 (console) 80 diam x55 h (head)	1.2	2570	Ranging automatic. or manually.
		B 360 F		●		10^{-3} lux	2.10^5 lux		model B only : Ec,Esc	1.5%	175x114x58 (console) 80 diam x55 h (head)	1.2	2860	Ranging automatic. or manually.
		L 1003	●			10^{-4} cd/m²	2.10^6 cd/m²	3°, 1°, 20' (selectable)		3%	240x160x110	2.4	7450	Ranging automatic. or manually. The head can be removed and connected with a cable. Digital display in view finder and at control panel.
MINOLTA (Japan) Europe representative : Kurt-Fischer-Straße 50 D-2070 Ahrensburg Germany Phone:+49 30 410 27 01 Fax: +49 30 410 27 03		T-1		●		10^{-2} lux	10^5 lux				170x72x33	0.22	724	Ranging automatic.

JOULE II Daylight Europe
Monitoring Subtask
Survey of Portable Light Measuring Instruments

manufacturer	photo	model	luminance meter	illuminance meter	chromameter	output range min	output range max	acceptance angle	optional measures w/ interchangeable sensors	V(λ) match (f1')	size (mm)	weight (kg)	apx. cost (ECU) (tax not incl.)	comments
		XY-1		●	●	10 lux 1600 K	2.10^5 lux 4.10^4 K				170x73x33	0.23	1730	The head can be removed and connected with a cable. Ranging automatic.
		LS-100	●			10^{-3} cd/m²	3.10^5 cd/m²	1°			208x79x150	0.85	2415	Digital display in view finder and at control panel. Ranging automatic.
		LS-110	●			10^{-2} cd/m²	10^6 cd/m²	1/3°			208x79x150	0.85	2415	Digital display in view finder and at control panel. Ranging automatic.
PRC KROCHMANN Genestraße 6 D-10829 Berlin Germany Phone:+49 30 751 70 07 Fax: +49 30 751 01 27		106 i & 106 e (both in standard or improved version)	● 106e only (with adapter)	●		10^{-1} lux	12.10^4 lux	5°	106e only : Ec, Esc, Eo, E2π	3.5% (std) 2% (imp)	145x80x37	0.30	1020 (imp) 880 (std)	Ranging automatic. On 106e a lens can be mounted on the illuminance sensor to measure luminances. A sighting telescope helps determining the evaluated area.
TEKTRONIX P.O. Box 500 Beaverton,OR97077-0001 USA Phone: +1 503 627 7111		J18 (main unit) + J1811 (detector)		●		10^{-2} lux	10^5 lux		chromaticity, L and radiance of CRTs, irradiance	3%	200x80x30	0.25	2740	Ranging automatic.

manufacturer	photo	model	luminance meter	illuminance meter	chromameter	min	max	acceptance angle	optional measures w/ interchangeable sensors	V(λ) match (f_1')	size (mm)	weight (kg)	apx. cost (ECU) (tax not incl.)	comments
TESTO (Germany) French representative: Testotherm S.a.r.l. 19, rue des Maraîchers B.P.100 Forbach Cedex Tel:+33.3-87 29 29 00 Fax:+33.3-87 87 40 79		0500		●		1 lux	10^5 lux			8%	160x85x30	0.20	270	3 ranges (manual) The head can be removed and connected with a cable. Ranging automatic.
TOPCON (Japan) French representative: Optilas CE 1834 91018 Evry Cedex Tel:+33.1-60 79 59 00 Fax:+33.1-60 86 96 33		IM-3		●		10^{-2} lux	2.10^5 lux				180x70x32	0.27	830	Finder view field is 5°. Ranging automatic. or manually
		BM-8	●			10^{-2} cd/m² ; 1 cd/m²	2.10^5 cd/m² ; 2.10^7 cd/m²	2° ; 0.2°			190x105x57	0.45	3020	
CEREP (France) 554, Alleé Gabriel Voisin Z.I. des Gâtines F78341 Plaisir Tel:+33.1-30 81 48 38 Fax:+33.1-30 81 97 98		FJ meter R453		● ●		1 lux ; 0.1%	4.10^4 lux ; 1000%		Indoor illuminance (lux) Outdoor illuminance (lux) Daylight factor value (%)		180x80x70	0.72	3000	Daylight factor meter consisting of 2 luxmeters connected by radio waves. Range approx. 700m.